32305

||||| ||| ||||| |||| |||||| || ||||| ||||| ||| |||||
320 973

☞ **W9-CHP-123**

32305

Can the Government Govern?

Can the Government Govern?

JOHN E. CHUBB
and
PAUL E. PETERSON
editors

THE BROOKINGS INSTITUTION
WASHINGTON, D.C.

22305

Copyright © 1989 by

THE BROOKINGS INSTITUTION

1775 Massachusetts Avenue, N.W., Washington, D.C. 20036

Library of Congress Cataloging-in-Publication Data

Can the government govern? / John E. Chubb and Paul E.
   Peterson, editors.
      p.   cm.
   Includes bibliographical references and index.
   ISBN 0-8157-1408-4 (alk. paper). ISBN 0-8157-1407-6 (pbk. : alk.
paper)
      1. United States—Politics and government—1945–   2. United
States—Economic policy.   I. Chubb, John E. II. Peterson, Paul
E.   III. Brookings Institution.
JK261.C36 1989
320.973—dc19   88-37652
                                                       CIP

9 8 7 6 5 4 3 2 1

The paper used in this publication meets the minimum
requirements of the American National Standard for Information
Sciences—Permanence of Paper for Printed Library Materials,
ANSI Z39.48-1984.

Set in Palatino
Composition by BG Composition,
   Baltimore, Maryland
Printing by R. R. Donnelley and Sons Co.
   Harrisonburg, Virginia
Book design by Ken Sabol

Foreword

Seeking more effective government has long been an American goal. Suspicious of authority and protective of liberty, Americans have had to work hard at building governmental institutions that provide both. The Constitution was the country's most dramatic—and successful—effort to create an effective framework that was nonetheless consistent with a traditional free-spirited independence. And it was Alexander Hamilton, the founder most concerned about institutional effectiveness, who said: "The true test of a good government is its aptitude and tendency to produce a good administration."

In recent years, changes in American political institutions seem to have violated Hamilton's precept. Indeed, the management of certain crucial contemporary problems has been disappointing for so many years that this volume has been prompted to ask: Can the government govern? The volume emphasizes how much we have yet to learn about making our governmental institutions more effective. In the three perhaps most troubling and important policy areas of the late twentieth century—energy, trade, and finance—the divisions of responsibility among Congress, the presidency, and bureaucratic agencies seem to work less well than we have a reasonable right to expect. What is more, if the two political parties are laying lasting claim to specific branches of government, as seems to be the case, institutional conflict could well become even more entrenched.

This is primarily a work of analysis, not of advocacy. Although the authors discuss a variety of policy and institutional reforms, their purpose here is not so much to insist on any particular reform as to explicate the causes and consequences of institutional intransigence, and to convince policymakers that the question of governmental effectiveness has become too critical to be ignored.

The editors, John E. Chubb and Paul E. Peterson, wish to thank many people who assisted in the volume's preparation. Barry P. Bosworth, I. M. Destler, Richard F. Fenno, Jr., Morris P. Fiorina, Robert A. Katzmann, Robert O. Keohane, Keith Krehbiel, William R. Lowry, Thomas E. Mann, Matthew D. McCubbins, Philip A. Mundo, Norman J. Ornstein, A. James Reichley, Bert A. Rockman, Allen Schick, Harold Seidman, Steven S. Smith, Thomas J. Weko, and Joseph White provided critical comments on some or all of the essays. John Coleman, Thomas Frank, Richard Phelps, and Bryan Sala served as research assistants. Nancy D. Davidson and James R. Schneider edited the manuscript, and Diana Regenthal prepared the index. Susan L. Woollen prepared the manuscript for typesetting. Peter Dombrowski and Richard Aboulafia verified the factual statements and citations in the papers. Renuka Deonarain, Sharon Hess, Barbara Johnson, Vida Megahed, and Eloise Stinger provided secretarial assistance.

Brookings and the Governmental Studies program owe a special debt of gratitude to the Ford Foundation and the Dillon Fund, whose generous financial support helped to make this volume possible. In addition, David B. Yoffie received financial assistance for his essay from the Harvard Business School's Division of Research.

The authors include John E. Chubb, senior fellow, the Brookings Institution; Samuel Kernell, professor of political science, University of California, San Diego; Terry M. Moe, associate professor of political science, Stanford University; Paul E. Peterson, professor of government, Harvard University; Mark Rom, social science analyst, General Accounting Office; Kenneth A. Shepsle, professor of government, Harvard University; and David B. Yoffie, associate professor, Harvard Graduate School of Business.

The interpretations and conclusions presented here are solely those of the authors and should not be ascribed to the persons whose assistance is acknowledged above, to any agency that funded research reported herein, or to the trustees, officers, or other staff members of the Brookings Institution.

BRUCE K. MACLAURY
President

November 1988
Washington, D.C.

Contents

ix

Part II: Institutions and Governance

Can the Government Govern?

American Political Institutions and the Problem of Governance

JOHN E. CHUBB and PAUL E. PETERSON

THE 1970s, a decade of stagflation and energy crises, may be revisited in the 1990s. The 1980s, a decade of relative prosperity, may turn out to be but a respite. During the 1980s several of the most troubling conditions of the previous decade improved: inflation, unemployment, and oil prices fell and remained low. But closely related conditions worsened. The United States ran record budget and trade deficits, reestablished its dependence on foreign oil, and continued to lag behind its major competitors in productivity growth. Although there is disagreement about precisely how and when these developments will affect the country, there is little doubt that they jeopardize national prosperity in the long run. To be sure, the country narrowed its deficits in the late 1980s and seems to be in no imminent danger of a major economic downturn or energy shock. But the problems that first appeared in the 1970s—falling growth rates, rising prices, and increasing vulnerability to international forces—are concerns for the future, not just the past.

When concerns as major as these mount, the people ordinarily blame the government. Voters throw out governments that preside during bad economic times and replace them with governments that promise to do better. And over the past two decades, the American people did just this. They awarded full control of the national government to the Democrats for four years, gave substantial control to the Republicans in the early 1980s, and opted for power sharing during the rest of the period. Yet the two political parties, working individually and together, failed to construct a set of policies to secure the country's economic future. When governments of quite different political combinations all fail to perform effectively, it is worth considering whether the problem is the government itself and not the people or parties that run it.

1

Specifically, the government may have a problem with its institutions. In carrying out permanent responsibilities such as stabilizing the economy, managing trade, and ensuring energy security, the government works through extensive—and complicated—institutional arrangements that require cooperative efforts among congressional committees, White House offices, and bureaucratic agencies. If these arrangements are not appropriately designed, the government will have difficulty adapting to new conditions and demands and making policy effectively. This appears to be the trouble with the national government today.

The problem, of course, is not simply one of institutional adaptability. The institutions of a democratic government must work with the demands that the public makes of them. Inasmuch as changes in the domestic and global economies have made it more difficult to satisfy pressing political demands without creating larger problems, institutions cannot be assigned all the blame for not responding adequately to all of society's troubles. And it must be said that during the 1980s the American public apparently made strikingly inconsistent demands upon its representatives in Washington. According to pollsters, Americans simultaneously opposed tax increases, supported most major government programs at existing or higher levels, and insisted upon the elimination of budget deficits. In a no less self-contradictory mood, the public also welcomed the plummeting price of gasoline, opposed a tax on its consumption, and wanted to be free from dependence on oil from the Middle East. If during this same period the government promoted an unsustainable economic expansion with budget deficits, foreign capital, and cheap energy, it was in part simply giving the public what it wanted.

It seems most unlikely, however, that the public has carefully and thoughtfully decided to sacrifice the long-run economic security of the country for temporary prosperity. More likely, it has not made any decisions on a set of difficult issues that cannot be resolved without detailed information, considerable expertise, and an ability to balance conflicting values. Inconsistencies in public opinion may well have made government decisionmaking difficult: choosing between special interests and general ones and between present benefits and future ones is never easy. But if governing institutions are not to lose the confidence of a public frustrated with their performance, they must not simply reflect specialized pressures and every change in public opinion, no matter how short-sighted and inconsistent. They must govern on behalf of the common good. What Hamilton wrote in defense of the Constitution two centuries ago seems as appropriate now as then:

> The Republican principle demands that the deliberative sense of the community should govern the conduct of those to whom they entrust the management of their affairs; but . . . when occasions present themselves when the interests of the people are at variance with their inclinations, it is the duty of the persons whom they have appointed to be the guardians of those interests to withstand the temporary delusion in order to give them time and opportunity for more cool and sedate reflection. . . .[1]

This book examines the problem of governance that the collision of new issues and established institutions may be creating for the United States. The essays in the volume address the problem by looking both at the specific ways government institutions are responding to major policy problems and at how American governmental institutions have been evolving in the late twentieth century. The first part of the book examines the institutions responsible for managing three of the most demanding economic problems of our time: energy, trade, and the stability of the macroeconomy. These essays consider the extent to which policy difficulties can be attributed to the character of the institutions responsible for them. In so doing, they take account of the changing economic conditions and political demands that have made contemporary governance more difficult. In the second part of the book, the essays step back from the particulars of specific policy arenas and assess the ways in which the presidency, Congress, and bureaucratic agencies have changed in recent decades, raising the question of whether these changes have contributed to more or less effective government. In this introductory essay we shall trace the long development of the contemporary governability problem. We shall also argue, drawing on the individual essays, that the problem is inherently and substantially institutional, and then discuss the politically difficult requirements for overcoming it.

---

1. *The Federalist,* no. 71.

POLITICAL INSTITUTIONS AND GOVERNMENT PERFORMANCE

The problem of governance in the United States is mainly one of creating institutions or governing arrangements that can pursue policies of sufficient coherence, consistency, foresight, and stability that the national welfare is not sacrificed for narrow or temporary gains. The United States has difficulty in arriving at such arrangements because it must fashion them out of three substantially autonomous political institutions: Congress, the presidency, and the bureaucracy. Because each institution represents different interests and holds different views of effective government, the development of governing structures, and consequently the management of ongoing problems, must always contend with political tension. This tension is a well-known part of the legislative process, such as in the making of the federal budget. But it is also manifest in battles between Congress and the president for control over bureaucratic agencies—how they should be set up, be reorganized, make decisions, and otherwise fulfill their routine responsibilities.

Historically, Congress and the president proved remarkably adept at building decisionmaking structures that could contain the political tensions between them and at the same time manage the major problems of the nation with reasonable effectiveness. During the nineteenth century, for example, the nation's affairs were managed quite effectively through a system of patronage shocking to most European observers. Yet when changing demands rendered patronage less effective and less politically useful, it was replaced by two very different but still distinctively American institutions: a civil service headed by a full tier of political appointees, and independent regulatory commissions given quasi-judicial status.

Such changes have not occurred easily, however. Most of the time, the vested interests that each of the competing institutions has in existing arrangements, and the differing objectives each would hope to satisfy through institutional change, keep established governing structures in place. When economic or other policy conditions change, Congress, the president, and the bureaucracy usually respond and adapt in ways that represent their respective interests and protect their respective powers. These ad hoc adjustments—recently, for example, the decentralization of

Congress and the centralization of the presidency—will often solve immediate political problems for each institution, and they may even amount to effective adjustments for the government as a whole. But in time, piecemeal institutional change can prove inadequate, for politics and for government performance, and conditions become ripe for more creative institutional change.

Perhaps the essence of the problem of governance today is that current administrative structures, erected mostly during the Progressive era and the New Deal, are so entrenched that their adaptations to new conditions contribute little to overall government effectiveness. Established structures no longer can contain political tensions between Congress, the president, and the bureaucracy, and, riven by conflict, they often do not permit successful management of the nation's problems.

These points are well illustrated in the three problem areas that perhaps most troubled the United States during the 1970s and 1980s. In the opening essay John Chubb shows that the United States still tries to manage energy supply and demand with an administrative structure that predates the twenty-year-old decline of domestic oil production and the consequent development of new energy issues such as rising prices and increasing threats to the environment. Although Congress and a series of presidents have long recognized that this structure is antiquated—for example, natural gas deregulation has remained on the legislative agenda for decades—they have been unable to agree on how to change it. Meanwhile, battles for control of this structure and efforts to keep it from collapsing have produced unsatisfactory results. Ultimately, both conservation and domestic energy production have been discouraged while energy consumption, especially of foreign oil, has been encouraged. If current trends continue, the United States will be nearly as vulnerable to an economically costly surge in world oil prices in the 1990s as it was in the 1970s.

Similarly, the government has been battling its record trade deficit with weapons forged in the 1930s. As David Yoffie points out in his essay, Congress and the president recognized in the midst of the Great Depression that the nation's economic welfare had been reduced by protectionist policies that exempted many U.S. industries from foreign competition. To encourage free trade, Congress passed the Reciprocal Trade Agreement Act, which shifted the responsibility for trade policy from the legislative branch, where political pressures for selective protection were most effective, to the executive branch, where institutions more committed to free trade could better resist industry pressure. As in the energy arena, the arrangement worked well until the issues began to change in the 1970s. As more U.S. industries became threatened by foreign competition and the trade deficit grew, the bargain between Congress and the president became strained by escalating demands for protectionism. Although the arrangement has not yet collapsed, it is no longer solving the problem. U.S. trade policy has not succeeded in easing out of existence many of the country's least promising industries nor has it worked well to open foreign markets to many of the nation's most dynamic industries. As Yoffie warns, U.S. trade policy may be an obsolete institutional bargain.

For most of the twentieth century the conduct of macroeconomic policy has also relied heavily on a fixed set of institutional arrangements. The Federal Reserve has long been responsible for monetary policy, and the president—with the steadily increasing assistance of the Bureau of the Budget and its successor, the Office of Management and Budget (OMB)—has taken charge of fiscal policy since at least 1920. As in the other policy arenas, the arrangements for both monetary and fiscal policy worked reasonably well and kept political pressures, for faster or slower economic growth, contained until the early 1970s. But here the story diverges somewhat from that in energy and trade policy. When economic issues began to change and the established institutions had to manage a decline in productivity, two oil price shocks, and unprecedented stagflation, one set of institutions—that for managing monetary policy—ultimately adjusted successfully. As Paul Peterson and Mark Rom argue, the ability of the Federal Reserve to stabilize the economy is testament to the effectiveness a governing institution can achieve when the president and Congress do not weaken its capacity for sustained and concerted action. The failure of the fiscal policy apparatus to avert record budget deficits is quite another matter, one consistent with the governing difficulties encountered in the energy and trade arenas. Institutional adjustments in the budgetary process have taken place, to be sure, but each has served more to strengthen the hand of one of the branches than to create an arrangement that will help the government restore its budget to balance and keep it there.

The difficulties encountered in energy, trade, and fiscal policy are not unique to these arenas. The political tensions between Congress, the presidency, and the bureaucracy have shaped governing arrangements in nearly every policy domain. And despite corrective measures that occur from time to time, the debilitating effects of these tensions are perhaps more evident today than they have ever been. It will come as no surprise, then, that the problem is not subject to a quick fix. Indeed, the problem of governance is such a pervasive part of the American political tradition that one can obtain the best understanding of the current predicament by initially considering its origins in the nation's constitutional history.

THE HISTORICAL LEGACY

Americans have always been better at representing than governing. The American Revolution was itself an attack on effective government. As Harold Laski observed, "Those who made the government arrangements were, out of actual and inferred experience, above all afraid of arbitrary power."[2] If the clarion calls of the colonials were "no taxation without representation" and "give me liberty or give me death," then the product of that revolution could hardly give priority to the needs of government.

The revolutionary leadership, as expressed through the Continental Congress, initially left matters of governance largely to the states, as the colonies were now to be called. Only the most urgent questions of mutual defense and foreign policy were to be considered by the Continental Congress, and these could be decided only with the consent of the individual states. Since the national government did not so much govern as represent the will of the states on a limited set of topics, it scarcely needed an executive officer. Policies could be determined by the Continental Congress, and these policies, the product of broad agreement, would be more or less self-enforcing.

The early years of the Republic gave ample testimony to the truth that representation alone was not sufficient for national unity. Under the Articles of Confederation, Congress could not contain the competitive instincts of the states—neither their over-

2. Harold J. Laski, *The American Presidency: An Interpretation* (New Brunswick, N.J.: Transaction, 1980), p. 155.

lapping claims on western lands nor their attempts to manipulate trade and tariffs for their individual benefit. Influential American leaders soon became aware that European powers had a vested interest in encouraging state rivalries, hoping to divide and weaken this new nation to the ultimate benefit of nations more studied in the art of statecraft.

The Constitutional Framework

To meet these domestic and foreign challenges, a call was issued for a national convention to consider revisions in the Articles of Confederation. The Constitution that emerged from this convention, it hardly need be said, was a tour de force, an extraordinary success in grafting upon a system of representation a governmental mechanism that survived a civil war, an industrial revolution, and the transformation of a fledgling republic into the world's richest and most powerful nation.

But for all its success, the Constitution still betrayed its origins in a revolution against executive power. Congress, the entity that most resembled the Continental Congress and state assemblies that had been the vehicles for revolution, was given pride of place in the new document. Its powers were carefully enumerated; its system of representation was spelled out in detail; its rules for meeting, recording activities, and adjourning were clearly set forth; and the division of responsibility between its upper and lower chambers was quite self-consciously delineated.

The executive branch, the one that was to administer the new government's policies, was treated summarily. The Constitution devotes less than half as much space to the executive's design as to the legislature's. Most of that space is devoted to the clumsy procedure by which the president is to be chosen, a procedure that was soon modified by the Twelfth Amendment and to this day is the subject of unremitting criticism. The only powers the president is specifically granted are the powers to command the armed forces, to make treaties and appoint officers (with the advice and consent of the Senate), to veto legislation (which, however, can be overridden by a two-thirds vote), to pardon offenses, to receive ambassadors from foreign countries, and to convene Congress. It is often remarked that little attention was given to the presidency because it was generally assumed that General George Washington would be chosen for the job. But reticence was more deeply rooted than that. In a country that had forsworn royalty, the role of executive power was expected to be very limited. As de Tocqueville observed, "the President is placed beside the legislature like an inferior and dependent power."[3]

Some have contended that a more expansive view of the presidency is inherent in certain brief phrases included in the Constitution. Much has been made, for example, of the clause that states "the executive power shall be vested in a president" and the statement that requires that the president "shall take care that the laws be faithfully executed." As the executive has gained in strength and independence, presidents have drawn upon these phrases to expand their prerogatives and justify actions they have taken. Relying on these provisions, Abraham Lincoln suspended the writ of habeas corpus, recognized rump bodies as state legislatures in seceding states, and freed slaves in rebellious parts of the nation. Harry Truman declared that powers inherent in the executive allowed him to declare a national emergency and seize the steel mills. Richard Nixon said that executive powers enabled him to impound funds that Congress had appropriated and gave him and his close White House aides the right to refuse Congress documents and testimony he regarded as privileged. While some of these and other claims of executive authority have been recognized by courts, most have been denied or subjected to stringent limits. And whatever might have been the intentions of the men who signed the Constitution, these clauses played almost no role in the early years of the American Republic.

The First Century

Both the executive branch and the national government as a whole played an abbreviated part in the nation's governance during the Republic's early years. Sectional conflicts were avoided by making government mainly a state responsibility. Trade and commerce flourished not because a national government nurtured economic growth, but in part because the Constitution prohibited the

3. Alexis de Tocqueville, *Democracy in America*, vol. 1 (Vintage, 1945), p. 128.

barriers to a national market that had existed under the Articles of Confederation. Twice Congress established a national bank that could provide such basic minimums for national commerce as a common currency and coordinated credit policies. But the effort at governance required too much, and both banks failed the political test, despite the unfortunate economic consequences of their demise.

On the first major occasion that the president acted as commander in chief, the War of 1812, the executive branch failed miserably. Even the declaration of war itself was a product of governmental ineffectiveness. President James Madison had been trying to counter British impressment of American sailors on the high seas with more effective enforcement of trade interdiction. But both Congress and the states had grown weary of trying to bring the British bulldog to heel by banning imports and exports. Because of cheating by American traders and availability of ample raw materials for the British in Canada, interdiction had been hurting the United States more than the British. The ultimate frustration, though, was Madison's. He could neither get Congress to pass tighter trade restrictions nor obtain effective enforcement of the laws already enacted.

War seemed the best way out. An attack on Canada could both eliminate a competing source of raw materials for foreign markets and add to the nation's territory. The only difficulty with this idea was Madison's inability to conduct the war. Congress did not want to spend money on armaments, and the states were slow to muster their militia and quarreled over their assigned quotas. By the time the political problems were solved and an army was raised, it was late in the autumn, and the invaders had to contend more with the elements than the enemy.[4] In the end it was not Montreal but Washington that was overrun. The burning of the nation's capital was not intrinsically significant, but it well symbolized the ineffectiveness of the national government. Peace was gratefully accepted on terms that failed to achieve any of the war objectives.

The question of effective government was no less the issue during the Civil War. When divisions between the North and South involved issues of representation, namely, the future of territorial acquisitions and the admission of new states, Congress found a

4. J. C. A. Stagg, *Mr. Madison's War: Politics, Diplomacy and Warfare in the Early American Republic, 1783–1830* (Princeton University Press, 1983), p. 271.

way to resolve them (for example, the Missouri Compromise and the Compromise of 1850). When governance was required, as in the case of the Fugitive Slave Law, the enforcement effort provoked riots, civil disobedience, and eventually a political protest that swept a new political movement, the Republican party, into power.

The Republican party's first president posed the question of effective government in the striking terms appropriate to his time: "Can a house divided against itself still stand? Can a nation survive that is half slave, half free?" For decades the country had dodged this question by pretending that government was unnecessary in this far-flung agrarian republic. But the nation's very success raised old problems anew in ever more pressing ways. Times were changing and the established institutional arrangements were straining to keep issues from spiraling out of control. Although the Missouri Compromise had finessed the slavery issues raised by the Louisiana Purchase, a similar solution could not be devised with respect to the acquisition of the Mexican territories stretching from Texas to California. The nation, moreover, was eager to exploit the new frontiers it had conquered. It had railroads to build, canals to dig, freeholds to distribute, and colleges to establish. The restless energy of a nation on the move could not be forever contained by a national government controlled by southerners whose major fear was the creation of national power. More than anything else, the Republican party of 1860 meant effective *national* government. To remain part of such a government would inevitably mean the South's absorption into a national polity that had no place for its peculiar institution.[5]

The nation learned more about effective government in four years than it had even guessed in the eighty that preceded them. Initially, the battles were fought by ill-prepared state militias often led by state politicians and prominent local citizens better appreciated for their public-spiritedness and desire for glory than their knowledge of military strategy. The War Department was divided into competing feudal baronies, and the actual authority of the so-called commanding general was anything but commanding. Not until the final year of the war did the North realize that military success could be achieved only by coordinating its superior economic power in such a way as to destroy the Confederacy's capac-

5. James M. MacPherson, *The Battle Cry of Freedom: The Civil War Era* (Oxford University Press, 1987).

ity to resist. Once a ruthless but effective strategy was designed, an outcome that had eluded Lincoln for three years became virtually inevitable.

The Civil War left an enduring mark on the American Constitution. Not only did three new amendments give the national government new authority over the states, but, equally important, meaningful executive authority had become an integral part of the nation's governing framework. A striking sign of this is the increasing use of the veto power of the president. Ulysses S. Grant vetoed 43 pieces of legislation, more than the total of all antebellum vetoes. Indeed, seven pre–Civil War presidents cast no vetoes at all. Several decades after the war, Grover Cleveland vetoed 358 measures, including many "private pension bills of an undefensible character" that were near and dear to many a congressman.[6] Presidential rhetoric, too, was undergoing change. Before the Civil War public speeches by presidents averaged less than three a year. Apart from inaugural and state of the union addresses, they consisted mainly of ceremonial speeches and "thank you's" at public occasions. Defense of presidential policies or promotion of legislative agendas were strictly beyond the political norms of the day. From the Civil War to the end of the century, presidential speeches numbered twenty a year, much less than that of modern presidents but considerably more than their antebellum predecessors. Gradually, these increasingly numerous speeches began to include partisan references and comments on issues pending before Congress.[7]

Congress did not acquiesce to these changes in constitutional practices easily, as the impeachment of President Andrew Johnson clearly illustrates. The radical reconstructionists in Congress not only objected to the president's dismissal of one of his cabinet members, an act later judged by the courts to be entirely constitutional, but they even condemned Johnson's rhetoric. As part of his campaign to save his presidency, Johnson embarked on a nationwide tour in which he defended his policies and prerogatives while attacking Congress. For his political stridency as much as for his alleged administrative misconduct, Johnson was impeached. But however crippled the Johnson presidency became, the longer-term struggle between the president and Congress in the last half of the

6. Laski, *The American Presidency*, p. 143.

7. Jeffrey K. Tulis, *The Rhetorical Presidency* (Princeton University Press, 1987), chap. 3.

nineteenth century took place on different terms from those that had prevailed in the antebellum period. If presidents were not yet the agenda setters that their twentieth century counterparts would become, they were no longer the place-holders that Tyler, Pierce, and Buchanan had been.

The Turn of the Century

As the nineteenth century drew to a close, problems of governance escalated. Industrialization was fast beginning to generate demands—for economic regulation and social amelioration—that only the federal government could fulfill. But the government was not well organized to respond to these concerns. Its administrative capacity, revealed by two wars to be limited, was insufficient to handle more than the most rudimentary domestic responsibilities. New forms of government organization, more permanent, professional, and powerful, were clearly needed. Yet establishing them would be difficult. Congresses and presidents, each responding to different constituencies, would have very different ideas about their design and supervision. In time, however, compromises among these divergent interests were reached, and a new administrative structure better suited to the changing requirements of effective governance was created. Although the emerging structure was the culmination of a series of political compromises and not the product of a coherent design, it included institutions that would become vital to government performance for a century to come. Perhaps the most important of these, and surely the most creative, were the civil service and the independent commission.

The Civil Service

Civil service reform pitted the interests of highly competitive, militant, patronage-hungry parties against the rising cadre of professionals eager to ply their trade in the public sector. Members of Congress, especially senators, were typically allied with party interests, particularly because senatorial courtesy gave senior senators great influence over executive appointments within their states. The position of the president was more ambiguous. On the one hand, the president was also the product of a party-controlled nominating process, and he could hardly ignore the forces that had placed him in office. On the other hand, civil service reform promised to give the president and his administrative aides more direct control over the bureaucracy than was possible in a system controlled by senators and the local politicos with whom they were connected. "By freeing the executive branch from the domination of party bosses in Congress, reform would give its leaders an opportunity to assert an independent control over government."[8]

The disjunction of interests between president and Congress was acknowledged by no less a product of the party system than Rutherford B. Hayes: "The end I have chiefly aimed at has been to break down . . . Senatorial patronage. . . . It seemed to me that as Executive I could advance the reform of the civil service in no way so effectively as by rescuing the power of appointing to office from Congressional leaders."[9] After the assassination of James Garfield by a rejected job hunter, pressures for civil service reform mounted, and the Pendleton Act, signed into law in 1883, established a civil service commission that initiated the long and laborious process of separating employment in the federal government from loyal work in the party apparatus.

Civil service reform has so often been cast as a struggle between parties and reformers that the contest between executive and legislative centers of power has been largely overlooked. But the champions of reform were not just Teddy Roosevelt and Woodrow Wilson. They also included Ulysses Grant, Chester Arthur, William Harrison, Grover Cleveland, and William McKinley. Not all of these chief executives were unabashed supporters of reform; loyalty to party and alliances with congressional leaders constrained their enthusiasm. But the steadiness with which an increasing number of federal positions were "blanketed in" to the civil service illustrates how presidents could combine political strategies with reform objectives.

Rearguard opposition to civil service reform was, of course, well entrenched on Capitol Hill. When Theodore Roosevelt's Commission on Department Methods recommended a broad range of sweeping reforms in 1907, "Congress rejected every one. . . . So vehement was the opposition that Congress even refused a public printing of the commission's final reports." Significantly, one Re-

8. Stephen Skowronek, *Building a New American State: The Expansion of National Administrative Capacities, 1877–1920* (Cambridge University Press, 1982), p. 55.

9. Ibid., p. 56.

publican senator denounced the schemes as an "executive encroachment on the sphere of Congressional action" that threatened to make Congress "a victim of a bureaucratic advance to
power."[10]

The bureaucratic advance continued into the twentieth century.
The Civil Service Commission standardized recruitment and promotion procedures, established a uniform pay schedule, and provided a pension fund and retirement system. The Bureau of the
Budget provided for centralized direction of agency requests for
funding, and the Governmental Accounting Office was created to
audit agency expenditures. All of these devices gradually rooted
out the most blatant forms of graft, corruption, and patronage that
had been a by-product of a legislative and party-controlled apparatus. But even though many civil service requirements spread
throughout the executive branch, they never culminated in the sort
of unified, merit-based, professional administration that Bismarck
created in Prussia—and that was being copied in virtually all indus-
trialized societies. To unify the civil service it would have been
necessary to establish public administration as a profession characterized by an integrated set of educational experiences, a narrow
channel for recruitment, a well-developed set of professional
norms, well-understood criteria for promotions across as well as
within administrative agencies, and access to all but the very highest policymaking positions of the government.

Canada, Japan, Britain, France, and Sweden were all finding
ways of integrating this Germanic administrative model with quite
different political systems. Woodrow Wilson thought Americans
could achieve similar results by drawing a sharp distinction between policy and administration. Congress was willing to agree to
only a portion of the reform agenda, however, for the very currency of its power base was control of the way in which federal
administrative actions affect states and communities. To concede
that control to the executive would have granted it control over the
local politics that was the congressional lifeblood.

The reform impulse was strong enough to eliminate overt political patronage from lower-level administrative agencies, thus reducing the most politically embarrassing instances of governmental incompetence and abuse of power. But the main policymaking

10. Ibid., p. 185.

positions of the executive branch remained exempt from civil service requirements. Job retention for the 3,000 or more appointees to these key positions depended upon sensitivity to the needs of political influentials in the White House, on Capitol Hill, or on the Republican and Democratic national committees.

This truncated civil service developed features very different from fully developed counterparts in other industrial societies. Lacking access to the highest policymaking positions, the civil service acquired little prestige. Lacking ready transfer and promotion across agencies, the civil service consisted of a host of departments, bureaus, agencies, and commissions, each with its own traditions, areas of expertise, and sources of personnel recruitment. Since entry into the civil service could be achieved by completing any one of a wide range of educational programs and passing a quite general examination, no common set of identifications and commitments developed. Even though each federal agency developed its own professional cadre—health care specialists, welfare workers, urban planners, engineers—the concept of a public administrator, someone who could perform effectively in a wide variety of executive positions, never really took hold. The experts were on tap, not on top. The study of public administration, once the darling child of the Progressive movement, became an orphan, scorned by the best universities as lacking in high academic standards and intellectual rigor.

The fragmentation of the civil service into professional subspecialties—networks of analysts with expertise in a particular domain—was quite consistent with the preservation of congressional prerogatives.[11] Although senators no longer controlled an array of lower-level patronage appointments, they still built close ties to those specialized professionals whose work impinged most directly on the political life of their states. The well-known iron triangle consisting of interest group, executive agency, and congressional committee could operate semiautonomously precisely because the professionals working within the triangle could not move beyond it easily. The bureaucracy could not develop a crosscutting set of loyalties and identifications that would have tied them together, connected them to their hierarchical superior—the president—and removed them from congressional scrutiny.

---

11. Hugh Heclo, *A Government of Strangers: Executive Politics in Washington* (Brookings, 1977).

Still, civil service reform was an important step forward. Although administration under the new civil service remained fragmented, it was also more expert, experienced, and objective than when bureaucracy was pregnant with patronage. This was vital to the success of the modern presidency, for stable and capable organizations were necessary if presidents were going to discharge effectively the new responsibilities an industrializing society was expecting of them. Managing the macroeconomy, regulating industries, and implementing trade policy were technically and administratively demanding tasks requiring professional expertise. Congress was willing to accept, and eventually embraced, this more professional system of administration as long as power remained functionally decentralized along the same lines as the legislature. Civil service reform, then, served the political needs of the president without jeopardizing those of Congress. It also facilitated the management of emerging national problems that, at least at that point, were not too complex and interdependent for a fragmented administration to handle reasonably well.

The Regulatory Commission

The independent regulatory commission is the second administrative institution that exemplifies the political bargain struck between Congress and the president during the first part of the twentieth century. Many of the responsibilities that the government was being asked to assume at this time required more than just narrow administrative competence. The government was taking responsibility for the behavior of business, industry, and the economy as a whole. If it was going to do so effectively, it would need to rely more on its power to direct members of the business community to perform their specific tasks in particular ways. This required the exercise of more of the government's power of coercion. Unlike traditional government responsibilities that could be accomplished through the adept provision of information, services, or grants to state and local governments, the responsibility for economic performance could not be fulfilled without the issuance of commands and the enforcement of them.[12] To be sure, when fiscal policy became a concern in the 1930s, it could be managed in traditional ways, through taxing and spending. But regulation was required

12. Theodore J. Lowi, *The Personal President: Power Invested, Promise Unfulfilled* (Cornell University Press, 1985), chap. 3.

to maintain a free economy, in which firms played by rules of fair competition, prices were not fixed, and society did not suffer from market by-products. Standards needed to be set and compliance monitored.

Standard setting had been mostly a legislative function, though, and even if Congress could not hope to set numerous detailed requirements in a wide range of policy arenas for many different industries, it was nonetheless wary of turning its legislative powers over to the executive. Since it was reluctant to delegate this power directly to the president, it therefore established "a headless fourth branch of government," a collection of regulatory commissions that operated semiautonomously of the president.[13] Within several decades these commissions included the Interstate Commerce Commission, Federal Reserve Board, Federal Trade Commission, Federal Power Commission, Federal Communications Commission, Securities and Exchange Commission, the National Labor Relations Board, Atomic Energy Commission, and a host of other regulatory bodies semi-independent in nature.[14]

Although these boards and commissions were established at different times, exercise different responsibilities, and vary in their constitutional design, most have several characteristics in common. They exercise direct authority over some economic or social activity. They thus can mandate a desired pattern of activity from particular firms or individuals. Ostensibly because this authority is deemed to be "quasi-judicial" in character, the commissions were set up in such a way as to limit executive control of them. The commissions do not have a single executive officer, but rather consist of five, seven, nine, or thirteen members who share responsibility for official action. "Boards and Commissions are unloved by everyone but the Congress," Harold Seidman has observed. "Plural executives may be inefficient administrators, but the Congress

13. The term was originally used by the President's Commission on Administrative Management, often known as the Brownlow commission. See Harold Seidman and Robert Gilmour, *Politics, Position and Power: From the Positive to the Regulatory State*, 4th ed. (Oxford University Press, 1986), p. 286.

14. For a more extended listing and classification of government agencies, see ibid., chap. 11. Not all regulatory agencies are independent. Although this mode predominated in the early twentieth century, in more recent years Congress has felt more comfortable with departmental exercise of regulatory powers. The Food and Drug Administration, the Federal Aviation Administration, and the Environmental Protection Agency all report to the president either directly or through a cabinet official.

is more concerned with responsiveness than efficiency."[15] Members are appointed by the president with the consent of the Senate for fixed terms rather than "at the pleasure" of the president. Often they have to come in more or less equal numbers from both political parties. Once appointed, the commissions can not be directed by the president to decide cases before them in any particular way nor are their decisions subject to anything other than judicial review.

Presidents have nonetheless been able to influence the work of these commissions.[16] The power of appointment can be used gradually to change the philosophical disposition of the commission. A new, politically astute chairman, who has direct access to staff resources, can shape the agenda of the board in ways consistent with a president's larger policy objectives. The commission budget is subject to review and approval by the OMB. A president can also dramatize issues in ways that constrain commission alternatives.

But Congress also has influence over these commissions. Subcommittees closely monitor their work, amend the statutes under which they operate, appropriate their funds, and influence (through the process of senatorial consent) the appointment of new members. Above all, commission independence legitimates an autonomous capacity for action that enables boards to respond to preferences from sources outside the executive branch. The result has been that agencies have developed close ties to the industries they regulate as well as to the relevant congressional committees, whose members typically have come from areas of industry concentration.[17]

In time such relationships became problems, and in the late 1970s and early 1980s several industries were deregulated in order to orient outcomes away from industry preferences and toward those of the general public. Still, for several decades independent agencies represented effective institutional compromises between Congress and the president, and in some instances this is still the case. That was plainly the experience of the agencies that controlled monetary, energy, and trade policy. Political problems in

15. Ibid., p. 61.

16. See, for example, Terry M. Moe, "Control and Feedback in Economic Regulation: The Case of the NLRB," *American Political Science Review*, vol. 79 (December 1985), pp. 1094–1116.

17. See Martha Derthick and Paul J. Quirk, *The Politics of Deregulation* (Brookings, 1985).

Congress and the White House were solved by delegating issues to bureaucrats who often turned out to have the resources to resolve them in ways that served the nation rather well. Only later, as the number of politically effective interests grew, and the issues that commissions considered began to expand, did the weaknesses of the independent regulatory commissions become fully apparent.

THE CONTEMPORARY SYSTEM

It may seem that the congressional reluctance to share power was the only force shaping the development of the government's administrative capacity. But if there had been no pressures countervailing those coming from Congress, the governing structure would have collapsed under the increasing burden of responsibilities assumed by the federal government in the late twentieth century. The countervailing force consisted of a succession of strong, administratively oriented presidents who asked for more mechanisms to help control the proliferating bureaus and agencies for which they were ostensibly responsible. By the 1980s presidents had succeeded in winning enough control over the departments so that the White House became a formidable competitor with the congressional system. Yet each advance in executive power was hedged with caveats and restrictions that left Congress with the continuing capacity to shape administrative actions. And it is precisely the even terms on which Congress and the president now compete for direction of the bureaucracy that raises anew the old question of governability. The tension between the branches, observed at periodic junctures in American history, has been steadily growing, but an institutional compromise that would resolve the tension has not yet been realized.

A Strengthened Executive

De Tocqueville recognized that the weak executive he observed in the 1830s was in good part due to the fact that "the United States is a nation without neighbors. Separated from the rest of the world by the ocean, and too weak as yet to aim at the dominion of the seas, it has no enemies, and its interests rarely come into contact with those of any other nation of the globe."[18] As these circumstances changed, the executive grew in strength: it is no accident that Abraham Lincoln, Theodore Roosevelt, Woodrow Wilson, and Franklin Roosevelt are all known both for enhancing the power of the Oval Office and for their wartime or imperial responsibilities. The role of the executive has also been changed by the alteration in public expectations about appropriate governmental responsibility for securing economic progress and domestic welfare. Theodore Roosevelt assumed greater responsibility for managing the public lands, Wilson for maintaining economic competition, and Franklin Roosevelt for establishing the welfare state and managing the national economy. In the postwar era, governmental activities in these areas—and many more—have been expanded and intensified.

The escalation of demands and the expansion of government institutions have both augmented the role of the president and given the presidency a distinctive institutional form. Undoubtedly, the seminal organizational advance for the contemporary presidency was the establishment of the Bureau of the Budget in 1921. Before the bureau's creation, budget making was an anarchical process with each department sending its own budget to Congress, leaving the resolution of competing priorities to the appropriations committees. After 1921 the Bureau of the Budget at least reconciled these departmental requests and submitted a single budget on behalf of the president. During and after World War II, the bureau grew in size, complexity, and responsibility. It acquired the power to approve virtually all agency proposals that had budgetary implications before they were submitted to Congress. It stepped up its scrutiny of departmental programs, calling upon agencies to justify in detail their proposed increases in expenditure. In recent years it has tightly reviewed the regulations agencies have proposed, instituted more uniform personnel policies across departments, and exerted even more stringent budgetary control.

But as the bureau (renamed the Office of Management and Budget), became increasingly powerful, it also became increasingly politicized.[19] Initially expected to be kept separate from more politi-

18. De Tocqueville, *Democracy in America*, p. 131.

19. Hugh Heclo, "Executive Budget Making," in Gregory B. Mills and John L. Palmer, eds., *Federal Budget Policy in the 1980s* (Washington, D.C.: Urban Institute,

cal concerns, the OMB director has in recent years become a top domestic policy adviser of the president, often superseding in influence the cabinet secretaries with operational responsibilities for domestic policy. Although this trend was significantly accelerated by Ronald Reagan, under future presidents the OMB will probably continue to be less neutral, less oriented toward helping the government to control and coordinate its expenditures, and more oriented toward helping presidents achieve programmatic and partisan goals.

Almost as significant as the OMB for the extension of presidential power has been the growth of the White House staff. In his essay, Samuel Kernell portrays the fundamental change in the size and organizational complexity of the group of advisers who work in closest proximity to the president. The existence of the staff was not formally recognized until 1939, when the Brownlow commission proposed that presidents have a small number of special assistants. Roosevelt used these assistants informally by assigning them on an ad hoc basis to pressing issues that did not fall within the domain of a particular department or agency. The staff has since grown to roughly five hundred members and contains well-organized units such as the Office of Personnel Appointments and Office of Communications. The growth of these and other offices within the White House staff has in fact been so extensive that a chief of staff, once a controversial position, is now accepted as a virtual necessity.

These changes, Kernell points out, are not simply due to presidential predilections, although the management styles of particular incumbents certainly affect the character of the staff. The growth in size and complexity has been continuous from one administration to another despite changes in party and personality. Admittedly, its size peaked during the Nixon administration. After Watergate the White House staff became so unpopular that both Ford and Carter made a point of reducing its political significance. Both committed themselves to cabinet government, and both made some efforts to carry out that intention. But the realities of governing precluded no more than marginal reductions in staff even in

---

1984), pp. 255–91; and Terry M. Moe, "The Politicized Presidency," in John E. Chubb and Paul E. Peterson, eds., *The New Direction in American Politics* (Brookings, 1985), pp. 235–71.

these worst of times. With Reagan's ascension to the presidency, the need for a strong president was boldly reasserted, and the influence and size of the White House staff reached new heights. The organizational and political aggrandizement of the White House staff, like the OMB, has been something of an inexorable response to the growing tension between Congress and the presidency, especially as manifested in the struggle for control of the administrative machinery of the government. As Kernell stresses, increases in political demands and decreases in the strength of the institutions that once relieved interbranch tensions, particularly political parties, have driven presidents to augment and institutionalize their own mechanisms of influence and control.

If the growth of the White House staff has been almost inevitable, so too, however, have been its problems. Watergate is not the only scandal that has touched the White House. Indeed, there is no other part of the executive branch so prone to become the object of press, congressional, and criminal investigations. The use of the National Security Council by John Poindexter, Oliver North, and others to conduct covert operations in Iran, Nicaragua, and elsewhere is the most recent example. But Truman was embarrassed by Harry Vaughan and George Allen, Eisenhower by Sherman Adams, Carter by Hamilton Jordan, and Reagan, in addition to the Iran-contra scandal, by Lyn Nofziger, Edwin Meese, and Michael Deaver.

The hint of scandal that always seems to hover about the White House testifies both to its political power and the informality with which individuals gain positions on its staff. What presidents want in their White House staff is loyalty. They can obtain this because few restrictions surround a staff appointment. Civil service requirements do not apply, senatorial advice and consent is unnecessary, and it is conventional practice to fill positions with staff from the presidential campaign. Committed to the president and convinced of the public support for his agenda, presidential staff members are usually eager to make sure the president's wishes (or what they think are his wishes) are fulfilled. Sophisticated about only the electoral side of politics, however, they are often less sensitive to the traditions, norms, procedures, and agendas of the entrenched agencies of the government and those agencies' patrons in Congress.

Prepared for the job or not, the White House staff is now expected to capture control of the government, and for this purpose the staff has fashioned ever more effective instruments. Departmental appointments increasingly are screened to ensure that the officers are loyal to the president—and not necessarily committed to departmental wish lists. New initiatives are more likely to emerge from discussions within the White House than from agency recommendations. Legislative liaison is a White House function; departments are often as little involved as possible. In the most extreme case (the Iran-contra scandal being the outstanding example), the White House staff is asked to carry out a major operational mission that the departments (State, Defense, CIA) are thought to be too clumsy, rule-bound—or astute—to attempt. Finally, the management of the president's direct relationship with the public, his ultimate and probably greatest source of political influence, has become something of a science. The president may not always convince the public, but he is routinely assisted by a standing army of pollsters, public relations experts, journalists, and speechwriters that strengthens his power of persuasion.

A Resurgent Congress

Congress has not allowed the centralization and politicization of executive power to progress unchecked. Although aggressive presidents and public emergencies have strengthened the presidency, Congress is too self-conscious of its own prerogatives to permit, for long, presidential intrusion on what it deems appropriate legislative domains. What James Bryce observed in the late nineteenth century is no less true today: "Men come and go, but an assembly goes on forever; it is immortal, because while the members change, the policy, the passion for extending its authority, the tenacity in clinging to what has once been gained, remain persistent."[20]

The techniques of congressional influence over agency activities are virtually infinite in number. Congressional appropriations often contain specific instructions on how—and especially where—monies are to be spent. Congress can also withhold appropriations from uncooperative agencies, though doing so can backfire if con-

20. James Bryce, *The American Commonwealth*, vol. 1 (Chicago: Charles Sergel, 1891), p. 223.

stituents are deprived of services. Agency administrators are frequently called upon to testify in oversight hearings on particular actions they have taken. New legislation is regularly accompanied by detailed committee reports that give specific instructions on the meaning of the new law, and courts have accepted these reports as documentary evidence of congressional intent.[21] Congress even incorporated into law provisions that allowed committees of either house to veto actions taken by executive agencies. These techniques are not all easy to employ, because except for oversight, they require the assent of the majority of the members of Congress.[22] Still, through the occasional use of these techniques and the continuously implied threat of exercising them again, Congress is well equipped to try to keep agencies within narrow bounds.

Perhaps as important as any technique, though, may be the constitutional conception that executive power does not inhere in the president himself but in subordinate heads of departments and bureaus. What Woodrow Wilson observed a century ago still remains substantially correct: Congress "does not domineer over the president himself, but it makes the secretaries (of the departments) its humble servants. Not that it would hesitate, upon occasion, to deal directly with the chief magistrate himself; but it has few calls to do so, because our latter-day presidents live by proxy; they are executives in theory, but the secretaries are executives in fact."[23] Today one would need to substitute for secretaries of departments bureau chiefs and agency heads, placing the president even more distant from the active agent in the government. As the Hoover commission complained in 1947, the "statutory powers often have been vested in subordinate officers in such a way as to deny au-

21. Appropriations committees often earmark appropriations for very specific activities in the reports accompanying their legislation. In the spring of 1988, James Miller, Reagan's OMB director, urged agencies to ignore hundreds of millions of dollars of such earmarks. He asserted, correctly, that they were not legally binding. But when members of Congress and agency officials severely criticized this "usurpation" of congressional power by the executive, Miller backed down. On the general question of committee reports, executive decisions, and judicial interpretation of legislative intent, see R. Shep Melnick, *Regulation and the Courts: The Case of the Clean Air Act* (Brookings, 1983); Robert A. Katzmann, *Institutional Disability: The Saga of Transportation Policy for the Disabled* (Brookings, 1986); and Katzmann, *Judges and Legislators: Toward Institutional Comity* (Brookings, 1988).

22. These are detailed and placed in proper perspective in Terry M. Moe, "An Assessment of the Positive Theory of 'Congressional Dominance,'" *Legislative Studies Quarterly*, vol. 12 (November 1987), pp. 475–520.

23. As quoted in Laski, *The American Presidency*, p. 126.

thority to the president or a department head."[24] This is additionally significant because the Congress has organized itself so that its system of committees and subcommittees is congruent with a decentralized executive.

Many of these mechanisms of legislative control are now hallowed by long tradition. But Congress has in recent years developed new and sometimes controversial techniques of legislative influence devised to keep an increasingly centralized and politicized executive from emasculating congressional power. Perhaps the most important of these is the Congressional Budget and Impoundment Control Act of 1974. Enacted in the aftermath of the Watergate scandal, it modifies an old interbranch practice, codified with legislation in 1950, that gave the president the right to impound funds whenever circumstances made it infeasible for expenditure to occur.[25] President Nixon interpreted this law in such a way as to give him the right to impound funds for practices that he felt were undesirable, unnecessary, or fiscally irresponsible. It was this substitution of the policy judgment of the president for that of Congress that angered congressional critics, who instigated lawsuits against the practice. The 1974 legislation ended the dispute by making it clear that Congress had delegated no such policymaking authority to the president. Of perhaps even greater importance, the act also attempts to make Congress a full and equal partner of the president in fiscal policymaking. It goes so far as to say that Congress will, through its budgetary and tax-writing processes, adopt a fiscal policy and coordinate federal activity, if necessary without the help of the president.

Congress has also subjected numerous authorizations of executive action to a provision that gives Congress the right to negate such action within a specific time period—the legislative veto. Congress initially reserved its grant of authority in this manner in 1932, when it gave President Herbert Hoover the right to reorganize the executive branch, subject to disapproval by either house within sixty days. As Congress began inserting this provision into an increasing number of legislative grants of power, presidents tried to resist this intrusion on executive prerogatives either by vetoing the legislation or by questioning the constitutionality of the provi-

24. As quoted in Seidman and Gilmour, *Politics, Position and Power,* p. 57.

25. James L. Sundquist, *The Decline and Resurgence of Congress* (Brookings, 1981), chap. 8.

sion. The device became increasingly popular during the Eisen-hower, Nixon, and Ford administrations, when Congress and the executive were controlled by different political parties, and reached its apogee during the Watergate crisis when the legislative veto "found its way into laws dealing with railroads, education, finan-cial aid for New York City, election finance, the disposition of Presi-dent Nixon's tapes and papers, the call-up of military reserve units or members, and advance payments or loans to military contrac-tors."[26] By 1976 the House Judiciary Committee was prepared to recommend a law that would have subjected all regulations by all governmental agencies to the legislative veto.[27]

To be sure, the proliferation of legislative veto provisions was not entirely a product of Congress's pursuit of control. Presidents sometimes invited the legislative veto as a way to get Congress to delegate more discretion to the executive. And at other times, it was only a minority within Congress, and not the institution as a whole, that demanded the veto, usually to satisfy newly regulated industries fearful of autonomous and antagonistic agencies. Never-theless, the legislative veto finally generated a reaction within the Department of Justice. With the aid of a public interest group known as the Public Citizen Litigation Group, a legal counterattack was mounted. A case involving a congressional veto of an Immi-gration and Naturalization Service decision to admit a foreigner, Jagdish Chadha, to permanent residence proved to be an ideal case for challenging the constitutional status of an increasingly perva-sive practice. The strategy succeeded in 1983 when the Supreme Court, deciding in favor of Chadha, declared the legislative veto unconstitutional. But inasmuch as *Chadha* was a rather extreme and particularistic instance of the use of the legislative veto, the applicability of the court decision to all legislative vetoes is not altogether clear. Many legislative vetoes still remain a part of the statutes, new ones have been enacted since *Chadha*, and this tech-nique of administrative control, though now of dubious constitu-tional status, remains partially in effect.

Legislation dealing with ethics in government and creating spe-cial prosecutors is another novel tool of legislative influence. The congressional purpose of these innovations, it is said, is to enhance

26. Ibid., p. 350.
27. Barbara H. Craig, *Chadha: The Story of an Epic Constitutional Struggle* (Oxford University Press, 1988), p. 56.

honesty and integrity among government officials. There is no reason to doubt that this is Congress's main motivation, but it is curious that the legislature has passed no comparable legislation applying to its own members. However, in many ways the ethics rules are a competitive response to the growth in the power and stature of the White House staff. The political efforts of this group of presidential loyalists are most likely to run afoul of government procedures and raise ethical questions. It is also this group that the president is most inclined to try to protect from embarrassing disclosures. The Watergate and Iran-contra scandals reveal that nothing weakens a presidential hand as quickly or decisively as the suggestion or reality of wrongdoing. At one time the president could count on his loyal attorney general to keep such scandals under control; now the selection of a special prosecutor, an increasingly pervasive governmental practice, makes this much more difficult. Between 1978 and 1988 there were ten separate investigations led by special prosecutors, each beholden to no clearly defined authority other than their own conception of their legal responsibilities. However much they and the ethical standards set by Congress may contribute to more honest government, both are significant new checks on executive power.

In addition to these legal checks on presidential authority, Congress has enhanced its own capacity to review, revise, and reinstruct the executive agencies. Congress has divided its work load into ever smaller bites by delegating more responsibility to a growing number of subcommittees. These subcommittees have been given bigger budgets, enabling them to hire additional staff. They have also been given more autonomous authority. Oversight of administrative agencies has been enhanced by an increasing number of hearings devoted to the review of agency activities.[28] At the same time, the staff and travel resources of individual members of Congress have been enhanced, facilitating congressional casework that mediates between administrative decisions and local constituents. These resources have also helped to spawn a profusion of special interest caucuses that monitor particular issues and policy domains. Finally, the research and investigative arms of Con-

---

28. Joel D. Aberbach, "Changes in Congressional Oversight," *American Behavioral Scientist,* vol. 22 (May–June 1979), pp. 493–515.

gress—the General Accounting Office, the Congressional Research Service, the Office of Technology Assessment, and the Congressional Budget Office—have gained new resources and prominence.

These developments have not helped Congress unambiguously, however. As Kenneth Shepsle stresses in his paper, they have come at the expense of Congress's ability to act decisively as an institution. Before the 1970s the locus of power in Congress was a level above the subcommittees, centered in the committees and their autocratic chairs. The work of Congress was divided rationally among committees, which although substantially autonomous, acted with the effective assent of the whole Congress. With the decentralization of power in Congress, the body came to speak with many voices on issues where it had once spoken with just one. This not only complicated and slowed the legislative process; it also changed the nature of congressional control of administrative operations. Agencies that once enjoyed the predictable congressional control that went along with the iron triangles found themselves subject to multiple and often conflicting jurisdictions in Congress. An able agency chief might well exploit this arrangement, playing one subcommittee off against another, to get from Congress what his agency wanted or needed. But many agencies have been hampered by the lack of clear direction that has emerged in both inconsistent enabling legislation and conflictual oversight.

Decentralization can also reduce congressional leverage with the president on major administrative matters such as the size of the budget deficit or the growth of the money supply. A president may be less willing to negotiate with congressional leaders when he knows that the institution is not fully behind them. As Shepsle also shows, Congress has taken steps to offset this and other consequences of decentralization by increasing the powers of congressional party leaders and by employing binding central decision-making procedures such as budget reconciliation. But these efforts, Shepsle concludes, have nevertheless left Congress better able to represent than to govern. Undoubtedly Congress has increased its ability to challenge the president for control of the bureaucracy. Still, the only certain effect of all of this is that during the 1970s and 1980s interbranch tensions grew more intense and the administrative structure of the national government became more unsettled.

The Partisan Dimension

In the first 150 years under the Constitution, the separation of powers was mitigated by the fact that the same political party regularly dominated both branches of government. As one well-known scholar of the American party system has observed, "From the time the two-party system settled into place in Andrew Jackson's time until the second election of Dwight Eisenhower, only two Presidents—Zachary Taylor, elected in 1848, and Rutherford B. Hayes, in 1876—had to confront immediately upon inauguration a House of Representatives organized by the opposition."[29] The Senate was equally likely to be held by the same party as the presidency—1848 and 1884 being the two exceptions.

Capture of both branches of government did not ensure harmonious cooperation. Civil service disputes between Republican presidents and Republican-controlled Congresses were endemic in the late nineteenth century. And Roosevelt's court-packing plan, reorganization schemes, and late New Deal initiatives went awry in an overwhelmingly Democratic Congress. Yet partisan loyalty, presidential coattails, and executive patronage facilitated concerted action by Congress and the president on such crucial occasions as the Great Depression and the beginning of the New Deal. In recent decades, however, unified government has been replaced by one in which each political party has acquired a distinctive grip on a particular branch of government: the Democrats on Congress and the Republicans on the presidency. As a result, the long-standing institutional contest for power has become intensified by the stake each of the two parties has in the outcome. Animated by both institutional and partisan interests, disputes between president and Congress have become not only a routinized component of American politics but the central issue of governance in the modern era.

The Republican party has called for changes in the Constitution that would strengthen the executive, such as the item veto, a balanced budget amendment, and repeal of the Twenty-second Amendment. Republican presidents have, moreover, pursued a governing strategy that has emphasized their administrative powers. They have attempted to centralize executive branch au-

29. James L. Sundquist, "Strengthening the National Parties," in A. James Reichley, ed., *Elections American Style* (Brookings, 1987), pp. 202–03.

thority by absorbing into the OMB budgetary and regulatory policymaking tasks once left to the departments. Under Reagan the
president's budget was largely prepared within the OMB, only to
be modified substantially on Capitol Hill by legislators who found
ready, if covert, access to disgruntled agency and department officers. Many new policies were initiated by White House task forces
who developed legislative programs quite independently of any
input from the departments expected to manage them. New regulations could not even be presented for public consideration until
the OMB had given them preliminary approval. Political appointments were made with less sensitivity to congressional wishes and
greater attention to the substantive policy commitments of the
appointee.

Democratic presidents have, of course, pursued some of their
goals administratively as well. Jimmy Carter, for example, appointed outspoken environmentalists and consumer advocates to
regulatory posts and tried to reshape agency decisionmaking with
zero-based budgeting. Still, the Democrats have been the party
more suspicious of executive power and they have led congressional efforts to limit it. They pushed through Congress legislation
limiting the power of the executive to impound appropriations.
They limited the authority of the OMB to estimate the revenues
and outlays of the federal government, asking it to share that responsibility with the Congressional Budget Office under the overall supervision of the quasi-independent General Accounting Office.[30] They subjected the executive to sunshine legislation,
freedom of information laws, a new code of ethics, and the inquiries of special prosecutors.[31]

Conflicts between the legislative and executive branches have
intensified in the past two decades as the Democratic party has
solidified its hold on Congress and the Republican party has dominated presidential contests. The Democratic party's hold on the
House of Representatives has, in fact, become almost ironclad: it
has lost control of the House in only four of the past fifty-five years
(1946–47 and 1952–53). Democratic control of the Senate is not quite

30. A provision in the Gramm-Rudman-Hollings deficit-reduction legislation,
later declared unconstitutional, created this novel arrangement.

31. Benjamin Ginsberg and Martin Shefter, "Political Parties, Electoral Conflict,
and Institutional Combat," paper prepared for the 1988 annual meeting of the
American Political Science Association.

as predictable: Republicans had a majority for the first six years of the Reagan administration and for six other years in the postwar era. But since it requires control of both houses to run Congress, the competitive position that the Republicans may have established in the Senate can hardly cause them to regard the legislative branch as the one more likely to protect their interests. If Republicans in Congress are going to tilt in one direction or the other on issues involving the balance of power, they will probably still favor the presidency, where they are truly competitive with, if not marginally stronger than, the Democrats.

The Democratic party's capacity to control Congress is due partly to historical accident, partly to its internal diversity, and partly to the fact that its weakness in presidential contests has strengthened its hand in Congress. The accidents of history have been of great benefit to the Democratic party on three occasions: the depression of the 1930s, the 1958 recession, and the Watergate scandal. In each case Republicans were blamed for a major misfortune, and Democrats were elected to both the Senate and House in large numbers. Once in office Democratic incumbents used their name recognition, constituent casework, legislative assistants, power of the frank, and other perquisites of office to solidify their electoral victories. Democratic advantages at particular historical moments thus became an entrenched component of overall governing arrangements.[32]

Apart from (or perhaps because of) these historical accidents, the Democratic party's congressional strength has been enhanced by its appeal for such diverse groups as urban ethnics, trade unions, blacks, Jews, Hispanics, southerners, environmentalists, farmers, and feminists. Many of these groups have little in common with each other, but all can find reasons for supporting the Democratic party. Each senator or representative emphasizes that face of the party that is most appealing to his or her constituents. And the very fact that each component of the party finds itself represented in Congress helps to perpetuate each group's identification with the Democrats. Historical accident, incumbency advan-

---

32. Thomas E. Mann, "Is the House Unresponsive to Political Change?" in Reichley, ed., *Elections American Style*, pp. 261–82. Mann argues that state legislative gerrymandering of congressional district boundaries seems not to be a major factor in sustaining a Democratic majority.

tage, and party diversity all reinforce one another and help make the Democratic party the majority party among voters nationwide.

Democrats in Congress also prosper because of (and not in spite of) their difficulty in capturing the presidency. Generally speaking, whoever carries the burdens of executive power loses ground in Congress in nonpresidential-year elections. At times—such as 1958 and 1974—congressional losses can be quite substantial. Republicans gain back some of the lost ground in presidential years, when their nominee pulls a number of senators and a few House members into office on his coattails. Eisenhower in 1952 and Reagan in 1980 had long enough coattails that they were able to capture control of the Senate for a portion of their presidential tenure. But presidential coattails have been less efficacious in House elections, and their overall effect has waned over time as more and more voters have acquired the political independence to split their votes between the parties in presidential and congressional races. In the end the congressional Democrats seem to benefit from discontent with incumbent Republican presidents. As one congressional scholar has observed, "House Republicans have been victims of their party's success in presidential elections."[33]

If Congress is a Democratic stronghold, Republicans may have the advantage in presidential contests. Republicans have held the White House for sixteen of the twenty years since 1968 and twenty-four of the thirty-six years since 1952. Although more Americans identify with the Democratic party than the Republican party, the large and, until recently, increasing number of voters who call themselves independents have tended to vote Republican in presidential elections. So too have many conservative southern Democrats, who have also begun to vote for Republicans in nonpresidential elections. Perhaps the most important reason for this is that the Republican party, somewhat more homogeneous and less dominated by assorted activists, has been able to unite behind candidates who are closer to the views of election-deciding voters, such as independents and conservative Democrats.

Conversely, Democrats find that the very diversity that helps solidify their hold on Congress undermines party unity in presidential contests. Members of Congress can appeal to different in-

33. Ibid., p. 277.

terests while still claiming loyalty to the Democratic party, but presidential candidates cannot follow this strategy without becoming accused of inconsistency, ambiguity, or playing into the hands of special interests. Bringing the diverse and often conflicting components of the party's constituency together into one national coalition has proven to be a formidable, if not impossible, task for Democratic presidential contenders.

Republicans also benefit from the electoral college system, which overrepresents small states (which are disproportionately Republican in orientation).[34] But not too much should be made of this point. History has shown that the Democrats can win the presidency if they nominate a candidate who is not outside the popular mainstream (1976) or is significantly closer to the mainstream than the Republican nominee (1964). And many of the key elections have been too close to conclude that one or the other party is the "natural" holder of the presidency. Still, if Republicans do not quite have a lock on the presidency in the way Democrats have one on the House of Representatives, the logic of the competitive situation in the postwar period is that each party has come to identify its interests with a particular branch of government. Republicans have a vested interest in strengthening the autonomous capacity of the executive branch, while the Democrats seek to conserve and extend congressional power.

In addition, each party is developing an internal coherence and partisan self-consciousness that makes it a particularly vigorous defender of its interests and priorities. The trend on Capitol Hill is described in Kenneth Shepsle's essay. Partisan voting in both the Senate and the House has increased steadily during the 1980s. In addition, power has shifted from the substantive committees to procedural committees, such as the House Rules and Senate Budget committees, where the party leadership exercises more direct authority. The party leadership is no longer just minding the legislative calendar; it is also mediating and resolving substantive issues.

As power has become more partisan, the Republicans in the House, frustrated with their "permanent" minority status, have

---

34. Rosenstone puts the advantage at 52 percent versus 48 percent of the respective shares of the popular vote that Democrats and Republicans have needed respectively to win an electoral college majority. See Steven J. Rosenstone, "Why Reagan Won," *Brookings Review*, vol. 3 (Winter 1985), pp. 25–32.

concentrated their political fire on the House Speaker, who at one time was treated as a figure who stood above petty party disputes. The process began during the term of Thomas P. O'Neill, who was increasingly attacked as a patronage-oriented politician from the state of "Taxachusetts." It intensified when Jim Wright became Speaker and Republicans discovered hints of impropriety in a number of his activities. The partisan spirit has become a pervasive part of the debate over budget resolutions, fiscal deficits, and automatic deficit-reduction procedures.

Vigorous partisanship on the presidential side once was thought to have reached its apogee during the Nixon administration. Assertion of the constitutional and legislatively delegated powers of the president was vigorous and controversial. Congress was denounced for passing liberal, spendthrift legislation. Congressionally appropriated funds were impounded; White House staff refused to respond to congressional inquiries: wage and price controls were established by presidential decree; the Domestic Council was created within the White House staff to coordinate legislative policy proposals; and covert actions, both legal and illegal, were organized by the White House to ensure the president's reelection.[35]

In the aftermath of the Watergate scandal, the intensity of the partisan debate between the president and Congress temporarily eased. Lacking electoral legitimacy, President Ford used the powers of his office more guardedly and signed congressional legislation for which he had little enthusiasm.[36] But after a Carter presidency that was similarly deferential to congressional powers, the Reagan administration intensified the partisan conflict between the branches in a systematic way that made the Nixon approach appear uncertain and ad hoc by comparison. The Reagan administration took office with an open call for public support for a strong, independently minded presidency. Loyalty to the Reagan movement was given top priority in selecting appointees not only for the White House staff but also for the OMB, the executive departments, agency heads, and members of regulatory commissions.

35. On the aggrandizement of presidential power during this period, see Arthur M. Schlesinger, Jr., *The Imperial Presidency* (Houghton Mifflin, 1973).

36. Even though he vetoed sixty-one bills, he still reluctantly signed such landmark pieces of "Great Society" legislation as the Education for All Handicapped Children Act.

The OMB drastically cut agency budgets to conform with the presidential commitment to reduced domestic spending. At the same time the president criticized Congress harshly for excessive spending, high deficits, and overregulation of the economy. Negotiations between president and Congress were often marked by mutual recriminations, allegations of malfeasance, and accusations of power usurpation. As the Reagan administration drew to a close, inherent tensions between the legislative and executive branches had been reinforced and heightened by conflict between the parties.

An Ineffective Bureaucracy

The congressional-presidential struggle for power has distinctively shaped the administrative structure of the national government. Although this influence is most obvious in the institutional arrangements that the two branches have devised to control how federal money is spent, the scars of the battle between Congress and the president are no less impressive in the bureaucratic institutions that ultimately do most of the nation's actual managing. In the volume's final essay, Terry Moe argues that Congress, responding to interest group demands, creates bureaucratic agencies and assigns them vital tasks, but then often fails to give them the requisite resources, authority, or autonomy to do their jobs effectively. Indeed, he argues, bureaucracy is not designed to be effective.

The demands to which Congress must respond are no more concerned with establishing bureaucratic agencies according to principles of rational administration than they are with fashioning public policies consistent with the national interest. Interest groups that want a federal agency created or reorganized by Congress are concerned that the agency not be diverted from serving their interests by presidents or even future Congresses of a different political makeup. They therefore want an agency insulated from day-to-day political control. Interest groups that oppose the agency will favor a different design, one that perhaps permits a legislative veto or places the agency close to the president. Meanwhile, Congress has its own structural interests: it wants bureaucratic agencies to resolve political conflicts that it cannot solve itself and tries to ensure that the agencies are as susceptible to congressional influence as to presidential influence.

Moe argues that the president's preferences for agency design stem mainly from his responsibility for the execution of policy and the overall performance of the government. The president's potential need to coordinate and control administrative decisionmaking leads him to resist the creation of independent agencies and the imposition of excessive constraints on agencies directly under his authority. The structure of bureaucratic agencies, like the content of national policy, is therefore a compromise, not only among society's interests but between the institutional interests of Congress and the president. The problem with this is that while a policy compromise may be necessary to solve the political conflict temporarily, an agency whose structural integrity is compromised or perhaps even sacrificed in the battle for political control cannot carry out the assigned policy effectively.

TOWARD A NEW INSTITUTIONAL EQUILIBRIUM

The subordination of the nation's governing structure to the presidential-congressional struggle is understandable. But it becomes increasingly difficult to defend when it leads to the design and implementation of short-sighted policies in such crucially important areas as energy, trade, and finance. To be sure, the conditions that the government must manage have become more difficult. A number of developments—including increased competition from Europe and Asia, the rise of the Organization of Petroleum Exporting Countries, and the aging of major domestic industries— eventually slowed the nation's economic growth and magnified the problems of governance. It is more difficult for a government to balance budgets, soothe dying industries, and ensure reliable energy supplies when its economy weakens and external threats strengthen simultaneously.

But U.S. policymakers responded to these changes by simply accelerating trends in institutional development that were already well under way. The presidency aggressively politicized the administrative processes of the executive branch. Congress fortified its defenses of the constituencies that it had increasingly taken responsibility to protect, while it searched for ways to defend its view of the national interest. And the two institutions struggled between themselves and with the bureaucracy to manage the nation's macroeconomy, foreign trade, and energy supply—in large part because the administrative arrangements that they were trying to manage with had become obsolete.

Domestic energy production and consumption were being regulated with procedures befitting energy industries of thirty or more years ago, giving too much authority to state governments and relying too little on the pricing of the market. Trade was being managed with an institutional arrangement designed in the 1930s; while still limiting protectionist claims with some success, it was not helping potentially competitive industries compete in markets closed by foreign governments. Deep, enduring deficits had become the trademark of fiscal policy, as both president and Congress discovered that "buy now, pay later" is the politically popular approach. Deficits had also been institutionalized through structural devices—for example, entitlement spending and tax indexing—that insulated past policy choices against future political attack.[37] Only the agency responsible for monetary policy, shielded from the petty bargaining between the two branches, seemed to have the farsightedness necessary to balance current concerns against long-term interests.

One can approach these policy problems with solutions specific to each policy arena, and at several points throughout the essays in this volume the authors have done just that. Yoffie recommends a strategic trade policy that would encourage free trade but would provide government assistance to domestic industries seeking better access to foreign markets. Peterson and Rom recommend that budget deficits be eliminated and that fiscal policy no longer be used as a mechanism for stabilizing the national economy. Chubb recommends the immediate deregulation of natural gas prices, the expedited deregulation of electricity production, reform of the process by which nuclear plants are licensed, and other policies designed to ensure that energy is produced and consumed as efficiently as possible.

None of these recommendations is new. Each already enjoys backing from many policy analysts. And yet, for reasons that go to

37. R. Kent Weaver, *Automatic Government: The Politics of Indexation* (Brookings, 1988).

the heart of congressional-presidential tension, none of these recommendations stands a good chance of being adopted, at least in a
form that is likely to work. Each proposal is justified by its long-run
contribution to the nation's welfare. But in the short run each
threatens to reduce the welfare of particular groups and perhaps
even society as a whole. As a result, each policy places a burden on
political institutions. If the policies are to become law, Congress
and the president must obviously stand up to the well-organized
interests supporting the status quo. But if the policies are going to
work, the institutions must also agree to a significant restructuring
of their own responsibilities and a new division of political power.
By and large, the policies recommended in this book will not work
under existing institutional arrangements. This may be the crux of
the current problem of governance. Institutional dysfunction helps
to stalemate congressional-presidential negotiations over policy
changes and to hamper the implementation of those policy
changes that do get made.

Consider several examples. If existing institutions were asked to
put into effect a strategic trade policy, it would likely degenerate
into a politically motivated program of protectionism. Congress
would demand that a variety of "deserving" industries benefit
from strategic assistance. The bureaucracy would be ill equipped to
defend itself against a new form of industry claims. And the president would not have the political support to thwart these pressures. Similar problems await a new energy policy. If the nation is
to produce, consume, and regulate energy more efficiently, it will
need to rely not only more on markets but also more on government authority, specifically the authority of the national government placed behind national standards. Unless administrative arrangements are reformed, however, a new national policy would
only have to approve a few nuclear power plants or utility rate
increases before political pressures would mount and congressional (and state) efforts to provide special dispensation would
prevail. Finally, there is the policy of a balanced budget. Here
institutional reform has been tried and tried again. It is true that
reforms of the budget process, perhaps especially those stimulated
by the Gramm-Rudman-Hollings bill, have marginally reduced the
size of the deficits. But presidential-congressional infighting over
tax increases, defense spending, and entitlement policy has limited

the progress toward a fiscally responsible budget, and, as a result, the deadline for a balanced budget has been repeatedly pushed into the distant future.

The specific institutional reforms that are needed to adopt and implement more effective economic, trade, and energy policies are varied and well beyond the scope of this book. But it seems clear that the United States needs institutions that have the responsibility and the authority, the incentives and the power, to pursue long-term national interests. If the problems of the last two decades have one element in common, it is the growing vulnerability of the United States to economic developments in the rest of the world. Since this interdependence is only likely to intensify, the country would do well to fashion institutions that can help policymakers give greater consideration to the national interest, a concept that acquires more specific meaning in an increasingly competitive environment.

The country has done this before. Wars and increasing foreign threats have led the nation to pursue less isolationist policies—and to reform its governing institutions. In the past the governing capacity of the country has been enhanced mainly by increasing presidential power and delegating responsibility to administrative agencies. That history unfolded in this way is testament to both the development of governing responsibilities more national and permanent in character and the adaptability of American political institutions. To be sure, this history has been marked as well by congressional resistance to institutional changes that might jeopardize representative democracy or create an imperial executive. Because of this important resistance, fundamental changes in governing arrangements have never come easy. Political tensions have always had to build to high levels, compromising not only government performance but also the political interests of Congress and the president, before action has been taken. Before fundamental arrangements could be changed, each institution has had to be convinced that its own actions were not sufficient to protect its interests or those of the country. But despite these obstacles, changes in parties and policymakers, coupled with the exigencies of critical historical moments, have in the past made possible new institutional bargains that have enhanced the authority of the executive branch while protecting the vital interests of the legislature.

Should the political opportunity for a new institutional bargain present itself—say, through an economic slump or crisis in the 1990s—the direction in which institutional change needs to move seems to be much the same as in the past. It is broad, long-term interests, not parochial and immediate ones, that need more protection from the day-to-day workings of the political system. And it is the presidency that is the institution best suited to safeguard these concerns. The presidency can take the broader view of national problems because it is the one office that has a national constituency, and it is the office best placed to find the appropriate balance between domestic and international concerns. The presidency as it is now constituted, however, is not up to these tasks. It does not have sufficient power to defend national interests, and it often fails to show adequate concern for the long term.

How is the presidency to develop greater strength and vision? And how are the interests that Congress represents to be protected in the process? Since these are questions that institutional reformers have considered for two centuries, there is no shortage of suggestions available. The more direct subordination of all administrative agencies to presidential control, a reduction in the number of congressional subcommittees and the size of congressional staffs, giving the president the item veto, and the coordination of presidential and congressional terms of office are all proposals that are currently being considered in spirited debates that are an essential part of the processes of institutional reform.[38]

Since the purpose of this volume is to analyze the problems of governance, not to advocate any particular solution, it would be misleading and distracting to endorse any of these suggestions. Finding the correct balance between governing on behalf of the national interest and representing the manifold special interests requires an attention to nuance and detail that requires an extended treatment of a particular proposal. In the end, the best approximation to the desirable balance should be sought in discussions that include not only scholars and institutionally minded citizens but also those who have immediate stakes in the institutional outcome.

But whatever is done to strengthen the presidential hand is not enough to protect national interests. Presidents can be nearly as shortsighted as Congress, as mounting deficits in recent years have

38. For an analysis of many of these suggestions and others, see James L. Sundquist, *Constitutional Reform and Effective Government* (Brookings, 1986).

amply demonstrated. Also needed are institutional changes that will remind presidents of their obligations to long-range national needs. Some have advocated repealing the Twenty-second Amendment, which shortens the president's outlook by limiting him to two terms. Others have suggested imposing constraints on certain presidential decisions that have large long-run effects, for example, ratifying a balanced budget amendment. Still others, hoping to protect the nonpartisan perspective of bureaucrats from White House political pressures, recommend including more key policymaking positions within the career civil service and subjecting the White House chief of staff to Senate confirmation.

All of these suggestions are worthy of consideration as devices designed to encourage presidents to think more about the long term and less about opinion polls and reelection strategies—things the White House is currently so well designed to consider. Yet each proposal has its shortcomings and none is endorsed here as a solution to the problems that have been identified. Once again, that is best left to the deliberative processes that are a constituent part of institutional change.

Some may argue that these kinds of institutional change are neither worthy of consideration nor necessary to address the policy issues of the 1990s. All that is needed, they say, are mechanisms by which leading politicians can get together and hammer out agreements that solve problems while taking into account political realities. The agreements on social security, tax reform, and the 1987 budget are cited as instances in which negotiated compromises solved policy dilemmas within the existing institutional framework.

One cannot help but applaud any efforts at policy compromise when so much of the contemporary scene has been marked by partisan acrimony, institutional confrontation, and unrestrained criticism of Congress, the bureaucracy, and the president by partisans in control of other institutions. But the institutional framework within which discussions take place necessarily shapes the balance of power within the negotiating group, and the outcomes that are fashioned in midnight meetings are usually consistent with the interests of the most powerful participants at the bargaining table. Political compromise is usually reached only after crisis is imminent, and the terms of agreement are often the least common denominator.

Onlookers may congratulate participants for any sign of the subordination of narrow interests and immediate concerns to long-range interests. But they do so only because such accomplishments are so rare. The relief with which the nation greeted a bipartisan agreement in 1987 to cut the budget deficit by a trivial amount in the midst of a colossal stock market crash illustrates how grateful even thoughtful observers can be when a country's politicians are taking only tiny steps in the right direction. If that is all that is needed, then institutional reassessment is hardly necessary. However, we think the essays that come will demonstrate that more is required.

Part I
Policy and Institutions

U.S. Energy Policy:
A Problem of Delegation

JOHN E. CHUBB

DURING THE 1990s the United States may experience a prolonged energy crisis. If this occurs, energy prices will escalate, economic growth will decline, and recovery will be slow and expensive. If current projections continue to hold, the growth of the country's energy needs will persistently exceed the development of its energy resources. To close the gap, the United States will turn increasingly to imports, especially oil.[1] This is socially desirable in the short run, but not in the long run. By the mid-1990s worldwide demand for oil is expected to push producers toward full capacity, return greater control over prices to the Organization of Petroleum Exporting Countries (OPEC), and perhaps drive prices up sharply. If this happens, the United States will have little choice but to pay high oil bills. In time, high prices will bring adjustments to reduce oil imports: conservation, alternative energy development, and fuel substitution. But while that is occurring, probably into the twenty-first century, energy costs will be a major drag on the U.S. economy and consequently a serious national problem.

What are the chances of avoiding this crisis? If history is a guide, not very good. The scenario for the 1990s is disturbingly similar to the experience of the 1970s. The United States was rocked by a pair of steep oil price hikes in 1973 and 1979 and saddled with nearly a decade of "stagflation" that energy prices helped to induce. The root cause was the doubling of the country's dependence on oil imports, peaking at nearly 50 percent of consumption, at a time when the world oil market was tightening and coming under the

---

1. Between 1985 and 1987 the nation's oil imports increased by 30 percent. U.S. Department of Energy, *Annual Energy Review 1987* (DOE, 1988), p. 107.

influence of OPEC.[2] This occurred for precisely the same reason it is occurring now. Domestic energy production, especially of oil, was unable to keep pace with demand, and oil imports offered the cheapest way to make up the difference. Eventually, through both energy development and conservation, the United States was able to cut its imports by nearly half, and similar developments worldwide caused real oil prices to fall almost to pre-1973 levels. But the costly adjustment took until the mid-1980s to complete. Throughout the 1970s Congress and the executive branch worked hard to speed the recovery and prevent a recurrence. In the end, however, it was essentially the discipline of the market that brought the country around.[3] As the market now lures the United States to increase its oil imports, there is little reason to believe the government will do any better at heading off a crisis the next time around.

Indeed, there are basic reasons to believe that the government may even do worse. The first is that many of its policies still discourage energy conservation and domestic energy development, both of which could replace imported oil. As the ability of United States to produce oil, its main source of energy, continues its slow decline, the country must turn to other energy resources and use all energy efficiently if it is not to depend increasingly on OPEC. Yet the country's production and consumption of the leading alternatives—natural gas, coal, nuclear power, and electricity from various sources—are governed by prices, set or influenced by the government, that tend to engender import dependence. To be sure, some of these government policies pursue goals, such as environmental and consumer protection, that may be at odds with the reduction of oil imports. But these other goals are often being pursued ineffectively or inefficiently.

Another reason for pessimism is that the politics of energy encourage the government to make and maintain these flawed poli-

2. Robert Stobaugh and Daniel Yergin, "The End of Easy Oil," in Stobaugh and Yergin, eds., *Energy Future: Report of the Energy Project at the Harvard Business School* (Random House, 1979), pp. 3-15; and Stobaugh, "After the Peak: The Threat of Imported Oil," in Stobaugh and Yergin, *Energy Future*, p. 18.

3. On the ineffectiveness of U.S. energy policy during the 1970s, see, for example, Pietro S. Nivola, *The Politics of Energy Conservation* (Brookings, 1986); George Horwich and David Leo Weimer, *Oil Price Shocks, Market Response, and Contingency Planning* (Washington, D.C.: American Enterprise Institute for Public Policy Research, 1984); Joseph P. Kalt, *The Economics and Politics of Oil Price Regulation: Federal Policy in the Post-Embargo Era* (MIT Press, 1981); and Paul W. MacAvoy, *Energy Policy: An Economic Analysis* (Norton, 1983).

cies. During the last two decades, the rise in energy prices and the intensification of energy resource development have raised the political stakes and exacerbated the political conflict associated with energy issues. Many existing policies enable Congress and the president to limit the political damage from these issues in ways that policies promising greater energy security simply do not.

What are these policies that are politically attractive but otherwise inadequate? They are principally those that regulate the development of the leading alternatives to imported oil: natural gas pricing, nuclear plant licensing, coal plant emission controls, and electricity pricing. For various reasons that will be detailed below, politicians value these policies. But a distinctive reason is that they delegate substantial decisionmaking authority to administrative agencies, thus shifting the blame for unpopular actions from politicians to bureaucrats. The Federal Energy Regulatory Commission, the Nuclear Regulatory Commission, the Environmental Protection Agency, and fifty state public utility commissions are left to shoulder political burdens that Congress and the president would rather not bear.

Of course, politicians have been delegating tough issues to agents for years, often without adverse policy consequences. Energy policy has always been substantially delegated. The problem is that delegation is a more efficient means of accomplishing policy goals under some conditions than under others. Generally, those conditions prevailed in the energy field before the 1970s, but have not since then. Delegation has consequently proven to be an increasingly less effective technique. It has not been replaced or substantially reformed, however. It is still too politically valuable for that.

In essence, much of the institutional structure of contemporary U.S. energy policy is ill designed for the problems of energy security in the 1990s and beyond. One purpose of this essay is to show how that structure has become inconsistent with an effective energy policy, at least if one of the policy's primary goals is the prevention of future energy crises. The other purpose of the essay is to explain, with reference to the political system that encourages delegation, why the institutional structure was created and persists. Before turning to these two tasks, though, it would be well to consider why the current rates of domestic energy production and consumption present a potentially serious national problem.

THE ENERGY SECURITY PROBLEM

For the better part of the twentieth century, the United States has relied on oil to meet the largest portion of its energy needs. Currently, oil's share is about 43 percent.[4] During most of the century, the United States also relied on oil for its incremental needs, which grew in tandem with the national economy. Until 1970 oil, both domestic and imported, was a reliable and inexpensive source of energy (its price was flat in real terms and it was cheaper than alternatives). After 1970 this all changed. After peaking in that year, domestic oil production began a decline that, except for a temporary boost from Alaskan oil, proceeded steadily and has no prospect of turning around.[5] To make up for the domestic drop-off and to satisfy the regularly increasing demand for energy, the United States stepped up its imports of oil. But that quickly proved disastrous. The demand for oil had been rising worldwide, and the OPEC oil cartel found itself in a position to exercise effective control over oil supplies and prices. The result was the first oil shock, a disruptive embargo on oil shipments from the Middle East and a quadrupling of crude oil prices in 1973–74.[6]

Initially, policymakers chose to view the energy crisis as a problem of price. The cartel price of imported crude was extortionary, imposing unacceptable burdens on consumers and rewarding American oil companies with windfall profits. The price shock was also expected to be short-lived: it was assumed that prices would collapse with the end of the embargo and the inevitable weakening of cartel discipline. As a result, the first significant policy response was a regime of oil regulations that placed a ceiling on domestic crude oil prices and allocated scarce supplies among various users, whose demand was stimulated by controlled prices. This counterproductive, though gradually weakening, regime remained in place until 1981, when President Reagan abolished it as the first act of his presidency. But long before its abolition, the view of the energy problem that justified it fell badly out of favor. By the mid-

---

4. Department of Energy, *Annual Energy Review 1987*, p. 11.

5. Stobaugh and Yergin, "The End of Easy Oil," p. 1; and Robert L. Hirsch, "Impending United States Energy Crisis," *Science*, vol. 235 (March 20, 1987), pp. 1467–72.

6. Richard B. Mancke, *Squeaking By: U.S. Energy Policy Since the Embargo* (Columbia University Press, 1976), pp. 3–20.

1970s it was generally recognized that the first energy crisis had exposed a fundamental problem with the country's mixture of energy production and consumption. The hard truth was that the days of reliable and inexpensive oil were over. If the nation did not want to import increasing quantities of oil, it would need to consume energy more efficiently, produce energy with fuels other than oil, or do both.

In Washington and throughout the country, agreement was strong that increasing dependence on OPEC oil—and even oil imports generally—was unacceptable. A fear of unstable supplies and escalating prices led to a consensus about the objective of reducing oil imports. But agreeing on an objective and agreeing on the means for accomplishing it turned out to be two very different things. Higher prices, the most effective conservation measure that could have been employed, were rejected as too controversial. And there were objections to the expedited development of the most readily available supply alternatives to oil—coal, nuclear power, and natural gas. The public's favorite energy alternative, solar power, unfortunately held little hope for improving the energy situation in the near future.[7] As a result, the nation embraced its least preferred energy source. Dependence on oil imports increased from 25 percent at the beginning of the 1970s to nearly 50 percent of oil needs by the end of the decade.[8] Therefore, when the Iranian Islamic revolution caused a mere 5 percent drop in U.S. oil supplies in 1979, the U.S. economy was shocked once again. Prices of crude oil tripled and, at least partially as a result, the economy was burdened with a recession as well as record-breaking inflation.[9]

The worst, however, was over. During the 1980s the most perceptible indicators of the country's energy situation improved markedly. Indeed, they improved so much that for at least the first half of the decade the energy problem seemed to be solved. Crude oil prices stopped climbing and began a slow retreat from roughly $40 a barrel in 1980 to $27 a barrel in 1985. Inflation eased in no small part because of this drop. And the U.S. economy, fueled by

7. Council on Environmental Quality, *Public Opinion on Environmental Issues: Results of a National Public Opinion Survey* (Government Printing Office, 1980), p. 22ff.
8. Stobaugh, "After the Peak," p. 18.
9. Ibid., p. 40; and Eric M. Uslaner, *Shale Barrel Politics: Energy Politics and Legislative Leadership* (Stanford University Press, forthcoming), chap. 1.

cheaper oil, rebounded for what was to become an extraordinarily long expansion. Oil imports' share of U.S. oil consumption returned to the comfortable level of 27 percent.[10] In just a few years the United States appeared to have turned around the problem that for the previous decade had seemed immovable. Appearances, however, can be deceiving.

The improvement in the U.S. energy situation in the early 1980s was the cumulative product of adaptations in the United States and throughout the world that took a decade to come to fruition. High world oil prices encouraged the more efficient use of all forms of energy and the development of alternative fuels as well as additional supplies of high-cost oil from such places as the North Sea and Mexico. These adjustments took time. Replacing capital that is energy inefficient (such as old buildings, machinery, trucks, and cars) takes years, as does the construction of electric power plants, transmission systems, and pipelines. But world and U.S. oil consumption, after continuing their historical increases in the 1970s, finally began to respond to these innovations and started to fall in the 1980s. Coupled with new oil production outside the United States, this trend created a glut of oil on world markets. The price began to fall, and the nations dependent on oil consumption began to prosper.[11]

The precise sources of this improvement are important to understand, for they establish the parameters of likely improvements in the future. From a global perspective, the most important development was the displacement of OPEC oil as the leading incremental energy source. As world oil consumption declined and new Western oil came on line, OPEC oil production fell by nearly half, and OPEC's share of the world oil market plummeted from 60 percent in 1974 to 35 percent in 1985.[12] As a result, the cartel lost its leverage over prices. The largest quantities of new non-OPEC energy after the first oil shock were provided by Western oil, representing 33 percent of all additions. Coal contributed 23 percent and nuclear power added 20 percent.[13] At the same time, energy of all sorts

10. Rochelle L. Stanfield, "Fillerup—With What?" *National Journal,* vol. 19 (July 25, 1987), p. 1895.

11. Edward R. Fried, "World Oil Markets: New Benefits, Old Concerns," *Brookings Review,* vol. 4 (Summer 1986), pp. 32–33.

12. Ibid., p. 33.

13. Mark P. Mills and Thomas R. Stauffer with Frank H. Lennox, "The Crash in World Oil Prices: An Analysis of Market Pressures on World Oil Prices," (Washing-

came to be used more efficiently—that is, without causing reductions in economic welfare. This reduced the demand for OPEC oil below what economic growth would otherwise have required. Although the contribution of efficiency is somewhat difficult to estimate, it was probably as important as the three leading sources of new energy combined.[14]

The United States enjoyed the lower oil prices that resulted from these global developments, and it also contributed to them. Although U.S. oil production declined, the country nevertheless reduced its imports of oil by nearly half by 1985, helping to swell world supplies. Again, it is difficult to estimate precisely the components of this response. But the three largest contributors, in order of importance, were conservation, coal, and nuclear power, each of which displaced at least a fifth of the oil that would otherwise have been imported.[15] In addition to its direct impact on oil consumption, conservation reduced the rate of growth in overall energy demand, enabling the United States to squeeze more economic output from each unit of energy input.

In anticipation of future developments, it is worth noting that the continued electrification of the United States played a significant role in reducing oil imports. Although the rate of growth in the demand for electricity fell sharply from its historical levels, electricity consumption continued to increase throughout the 1970s and 1980s, generally keeping pace with economic growth, as overall energy consumption flattened.[16] Through increased use of electricity, the United States was able to exploit alternative fuels, principally coal and nuclear power.[17]

ton, D.C.: Science Concepts, 1986), p. i; and Walter J. Mead, "The OPEC Cartel Thesis Reexamined: Price Constraints from Oil Substitutes," *Journal of Energy and Development*, vol. 11 (Spring 1986), pp. 213–41.

14. Mills and Stauffer with Lennox, "The Crash in World Oil Prices," p. 1; Fried, "World Oil Markets," p. 32; and Hirsch, "Impending United States Energy Crisis," p. 1467.

15. Mills and Stauffer with Lennox, "The Crash in World Oil Prices," pp. 1–2; Frank H. Lennox and Mark P. Mills, "An Analysis of the Role of Nuclear Power in Reducing U.S. Oil Imports," (Washington, D.C.: Science Concepts, 1987), pp. 1–21; and Steven Prokesch, "Wastrels No More in Energy: U.S. Practices Conservation," *New York Times*, February 12, 1986, pp. D1, D5.

16. U.S. Department of Energy, *Energy Security* (DOE, 1987), pp. 130–60; and "Annual Industry Forecast," *Electrical World*, vol. 201 (September 1987), pp. 37–42.

17. As a result, the share of U.S. electricity generated with oil fell from 17 percent in 1973 to 5 percent in 1987 while the shares generated by nuclear power (by 1987 the second most important source of electricity) were essentially the opposite of these

Given these adjustments, where is the problem? Why should the United States be concerned about another energy crisis in the 1990s? The answer begins with world oil markets, which since 1985 have been giving off dramatically different signals than they did during the early 1980s. After declining at a comfortable pace through mid-1985, world oil prices collapsed to $10 a barrel in mid-1986. The immediate cause was the decision of Saudi Arabia, the OPEC member most capable of restricting its output, to triple its production in order to reclaim its severely diminished market share and augment its dwindling oil revenues. The collapse, however, was short-lived. By virtue of renewed OPEC cooperation, prices recovered to $18–$20 a barrel by late 1986 and have remained there, except for occasional dips, ever since. The price is nevertheless well below that of the mid-1980s and highly significant for the world's energy future. The new price signals a change in the prevailing attitude within OPEC, an acceptance (or resignation) among enough OPEC members that stable, low prices are better for the cartel in the long run. In the short run, while oil is plentiful, strict production agreements are difficult to maintain and unlikely to boost world prices substantially. But over the long haul, low prices will increase world oil demand, and, as new Western oil continues to dry up, enable OPEC to regain a dominant market share and real price leverage. Working on the assumption that OPEC will follow this patient course, forecasters generally expect oil prices to increase only gradually into the early 1990s and then to gain more rapidly.[18]

To be sure, oil price forecasts are notoriously unreliable, and

---

figures. Coal increased its share of the electricity market from 46 percent to 57 percent. Department of Energy, *Annual Energy Review 1987*, p. 193.

18. On the machinations within OPEC, see Sarah Miller and Jonathan Birchall with Terri Thompson, "OPEC Pulls Off a Small Miracle," *Business Week* (August 18, 1986), pp. 34–35; and Fried, "World Oil Markets." The more ominous forecasts are found in Hirsch, "Impending United States Energy Crisis"; William W. Hogan and Paul N. Leiby, "Oil Market Risk Analysis," Discussion Paper H-85-03 (Harvard University, John F. Kennedy School of Government, December 1985); Dermot Gately, "Lessons from the 1986 Oil Price Collapse," *Brookings Papers on Economic Activity*, 2: 1986, pp. 237–82; George C. Georgiou, "Oil Market Instability and a New OPEC," *World Policy Journal*, vol. 4 (Spring 1987), pp. 295–312; and John Paul Newport, Jr., "Get Ready for the Coming Oil Crisis," *Fortune* (March 16, 1987), pp. 46–57. Less ominous forecasts are found in Fried, "World Oil Markets"; Philip H. Abelson, "Energy Futures," *American Scientist*, vol. 75 (December 1987), pp. 584–93; and Mead, "The OPEC Cartel Thesis Reexamined."

jumps in price may be avoided, may come somewhat later, or may hit sooner. Still, dependence on imported oil is no better an idea for the 1990s than it was in the 1970s. The OPEC nations virtually monopolize proven oil reserves in the non-Communist world, a fact that enhances their ability to act as a cartel.[19] The production costs of OPEC oil are only a fraction of those of American oil, a blessing that provides OPEC great flexibility in pricing and a means of undercutting conservation and alternative fuel development in the United States.[20] The OPEC nations also remain politically unstable, posing a problem for their reliability as energy suppliers. Were market forces capable of moving the United States rapidly and inexpensively away from oil once OPEC regained market control, there would be less to fear from oil imports. But as the United States discovered in the 1970s, oil is difficult to displace once it becomes integral to the economy. It is disturbing, therefore, that oil imports rose to over 40 percent of U.S. oil needs in 1987 and are projected to reach 50 percent in the 1990s.[21] Once again, the United States is on the slippery slope toward excessive import dependence.

The principal cause of this backsliding is the switch in oil price signals. In real terms, oil prices have lost most of what they gained during the decade following the first oil shock. Some of the once powerful incentives to produce and conserve energy domestically have weakened with them. Domestic oil production—from costly low-yield wells—has consequently fallen by about 10 percent.[22] Industries are finding it profitable to substitute oil for other fuels, particularly natural gas.[23] Economic growth, stimulated by cheap oil, is causing overall energy demand to rise once again, and the demand for electricity, which has always kept pace with the econ-

---

19. According to recent estimates, OPEC controls 82 percent of the world's recoverable oil reserves. "New Data Lift World Oil Reserves by 27%," *Oil and Gas Journal* (December 28, 1987).

20. Department of Energy, *Energy Security*, p. 23; and James R. Schlesinger, "Oil Euphoria Obscures Potential Political Problems," *Financier* (April 1986), p. 17.

21. Department of Energy, *Annual Energy Review 1987*, p. 107; Hirsch, "Impending United States Energy Crisis," p. 1472; and many of the forecasts cited in note 18.

22. Department of Energy, *Energy Security*, pp. 22–23; Abelson, "Energy Futures," p. 584; and Newport, "Get Ready for the Coming Oil Crisis," p. 47.

23. Hirsch, "Impending United States Energy Crisis," p. 1471; Schlesinger, "Oil Euphoria Obscures Potential Political Problems," p. 17; and John Burnstein, "The Hidden Dangers of Cheaper Oil," *Houston Post*, March 18, 1986.

omy, to rise even faster.[24] Oil is meeting much of this new demand, even that for electricity, where some of the largest reductions in oil consumption had been registered. Because oil prices will probably remain low in the near term, these developments are likely to continue, becoming essential to economic activity and thereby resistant to rapid change.

Market forces, however, are not the only reason for increasing import dependence. Government policies, to a significant extent, still stimulate energy demand, and, to an even greater extent, discourage domestic energy supply. This is especially true of energy regulatory policies that enhance the appeal of oil imports on both sides of the economic equation. To be sure, regulation on the demand side has been improved. Oil prices are no longer held below market level, encouraging consumption and subsidizing imports. When world oil prices rise, the demand for oil will be efficiently discouraged. Natural gas prices are also closer to market levels than in the past as a result of partial deregulation. But in some parts of the country the consumption of natural gas is still subsidized, increasing the demand for a fuel for which oil imports are a close substitute. Finally, electricity consumption, by virtue of regulated prices that fall short of covering replacement costs, is also subsidized.

On the supply side, improvements are harder to find.[25] The production of natural gas, coal, nuclear power, and electricity from other sources is discouraged in various ways by government regulation.[26] If regulation were producing benefits generally considered to exceed those of reduced import dependence, or if the benefits of regulation were at least being produced at costs competitive with those of alternative policies, the discouragement of domestic en-

24. "Annual Industry Forecast," p. 37; "Annual General Construction Survey," *Electrical World* (January 1988), p. 45; Department of Energy, *Energy Security*, pp. 130–60; and Ahmad Faruqui, "U.S. Electricity Use: 1950–2000," *Forum for Applied Research and Public Policy* (Winter 1986), pp. 56–61.

25. Although oil prices are no longer regulated, a windfall profits tax will act much like price regulation in discouraging domestic oil production when world oil prices rise.

26. While it is also true that the government encourages energy supplies with various tax incentives and R & D subsidies, this does not balance policies that discourage supplies in the ineffective or inefficient pursuit of other goals, such as consumer protection. Tax incentives and R & D subsidies have also been reduced in the 1980s.

ergy production would be acceptable. As will become clear, however, these conditions are not being met.

The United States may therefore have to wait for the price of OPEC oil to reach unnecessary heights before energy development and conservation, so vital in the 1970s, become more economical and gain pace. Because so much of the new energy development is again likely to require the addition (or replacement) of electric power capacity, which can take a decade or more to bring on line, and because so little of that development is now under way, the country may also have to pay OPEC oil prices for an unnecessarily long time.[27] The government could help to spare the country from these costs with various measures, including, but not limited to, regulatory reform. The other most promising approaches are probably taxes on gasoline or imported oil. Both would directly deter oil imports, and the latter would encourage domestic oil production. The development of fuel substitutes for gasoline and oil would also be stimulated. Given the large federal budget deficit, there is reason to believe that the negative economic effect of increased taxation would be offset by the eventual economic benefits of a more balanced fiscal policy. Still, there are problems with both measures and obstacles to their adoption that are beyond the scope of this analysis.[28] Regulatory reform, the measure addressed here, also has substantial potential for increasing energy security—and raises issues of its own. These issues, however, tend to be political rather than technical.

THE DELEGATION PROBLEM

All of the United States' most promising energy sources are controlled directly or indirectly by administrative agencies. Natural

27. Department of Energy, *Energy Security*, pp. 130–60; Mark P. Mills, "A Return of the Age of Oil for the U.S. Electricity Supply System?" *Public Utilities Fortnightly* (February 6, 1986), pp. 33–39; and Martin L. Baughman, "What Cheap Fuel Will Do to Electricity and the Economy," *Electric Perspectives* (Fall 1986), pp. 16–27.

28. The adverse economic consequences of energy taxes are analyzed in Fried, "World Oil Markets," p. 38; Congressional Budget Office, "The Budgetary and Economic Effects of Oil Taxes" (CBO, 1986); Stanley Reed, "Why an Oil-Import Tax Would be a Mistake," *New York Times*, February 7, 1986; and Richard J. Gilbert and Knut Anton Mork, "Will World Oil Markets Tighten Again? A Survey of Policies to Manage Possible Oil Supply Disruptions," *Journal of Policy Modeling*, vol. 6 (February 1984), pp. 111–42.

gas is governed mainly by the pricing regulations of the Federal Energy Regulatory Commission (FERC). Nuclear power is subject to licensing by the Nuclear Regulatory Commission (NRC). Coal-fired electricity is affected by various federal agencies, perhaps most significantly the Environmental Protection Agency (EPA), which regulates coal emissions and air quality. In addition, electricity generated by any means must be approved by state public utility commissions that have authority over supply, price, and, often, power plant location. Electricity is also governed by interstate transmission and cogeneration rules administered by FERC. Because many of the less immediate energy alternatives—solar, wind, biomass—are intended to produce electricity, they also will come under the influence of many of these agencies. These are not the only agencies that affect the production and consumption of energy supplies; they are only the most consequential.

Subjecting energy supplies to administrative supervision is not new to U.S. policy. Natural gas has been regulated at the national level since FERC's predecessor, the Federal Power Commission (FPC), was authorized in 1938 and at the state level for much longer. Nuclear power has been tightly controlled since the Atomic Energy Commission (AEC), the NRC's forerunner, was chartered in 1946. State regulation of electricity is almost as old as the energy source itself. And the nation's oil supply was managed by a few state conservation agencies until the early 1970s and by several federal regulatory bodies until 1981. Some energy regulation, primarily that administered by the EPA, is relatively new. But most of it is not. What is new is the diminishing caliber of its performance, its increasing inability to fulfill the objectives of policy effectively or efficiently.

This raises key questions. Why should an administrative solution that worked for years stop working? Why should it prove increasingly unsatisfactory to delegate control over key energy supply problems to administrative agencies? A good part of the reason is that the administration of energy supplies, while inherently difficult, has grown steadily more troublesome over time. Since the advent of domestic oil scarcity, moreover, the growth of problems has accelerated.

The U.S. energy supply system has traditionally been considered ripe for regulation. The transmission systems and pipelines that distribute electricity, natural gas, and oil exhibit many of the characteristics of natural monopolies, for example, large economies of scale and declining marginal costs. If the government licenses a single firm to control distribution, subject to publicly established prices, the public may be better served by monopoly than by competition. The processes that produce energy—oil drilling, coal burning, atom splitting—also indicate a need for regulation. The market alone may not encourage energy producers to limit some of the by-products of their activities to socially acceptable levels. The government may therefore be able to increase the public welfare by forcing producers to internalize safety or cleanup costs that would otherwise be external to energy transactions. These and other classic failures of free markets have long justified government intervention in the supply of energy. To be sure, these conditions have undergone steady change, usually in the direction of weakening the justification for intervention. But setting that issue temporarily to the side, there is the equally important issue of the form government intervention should take when it is judged to be warranted.

This issue has prompted debate among various experts, but very little among politicians. In the view of politicians, the appropriate form of intervention has been as clear-cut as the justifications for it. Congress and the president, or sometimes the courts, should establish the objectives of the intervention and then turn over the job of accomplishing them to an administrative body. The explicit reasons for this are quite sensible. Politicians have neither the expertise to design policies in adequate detail nor the capacity to acquire greater expertise in every area in which they must act. The situations that policies address are subject to change, and politicians are not in a position to revise laws as needed. Even if the issues do not change, they often involve questions of fact more than of value, and therefore require little political judgment. There is also something to be said for protecting questions of fact from answers that are slanted by political bias. Administrative agencies, specialized to bring expertise to their tasks, organized to make the complex manageable, and staffed impartially to ensure objectivity, can carry out policies with a level of effectiveness and efficiency that politicians (or courts) cannot.

Of course, politicians may not fully accept this line of reasoning, and they have other motives (discussed below) for favoring delegation. But for decades, beginning in the late nineteenth century, politicians were bombarded by Progressives, management "scientists," and interest groups with this "good government" rationale.[29] And they responded as if they were persuaded. From the turn of the century through the New Deal, delegation to administrative agencies became a standard formula for public problem solving. When the problem required market regulation—the case with energy production—the formula was followed almost without exception.

The formula, however, has inherent problems. They start with the fact that once a problem is delegated, its solution may not square with the preferences of those who did the delegating. There is no guarantee that bureaucrats will do what politicians want, even on matters involving the basic values intended for protection by the policy. Thus society may not get the outcomes its elected officials bargained for. The market may be corrected to the satisfaction of the experts, but not to that of the general public.

This problem is especially likely to crop up in delegated interventions into energy markets. The reason is that energy issues are unusually complex and technical, giving bureaucratic experts important advantages over political generalists in negotiations over how policies are being administered. Politicians lose much of their ability to challenge the merit of bureaucratic decisions, actions, or requests. Indeed, politicians are at risk of being deceived about much of what their agencies are doing. Unless politicians are willing to invest heavily in alternative sources of information (a strategy which creates control problems of its own), they will need to defer to the judgments of administrative agencies on a wide range of key energy decisions: the safety of nuclear power plants, the contribution of coal-fired power plants to lake acidification, the equity and efficiency of natural gas prices, the adequacy of electric generating capacity, and much more.

However, even if this "asymmetry of information" between politicians and bureaucrats is severe, politicians need not lose control of their administrative agents.[30] That depends *ex ante* on the

---

29. On this political movement, generally, see Stephen Skowronek, *Building a New American State: The Expansion of National Administrative Capacities, 1877–1920* (Cambridge University Press, 1982). On the establishment of the regulatory agencies, see Marver H. Bernstein, *Regulating Business by Independent Commission* (Princeton University Press, 1955).

30. The concept of information asymmetry is one of the fundamentals of principal-agent theory, a family of economic models of organization. That theory, which guides the following discussion of the delegation problem, is reviewed and applied

degree to which the interests of politicians and bureaucrats are also in conflict. Inevitably there will be some conflict. Bureaucrats almost naturally prefer more discretion and resources—what theorists usually call "slack"—than politicians would like them to have. This has important consequences, for example, for government expenditures. But conflict beyond this basic level, on crucial matters of policy objectives and the means for accomplishing them, is more variable. Some agencies seem to be repeatedly at odds with political overseers. The Federal Energy Administration, which administered oil price regulations during much of the 1970s, is a glaring example. Other agencies, such as the U.S. Geological Survey, responsible for estimating energy reserves, seem to stay constantly in tune with their political environments, playing precisely the roles that are expected of them. Variation also occurs over time. A revered agency such as the Atomic Energy Commission may fall into irreconcilable conflict with political authorities and become a reviled agency like the Nuclear Regulatory Commission. Agencies that enjoy the advantages of asymmetric information—such as energy agencies—are not inevitably problems for politicians who delegate responsibility to them. Much depends on the degree of conflict of interest.

Much also depends on the measures that politicians take to overcome information asymmetries and conflicts of interest when they occur. Unfortunately for politicians, the repertoire of measures available to them is logically pretty limited. Politicians can staff an agency with sympathetic bureaucrats. They can structure agency behavior with rules and incentives that aim to channel bureaucratic interests in politically desirable directions. And they can monitor agency activities and their outcomes, instilling in bureaucrats concern for detection and creating an incentive for appropriate behavior. In practice, politicians end up employing a mixture of all three of these instruments of control.

What is important is that the mixture can have significant consequences, intended and unintended, for the outcomes of delegation. This is especially clear if the delegation is prompted by the complexity or technical difficulty of a policy problem. In such cases, politicians delegate in recognition of their own ignorance

---

to public bureaucracy in Terry M. Moe, "The New Economics of Organization," *American Journal of Political Science*, vol. 28 (November 1984), pp. 739–77.

and incompetence. In practice, this often means that problems are handed over to professionals—in energy agencies, most commonly economists, physicists, engineers, biologists, and lawyers. This has many virtues, especially the integrity that professionalism lends to agency decisions. Politicians may turn problems over to other kinds of experts as well, for example, interest groups or lower governments, both of which have specialized information about their spheres of influence. The key is finding a repository of expertise in which public responsibility can also be vested without fear that interests contrary to those of the public (or at least the politicians' view of the public interest) will be pursued by the experts.

The major difficulty arises when politicians cannot find appropriate experts, or at least experts that are acceptable to all of the interests at stake in the policy dispute. In that event, the politicians must begin substituting their judgment, however uninformed it may be, for the judgments of those more competent to make technical decisions. This they do by constraining agency behavior and decisions, principally through monitoring and regulation. Both approaches, however, have pitfalls. Direct monitoring, through oversight hearings and investigations, for example, is costly, and requires a level of staffing that creates delegation problems of its own.[31] Indirect monitoring, relying on the complaints of groups and constituents subject to agency decisions, is relatively costless, but the quality and balance of the intelligence that it offers are inevitably suspect.[32] Direct regulation tends to be undermined by its information requirements, which by definition are too demanding for politicians to satisfy completely. Still, political circumstances may preclude the delegation of broad responsibility for even the most complex and demanding problems. The task for politicians, then, is finding ways to monitor and regulate without so interfering that a policy becomes ineffective or inefficient. Although politicians have in fact found various ways of resolving this problem, the more they find themselves facing it, the more delega-

31. On the difficulties of direct oversight, see especially Morris S. Ogul, *Congress Oversees the Bureaucracy* (University of Pittsburgh Press, 1976).

32. On the potential for indirect oversight, see especially Matthew D. McCubbins and Thomas Schwartz, "Congressional Oversight Overlooked: Police Patrols Versus Fire Alarms," *American Journal of Political Science*, vol. 28 (February 1984), pp. 165-79.

tion is likely to get into trouble.[33] This is essentially what has happened with the administration of energy supplies.

The administration of energy supplies has gradually evolved from reliance on broad delegation to trusted experts and agents into more circumscribed and supervised delegation to suspect bureaucrats. It has generally shifted from what I shall call the "old delegation" to the "new delegation." With this shift, all of the conditions that can plague delegation, rendering it less effective or efficient, have been exacerbated. From one energy supply issue to the next, the conditions have varied. But a general pattern is plain. The conditions that logically need to be satisfied if delegation is to work are being satisfied less well now than in the past.

THE OLD DELEGATION

The two domestic energy sources that stand to provide the greatest relief from oil imports as the United States moves into the twenty-first century have been regulated by government agencies since the beginning of the twentieth century. Electricity, the demand for which is expected to constitute the bulk of the nation's new energy needs, can be generated by fuels other than oil. It came under the control of state public utility commissions (PUCs) during the Progressive Era and federal commissions during the New Deal. Natural gas, which is a close substitute for oil in many applications and is not in immediate decline, shares electricity's regulatory origins. Both also share a history of diminishing regulatory effectiveness, traceable to the delegated structure of responsibility for their development.

Government control over U.S. electricity and natural gas supplies is delegated in two ways: in the customary manner from politicians to bureaucrats, and in a more distinctive fashion from national authorities to state officials. Over the years, both delegation relationships have become plagued by conflicts of interest and impaired by the efforts of the respective sides of the conflicts to achieve their own ends. But initially relationships were harmonious and delegation reasonably successful.

33. On the problems of political control of the federal bureaucracy, see Terry M. Moe, "An Assessment of the Positive Theory of 'Congressional Dominance,' " *Legislative Studies Quarterly,* vol. 12 (November 1987), pp. 475–520.

Both electricity and natural gas first came under state control, not by explicit delegation of responsibility from the federal level down, but by state intervention in energy markets that the federal government saw no need to occupy.[34] In its first decades of widespread use, beginning in the late 1800s, electricity was generated and distributed on a local basis, usually by several private firms. Towns, cities and states were not interconnected, as they are today; hence the problems associated with electric power could be resolved without mediation by the national government. The primary problem was monopolization. Competition among electric companies turned out to be unstable, with firms gaining continuous advantage through economies of scale and mergers. As competition declined and electric rates rose to monopoly levels, customers pressured the lower governments for relief. The response, after assorted experiments with local regulation and municipal power companies, was essentially the same throughout the nation. Between 1907 and 1922, forty-seven state governments established public utility commissions to regulate the generation and transmission of electricity as a natural monopoly.[35] When natural gas began to be provided by local power companies in the 1920s and 1930s, its distribution came under PUC regulation for the same economic reasons.

The establishment and operation of state PUCs were fairly consistent with a model of effective delegation. There were no significant conflicts of interest between the federal government and the states who were carrying out the new regulatory policy: both were interested in the growth of electricity (and later, natural gas) supplies at fair prices. The creation of independent bodies of experts at the state level went a long way toward protecting regulation from the political interference that could have been expected from the local political machines that ran the cities of the day. And regulating the profits of natural monopolies is a reasonably straightforward technical task that experts can be expected to perform ably.[36]

34. Histories of public utility regulation can be found in David Howard Davis, *Energy Politics*, 3d ed. (St. Martins, 1982), pp. 130–204; and Douglas D. Anderson, *Regulatory Politics and Electric Utilities: A Case of Political Economy* (Auburn House, 1981).

35. Davis, *Energy Politics*, p. 170.

36. Standard methods of rate-of-return regulation are reviewed in Michael A. Crew and Paul R. Kleindorfer, *The Economics of Public Utility Regulation* (MIT Press, 1986). Complications are summarized in that volume and in Paul L. Joskow and

State PUCs did present problems of political control that the Progressive politicians who created them did not anticipate. The power companies enjoyed sizable information advantages over the PUCs and their overseers—legislators, governors, and voters—that sometimes enabled utilities to "capture" PUC decisionmakers.[37] But the pro-industry biases that this ordinarily entails were appreciably mitigated. The power companies tended to accede to PUC regulation, finding it far preferable to the government takeovers with which they were first threatened. Utilities also enjoyed the protected profits they received from their agreement to provide reliable service. But most important, the state PUCs found it possible to provide utilities handsome rates of return without imposing any obvious costs on consumers. Indeed, the PUCs may scarcely have limited profits at all.[38] Until the late 1960s utilities were able to exploit economies of scale and flat fuel costs to deliver electricity at rates that actually declined in real terms for half a century.[39] Avoiding battles with power companies over their profits and with customers over their bills, PUCs were able to satisfy state political interests and to provide the nation with an economical and modern power supply that grew at roughly twice the rate of the economy.

By and large, the federal government permitted PUC regulation, at least of electricity, to proceed unfettered until the 1960s. When it had problems with PUC policy—which it did, selectively—the federal government worked around the regulated system of private power rather than through it. During the Depression, the Roosevelt administration was disturbed that private utilities found

Roger G. Noll, "Regulation in Theory and Practice: An Overview," in Gary Fromm, ed., *Studies in Public Regulation* (MIT Press, 1981), pp. 1–65. The key complication is that while rate-of-return regulation is a straightforward method of protecting consumers against monopoly prices, it is an ineffective tool for ensuring the socially efficient pricing of electricity, that is, at marginal cost. Thus, while the early PUCs were an effective use of delegation for regulating monopoly, they were an ineffective use of it for promoting the efficient production and consumption of electric power.

37. Anderson, *Regulatory Politics and Electric Utilities*, pp. 1–88. On the theory of capture and the alternatives to it, see Roger G. Noll, "Government Regulatory Behavior: A Multidisciplinary Survey and Synthesis," in Noll, ed., *Regulatory Policy and the Social Sciences* (University of California Press, 1985), pp. 9–63.

38. Paul L. Joskow, "Inflation and Environmental Concern: Structural Change in the Process of Public Utility Price Regulation," *Journal of Law and Economics*, vol. 17 (October 1974), pp. 291–327.

39. Anderson, *Regulatory Politics and Electric Utilities*, pp. 61–88.

it uneconomical to provide electricity for many rural areas and farming communities. Thus Roosevelt and the Democratic Congresses created the Tennessee Valley Authority and the Rural Electrification Administration to provide power publicly. The federal government also used its authority over interstate waterways and hence hydroelectric power to set up federal power administrations (such as Bonneville) to provide electricity directly. These endeavors avoided the frictions and delays that would likely have resulted from efforts to work within the state regulatory framework. And they produced very little friction of their own: they were promoted by enthusiastic members of Congress who were delighted to provide jobs and cheap power to grateful constituents.

When it came to natural gas, the federal government did become involved in PUC regulation. But its involvement, at least initially, was fully consistent with the states' objective of managing a natural monopoly. Many PUCs had encountered a problem in controlling gas prices that was not presented by electricity. Most states did not produce their own natural gas, but had to import it from Texas, Louisiana, Oklahoma, California, or a few other gas-producing states. Local gas companies actually purchased their supplies from interstate pipelines that bought and gathered the gas from producers. The local gas companies usually could not shop for the cheapest gas, however, because interstate distribution systems developed along the lines of natural monopolies, serving each city or town most efficiently with a single pipeline. State PUCs consequently found it impossible to control retail gas prices: pipelines were relatively free to set wholesale prices at rent-seeking levels.[40] The PUCs' problem was exacerbated by an unusual degree of concentration in the gas industry in the 1920s and 1930s: pipelines and producers were organized into giant holding companies, four of which controlled nearly 60 percent of gas distribution.[41]

The federal government moved to facilitate state price regulation with two restraints on monopoly. The Public Utility Holding Company Act of 1935 limited to two levels the integration of gas companies and, with the supervision of the Securities and Exchange Commission, reduced the gas giants to regional companies whose market power was lessened and whose financial accounts

40. Stephen G. Breyer and Paul W. MacAvoy, *Energy Regulation by the Federal Power Commission* (Brookings, 1974), pp. 56–88.

41. Davis, *Energy Politics*, pp. 136–38.

were simpler to monitor. This soon became important, for in 1938 the Natural Gas Act gave the Federal Power Commission responsibility for regulating pipeline construction and gas transmission rates. Both of these laws passed amid intense political conflict between industry and local government. But the forms that both laws took, especially the Natural Gas Act, were fairly noncontroversial. Because of their natural monopoly characteristics, gas pipelines were to be regulated by experts who would determine when the public would benefit from construction of a new pipeline and what rates the pipeline could fairly charge for its services. Providing little guidance other than the standard mandate to protect consumers, Congress delegated control over pipelines to the FPC. As with PUC regulation of electricity, FPC regulation was vulnerable to capture. But the gas industry was more concerned with protecting its producer prices from regulation than with fighting the more justifiable regulation of its pipelines. The Supreme Court, moreover, reinforced Congress's intent by giving the FPC ratemaking standards, generally favorable to consumers, that enabled the FPC to perform its rather unexceptional function with confidence.[42]

By the end of the New Deal, the basic structure of electricity and gas regulation, still operative today, was in place. Just before passage of the Natural Gas Act, Congress had completed the regulatory structure for electricity by delegating control over the rates for interstate transmission—still an uncommon and noncontroversial enterprise—to the FPC. The structure governing gas and electricity was a simple one, based on sound principles of regulation and delegation. State governments were the appropriate focus for most ratemaking because local conditions—for example, the fuels for generating electricity—varied widely. The federal government had an inevitable role to play in resolving interstate issues. And experts could be counted on to make the technical determinations to constrain, if not dictate, the prices appropriate for natural monopolists operating within states or between them. From its Progressive political roots to its harmonious administrative design, the system for electricity and gas regulation exemplified the old delegation.

So too did the system established soon thereafter to govern nuclear power, a much more challenging problem of democratic

---

42. In *FPC* v. *Hope Natural Gas Company*, 320 U.S. 591 (1944), the Supreme Court gave the FPC a mechanical method—a "rate-of-return" formula—for pricing pipeline services based on "actual legitimate cost."

control than natural gas or electricity. Nuclear energy, a promising but untested source of electric power, raised profound issues of public safety and national security, unlike any that were addressed by the agencies then responsible for electricity. Indeed, the only agencies of the government experienced with these issues were part of the military. Since the harnessing of atomic energy had resulted from the development of nuclear weapons during World War II, there was a distinct possibility after the war that the development of nuclear energy for all purposes would remain securely under military control. Although that proved politically unpopular, the security concerns that justified military control determined the organization of responsibility for nuclear power development. Nuclear power, from the enrichment of uranium through the construction and operation of reactors to the disposal of wastes, was to be monopolized by the federal government. Lower levels of government and the private sector were to be excluded. Pursuant to this, the 1946 Atomic Energy Act gave complete control over nuclear power to a single federal agency, the Atomic Energy Commission, and made it subject to the authority of but one committee in Congress, the Joint Committee on Atomic Energy (JCAE)—the only congressional committee to derive its powers from a permanent statute rather than the more flexible rules of Congress.

The delegation of power to the AEC was as simple in structure as the federal government permits: a pair of political sovereigns— one committee of Congress and the president—and one federal agency, without obligations to other agencies at any level. But it was not a delegation without problems. Never before had political sovereigns been so utterly lacking in expertise to guide or control an agency's behavior. Having decided not to give control over the new source of power to the military, however, Congress and the White House had little choice but to place their trust in the only other available experts, the nuclear scientists. During its early years, the AEC was therefore run by (and for) the scientists who staffed the agency and were constituted as the General Advisory Council to "assist" the inexpert AEC commissioners.[43]

By the early 1950s, however, the JCAE, especially its Democratic

43. On the process and politics of AEC–NRC decisionmaking see Joseph P. Tomain, *Nuclear Power Transformation* (Indiana University Press, 1987); John E. Chubb, *Interest Groups and the Bureaucracy: The Politics of Energy* (Stanford University Press, 1983), pp. 89–125; and Davis, *Energy Politics*, pp. 205–42.

members, challenged the scientists' view of the AEC's mission. For politicians accustomed to the administrative pace of the New Deal (and fearful of the Soviet Union, which had—to the scientists' surprise—entered the nuclear age itself), the AEC scientists were too slow and conservative. The development of atomic energy needed to involve more than pure research and military applications, for example, atomic submarines. In Congress's view, atomic energy should also be developed for practical civilian purposes, certainly electric generation, and preferably through public works projects along the lines of the TVA or federal hydroelectric power. Although politicians still lacked the expertise to determine independently what new applications were technically feasible (the JCAE even had to borrow staff from the AEC), Congress had the power to force the AEC to try new applications. This power was exercised in the Atomic Energy Act of 1954.

A compromise between the Eisenhower administration, which opposed additional public power projects, and the Democratic Congress, intent on civilian nuclear power, the new legislation established the basic structure of nuclear power development that remains in place today. The act gave the AEC complete responsibility for supervising the development of commercial nuclear power. The only means specified in the statute for doing this was for the AEC to issue licenses for reactor construction and operation. Consistent with Congress's lack of expertise and the inherent difficulty of forecasting the needs of a new technology, the act gave the AEC only rough performance standards—ensuring the public health and safety—and few procedural standards other than holding hearings. In addition, Congress asked that industry be permitted into the AEC's exclusive scientific circle, and it authorized the AEC to subsidize the construction of experimental reactors—that is, to promote, and not simply to regulate, nuclear power's development.

With the assignment of these new responsibilities in 1954, the relationship between the AEC and the Congress and president settled into the pattern of the old delegation, where it was to remain for nearly twenty years. Politicians agreed that the country should be developing nuclear power through private initiative but with public supervision. It was also agreed that the most effective form of supervision would be by a single agency staffed by scientists, and later engineers, who were uniquely qualified to evaluate the safety and other attributes of nuclear reactors and their associated power systems. While technical considerations demanded that the delegation to the AEC be rather complete, based more on trust than regulation, Congress organized itself, through the unusually specialized JCAE, to maximize its expertise and intelligence and to focus its authority and potential control.

Knowing that its mistakes might well be detected and result in limits on its autonomy, the AEC used its delegated powers to fulfill political expectations to a large extent. By the end of the 1960s ten commercial reactors were in operation, several of which had been operating safely for a decade. The reactors were being brought into operation roughly on schedule, about six years from start to finish.[44] And most important, nearly one hundred reactors were under construction or on order, suggesting that nuclear power was on its way to displacing oil as the dominant U.S. fuel. To be sure, there are reasons for this performance that go well beyond the harmonious structure of regulation—for example, the "turnkey" contracts of nuclear vendors.[45] But as the changes that were to come with the new delegation will make clear, the old delegation certainly facilitated the successful introduction of nuclear technology into the nation's electricity supply system.

THE NEW DELEGATION

While the old delegation remained essentially intact until the mid-1970s, the transition to the new delegation began much earlier, with the growth of discord between national political authorities and the agents who were delegated regulatory responsibility. The discord developed out of changes in both groups' interests. Political authorities moved to resolve emerging conflicts not by eliminat-

44. Author's calculations from data in NRC Licensing Reform, Hearing before the Subcommittee on Energy Conservation and Power of the House Committee on Energy and Commerce, 98 Cong. 1 sess. (GPO, 1984), pp. 506–15; and Martin B. Zimmerman, "Learning Effects and the Commercialization of New Energy Technologies: The Case of Nuclear Power," Bell Journal of Economics, vol. 13 (August 1982), pp. 297–310.

45. A "turnkey" contract is an agreement by a nuclear reactor vendor to build a reactor at a guaranteed price and then "turn the key" over to the utility. This early practice protected utilities from cost overruns, which were to become enormous. On the promotion of nuclear power by government and industry, see Tomain, Nuclear Power Transformation, pp. 6–28.

ing or restructuring delegation but by intervening in the extant systems of regulation ever more extensively. The unintended consequences of this include many of the energy regulatory problems of today.

Natural Gas

Significant discord developed first in the regulation of natural gas. When the FPC began regulating natural gas, its responsibilities were limited to the licensing and pricing of gas pipelines, manageable tasks that could be guided by standard models of public utility regulation and that were generally supported by Congress and a series of presidents. The tasks were not easy, for even with political and then judicial support, pricing required a certain amount of nontechnical balancing of consumer and industry interests. But even though natural gas consumers were well organized—through local gas distribution companies—their differences with gas pipelines were in principle and in practice resolvable. The problem was that the fair and effective regulation of gas pipelines did not guarantee cheap gas, which was what consumers and state and local governments, the political forces behind the 1938 Natural Gas Act, really wanted. Cheap gas could not be guaranteed unless the price charged at the wellhead by natural gas producers was also regulated. From the outset, the FPC contended that it did not have the authority to set wellhead prices, and Congress backed its agency on this point. But the FPC's political superiors in the other two branches disagreed, siding instead with consumers, and the seeds of discord were sown.

Natural gas producers enjoyed strong support in Congress through the 1940s, 1950s, and 1960s. When pressure for the FPC to regulate wellhead prices was approaching its zenith, the key Senate subcommittee, chaired by Lyndon B. Johnson, from the producing state of Texas, was solidly on the industry's side. In 1949, for example, it rejected President Truman's renomination of Leland Olds, the FPC's most proconsumer commissioner, and was supported by the full Senate by a vote of 53–15.[46] One year later, though, Truman retaliated by vetoing the Kerr bill, which Congress had passed to limit the FPC's jurisdiction to pipelines.

46. Davis, *Energy Politics*, p. 142.

President Truman was not Congress's only adversary, however. In 1945 the Supreme Court had extended FPC regulation to cover the wellhead price of gas produced by subsidiaries of the pipelines, and in 1954, in *Phillips* v. *Wisconsin,* it stretched it to cover all gas produced for interstate sale.[47] The FPC was thereby delegated an enormous responsibility—pricing the products of thousands of producers—that most of its commissioners and staff had long resisted and that its superiors in Congress continued to reject forcefully throughout the 1950s. Indeed, were it not for several scandalous incidents of gas industry lobbying, legislation probably would have terminated wellhead regulation before it had really started.[48]

The lack of strong political support and clear direction steadily took a toll on FPC performance. Wellhead price regulation was technically more difficult than pipeline regulation, for it applied to far more firms and addressed issues distinct from those of natural monopoly. The gas-producing industry was effectively competitive, so prices would be difficult to administer very efficiently. Without statutory guidelines or much in the way of economic precedents and principles, the FPC charted a cautious course—not only with respect to the technical matter of gas pricing but also in relation to its divided political superiors. After setting temporary prices nationwide, it embarked on a careful case-by-case review of the evidence concerning appropriate pricing for each gas producer. This procedure, in effect dictated by the FPC's vague new mandate, protected the FPC from charges that its decisions were governed by considerations that did not derive from the merits of each case. Through adjudication, the FPC minimized the conflict of interest between itself and its political sovereigns, whose loyalties were divided between producers and consumers.

The key problem with this resolution of the delegation problem is that the adjudicatory process was slow. By 1960 the FPC had not settled the 1954 Phillips case, and it was backlogged with additional cases beyond any hope of effective resolution. To ameliorate the

47. The 1945 case, *Colorado Interstate Gas Co.* v. *Federal Power Commission,* 324 U.S. 581 (1945), and the more significant *Phillips* case, *Phillips Petroleum Co.* v. *State of Wisconsin,* 347 U.S. 672 (1954), are discussed in Ralph K. Huitt, "National Regulation of the Natural Gas Industry," in Emmette S. Redford, ed., *Public Administration and Policy Formation* (University of Texas Press, 1956), pp. 53–116.

48. Davis, *Energy Politics,* pp. 144–45, recounts two notorious episodes of alleged attempts at bribing legislators.

situation, the FPC established new interim prices (a higher price for new production and a lower one for existing production, which was to become a troublesome precedent), and it initiated a new case-by-case process to determine prices on a more general, areawide basis. But by the end of the 1960s this procedure also proved to be too cumbersome. Cases continued to drag on for five years, and regulated producer prices lagged badly behind changes in supply and demand.[49]

The FPC's cautious response to its delegation problem was ultimately undermined by the peaking of U.S. natural gas production in 1971. During the 1950s and 1960s, lags in FPC decisionmaking led gas producers to shift much of their supplies from regulated, low-priced interstate markets to unregulated, higher-priced intrastate markets. Until 1970 there was sufficient gas for interstate markets, even at the FPC's low prices, after the more profitable intrastate markets were serviced. But in the 1970s, with no additional production, the rising demand at controlled prices could no longer be fully satisfied. The FPC therefore needed a new strategy. With its existing authority, however, there was only one available to it: raising interstate prices to levels competitive with intrastate prices. There was no strategy that would both eliminate shortages and continue to provide interstate consumers with low prices. When the FPC turned to its political sovereigns for a way out of its dilemma, they offered none. The energy crisis had made Congress and presidents wary of subsidized prices that encouraged excessive gas consumption. But the crisis had not lessened political concern about interstate consumers who would protest the loss of their long-time FPC subsidy. As a result, the government could not agree on any change in pricing policy and left the problem of shortages to the FPC. The agency's inevitable response was a series of price hikes that relieved the shortages but brought a rain of protests down upon the agency. Not until 1978 was the FPC—by then reconstituted as the Federal Energy Regulatory Commission—delegated new authority, more consistent with the limitations of the country's natural gas resources.

The Natural Gas Policy Act of 1978 did not resolve the problems

---

49. Adjudication and its attendant regulatory lags are blamed for most of the FPC's pricing problems in Breyer and MacAvoy, *Energy Regulation by the Federal Power Commission*, pp. 61–88, 135–65.

of wellhead pricing, however. It added to them. The act gave FERC responsibility for the wellhead prices of intrastate gas to eliminate the bias against interstate markets and mandated different prices for roughly two dozen different kinds of gas, varying mainly in age of discovery and depth of production. Because the act also called for the deregulation of all but the oldest gas (still a large portion of all production) in 1985 and of some new gas immediately, it was a compromise between consumer interests in low prices, industry interests in competitive rates of return, and national energy interests in maximizing gas production and its efficient use. The act was not a classic compromise in which these interests would be balanced by administrative experts, however. It was a compromise in which many of the participants insisted that their interests not be placed at the mercy of administrators and experts. Congress and the president, therefore, sought to legislate prices and the conditions for their increase—but only to a point. FERC was delegated the responsibility for ensuring that the statute effectively served the interests of consumers, industry, and the nation generally.

The detail of this delegation had the virtue of providing FERC the kind of technical guidance and political protection that the FPC never had. But it also threatened to produce unintended consequences that FERC would be too constrained to correct or accommodate. To date, unintended consequences have been the hallmark of this new delegation. As oil prices fell, so did the attractiveness of gas selling at high prices that were fixed by law or long-term contract (encouraged by legislated price increases) or driven by deregulated new production. Large industrial and commercial gas users with the ability to switch to oil did so. Because pipelines had contracted to buy gas for years to come at high prices, expensive gas was nevertheless being produced in large quantities. This caused a serious problem for pipelines. They had to try to sell the overpriced gas to local gas companies whose captive customers, residential and small business consumers, did not have the luxury of switching to oil. Since many local gas companies could not choose among gas suppliers, pipelines sometimes succeeded in passing high gas prices on. Not all gas users were victimized by the law, however. In some parts of the country, gas companies and large users, such as electric utilities, had access to regulated "old gas" priced well below market levels.

All of this made the consequences of natural gas policy perverse.[50] While the nation was expressly concerned with utilizing its most attractive alternative to imported oil efficiently but without exposing consumers to hardship, it was accomplishing neither goal very successfully. The policy discriminated arbitrarily among small consumers who were trapped by supply systems, giving some protection from market prices but forcing others to pay high regulated prices. The policy had a somewhat different effect on large users, providing a subsidy to some but driving many of those who faced high prices to switch to imported oil. To be sure, any policy that pursues equity and efficiency simultaneously will produce compromised outcomes to some degree. But the dual inefficiencies of natural gas policy—some gas users are encouraged to substitute imported oil and others to waste gas—are not being counterbalanced by equity; that is, controlled prices help some consumers while indiscriminately hurting others.

Since its creation, FERC has had to devote much of its time to undoing these unintended consequences. This has involved the issuance of a series of regulations or "orders" aimed at lowering artificial gas prices and thereby eliminating the inadvertent gas surplus. FERC's basic approach has been to facilitate direct purchases of cheaper wellhead gas by large commercial and industrial users who were switching to oil. To be equitable, this approach has also tried to provide local gas distribution companies the same opportunity to "shop" for the lowest-priced gas. Thus far, the approach has made only halting progress because it tends to leave pipelines, which are effectively being asked to work as common carriers, with old contractual obligations for expensive gas that they will not be able to sell in a new market.

The Natural Gas Policy Act does not delegate FERC sufficient latitude to progress much further, however. FERC lacks the author-

---

50. The labyrinth of natural gas regulation is well analyzed in Stephen F. Williams, *The Natural Gas Revolution of 1985* (Washington, D.C.: American Enterprise Institute for Public Policy Research, 1985); Edward J. Mitchell, ed., *The Deregulation of Natural Gas* (Washington, D.C.: American Enterprise Institute for Public Policy Research, 1983); Henry G. Broadman, "Natural Gas Deregulation: The Need for Further Reform," *Journal of Policy Analysis and Management*, vol. 5 (Spring 1986), pp. 496–516; Pietro S. Nivola, "The Political Economy of Deregulation in the Energy Sector," paper prepared for the McNaughton Symposium, November 4–5, 1987; and Department of Energy, *Energy Security*, pp. 114–25.

ity to raise the price of old gas to levels that would encourage producers to supply more of it and to renegotiate long-term pipeline contracts for overpriced new gas. It also lacks the power to require pipelines to transport gas as common carriers and the discretion to certify enough new pipelines to permit the gas transmission system, like the system for oil, to operate competitively. FERC's hands are legally tied, and its actions are repeatedly second-guessed by divided political overseers. The Reagan administration has pushed FERC toward market pricing. Congress speaks with many voices, but by repeatedly failing to deregulate, it has conveyed its general suspicions about competition. Meanwhile, the courts have overturned FERC orders for exceeding statutory authority. The agency is consequently left little alternative but to fall back on its traditional strategy of case-by-case negotiations with producers, pipelines, and consumers.[51] Progress is being made.[52] But FERC alone cannot eliminate the perverse inefficiencies of natural gas production and consumption or ensure against excessive dependence on imported oil or natural gas.

Coal-fired Electricity

The experiences of natural gas regulation, though unique in certain details, have been replayed in the regulation of electricity and the fuels that are used to generate it. Conflicts of interest, ultimately deriving from the increasing scarcity of domestic oil, began to plague old delegation relationships. To protect their interests, national political authorities began to impose new demands on these relationships, which ultimately failed to serve them. The new forms of delegation did produce important results desired by national authorities, but not without unintended consequences

51. The politics of the stalemate are highlighted in Burt Solomon, "Ganging Up," *National Journal*, vol. 18 (July 19, 1986), pp. 1778–81; and Nivola, "Political Economy of Deregulation in the Energy Sector," pp. 7–8.

52. In 1987 the Congress repealed the Fuel Use Act, which for a decade had prevented utilities and industry from building new gas or oil-fired boilers. This will help clear the way for greater use of the country's natural gas resources, which recent estimates indicate are large enough to maintain current production levels for thirty-five years. In addition, gas pipelines are transporting more gas for others: 57 percent of their through-put in the last quarter of 1987, up from 42 percent a year before. On the most recent developments, see Rochelle L. Stanfield, "Gassing Up," *National Journal*, vol. 20 (June 11, 1988), pp. 1538–40.

that were injurious not only to electricity supplies but also to the interests that national intervention sought to protect.

The first source of conflict was the division of regulatory responsibility between the national government and the states, initially pertaining to the issue of air quality but then expanding to include the gamut of issues from electricity pricing to evacuation planning for nuclear power emergencies. Until the 1960s the states had been left almost solely responsible for protecting air quality. The causes and consequences of pollution were deemed to be mostly local and the appropriate remedies highly variable. Federal involvement was unnecessary and unpromising. With the Clean Air Act of 1970, however, these views changed abruptly. The act made air quality a largely national concern. State concerns were declared to be insensitive to the consequences of pollution for neighboring states and solicitous toward polluters who happened to be major employers within particular states. The national government would henceforth establish permissible levels of air pollutants in every part of the country, leaving the states only the discretion over how to reach them.

This was a sharp break with precedent in environmental regulation. But with respect to administrative structure it was not. The Clean Air Act followed a model of cooperative federalism—a marriage of federal control over ends and state control over means—that was already in widespread use, though encountering widespread problems.[53] The Clean Air Act anticipated and attempted to avoid some of these problems, but ultimately encountered them all. Fearing resistance from the states and capture of the Environmental Protection Agency, the fledgling federal agency responsible for monitoring the states, Congress wrote an unusually detailed regulatory statute. It established scores of quality control regions and explicit criteria for the ambient levels of numerous pollutants within those regions. It also laid down guidelines for state implementation plans and prescribed EPA planning where state approaches failed to satisfy federal standards. Both the EPA and the states were unusually constrained by this piece of new delegation.

53. On the politics of air pollution control, see Bruce A. Ackerman and William T. Hassler, *Clean Coal/Dirty Air* (Yale University Press, 1981); and Charles O. Jones, *Clean Air: The Policies and Politics of Pollution Control* (University of Pittsburgh Press, 1975). On the problems associated with implementing pollution control through the federal system, see Peter Huber, "Electricity and the Environment: In Search of Regulatory Authority," *Harvard Law Review*, vol. 100 (March 1987), pp. 1002–65.

Nevertheless, Congress preferred delegating a considerable measure of authority to the states instead of simply making the policy a federal responsibility.

Throughout the 1970s resistance to the Clean Air Act occurred as predicted. For a time the EPA was allowed to try to negotiate cooperation from recalcitrant states. But eventually federal-state conflict led to additional constraints. Especially in the portion of the act that addresses pollution by electric utilities, Congress became extraordinarily specific about pollution remedies to be implemented by the states. Utilities burning coal were singled out (appropriately) as major polluters and required to reduce pollution, not just to specified levels, but by specific technological means, which the EPA interpreted as requiring smokestack scrubbers. Mandated scrubbers are an inefficient approach to regulation, forcing one solution on a problem that has many locally variable remedies, including the use of alternative fuels.[54] But however burdensome this approach may be on ratepayers and utility stockholders, scrubbers significantly improved air quality. The problem is that the constrained and conflict-ridden process has not been able to resolve an additional issue vital to air quality: acid rain. Left unresolved, the acid rain issue creates tremendous uncertainty about the costs of developing future electricity supplies from coal, inflates the risks of investment in coal power plants, and thereby discourages generating capacity development.[55]

Acid rain, as it is popularly called, is not fully controlled by the existing regulatory system because a significant portion of the sulfur pollutants that fall with rain into lakes or waterways originates from sources distances away, where ambient air standards are being met. In other words, the existing system permits—even encourages—states to export some pollutants to other states and nations. Ambient air standards can be met by dispersing pollutants as well as by limiting their production. Utilities have consequently increased the heights of their smokestacks (tripling them between 1975 and 1985) in compliance with EPA regulations. Many states, recognizing that they have little to gain and much to lose from

54. Robert W. Crandall, *Controlling Industrial Pollution: The Economics and Politics of Clean Air* (Brookings, 1983).

55. Although acid rain regulation might well make coal power more expensive, it is not clear that the additional financial costs would exceed the gains from eliminating current financial risks of unsettled regulation.

limiting such practices, have not intervened. The Clean Air Act does give the EPA authority to restrict pollution exports.[56] But the authority is arguable and ambiguous. Environmental groups have been pressuring the EPA and working through the courts to force the EPA to use its authority to control pollution exports.[57] Utilities, generally interpreting the Clean Air Act as a compartmentalized approach to pollution control, have worked vigorously on the other side. Caught in the middle, the EPA has not moved to resolve the acid rain issue.

The EPA's inertia is more deeply rooted than this, however. It grows out of the conflicting signals and directives that it receives from political authorities. The White House has whipsawed the agency with political appointees that have ranged from the environmental activists of the Carter years to the antiregulation zealots of the early Reagan years back to the more even-handed managers of the mid-1980s. The agency has also listened to a cacophony of voices from Congress. Since 1981 Congress has been working on a reauthorization of the Clean Air Act driven in large part by the acid rain issue. The task has proven enormously divisive, overlaying the usual partisan and ideological disputes about regulation with intense regional conflicts between pollution exporters and "importers." Bills have seldom been recommended out of committee and have never passed either house of Congress. If they had passed, President Reagan, who favors the extant act, would have been waiting with a veto.[58] As this debate has raged on, and the participants have argued over what the EPA can and cannot, and should and should not, do about acid rain, the agency has been left uncertain how to proceed and also rather certain that however it did proceed, it would be redirected by the pending changes in its authorizing legislation. Although Congress and the president continue to cling to the old system of responsibilities delegated to the EPA and the states, it is little wonder that that system has failed to resolve a key environmental issue. Both the improvement of water quality and the development of electricity from coal have suffered as a result.

56. Huber, "Electricity and the Environment," pp. 1034–35.

57. Rochelle L. Stanfield, "Environmentalists Try the Backdoor Approach to Tackling Acid Rain," National Journal, vol. 17 (October 19, 1985), pp. 2365–68.

58. Eight years of political stalemate are summarized in Rochelle L. Stanfield, "Punching at Smog," National Journal, vol. 20 (March 5, 1988), pp. 600–602.

Nuclear Power

The problems that the regulatory structure has created for coal production have been mirrored and magnified in the regulation of nuclear power. This comes as some surprise since nuclear regulation was organized from the start to minimize conflict. Congressional control was centralized, the AEC's expertise was trusted and respected, and no authority was delegated below the federal level. Yet, by the mid-1970s the old delegation relationship had become riven with conflict, including disputes involving the states. And today there is consensus among supporters and opponents of nuclear power alike that the nuclear regulatory system, now modeled after the new delegation, will need to be changed before nuclear power develops any further.[59]

The old delegation was partially a victim of its own success. Its tightly controlled process, simultaneously regulating and promoting nuclear power, helped convince utilities in the 1960s that electricity could be generated more economically, cleanly, and safely with nuclear power than with any of the alternative fuels. Coming at a time when domestic oil and gas production were peaking and coal-fired power plants were running into environmental attacks, utilities welcomed the promising news from the AEC. From the late 1960s until the first oil shock, utilities across the United States were ordering nuclear reactors of increasing generating capacity at the rate of about twenty-five a year. Operational reactors were expected to number over 200 by the end of the 1980s and to be producing perhaps 40 percent of the nation's electricity.[60] Today, those expectations are still far from being realized. With a little over 100 plants producing electricity and a dozen or so awaiting completion, nuclear power's contribution to the nation's electric supply will soon exceed the combined contributions of all fuels other than coal, but its share of the electricity market will peak at about 20 percent.[61] The reasons for nuclear power's unfulfilled promises are many. It can be argued, however, that they begin with breakdowns

59. *Proposed Changes in the Nuclear Powerplant Licensing Process,* Committee Print, Subcommittee on Energy Conservation and Power of the House Committee on Energy and Commerce, 99 Cong. 2 sess. (GPO, 1987), pp. 1–16.

60. Tomain, *Nuclear Power Transformation,* pp. 10–11; and I. C. Bupp, "The Nuclear Stalemate," in Stobaugh and Yergin, eds., *Energy Future,* p. 108.

61. Department of Energy, *Energy Security,* pp. 182–95.

in the regulatory process prompted by nuclear energy's remarkable early success.

Once the AEC succeeded in transforming nuclear power from a distant hope to an immediate promise, it inevitably began to attract greater attention, especially from the hundreds of communities about to become homes to nuclear power plants.[62] The environmental movement also took interest, raising new issues such as thermal water pollution and helping to politicize the key local issue, nuclear safety. Previously quiescent, these interest groups had not played a significant role in nuclear regulation, neither stimulating political oversight nor working directly with the AEC. The AEC's rules of procedure permitted public participation, but during the 1960s the opportunity was rarely taken. The regulatory process essentially involved nuclear experts from government and industry working together to design plants that in their view were both safe and efficient. The formal procedure for this was licensing, first of plant construction and then of full power operation.

To accommodate the great uncertainties of a new technology, the process was kept flexible. General rules for reactor design were few, permitting utilities to tailor plants to local circumstances and to choose among alternative reactor technologies and vendors. Designs were also permitted to be incomplete during construction licensing, allowing for innovations and learning that would likely occur while plants were built. In the view of the AEC and the JCAE, this unstandardized, design-as-you-go process increased the efficiency and effectiveness of nuclear plants in all respects, including their safety. In the view of many outside the regulatory system, the process simply catered to utilities, who were suspected of caring little about safety or the environment.

Around 1970, when nuclear power development began to escalate, increasing numbers of once-dormant interest groups began to question the integrity of the regulatory process. Despite the relatively smooth performance of the reactors brought into commercial operation by the AEC during the 1960s, experts were not going to be entrusted so completely now that their decisions promised to have such a widespread effect. Under pressure from the environmental movement and groups of local activists, the old delegation

---

62. The following discussion draws on Chubb, *Interest Groups and the Bureaucracy*, pp. 89–125.

rapidly began to give way. In 1971 the Supreme Court decided that the National Environmental Policy Act required the AEC to prepare environmental impact statements before granting construction licenses. In 1974, partly in response to environmental protests and partly in response to the first oil shock, the AEC was divided in two. An Energy Research and Development Administration would assume all responsibilities for commercializing alternative fuels. The Nuclear Regulatory Commission would handle only the AEC's regulatory responsibilities and be free from all promotional conflicts of interest. In 1977 the JCAE was disbanded after it had already lost battles with the rest of Congress over the AEC, its commissioners, and its responsibilities. The joint committee's responsibilities were turned over to five congressional committees; the leading two, House Interior and Senate Environment, had not previously exercised jurisdiction over nuclear power promotion, only environmental regulation. The divisions of opinion about how nuclear regulation should proceed were now embodied in the NRC's congressional oversight structure. In the 1980s these divisions only intensified. The 1979 Three Mile Island accident, although contained, strengthened political demands for tougher NRC regulation and weakened public support for nuclear power.[63] The accident at Chernobyl in the Soviet Union in 1986 had much the same effect, despite the fundamental differences in American and Soviet reactors.[64]

The old system of delegation was substantially changed, then, during the 1970s and 1980s. But a vital part of it was left completely intact. Reactor licensing continued to follow the ad hoc procedures that were authorized by the 1954 Atomic Energy Act and designed for nuclear power during its infancy. Despite criticism of the procedures, first from environmentalists and local activists and then, beginning in the mid-1970s, from the nuclear industry itself, the

63. Many of the demands for change are summarized in the report of the commission that President Carter appointed to investigate the 1979 Three Mile Island accident, the Kemeny commission report. After the accident, the portion of the public "favoring the building of more nuclear power plants in the United States" fell steadily from a strong majority to a small minority. Nevertheless, other surveys suggest that the public is now essentially ambivalent about nuclear power. For a review of the surveys, see William Schneider, "Public Ambivalent on Nuclear Power," *National Journal*, vol. 18 (June 21, 1986), pp. 1562–63.

64. On the technical implications of the Chernobyl accident for the American nuclear power program, see Richard Wilson, "Chernobyl: Assessing the Accident," *Issues in Science and Technology* (Fall 1986), pp. 21–29.

adjudicatory licensing process survived the demise of the old delegation. But under the new delegation, the process became increasingly troublesome. Flexibility, once a virtue of the system, became a liability.

Nuclear power projects had always been vulnerable to delays and design changes because the open-ended, case-by-case regulatory process invited them. With NRC regulation, these interruptions became more frequent.[65] Unlike the AEC, which was relatively free to evaluate prospective changes in plant construction and operations on their merits and to do so expeditiously, the NRC was relatively constrained. It lacked strong political support, served many political masters, and was subject to swift political reprimand if it failed to respond satisfactorily to a complaint against a nuclear plant or construction project. It also could count on its decisions being reported back to politicians, for its activities were monitored, however inexpertly, by interest groups that the AEC never had to deal with.

Among these groups, perhaps the most important were state and local governments, which had always had the right to participate in the licensing process and subsequently laid claim to the right to control evacuation planning for nuclear accidents. In 1987 the NRC attempted to wrest this control away from two states, New York and Massachusetts, which had refused to cooperate with emergency planning and were thereby blocking the operation of two completed power plants. Congress nearly passed legislation prohibiting the NRC from preempting state actions—in just these two cases.[66] While this is the farthest Congress ever went to control specific NRC decisions, it is representative of the change in attitude among the political overseers of nuclear power that took place in the 1970s and 1980s. Indeed, one of the leading nuclear overseers in the House of Representatives today, former Conservation and Power Subcommittee Chairman Edward Markey, led the battle against NRC preemption.

Also indicative of the change in Congress is the incessant legislative debate over how to reform the licensing process. Beginning

65. Department of Energy, *Energy Security*, pp. 182–210; *Proposed Changes in the Nuclear Powerplant Licensing Process*, Committee Print; and Charles Komanoff, *Power Plant Cost Escalation: Nuclear and Coal Capital Costs, Regulation, and Economics* (New York: Komanoff Energy Associates, 1981).

66. Martha Bridegam, "House Refuses to Block Nuclear Plant Openings," *Congressional Quarterly Weekly Report*, vol. 45 (August 8, 1987), pp. 1797–99.

during the Carter administration and continuing to the present, Congress has regularly proposed wholesale changes in nuclear licensing.[67] To be sure, the old process remains intact, and the NRC continues to receive all of the formal professional autonomy enjoyed by the AEC. But the NRC's effective autonomy has been much less; it has been subject to altogether different political controls. In some consequence of this, the NRC has been more prone than the AEC to occupy itself, often at great length, with issues of ongoing plant construction and operation and to demand changes at nuclear facilities, often requiring backfitting, rebuilding, and great expense.[68]

There is little doubt that this shift in the regulatory process has increased the cost of nuclear power in the United States. Increases in mandated design changes and new construction add directly to plant costs. Delays of any kind increase the costs of plant financing. Since the early 1970s the capital costs of U.S. nuclear plants have increased up to sevenfold, and their construction times have doubled to fourteen years.[69] This is partly the fault of utilities and the nuclear industry. Some construction projects were mismanaged, and technical problems associated with the size and complexity of nuclear plants were poorly foreseen. However, part of the costs and delays is nobody's fault. Utilities began construction on many reactors in the early 1970s based on generally accepted forecasts that electricity demand would continue to rise at historical rates of 7 percent. When the oil shocks depressed demand growth to unprecedented lows, utilities had to slow the construction of reactors. Unfortunately, the time during which construction was slowed was one of record high interest rates, escalating the costs of capital financing.

But not all of nuclear power's costly delays are due to industry mismanagement or unforseeable events. Delays in the awarding of nuclear plant operating licenses did not increase sharply in response to either the oil shocks or their inflation spikes. Rather, the delays grew steadily from an average of less than twelve months in the late 1960s to an average of sixty months for the plants most

67. At least fifty licensing reform bills have been introduced since 1976. *Proposed Changes in the Nuclear Powerplant Licensing Process,* Committee Print, p. 2.

68. Komanoff, *Power Plant Cost Escalation.*

69. Department of Energy, *Energy Security,* p. 189.

recently completed.[70] This gradual pattern of growing delays is fully consistent with the steady deterioration of the licensing process and of the political support for it. In addition, there is ample evidence that the industry learned from its early construction experiences and, all things being equal, developed a better, not a worse, construction record over time.[71] The problem is that all things were not equal—the status quo was undermined by declining electric demand, accelerating inflation, halting and shifting regulation, and changes in political control.

While the changes in plant design and operation produced by the regulatory process have enhanced nuclear safety (especially those pertaining to operator training prompted by the 1979 Three Mile Island accident), it is clear from the case-by-case procedures behind them that those changes were not made efficiently. The same conclusion is warranted by comparison of U.S. plants with those put into operation by other countries. Equivalent to American reactors in quality and safety, foreign power plants have been built in much less time and at far lower cost.[72] The key difference between U.S. and foreign plants is that the former are products of a unique regulatory process, relying on antiquated, unstandardized, design-as-you-go procedures. With a clear mandate and strong political support, such a process may still have a chance of working effectively. But under current conditions, it inflates costs and risks to such an extent that nuclear power may remain an

70. Nuclear plants predicted to be completed in the following years met with delays that averaged the number of months shown in parentheses: 1960 (12 months early), 1961 (10 months early), 1963 (10 months early), 1966 (3), 1967 (10.5), 1968 (9), 1969 (21.0), 1970 (15.2), 1971 (18.1), 1972 (23.0), 1973 (33.5), 1974 (21.8), 1975 (40.2), 1976 (32.0), 1977 (65.2), 1978 (56.3), 1979 (72.2), 1980 (46.6), 1981 (56.0). Delay is classified as the time between the predicted date of operation when the construction permit was issued and the actual date on which an operating license was issued. Averages are based on author's calculations from data in NRC Licensing Reform, Hearing, pp. 506–15. For plants completed after 1982, the dates that operating licenses were issued are assumed to be six months before the dates of commercial operation, as reported in Atomic Industrial Forum, Inc., "Nuclear Power Plants in the United States," Infodata (July 1, 1987), pp. 1–10. The figures for 1971 and 1974 do not include extraordinarily long delays for Diablo Canyon reactors. Reactors encountering lengthy delays but not yet licensed to operate—for example, Seabrook and Shoreham—are not included in the calculations. This omission, plus the use of estimated dates for the operating licenses of later plants, causes delay to be underestimated in recent years.

71. Komanoff, Power Plant Cost Escalation; and Zimmerman, "Learning Effects and the Commercialization of New Energy Technologies."

72. Department of Energy, Energy Security, p. 189.

unattractive investment until the process changes. Whether nuclear power is ultimately embraced by the United States for its still considerable long-run cost advantages or is phased out for insuperable concerns over its safety, Americans would be better off making those decisions based on a knowledge of the price, unbiased by an inefficient regulatory process.

Electricity

Federal regulation by the NRC and the EPA is by no means the only significant regulatory obstacle to the avoidance of shortages in electric generating capacity. State regulation by public utility commissions has also caused problems by placing additional hurdles in the way of coal and nuclear power, discouraging additions to electricity capacity generally, and encouraging inefficient (that is, excessive) amounts of consumption. The once cooperative relationships between the federal government and the states and between state politicians and their PUCs have broken down. Washington has become dissatisfied with the electricity pricing policies pursued by the states and is no longer allowing them to operate as independent agents. The states have become intolerant of PUCs that are too cozy with utilities and have taken measures to discourage those arrangements. The result of this new delegation is the uneasy coexistence of an institutional structure put in place at the turn of the century and a variety of innovative strategies to make that structure work in the next century.

The traditional delegations of authority over the supply of electricity began to create problems in the early 1970s. First, state PUCs began to come into conflict with their immediate political overseers—governors, state legislators, and, ultimately, voters. As a result of rising inflation, soaring interest rates, and slowdowns in construction resulting from new environmental regulations, electric power plants, though still realizing economies of scale, were being completed at costs that began to require real rate increases.[73] Public utility commissions were consequently forced to make difficult decisions that they had previously been able to avoid. The utilities needed rate increases for new plants, and they needed

---

73. Anderson, *Regulatory Politics and Electric Utilities*, pp. 61–88; and Mancke, *Squeaking By*, pp. 133–44, are key sources for the following discussion.

them fast: by law, costs could not be recovered until projects began producing electricity. The appropriate size of the increases was a tough issue, though. If the PUCs acceded to the demands of the utilities, as had often been their practice, they would incur the wrath of politicians responding to the outcries of consumers and perhaps have their independence limited. Hoping to temporize, PUCs sought refuge in formal review procedures and economic analysis. But these were activities for which they were often inadequately staffed. The resulting delays in PUC decisions antagonized utilities desperate for relief.

The conflicts faced by the PUCs only worsened thereafter. The oil shocks raised fuel costs to exorbitant levels for utilities reliant on oil and natural gas. But the burden of the oil shocks fell mostly on consumers because PUCs permitted fuel costs to be passed through more or less automatically in higher rates. Consumers consequently stepped up their involvement in PUC ratemaking and their political pressure on PUC overseers. The oil shocks also depressed electricity demand, forcing utilities to delay the completion of coal and nuclear projects and driving up the ultimate costs of those plants through higher finance charges and inflated capital costs. By the 1980s, then, PUCs were facing utility rate requests for completed power projects well over budget—occasionally by several billions of dollars—and intensified consumer and political pressure for rate protection. While the PUCs had acquired more of the resources necessary to resolve these conflicting demands professionally, they were nevertheless burdened with inherently political issues that could not be settled analytically. The immediate consequence was a slowdown in ratemaking processes as PUCs struggled to strike balances between the disparate interests of consumers and utilities.

The longer-term consequence may be somewhat different, however. Utilities have been chastened by their experiences with PUCs over the last ten or fifteen years and recognize that they are no longer their partners in power development. PUCs are now willing to declare that construction costs were "imprudently incurred" and should not be recovered from ratepayers. The ratemaking process can now delay returns on investment so long that electric power investments are rendered unprofitable. And the sheer uncertainty of both the process and its outcome makes capital-intensive projects additionally risky. Add to this the uncertain costs of federal regulation by the EPA and the NRC and continuing doubts about the resurgence of electric demand, and it is little wonder that investment in electric supply capacity for the 1990s and the twenty-first century is lagging behind projections of demand.[74]

Utilities hope that by managing demand for their power—using price incentives to shift usage to off-peak periods and encourage conservation—they can provide an adequate electric supply with existing capacity, at least for the immediate future. But PUCs are not fully cooperative with this approach either. Demand management is essentially an effort to price electricity efficiently, at the marginal cost of providing additional electricity at different times of day and ultimately at the cost of replacing incremental power with new capacity. More efficient pricing would cut electricity demand in many parts of the country and help to ensure that additions to capacity were really needed. But however beneficial efficient electricity pricing might be to a national energy policy, it is potentially costly to a state PUC. Not only does it create technical problems that are yet unresolved, it also generates political opposition from ratepayers accustomed to subsidized prices. The conflict can conceivably reach the point that the time and money invested in the battle by consumers, industry, utilities, and the government will outweigh the economic benefits of more efficient pricing.[75]

If demand cannot be effectively managed, the supply alternatives that utilities are most likely to pursue include increased purchases of electricity cogenerated by industry, imports of power from Canadian utilities or neighboring utilities with surpluses, and the restarting or construction of combustion turbines fueled by oil or natural gas.[76] In the long run all of these alternatives are likely to be more expensive for consumers than more capital-intensive plants using coal or nuclear power.[77] The variable costs of the alternatives are larger and more likely to escalate than those of capital-intensive plants. But all of the alternatives avoid what utilities and

74. Department of Energy, *Energy Security,* pp. 130–60.

75. Crew and Kleindorfer, *Economics of Public Utility Regulation,* pp. 120–209.

76. Huber, "Electricity and the Environment," pp. 1044–53; and Department of Energy, *Energy Security,* pp. 130–60.

77. The alternatives vary widely in their prospective costs. The most promising of the alternatives is the new "combined cycle" gas technology that uses gas much more efficiently than traditional gas combustion plants. On long-term costs, see Frank H. Lennox and Mark P. Mills, "Electricity from Nuclear Energy: Burden or Bargain?" (Washington, D.C.: Science Concepts, 1987), pp. 1–18.

their investors perceive to be enormous regulatory risks associated with major capital projects. While PUCs are supposed to heed the signals of the long run, they too would prefer to avoid conflicts threatened by projects of greater scope.

The federal government is increasingly concerned with how state officials and utilities have accommodated themselves to the new conflicts over power development.[78] The prospect of increasing oil and gas usage is especially alarming, for the displacement of oil and gas from electric power generation has been an important means of reducing oil imports. But politicians in Washington have a greater stake in the level of oil imports than do politicians in the state capitals. While the state officials must worry that future oil price hikes will drive up electric rates and hurt local businesses, national officials must worry about these effects plus the effects on the macroeconomy and national security. States can—and do—pursue their parochial interests without concern for these national interests. With state decisions about electricity supply and demand threatening to increase oil dependence, another fundamental conflict of interest is emerging in the traditional system of delegated control.

In fact, the conflict has been developing since the early 1970s. After the first oil shock, federal officials began questioning PUC policies that exacerbated the energy supply problem. For example, large electricity consumers were typically given volume discounts that discouraged them from using electricity with greater efficiency. And industries that produced vast quantities of waste heat were discouraged from using it to generate electricity (cogenerating) by policies that provided them no market for the power they could not themselves use. These policies and others like them were the product of the marriage between monopoly utilities interested in expansion and cooperative PUCs dedicated to maintaining flat rates for consumers. The policies were consequently slow to change—too slow for the federal government. Hence, after a pitched ideological battle over states' rights, Congress passed and President Jimmy Carter signed the Public Utility Regulatory Policies Act (PURPA) of 1977, the first major intrusion of the federal government into this traditional area of state prerogatives.

PURPA gave the states considerable flexibility: it made PUC rate

78. Nivola, *Politics of Energy Conservation*, pp. 151–93; and Huber, "Electricity and the Environment."

reform voluntary (volume discounting and marginal cost pricing were encouraged but not required) and gave PUCs control over the "avoided cost" (replacement cost) prices to be charged for the cogenerated or independently generated power that PURPA required the utilities to buy. However, the states opposed the new law's implementation strenuously. Ultimately, the Supreme Court upheld the federal government, but until the early 1980s state compliance was slow.[79] Even now, the PUCs continue to prove more resistant than responsive. While many states have eliminated their most egregiously promotional rates, few have adopted the kind of marginal cost pricing that PURPA proposed to encourage efficiency in electricity usage.[80] Cogenerated and independently generated power have grown to 4 percent of the nation's electric supply, but a few states—notably California and Texas—account for much of that growth, as most states have set "avoided cost" prices too low to attract competitors to public utilities.[81]

Generally speaking, state PUCs, struggling to satisfy angry consumers and utilities, have found that federal efforts to encourage efficient production and consumption only exacerbate their problems. Rate reform threatens users, large and small, with higher costs. Cogeneration threatens utilities with the loss of large customers (who can generate their own power) and with the need to make up for their losses by charging small consumers higher rates. What is more, the technical challenge to PUCs attempting to price electricity at its full cost of replacement is formidable: there is nothing resembling a market in electric generation to help PUCs make such estimates.[82] Federal goals are consequently not being fulfilled.

The federal government has not acted forthrightly, however, to achieve its electricity objectives. Congress and the president have delegated to the Federal Energy Regulatory Commission the tough job of accomplishing more. Under the leadership of several Reagan appointees, FERC has taken innovative measures to encourage electricity pricing that is more responsive to the threatening world market the United States now faces. If pursued to their logical

---

79. *FERC* v. *Mississippi*, 456 U.S. 742 (1982).

80. Nivola, "Political Economy of Deregulation in the Energy Sector," p. 12.

81. Andrew Pollack, "Non-Utility Electricity Rising," *New York Times*, August 12, 1987, p. D1.

82. On the general issue of reforming utility ratemaking in the direction of replacement cost pricing see Richard L. Gordon, *Reforming the Regulation of Electric Utilities: Priorities for the 1980s* (Lexington Books, 1982).

conclusion, these measures would transform the electricity supply system from a set of local monopolies to a competitive market in which electric generation would be a for-profit enterprise, offering better rewards for firms developing new generating capacity efficiently. Only residential distribution, and perhaps electric transmission, would be treated as a natural monopoly. Such a transformation of the nation's electric supply system is a long way off, however. FERC has limited authority in this realm, as it does in the field of natural gas. Until it receives more unified support from its political overseers, it is apt to preside with caution over the interest conflicts and unintended consequences for which it has been delegated responsibility.

THE POLITICS OF DELEGATION AND THE OBSTACLES TO REFORM

The organization and performance of the policies governing each of the energy supplies that will be vital to the United States in the 1990s and beyond have followed a similar pattern of development. Each policy has required for its effective implementation the exercise of considerable independent, expert judgment. The policies have not been self-implementing, in the manner of, say, a gasoline tax. By necessity, the agencies responsible for them have not been given strict marching orders. In essence, every policy has employed a professional model of administration. But over time the structure of this model has changed significantly.

The most important change, the one that drove all others, was an increasing conflict of interest between national political authorities and their administrative agents. In large part this developed because of changes in national political interests. The 1973–74 energy crisis raised issues of price, national security, income distribution, and environmental protection to new heights and forced presidents and members of Congress into unaccustomed action. Presidents, suddenly held publicly responsible for the nation's vulnerability to a foreign oil cartel, began bringing the energy agencies more directly under their control.[83] Through reorganizations that culminated in the creation of the Department of Energy in 1977 and

83. For details, see Chubb, *Interest Groups and the Bureaucracy*, pp. 58–85; and Charles O. Jones and Randall Strahan, "The Effects of Energy Politics on Congres-

administrative appointments that placed vigorous leaders at the helms of many of the energy agencies, presidents became a new and important force in administrative affairs. As their energy policies oscillated, however—from the market orientation of Ford to the more regulated approach of Carter to the radical private enterprise thrust of Reagan—presidents became an intensified source of conflict.

In Congress the response to the new issues was quite different, but the effect was much the same. Whereas presidents centralized, Congress decentralized. By 1981 Congress had divided up authority over energy policy among forty-three subcommittees, more than double the number of a decade before. This increased by 100 percent the numbers of senators and representatives with some authority over the energy agencies and increased by at least that amount the number of interests to which the agencies were expected to respond. It also institutionalized the inconsistent demands upon administrative agencies—for example, for both higher and lower gas prices and electric rates and more vigorous or more flexible regulation of coal and nuclear power. To help ensure administrative responsiveness—to exactly what, it was unclear—Congress added more than 400 staff members to the key energy committees.[84] Because federal energy agencies were continuing to pursue their traditional interests and state agencies were becoming more parochial, the changes in Congress and the presidency introduced conflict into the various delegations of authority.

Congress and several presidents tried a variety of measures to resolve these conflicts and achieve new results. They rewrote the policies governing natural gas prices, electricity prices, and air pollution, placing stricter statutory limits on agency discretion. They watched agency behavior more closely, using not only their own staffs but interest groups that had stepped up their monitoring. They demonstrated an increased willingness to reproach agencies

---

sional and Executive Organization in the 1970s," *Legislative Studies Quarterly*, vol. 10 (May 1985), pp. 151–79.

84. Jones and Strahan, "Effects of Energy Politics," pp. 164, 165–66, 169. The decentralization in Congress and the centralization in the executive branch were also parts of more general institutional trends, as discussed in Steven S. Smith, "New Patterns of Decisionmaking in Congress," and Terry M. Moe, "The Politicized Presidency," both in John E. Chubb and Paul E. Peterson, eds., *The New Direction in American Politics* (Brookings, 1985), pp. 203–71.

for specific actions, such as NRC licensing decisions or EPA enforcement efforts. And they regularly threatened each agency with a major overhaul of its authority. While each policy continued to be premised on the need for substantial administrative flexibility and expert judgment, the harmony and trust that characterized the old form of delegation gave way to the discord and suspicion of a new form. In this new delegation, politicians repeatedly substituted their own judgments for those of administrators, who in principle were still considered the more capable decisionmakers. And politicians struggled among themselves to push administrators in differing directions.

The new delegation did have at least one of its hoped-for effects. It increased the number of interests somehow incorporated into the administration of energy supplies. It did so, however, with limited efficiency and effectiveness. Indeed, it is fair to say that the hallmarks of performance by the new delegation have been costly delays and unintended consequences. Among these consequences, moreover, is the very real prospect of another energy crisis, heightened by policies that unnecessarily impede the production and conservation of domestic energy supplies.

This, of course, is a serious consequence and it raises an important question. Why, in light of its many problems, is the new delegation the primary method by which U.S. energy supplies are regulated? To begin, the answer is not a lack of alternatives. National policymakers are not stuck on the horns of a dilemma. They are not forced by the technical demands of energy supply issues to delegate broad authority to experts and then compelled by the political pressures of constituents to intervene, ultimately with frustration, in the exercise of this authority. To the contrary, reforms are available that could relieve many of the problems that the new delegation has created for members of Congress, presidents, and administrators.

Many of the perverse conditions in natural gas markets—for example, excessive consumer prices and oil substitution on the one hand and depressed prices and excess consumption on the other—could be eliminated through the immediate decontrol of the wellhead price of all natural gas. Decontrol would reduce FERC's natural gas responsibilities to the more manageable task of certifying and pricing pipelines. Such a move has long been recommended by economists who stress that natural gas production is competitive and that market pricing would encourage gas to be produced and consumed efficiently.[85] In the short term that would probably mean a decrease in overcommitments to natural gas in some parts of the country and a decrease in oil imports in other parts.[86] It would also mean higher prices for some consumers but lower prices for many others, whom natural gas policy has only hurt. In the longer term, Congress might well be able to enhance these processes and relieve FERC of all of its natural gas obligations by deregulating natural gas pipelines. This has been done for oil pipelines and would permit gas distribution companies, like oil resellers, to shop for producers offering the lowest wellhead prices.[87]

Inefficiencies in the supply of electricity could be alleviated by similar means, and the burdens on PUC decisionmaking would be lifted simultaneously. With the expansion and interconnection of the electricity transmission system, it has become possible for electric power produced in one part of the country to be consumed in another part, even hundreds of miles away. Power is increasingly "wheeled" from one utility to the next.[88] With the development of cogenerated and independently generated power, moreover, it is not only utilities that are producing the power that is wheeled. As a result, it is more than conceivable that the electric power industry could be deregulated and restructured along the lines of the telecommunications industry. Utilities, or some such regulated entity, would transmit electricity from producers to users for a regulated transmission fee. Producers would be free to earn unregulated profits for generating electricity efficiently. And large users, as well as local distribution companies, would be able to shop for the lowest-priced power.

There are still questions about the adequacy of the current transmission system and the reliability of unregulated supplies that must be answered before the total deregulation of electricity gener-

85. See, for example, Breyer and MacAvoy, *Energy Regulation by the Federal Power Commission;* Mitchell, ed., *Deregulation of Natural Gas;* and Williams, *Natural Gas Revolution of 1985.*

86. Department of Energy, *Energy Security,* pp. 114–28.

87. A persuasive argument for pipeline deregulation is provided in Arlon R. Tussing and Connie C. Barlow, *The Natural Gas Industry: Evolution, Structure, and Economics* (Ballinger, 1984), pp. 236–37.

88. Andrew Pollack, "Shopping Around for Electric Power," *New York Times,* August 13, 1987, p. D1.

ation will command the kind of analytical support enjoyed by natural gas deregulation.[89] But there is widespread acknowledgement that experimentation in this direction is desirable. And there is little question that reform in this direction would help to resolve much of the conflict surrounding state PUCs. The federal government, as well as PUC constituents, would have less reason to question PUC rates if those rates were guided by competitive producer bids to supply a utility with power or set by a free market in electricity without PUC determinations. During the 1980s FERC has issued orders to move PUCs voluntarily toward competitive pricing, but without congressional action those efforts have not yet had great force.[90]

Were the generation of electricity significantly deregulated, electricity would come to be priced more closely to its replacement cost and thereby consumed more efficiently. Such pricing would also provide new incentives—to make unregulated profits—for power producers to minimize the costs of supplying power. Whether this would lead to the development of more cogenerated or small-scale power or more large-scale generating capacity is unclear. Much will depend on the prices of oil and natural gas, the fuels for most small-scale power today. But assuming that the prices of oil and gas escalate and alternatives such as coal and nuclear power become more attractive, a new system of regulation would ensure that alternative power projects would be completed at lower cost than has been the case recently.

Incentives to invest in new capacity could be increased by less radical means, however. Investments in coal and nuclear projects are discouraged by the uncertainties of regulatory environments that leave final costs and timetables not only unattractive but open-ended. Congress and the president could go a long way toward reducing these uncertainties by fundamentally reforming the unstandardized, design-as-you-go nuclear licensing process and by removing the states' effective jurisdiction over acid rain. The particulars of how these changes should be made are debatable. But almost any such reform would help to alleviate the administrative

89. See, for example, Gordon, *Reforming the Regulation of Electric Utilities*; Brent Barker, "Deregulation: Facing the Big Question," *EPRI Journal* (March 1988), pp. 1–23; and Sarah McKinley, "Zausner: How Utilities Can Survive (and Even Thrive on) Deregulation," *Energy Daily*, vol. 13 (December 16, 1985), p. 1.

90. Nivola, "Political Economy of Deregulation in the Energy Sector," pp. 3–8.

delay and confusion that the implementation of nuclear safety and air pollution regulation currently invites. There is no shortage of technically feasible proposals—for example, preapproved, standardized reactor designs, with one-step licensing, and assorted incentive systems to encourage coal users to reduce pollutants efficiently at their source, rather than dispersing them into the distant air.[91] But technical feasibility is not the key obstacle to reform in any of these areas.

The major obstacle is political. The new delegation came into being and remains in place because it, better than any of the technically superior alternatives, works politically. Members of Congress especially, but presidents too, are in the business of winning elections. Whatever they hope to accomplish in office—and this includes the noblest aspirations to serve the public interest—politicians cannot accomplish if they fail to be elected and reelected. To do this, they look for ways of solving constituents' problems that do not produce obvious problems for other constituents. They look for policies or actions that do not create big losers at the same time they create winners. In other words, they look for options that do not lose as many votes as they gain.

Traditionally, politicians have found such options in pork barrel policies. These policies provide large benefits to particular constituencies and then spread the costs over all other constituencies or over a long period of time. In the aggregate, the costs and benefits of these policies may be nearly equal. But the public perception is likely to be quite different because only the benefits are easy to perceive. In years past, energy policy often made use of this technique. The TVA and the country's hydroelectric power plants were early products of the pork barrel. And during the 1970s a boom in energy research and development spending resulted from the same political calculations.[92]

Occasionally, however, problems arise that cannot be solved with such politically attractive approaches. Solutions to these problems almost inevitably create clear winners and losers and place politicians at great electoral risk. The energy supply issues are

91. See, for example, Huber, "Electricity and the Environment;" *Proposed Changes in the Nuclear Powerplant Licensing Process*, Committee Print; and Crandall, *Controlling Industrial Pollution*, pp. 156–70.

92. On the politics of escalating R & D spending, see Chubb, *Interest Groups and the Bureaucracy*, pp. 181–222.

perfect cases in point. Since the economic, distributional, and environmental costs of energy development were driven up by the onset of oil and gas scarcity in the early 1970s, the implications of every energy policy decision have increased enormously. Thus natural gas deregulation might substantially increase the gas prices paid by certain consumers. Nuclear licensing reform might lead utilities to propose building new reactors that would have to be sited in somebody's "backyard." Acid rain legislation might make high-sulfur coal unattractive and cost jobs in eastern mines. And electricity deregulation might raise rates for residential consumers in the short run. In the long run, all of these policies promise large benefits in the form of secure and efficient energy supplies and greater economic growth. But between now and the always-looming next election, long-term benefits offer few political rewards. It is policies' immediate consequences, which may be large, that politicians must be concerned with.

One way politicians can reduce this concern is through delegation. By turning over a large measure of responsibility for solving a problem to an administrative agency, politicians create uncertainty about how the costs and benefits of a policy will ultimately be allocated.[93] Politicians can exploit this uncertainty, moreover, using it to mold the expectations of constituents or interest groups about policy effects. When the responsibilities of FERC were revised in 1978, for example, politicians were able to satisfy consumers that the prices of gas would be lower as a result of the legislation, even though they proved to be higher in some places in the 1980s. Delegation is also useful in limiting responsibility for policy effects, whatever their distribution, when they ultimately occur.[94] When the NRC decides to approve or disapprove the start-up of a controversial power plant, it is the agency that bears the brunt of political protests, not the Congress or the president, even though they are

93. On the role of uncertainty in delegation, see Morris P. Fiorina, "Legislator Uncertainty, Legislative Control and the Delegation of Legislative Power," paper prepared for the Conference on Adaptive Institutions, Stanford University, November 9, 1984.

94. See R. Kent Weaver, "The Politics of Blame Avoidance," *Journal of Public Policy*, vol. 6 (October–December 1986), pp. 371–98; Morris P. Fiorina, "Legislative Choice of Regulatory Forms: Legal Process or Administrative Process," *Public Choice*, vol. 39 (1982), pp. 33–66; Fiorina, "Group Concentration and the Delegation of Legislative Authority," in Noll, ed., *Regulatory Policy and the Social Sciences*, pp. 175–97; and more generally, Theodore J. Lowi, *The End of Liberalism: The Second Republic of the United States*, 2d ed. (Norton, 1979).

ultimately responsible for the decision. Finally, delegation permits politicians to have the best of two worlds. It relieves them of much of the blame for making unpopular decisions about general policy and provides them the opportunity to claim credit for helping constituents who run into problems with the agency as it carries out an ill-defined policy.[95] When many of the representatives from New York and Massachusetts attempted to block the NRC from expediting evacuation planning for the Shoreham and Seabrook nuclear power plants, they stood to earn the kind of praise from their constituents that their participation in comprehensive licensing reform could never produce. The exploitation of the opportunity to intervene selectively in administrative decisionmaking is one of the distinguishing features of the new delegation from the old.

Another distinguishing feature arises when politicians are not completely free to delegate their way out of no-win political situations. Well-organized constituents may not be deceived by delegation and may consequently insist that their interests be protected more explicitly by law. In these situations, Congress and the president may be forced to write policy in greater detail, leaving only some of the tough decisions to administrators. This was clearly the case with the drafting of air pollution and natural gas legislation in the 1970s, and it continues to be evidenced in the rewriting of acid rain and nuclear licensing bills in the 1980s. Congressional freedom may also be limited in the other direction. Groups long accustomed to a delegated arrangement may strongly resist restrictions on discretionary authority. Congress has faced this opposition from state governments when it has been pushed to consider reforms of electricity pricing. But while politicians may find their ability to structure delegation to their full advantage increasingly constrained, they also continue to find delegation politically valuable. Even as politicians have been forced to intervene in administrative affairs, gradually transforming delegation from the old to the new and causing myriad problems of performance, they have discovered that restricted delegation is better than no delegation at all. Thus far the new delegation has enabled Congress to reduce the political

95. On this ombudsman strategy, see generally David R. Mayhew, *Congress: The Electoral Connection* (Yale University Press, 1974); Morris P. Fiorina, *Congress: Keystone of the Washington Establishment* (Yale University Press, 1977); and Bruce Cain, John A. Ferejohn, and Morris Fiorina, *The Personal Vote: Constituency Service and Electoral Independence* (Harvard University Press, 1987).

costs of unpopular issues, in the various ways mentioned above, without creating enough new political costs, in poor policy performance, to offset them.

What are the chances, then, of Congress and the president finding it politically advantageous—or at least acceptable—to reform these flawed delegations of authority over energy supplies? If the 1990s bring another energy crisis, the chances for change will increase substantially. Then the adverse consequences of current policies would become clear, and politicians would have an easier time defending reforms that could overcome regulatory obstacles to more efficient energy production and consumption. Short of another crisis, though, there is but one development that holds any hope for moving national policymakers toward significant reform. That is the leadership of the administrative agencies themselves. Despite the constraints that have been placed upon them, the FERC, especially, and the NRC, to a lesser extent, have been experimenting administratively with the most promising kinds of reform—procompetitive deregulation and plant standardization.[96] Although these reforms will require congressional and presidential support to come to fruition, the experimentation may prove politically valuable. The same kind of experimentation preceded the overhaul of regulation in the airline and trucking industries, serving to demonstrate the technical feasibility and political acceptability of ideas politicians had considered too controversial to entertain seriously.[97] Still, there is only rather faint hope of this happening through the energy agencies. Buffeted by criticism, and constrained by various limits on the use of their expertise, the energy regulatory agencies are more likely to try to temporize than to revolutionize, leaving the big changes in energy policy for the next energy crisis.

96. See, for example, Barbara Rosewicz, "FERC Seeks Wider Corridors of Power: Plan Calls for New Breed of Electricity Maker," *Wall Street Journal*, March 15, 1988.

97. Martha Derthick and Paul J. Quirk, *The Politics of Deregulation* (Brookings, 1985).

American Trade Policy: An Obsolete Bargain?

DAVID B. YOFFIE

EACH YEAR from 1983 to 1987 the United States experienced the largest national trade deficits the world has ever seen. The economic consequences of these deficits have been far-reaching: after being the world's largest creditor for half a century, America has become the world's largest debtor, and U.S. export industries lost world market shares in all regions of the globe and virtually all industrial sectors. The political consequences of the deficits have also been significant. Although American trade policy has not caused the deficits, calls for tariffs and other restrictions on imports have become increasingly vocal.

Despite these economic problems and political pressures, American trade institutions have not embraced a sweeping or hurriedly improvised protectionism. The policy of favoring liberal trade, which has worked well to help expand the U.S. economy in the past fifty years, has not been seriously compromised. Through 1987 Congress refrained from passing legislation that would have raised import barriers and seriously damaged the international trading system. Even the 1988 trade bill will not have a wide-reaching effect on U.S trade policy or alter the political balance between free traders and protectionists. And while the executive has become more aggressive in international negotiations, increasingly threatening trade retaliation against countries such as Japan, American trade policy has remained remarkably liberal.

The growing political onslaught of protectionist and other trade pressures, however, is causing American trade institutions and the postwar strategy to liberalize international trade to lose their viability. The foundation of both the institutions and the strategy has been the bargain struck between Congress and the president with the signing of the Reciprocal Trade Agreements Act in 1934. The bargain has allowed presidents to liberalize trade as long as they shielded Congress from domestic pressures to restrict it, which they have done through limited and largely symbolic protectionist actions. But the pressures of the 1980s may have made the bargain obsolete. Mature industries, unable to compete and disappointed by what they perceive to be mere gestures of aid, have been laying siege to Congress, the International Trade Commission, and other trade institutions. These hard-core groups of firms have become chronic protectionists, repeatedly bombarding different agencies under different trade laws with requests for protection. Newer, more competitive industries have also become a source of instability for American trade institutions. These firms, which historically supported unconditional free trade at home as well as government efforts to liberalize international markets, are now demanding that sanctions be imposed selectively against countries with closed markets, a policy that cannot easily be accommodated by existing institutions. Finally, for the first time since the 1930s a respectable school of theory, called the new trade theory or strategic trade policy, has questioned whether a blanket commitment to free trade is the best course for the United States. Such theories, if imperfectly understood or willfully misapplied, could provide a new president a base of seeming legitimacy for pursuing strongly protectionist policies.

The consequence of these political and academic assaults is that many U.S. trade policies and institutions have become confused and their goals have become uncertain. Uncompetitive declining industries have received increased protection while policies for aiding emerging industries have been uncoordinated and contradictory. And the problems may be difficult to solve. Neither Congress nor the executive branch has actively pursued reasoned alternatives to these ad hoc reactions, and there is little evidence that they would or could implement the alternatives if they had them. Congress, after all, took three years to write the 1988 trade bill, and its labors produced only marginal changes in the statutes. But without a new and more stable bargain and a clearer vision, the institutional inertia and the mere fiddling with details of the statutes will ensure that U.S. international trade policy becomes more and more ineffectual.

TRADE PROBLEMS AND TRADE POLICY

U.S. domination of world trade has been diminishing for more than thirty years. In 1950 America supplied 20 percent of total world exports, almost 30 percent of world manufactures, and 50 percent or more of many capital goods and other manufactured products.[1] Although the United States has remained the largest exporter in the world, by 1980 its exports had dropped to 11.6 percent of the world total and its share of world manufactures had fallen to 17 percent.

Before the 1980s this slippage was not widely viewed with alarm. Much of the decline was an inevitable correction promoted by the government: it was in America's interest for the industrial nations of Europe and Japan to regain some of the world market shares lost to the United States because of the devastation of World War II. Although poor productivity growth continued to weaken the U.S. competitive position during the 1970s, America's balance of payments remained stable. Despite two oil shocks, the current account hovered near zero, and for seven of the ten years the United States had a surplus on its balance of goods and services and a surplus in manufacturing trade.[2]

It was not until the 1980s that the American trade position collapsed. A $1.8 billion annual surplus in the current account in 1980 became a $141 billion annual deficit by 1986 (see figure 1). In addition, trade in manufactures fell from a surplus of $18.6 billion to a deficit of $133.4 billion, and America's share of world imports grew from 13.2 percent to 18.7 percent. Estimates suggest that the United States will owe more than one-half trillion dollars to the rest of the world by the end of the 1980s, which will require tens of billions of dollars in annual exports merely to service the debt.[3] By the mid-1990s it will have to run a sizable trade surplus to restore balance.

The roots of today's budget crisis and growing oil dependence, discussed in other chapters, can be found in failed fiscal and energy policies. Most analysts agree that the trade imbalance is a consequence of the burgeoning budget deficit and high American

1. David B. Yoffie, "Protecting World Markets," in Thomas K. McCraw, ed., *America Versus Japan: A Comparative Study in Business-Government Relations Conducted at the Harvard Business School* (Harvard Business School Press, 1986), pp. 35–75.

2. *Economic Report of the President, February 1988*, p. 368.

3. C. Fred Bergsten, "Economic Imbalances and World Politics," *Foreign Affairs*, vol. 65 (Spring 1987), p. 770.

FIGURE 1. *U.S. Trade and Current Account Balances, 1979–87*[a]

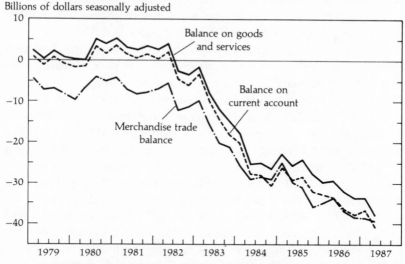

Billions of dollars seasonally adjusted

SOURCE: Council of Economic Advisers, *Economic Indicators*, prepared for the Joint Economic Committee, 100 Cong. 1 sess. (Government Printing Office, 1987), p.36.

a. Figures are quarterly balances: four consecutive quarters equal the annualized rate.

interest rates in the early 1980s that led to a 70 percent appreciation of the dollar.[4] The rising dollar increased American prices compared with those of all major foreign producers, causing U.S. exports to suffer while imports ballooned. Trade performance also suffered from the international debt crisis and global macroeconomic imbalances. As capital flows to developing countries contracted, they were forced to cut back on imports and increase exports to service their debts. The $20 billion surplus that the United States had with Latin America in 1980, for instance, had turned into a deficit of $13.5 billion by 1986.[5] In addition, because the U.S. economy was growing faster than the economies of most industrial countries, America consumed increasing quantities of imports, while its trading partners bought fewer U.S. exports.

Although trade policy did not cause the trade imbalance, the

4. Martin Feldstein, "Correcting the Trade Deficit," *Foreign Affairs*, vol. 65 (Spring 1987), p. 796. See also Rudiger Dornbusch and Jeffrey A. Frankel, "Macroeconomics and Protection," in Robert M. Stern, ed., *U.S. Trade Policies in a Changing World Economy* (MIT Press, 1987), pp. 77–130.

5. U.S. Department of Commerce, Bureau of the Census, *Highlights of U.S. Export and Import Trade* (Government Printing Office, 1987), table 3.

government's failure to reduce the deficits has had significant effects on trade politics and policy. There has been a growing demand for protection as well as an increasing readiness to supply it. At the same time, the perceived need in some industries for large-scale production that must be exported, combined with their perception that markets overseas are closed, has produced new demands for reciprocity in trade relations. And finally, the failure of the deficit to respond quickly to the depreciation of the dollar has raised new debates about the efficacy of liberal trade. Between September 1985 and September 1987 the dollar depreciated 26.9 percent against a basket of all European currencies and 40 percent against the Japanese yen. Even after taking into account the expected lags of the J curve, most economists predicted significant improvement in the trade figures by late 1987.[6] But although the volume of U.S. exports improved dramatically in the second and third quarters of 1987, the trade deficit measured in dollars continued to expand, hitting an all-time monthly high of $17.6 billion in October. The figures improved through the first six months of 1988, and most economists agree that further exchange rate adjustments will eventually reverse the growth of the deficit. However, the lags and the potential costs of the dollar's devaluation have shaken confidence in standard solutions.

The trade deficit has affected other important areas of U.S. trade policy, such as its movement toward bilateral trading arrangements with countries like Israel and Canada instead of multilateral trade liberalization. The remainder of this chapter, however, focuses on the domestic politics of import protection, especially in manufactured goods.

PROTECTION: DEMAND AND AVAILABILITY

For the first 150 years of its history, the United States, except for a few pauses, was a protectionist nation. Although Alexander Hamilton's *Report on the Subject of Manufactures* failed to convince

6. Economic theory has long argued that devaluation of a nation's currency leads to an immediate deterioration in the balance of trade followed by a steep improvement. Therefore the trade or current account balance will trace a J-shaped curve. See, for example, Peter B. Kenen, *The International Economy* (Prentice-Hall, 1985), p. 331.

the House of Representatives when it was presented in 1791, protectionism became America's primary trade policy after the passage of the tariff of 1816.[7] The Constitution had given Congress
exclusive authority to set tariffs and, acting like the typical government of a developing country, Congress erected high tariffs to
promote infant industries and raise revenues to support the federal
government.

In the 1890s, however, as some U.S. industries became more
competitive in world markets, Congress began to face increased
pressure to facilitate exports and help firms penetrate foreign markets. To accomplish this objective, the United States had to negotiate with trading partners—a responsibility that rested with the
executive. Even though trade powers constitutionally rested with
the legislature, Congress was willing to cede some authority because tariffs were becoming less important as a source of revenue
and Congress retained virtual veto powers over executive actions.
The actual delegation of responsibility began in 1897 when the
Dingley Tariff Act gave the president the power to negotiate bilateral trade treaties and to impose countervailing duties to offset
foreign export subsidies.[8] Although Congress refused to ratify any
of the initial treaties negotiated by the executive, delegation continued with the formation of the International Trade Commission in
1916; the passage of the Ford-McCumber Bill in 1922, which empowered the president to adjust tariffs on the basis of production
costs and to negotiate unconditional most-favored-nation treatment; and ultimately the passage of the Reciprocal Trade Agreements Act of 1934.[9]

The RTAA established the institutional framework for American
trade policy for the next fifty years by providing the president with
authority to negotiate tariff levels. This unusual delegation of congressional power came about partly because members of Congress
wanted to avoid repeating the process that had created the Smoot-
Hawley tariff of 1930, which had raised tariff levels to their highest

7. Robert A. Pastor, *Congress and the Politics of U.S. Foreign Economic Policy, 1929–
1976* (University of California Press, 1980), p. 75.

8. Robert E. Baldwin, *The Political Economy of U.S. Import Policy* (MIT Press, 1985),
p. 34.

9. The International Trade Commission was known as the United States Tariff
Commission until the Trade Act of 1974. "Most favored nation" (MFN) means that
once a tariff is imposed or cut between two nations, all other nations are entitled to
equal tariff treatment.

point in American history and was widely perceived to have aggravated the Great Depression. As one senator described Smoot-Hawley during the 1934 debate on the RTAA, "Logrolling is inevitable, and in its most pernicious form. We do not write national tariff law. We jam together, through various unholy alliances and combinations, a potpourri or hodgepodge of sections and local tariff rates, which often add to our trouble and increase world misery."[10] In addition, the despair and crisis atmosphere created by the depression disrupted the historical pattern of trade politics, making it easier for Congress to change policy. Import-competing industries found they had less to fear from lower tariffs, while export interests suddenly found they had more to gain. U.S. exports had been particularly hard hit by the global slowdown and foreign retaliation against Smoot-Hawley: while world exports dropped 50 percent between 1928 and 1932, American exports dropped 66 percent. The devaluation of the dollar in 1933 did give U.S. firms an opportunity to recoup some of their losses: import-competing industries, in effect, received increased protection, and exports almost doubled. But without reductions in foreign tariffs, further export expansion was likely to be stifled, and foreign governments would reduce their tariffs only if the United States offered reciprocal treatment.

The strengthening of exporting interests, the weakening of domestic arguments for protection, and the widespread perception of crisis helped Cordell Hull, President Roosevelt's secretary of state, persuade Congress that the United States needed "an emergency measure to deal with a dangerous and threatening emergency situation."[11] Hull was a fervent believer that free trade was inextricably intertwined with peace and prosperity, and although Congress never fully accepted his philosophy, there was greater support for it than during any previous era in American trade history.[12]

The result was the RTAA, a bargain that gave the executive branch added trade powers in exchange for an implicit promise that it would protect members of Congress from the inevitable

10. Quoted in John H. Jackson, "Anticipating Trade Policy in 1987," *Looking Ahead*, vol. 9 (Winter 1987), p. 3.

11. Quoted in Stephen Haggard, "The Institutional Foundations of Hegemony: Explaining the Reciprocal Trade Agreements Act of 1934," *International Organization*, vol. 42 (Winter 1988), p. 111.

12. Cordell Hull, *The Memoirs of Cordell Hull*, vol. 1 (Macmillan, 1948).

pressures of special interests seeking trade barriers.[13] The act gave the executive the authority to negotiate reciprocal trade agreements that raised or lowered tariffs by up to 50 percent without the advice and consent of the Senate. From the beginning, Congress never intended to forfeit much power. It retained its oversight powers and maintained channels outside Congress for business groups to seek trade barriers. It also limited the duration of the president's authority and continued to hold this knife over presidential powers thereafter. Its goal was to create a system that would allow industries in distress to appeal individually for help without the extensive logrolling engendered by the Smoot-Hawley Act, but at the same time allow the executive to define the national interest in trade more broadly. Congress did not ban protection; it simply made protection the exception rather than the rule. In effect, the new bargain allowed trade liberalization and selective protection to coexist.

Through the end of World War II the effects of the Reciprocal Trade Agreements Act were modest. Although the United States negotiated several bilateral treaties to reduce tariffs on a reciprocal basis, there is considerable debate as to whether the level of protection in general fell.[14] By the end of the 1940s, however, the executive branch sought to use its authority under the RTAA to implement a clearly defined liberal trade strategy. A strong consensus emerged that the best possible system was "openness in general, a trade world where American products and firms could compete as freely as possible with others. It was assumed that the United States as a whole would do well in such a world; others would gain, but so would we, and we would remain in the front economic

13. Thousands of pages have been written about the politics of Smoot-Hawley and the RTAA. The most well known works include E. E. Schattschneider, *Politics, Pressures and the Tariff: A Study of Free Private Enterprise in Pressure Politics, as Shown in the 1929–30 Revision of the Tariff* (Prentice-Hall, 1935); Henry Joseph Tasca, *The Reciprocal Trade Policy of the United States: A Study in Trade Philosophy* (University of Pennsylvania Press, 1938); and Raymond A. Bauer, Ithiel De Sola Pool, and Lewis Anthony Dexter, *American Business and Public Policy: The Politics of Foreign Trade*, 2d ed. (New York: Aldine de Gruyter, 1972). For more recent expositions see I. M. Destler, *American Trade Politics: System Under Stress* (Washington, D.C.: Institute for International Economics, 1986), pp. 9–36; and Haggard, "The Institutional Foundations of Hegemony," pp. 91–119.

14. John A. Conybeare, *Trade Wars: The Theory and Practice of International Commercial Rivalry* (Columbia University Press, 1987), argues that effective protection actually increased during the 1930s.

rank. Trade was a positive-sum game, and liberal policies would make everyone better off, ourselves included."[15]

Congress, however, never gave the executive a free hand. Although the RTAA made it difficult for firms and labor groups to follow the old pattern of asking their congressional representatives to logroll for trade barriers, interest groups—particularly in the manufacturing sector—could still seek protection outside Congress.[16] Trade statutes allowed any individual industry to appeal to the International Trade Commission or to the president for protection.

To understand the implications of the RTAA for the stability of trade politics, it is useful to make some assumptions about the conditions under which industries sought protection and under what conditions the executive erected trade barriers. Underlying these assumptions is an implicit, simplified model of protection that considers American trade barriers a function of the intensity of group demands mediated by an executive that has its own rules for choosing among competing interests.

Before the passage of the RTAA, business executives could go to their local congressional representatives to ask for a tariff, whether or not they were hurt by imports. After World War II, decisions on whether to provide protection were made by the president, usually after a recommendation by the International Trade Commission. Since trade statutes directed the ITC to recommend protection only if an industry was being injured by foreign competition, interest groups were now faced with institutions that made protection a special circumstance. Hence one can assume that demand for trade barriers would vary directly with the degree of an industry's economic distress. That is, firms are most likely to request trade barriers only when they confront declining production and profitability in conjunction with import competition.[17]

I also assume that the executive provided trade barriers only

15. Destler, *American Trade Politics*, p. 96.

16. Since the end of World War II, agriculture has been treated as an exceptional case. Congress maintains a more extensive role in agricultural trade policy. In addition, from the very inception of the General Agreement on Tariffs and Trade, the United States wanted to exempt its own agriculture from the rules governing manufacturing trade, especially the prohibition on quantitative restrictions. See Richard N. Gardner, *Sterling-Dollar Diplomacy: The Origins and Prospects of Our International Economic Order* (McGraw-Hill, 1969), pp. 149–50.

17. Timothy J. McKeown, "Firms and Tariff Regime Change: Explaining the Demand for Protection," *World Politics*, vol. 36 (January 1984), pp. 215–33.

after balancing the economic and foreign policy costs of protection against the legitimate complaints of domestic groups. The logic underlying this assumption is that even though Congress abdicated direct responsibility for trade policy, it could have reversed that decision at any time. The president therefore had to prove to Congress that he could shield legislators from protectionist pressures, which could only be done by buying off selected industries with limited import protection.

The president ensured that economic and foreign policy costs would be considered in making trade decisions by the way trade issues were treated within the bureaucracy. At first, the State Department under Cordell Hull handled these issues. After World War II, under pressure from Congress, trade recommendations were made to the president by interagency committees that included the State Department, Treasury, and the Council of Economic Advisers, as well as Commerce, Labor, and, after 1962, the U.S. trade representatives. The State Department predictably opposed restrictions because of their potentially harmful effect on foreign relations; Treasury and the Council of Economic Advisers opposed them because they could lead to inflation and potential efficiency losses.

Trade laws negotiated between Congress and the president provided the rules for determining who would get protection. The first rule was that the industry had to be in distress (as defined by low profitability and declining employment): the executive would not provide protection to promote growth industries. The second rule was that if U.S. firms faced "unfair" trade practices from overseas, those practices should be "countervailed."[18] It was good politics for the president to temporarily protect industries in distress or countervail unfair foreign subsidies to buy off the individual losers in international trade and keep them from building coalitions for protection. At the same time, the interagency structure of decision-making in the executive branch ensured that the president would limit the restrictiveness of any trade barriers to reduce foreign policy complications and inflationary costs.[19]

18. Judith Goldstein, "The Political Economy of Trade: Institutions of Protection," *American Political Science Review*, vol. 80 (March 1986), pp. 161–84; and Baldwin, *Political Economy of U.S. Import Policy*.

19. This highly simplified supply and demand model for U.S. trade policy is generally consistent with the mainstream literature on the political economy of protectionism. Similar theories have attributed the demand for protection to crisis

Although this implicit model of protection is simplified, its logic leads to some important conclusions about the stability of institutional arrangements governing international trade policy in the 1980s. As long as demand for trade barriers was a function of industry distress, pressures for protection would decrease during periods of significant domestic economic growth and domestic competitive strength in international markets. If competitiveness declined or growth slowed, or both, pressures for protection would increase. As long as the executive weighed the benefits of barriers against the costs of domestic inflation or of foreign diplomatic complications, restrictions would always be less rigorous than the industry desired. If the executive branch failed to buy off disaffected groups, however, it would also fail to shield Congress from protectionist pressure.

The strong competitive position of the United States after World War II meant that there was relatively little protectionist activity through the early 1960s. Since the country was running large trade surpluses and the primary trade problem was foreign tariff and quota barriers against American exports, Congress was willing to delegate increasing trade authority to the executive to liberalize trade. The Trade Expansion Act in 1962 marked the pinnacle of this delegation of powers (table 1).

The U.S. trade position began to weaken by the mid-1960s, but the demand for protection remained subdued. With nearly full employment, the Kennedy round of trade negotiations under way, and corporate profitability reaching all-time highs, efforts to expand trade barriers would have been hard to justify.[20] Even as the economy slowed during the 1970s and import penetration rose, protectionist pressure did not become acute. As one recent study has shown, divisions between multinationals who supported freer trade and purely domestic firms in the same industries that pre-

---

conditions in industries and associated it with product markets rather than factor markets. For a review of this literature, see Douglas Nelson, "Endogenous Tariff Theory: A Critical Survey" (World Bank, 1987).

20. Even restrictions on foreign textiles, in effect since 1957, came under attack. Because domestic firms could not supply the needs of the military, the government unofficially loosened quotas in 1966–67. David B. Yoffie, *Power and Protectionism: Strategies of the Newly Industrializing Countries* (Columbia University Press, 1983), chap. 4.

TABLE 1. *Major Changes in U.S. Trade Acts, 1948–84*

Year	Increases in presidential authority for liberalizing trade	Protectionist provisions mandated by Congress
1948	Trade Act extended one year	Peril point provision added: Tariff Commission to investigate anticipated tariff adjustments to determine at what point a domestic industry might be seriously injured
1949	Peril point provision repealed	
1951	President given discretion regarding the Tariff Commission's escape clause verdict (also 1962)	Congress mandates escape clause into law for "serious injury." Commission has 12 months to decide. Law prohibits any reduction in rate of duty when an imported product causes or threatens serious injury to a domestic industry
1955	President given three years' authority to reduce any tariff by 15 percent of January 1955 rate	Escape clause changed to allow small segments of an industry rather than an entire industry to seek tariff relief if it can show injury
1962	President given five-year authority to reduce any tariff by 50 percent and to negotiate elimination of tariffs on some broad categories of goods Escape clause relief granted only if imports are a "major factor" causing or threatening serious injury	President can restrict imports from any country maintaining unreasonable restrictions against U.S. exports President must submit list of articles to be negotiated for Tariff Commission's review Escape clause override of presidential decision reduced to majority vote of the authorized membership of each house
1974	President given five-year mandate to enter into trade agreements to reduce all tariffs above 5 percent ad valorem by as much as 60 percent President authorized to negotiate agreements to harmonize, reduce, or eliminate all barriers to free trade	Escape clause eligibility broadened Establishes 45-member advisory council consisting of government, labor, business; also authorizes private-sector advisory councils President expected to provide import relief recommended by ITC unless he has reason to believe it is not in U.S. national economic interests Protection allowed without a connection between increased imports and previous tariff concessions, and increased imports only have to be a "substantial cause" of serious injury Shorter time limits for Treasury to decide on subsidy and dumping cases

TABLE 1 *(continued)*

Year	Increases in presidential authority for liberalizing trade	Protectionist provisions mandated by Congress
		Majority of those present and voting in each house can override presidential decision rejecting an affirmative escape clause finding
		Rename, reorganize, and expand power of ITC
		A new fast-track procedure for handling dumping cases
1979	U.S. countervailing duty laws overhauled; must show serious injury	Definitions of subsidy made more inclusive
		Loosening of definition of "material injury" regarding effect of subsidies
		If ITC divides evenly on a subsidy case, that is to be taken as an affirmative finding
		Administration of antidumping laws go from Treasury to Commerce
		ITC to determine whether dumping occurred, not Treasury
		ITC to expedite dumping and subsidy cases by having preliminary investigations
1984	The president can veto a congressional override of his decision to ignore ITC recommendation (restores constitutional right)	If president rejects affirmative ITC decision, the ITC's recommendation to remedy the injury will take effect if both houses pass a joint resolution disapproving the president's action

SOURCES: Robert E. Baldwin, *The Political Economy of U.S. Import Policy* (MIT Press, 1985); and Robert Z. Lawrence and Robert E. Litan, *Saving Free Trade: A Pragmatic Approach* (Brookings, 1986).

ferred protection fragmented support for barriers during most of the decade.[21]

But while the aggregate demand for protection remained low, falling tariffs in the wake of the Kennedy round of trade talks, combined with slower economic growth, led an increasing number of individual industries, such as steel, textiles, and footwear, to lobby for restrictions. Despite the weakening of its committee system and party leadership, Congress was able to fend off most of

21. Helen Milner, "Resisting the Protectionist Temptation: Industry and the Making of Trade Policy in France and the United States during the 1970s," *International Organization*, vol. 41 (Autumn 1987), pp. 639–65.

the demands. While highly protectionist bills, such as Burke-Hartke in 1971, received serious support from legislators, no product-specific protectionist legislation was passed. At the same time, congressional attempts to reassert control over the executive in the wake of Watergate were reflected in trade issues. In the 1974 Trade Act Congress granted the executive the authority to continue liberalizing trade, but it also made it easier for industries in distress to appeal for protection. This trend became more apparent in the Trade Act of 1979, which reduced the president's discretion and further loosened the eligibility criteria for receiving certain types of protection. These provisions took some of the initiative for trade policy away from the executive branch and put it into the hands of the private sector.

Changes in the trade laws, combined with growing industry distress in the 1980s, inevitably heightened the demand for protection. One indication of the increase was that trade became a more active issue in Congress. During the Ninety-ninth Congress (1985–86), 782 trade bills were introduced, 248 with explicit protectionist provisions; there were only 249 similar proposals during the Ninety-third Congress. According to a different measure, members of the House of Representatives introduced 127 restrictive trade bills in the Ninety-sixth Congress (1979–80), 137 in the Ninety-seventh, and 144 in the Ninety-eighth.[22]

Even more significant were increases in the number of applications for protection. Under law, industries had four principal avenues of appeal or means of relief from fair and unfair import competition: escape clause actions (section 201 of the 1974 Trade Act), national security considerations (section 232 of the 1962 Trade Act), countervailing duties (section 303 of the 1930 Tariff Act), and antidumping duties (section 731 of the 1930 Tariff Act) (see table 2).[23] While escape clause petitions fell from 41 filed between 1975 and 1979 to only 17 between 1980 and 1985, the demand for action under

22. Patricia I. Hansen, "Defining Unreasonableness in International Trade: Section 301 of the Trade Act of 1974," *Yale Law Journal*, vol. 96 (April 1987), pp. 1122–46; Stephen L. Lande and Craig Van Grasstek, *The Trade and Tariff Act of 1984: Trade Policy in the Reagan Administration* (Lexington Books, 1986), p. 9; and Destler, *American Trade Politics*, p. 75.

23. Other available avenues included section 301 of the 1974 Trade Act, which gave the president the right to retaliate against such unfair practices as denial of access to foreign markets or failure to abide by negotiated trade treaties, and section 337, which allowed the government to restrict imports when infringement of patents or trademarks caused material injury.

TABLE 2. *Provisions of Most Commonly Used U.S. Trade Laws* [a]

Provision	Escape clause	National security clause	Countervailing duties	Antidumping	Unfair trade
Section and law	Section 201, 1974 Trade Act	Section 232, 1962 Trade Act	Section 303, 1930 Tariff Act	Section 731, 1930 Tariff Act	Section 301, 1974 Trade Act
Year modified	1979, 1984	1974, 1979	1974, 1984	1974, 1979, 1984	1984
Rule for implementation	Increased imports cause or threaten to cause substantial injury	Imports threaten to impair national security by weakening vital domestic industry	Export subsidy causes or threatens to cause material injury	Price below "fair market value" causes or threatens to cause material injury	Barriers restrict U.S. commerce; no injury test required
Penalty	Duty, quota, orderly marketing agreement, or trade adjustment assistance	At president's discretion	Tariff that offsets subsidy; negotiated settlement	Tariff that raises price to fair market value; negotiated settlement	President's discretion
Investigating agency	ITC	Commerce (ITA)	Commerce (ITA) and ITC	Commerce (ITA) and ITC	U.S. trade representative
Recommendation due	6 months	No deadline	160–300 days	235–420 days	9–14 months
Decisionmaker	President	President	Commerce (ITA)	Commerce (ITA)	President
Decision due	60 days	No deadline	On recommendation	On recommendation	21 days
Congressional override	Yes, within 90 days if president rejects	No	No	No	No

Sources: Stephen L. Lande and Craig Van Grasstek, *The Trade and Tariff Act of 1984: Trade Policy in the Reagan Administration* (Lexington Books, 1986), pp. 113–14; and U.S. Commerce Department, Office of Industrial Resource Administration, *The Effect of Imports on the National Security* (Government Printing Office, 1984).

a. Excludes the revisions under the 1988 trade law.

TABLE 3. *Trade Cases Filed, by Type of Petition, 1979–85*

Type of petition	1979	1980	1981	1982	1983	1984	1985	Total
Antidumping duties	26	46	15	65	48	76	66	342
Countervailing duties	40	10	27	146	30	55	43	351
Escape clause	4	2	1	3	0	7	4	21
National security clause	1	0	2	2	1	1	0	7
Total	71	58	45	216	79	139	113	721

SOURCES: Compiled from I. M. Destler, *American Trade Politics* (Washington, D.C.: Institute for International Economics), pp. 223–342; and Department of Commerce, *The Effect of Imports on the National Security*.

the other three laws ballooned.[24] Petitions for antidumping and countervailing duties increased most. During the 1970s industries did not use these laws because, to increase U.S. negotiating authority in the Tokyo round of trade talks, Congress gave the executive the power to waive application of existing statutes, which deterred industries from filing petitions.[25] However, once Congress ratified the Trade Act of 1979, industries were given clear guidelines for appealing for countervailing and antidumping duties. From 1979 to 1985, 693 of these petitions were filed, an average of 55 annually the first three years and 132 annually in the next four (table 3). Petitions filed under the national security clause averaged about 1 every two years from 1962 to 1979, but 6 petitions were filed in the following four years.

Because increasing distress in particular industries and growing evidence of foreign dumping and subsidies are sufficient condi-

24. The purpose of the escape clause was to provide temporary protection for industries injured by previous tariff cuts. The decline in these petitions was probably a function of the presidential record for awarding relief under the clause. Because the president had more discretion in escape clause cases than in countervailing and antidumping cases and often exercised that discretion by not providing relief, industries had incentives to use alternative channels. For instance, between 1971 and 1977, 57 escape clause cases were filed and 27 reached the president's desk, but only 4 led to import barriers. Bahram Nowzad, *The Rise in Protectionism* (International Monetary Fund, 1978), p. 27. See also Alan V. Deardorff and Robert M. Stern, "Current Issues in Trade Policy: An Overview," in Stern, ed., *U.S. Trade Policies*, pp. 15–68; and Goldstein, "Political Economy of Trade."

25. Before 1979, U.S. law did not require industries to prove they had been injured before countervailing or antidumping duties were applied. Because many U.S. trading partners did require such proof, they refused to negotiate a code for handling subsidies under the GATT unless the United States agreed not to impose duties during the Tokyo round.

TABLE 4. *Nonsteel and Nontextile Trade Petitions Filed, 1979–85*

Petitions[a]	1979	1980	1981	1982	1983	1984	1985
Nonsteel and nontextile petitions filed	54	21	29	40	38	42	47
Petitions receiving positive action	7	7	6	12	16	13	22
Petitions receiving positive action (percent)	13.0	33.3	20.7	33.3	42.1	31.0	46.8

SOURCE: Calculated from Destler, *American Trade Politics*, pp. 223–334.
a. Filed under antidumping, countervailing duty, and escape clause provisions.

tions for the executive to supply protection, one should have expected to see rising trade barriers in the 1980s. Not surprisingly, the
Reagan administration did grant more protection than previous
administrations. While only 13 countervailing duties were in effect
in 1968, and only 30 had been imposed in the previous thirty-four
years, the Customs Department was collecting countervailing duties on 56 items in the first half of 1983. Meanwhile, only 12 antidumping cases were acted on between 1955 and 1968, compared
with 137 in late 1983.[26] Although the total can be somewhat misleading because the steel and textile industries, which had been receiving some form of protection for several years, filed multiple petitions, table 4 shows that even when textile and steel petitions are
excluded, the percentage of other petitions that received positive
action from the executive increased dramatically after 1979.

Other studies have reported similar results. The Institute for
International Economics reported that the value of imports subject
to special restrictions grew from $0.6 billion in 1955 to $28.9 billion
in 1980 and $67.1 billion in 1984. When automobiles (more than $36.5
billion in imports in 1985) are added, the percentage of total imports
($345 billion in 1985) subject to protective measures increased by 10
percentage points over what it had been in the late 1970s.[27]

This increase in protection has to be put into context. Even
modest restrictions of an imported product can have an enormous
impact on a particular foreign industry because the United States is

26. Destler, *American Trade Politics*, pp. 113, 125.
27. Gary Clyde Hufbauer, Diane T. Berliner, and Kimberly Ann Elliott, *Trade Protection in the United States: 31 Case Studies* (Washington, D.C.: Institute for Inter-national Economics, 1986), p. 20; and U.S. Department of Commerce, *Statistical Abstract of the United States* (GPO, 1987), p. 791.

such a large market. But to measure the significance of rising American protection, one has to go beyond the dollar value of imports subject to some form of restraint. A 1 percent tariff on all U.S. imports, for example, could be counted as a massive increase in protection if one counts the sectors restricted. Yet it would not have an important effect on the terms of trade, the gross national product, the growth of imports, or the demand for protection. It is even possible that increased protection could improve social welfare. Paul Krugman has estimated that if the United States raised tariffs and there was no retaliation, it could be better off. Even if others retaliated, causing U.S. firms to face a 10 percent tariff, the welfare losses would amount to only 0.2 percent of GNP.[28]

Using broader measures of protectionist policies, most economic studies of American trade restrictions on manufactures have suggested that the United States has remained more liberal than most of its trading partners (many of whom have large trade surpluses), and the total cost of American protection has been low.[29] Although protectionist activity has been increasing, many of its effects have been overrated. The most obvious indicator of the limited impact of American trade barriers is that from 1980 to 1986 the growth in U.S. imports outstripped the growth of world imports seven to one.[30] In addition, the costs of specific policy tools, such as countervailing and antidumping duties, have been exaggerated. Although rising numbers of petitions harass foreign exporters, between 1982 and the first half of 1985 only $2.9 billion worth of imports were actually subject to these duties.[31] This amounted to less than 0.5 percent of

28. Paul Krugman, "Comments and Discussion," *Brookings Papers on Economic Activity*, 1: 1987, pp. 346–47.

29. Seventeen percent of U.S. manufactures were subject to nontariff barriers in 1983 compared with 19 percent for the European Economic Community. Julio Nogues, Andrej Olechowski, and L. Alan Winters, "The Extent of Non-Tariff Barriers to Imports of Industrial Countries," working paper 789 (World Bank, 1986).

30. U.S. imports grew at a compound growth rate of 7 percent while world imports grew by only 1 percent. These numbers are calculated from International Monetary Fund, *Direction of Trade Statistics: 1987 Yearbook* (IMF, 1987), pp. 2, 405. While the orders of magnitude are a function of higher growth in the United States, and some might argue correctly that U.S. imports would have grown faster in a freer trade environment, protectionism clearly has not had a significant effect on American trade flows.

31. Alan A. Rugman and Andrew Anderson, *Administered Protection in America* (Methuen, 1987), have made a strong case for administered protection as a form of foreign harassment. The $2.9 billion figure comes from Lande and Van Grasstek, *Trade and Tariff Act of 1984*, p. 19.

total imports over the period. And while systematic studies have shown that restrictions in textiles, apparel, steel, and autos cost consumers more than $33 billion a year in the mid-1980s,[32] "all empirical estimates of the social costs of protection, with few exceptions, arrived at low values compared with gross national product."[33] Clearly, American protectionism has not been as severe or damaging as some have claimed.

AN OBSOLETE BARGAIN?

American trade institutions have failed to maintain purely liberal trade policies, but it would be politically naive to believe that when trade deficits and exchange rate disequilibrium are as severe as they have been in the 1980s, any set of democratic institutional arrangements in a large country would have done significantly better. When the volume of imports rises by 50 percent more than domestic production in the span of a few years—from 11.4 percent in 1980 to 15.7 percent in 1985—a political reaction would seem inevitable.[34] Yet despite the increasing imports and unprecedented trade deficits, the executive has been able to avoid wholesale increases in trade restrictions. The president did provide limited protection for sectors such as autos and machine tools so as to buy off Congress, but he refused protection for other sectors such as copper and footwear. In the meantime, Congress continued to tighten laws against unfair trade practices and to restrict presidential discretion while shying away from legislating product-specific protection.[35]

The ability to maintain control of policy in the face of such se-

32. William R. Cline, *The Future of World Trade in Textiles and Apparel* (Washington, D.C.: Institute for International Economics, 1987), p. 14; and Hufbauer and others, *Trade Protection in the United States*, p. 13. See also William R. Cline, *Exports of Manufactures from Developing Countries: Performance and Prospects for Market Access* (Brookings, 1984); and William R. Cline and C. Fred Bergsten, "Trade Policy in the 1980s: An Overview," in William R. Cline, ed., *Trade Policy in the 1980s* (Washington, D.C.: Institute for International Economics, 1983), pp. 59–98.

33. Bruno S. Frey, *International Political Economics* (Blackwell, 1984), p. 18.

34. Destler, *American Trade Politics*, p. 170.

35. Two exceptions to this pattern were the Jenkins Bill of 1985, which passed both houses and legislated quotas on textiles and apparel, and a trade bill passed in the summer of 1988 that restricted textiles, apparel, and footwear. Both were vetoed; and both times Congress failed to override the veto.

vere pressures might suggest great resilience in trade institutions. For instance, members of Congress in both 1984 and 1988 loaded the House and Senate trade bills with highly protectionist amendments, but conference committees were able to eliminate them. This institutional adaptation has led some analysts to argue that trade institutions are fundamentally sound and that it would be premature to propose significant changes because the declining value of the dollar will reduce the volume of imports, expand exports, and alleviate protectionist pressures.[36]

An alternative hypothesis is that important trends, many of them unrelated to the value of the dollar, are making the historical bargain between Congress and the executive branch obsolete. Should this be the case, devising effective trade policy will become more difficult, even if the dollar's decline improves the trade deficit. The strategy of the past fifty years—to liberalize trade and use temporary trade barriers to protect Congress from interest group pressures—was premised on certain assumptions about how the world worked. It assumed that dynamic American firms could compete in a world with lower tariffs and that noncompetitive basic industries would be phased out after a transition period, with assets relocated according to comparative advantage. These assumptions were politically important because the executive depended on dynamic, internationally oriented industries to support free trade initiatives; and the ultimate disappearance of industries that could no longer compete was the best way to protect Congress against protectionist pressure.[37]

In the past several years these assumptions have been challenged. A growing trend toward recidivism among industries demanding relief has made it more difficult to shield Congress from chronic protectionist pressures. In addition, some of the most technologically advanced American industries no longer unconditionally support free trade. These capital-intensive industries are also placing new demands on policymakers that are difficult to accommodate without changing trade institutions and compromising a

36. This position is most strongly represented by I. M. Destler, C. Fred Bergsten, William R. Cline, and others at the Institute of International Economics.

37. The United States need not be totally dependent on the market to eliminate uncompetitive industries. Robert Z. Lawrence and Robert E. Litan, for example, have argued that trade adjustment assistance can help this process. See *Saving Free Trade: A Pragmatic Approach* (Brookings, 1986).

liberal trade strategy. Finally, protectionist arguments have achieved a new legitimacy. While the forty-year academic consensus on trade liberalization is not yet at risk, recent protectionist theories provide a basis for challenging the status quo.

Growing Recidivism

Perhaps the most important feature of the executive's trade strategy since the 1950s is that it has seldom given those industries demanding protection as much as they wanted. The executive has always been willing to consider restrictions in order to shield Congress from advocates of protectionism, but it has been difficult for many industries even to meet the criteria for consideration. Furthermore, as long as the president considers such factors as America's obligations under the General Agreement on Tariffs and Trade, the potential for protection to increase domestic inflation, or the possible diplomatic costs of restricting imports from allies, interest groups will probably not receive the high tariffs or the tight quantitative restrictions they usually request. The GATT, for instance, requires a country to compensate its trading partners (or accept retaliation) if it imposes tariffs or quotas. And since the inflationary costs of tariffs and quotas are relatively easy to identify, there are political incentives to avoid them.[38]

When the executive branch has given in to protectionist demands, it has historically done so by imposing very low tariffs or negotiating settlements with foreign suppliers, usually after lengthy procrastination.[39] Through the late 1970s, when industries applied for countervailing or antidumping duties, the Treasury Department at times postponed decisions for years and even then

38. C. Fred Bergsten and others, *Auction Quotas and United States Trade Policy,* Policy Analyses in International Economics 19 (Washington, D.C.: Institute for International Economics, 1987).

39. The most notable exception was Harley Davidson's 1982 petition for protection under the escape clause. The ITC recommended 40 percent tariffs on motorcycles, which would decline over five years. Although the administration devised a mechanism to exclude European motorcycles from the tariff, it otherwise gave this one-company industry exactly what it sought. One of the members of the Council of Economic Advisers reported in a personal interview that even the CEA—usually the strongest opponent of any barrier—did not oppose the tariff because Harley Davidson was nearly bankrupt and protection would hurt only users of large motorcycles, such as Hell's Angels.

would reduce the requested duties to trivial levels.[40] But in 1979 Congress reassigned responsibility for these cases to the International Trade Commission and the Department of Commerce, ostensibly to create a more impartial judge (the ITC) of whether an industry was injured and an agency (Commerce) more partial to business concerns. Even after the reassignment, however, investigations would often last more than a year, and in the large cases, such as the steel petitions of 1982 and 1984, Commerce chose to negotiate a settlement rather than impose prohibitive duties.

This search for protectionist solutions that would be less offensive to U.S. trading partners and have less transparent inflationary costs produced such creative trade barriers as trigger price systems and voluntary export restraints.[41] Voluntary export restraints, in particular, have been a favorite U.S. trade policy and have been used on behalf of dozens of small industries as well as every large one that has received some protection, including textiles, steel, footwear, color TVs, autos, and machine tools. From the executive's point of view, voluntary restraints are very useful. Because they are not covered by the GATT, the president can negotiate them to appease domestic interest groups without violating international obligations. In addition, the restricted country rather than the United States captures any additional profits generated by protection, and many restricted countries have found ways to use the restraints to their advantage.[42] Although no country wants to be subject to them, the restrictions sometimes lead to increased export earnings, which reduces U.S. foreign policy costs. The executive

40. The classic example of this behavior was the Treasury's approach to the multiple petitions filed by Zenith Corporation between 1971 and 1977. Despite several rulings that Japan had violated American trade laws, importers of Japanese electronics ultimately had to pay a fine of only ten cents on the dollar, and this almost a decade after the initial verdicts. See David B. Yoffie, *Zenith and the Color Television Fight*, Harvard Business School case no. 383-070 (1982).

41. The trigger price system was used between 1977 and 1981 in the steel industry. If steel imports entered the country below the trigger price, the government would immediately launch a dumping investigation. Voluntary export restraints, also called voluntary restraint arrangements, are tacit agreements with particular foreign suppliers to restrict exports. More formal legal versions of these deals are called orderly marketing agreements. See John Zysman and Laura Tyson, eds., *American Industry in International Competition: Government Policies and Corporate Strategies* (Cornell University Press, 1983).

42. Bergsten and others, *Auction Quotas*, discusses the distribution of rents; Yoffie, *Power and Protectionism*, discusses voluntary export restraints as tools of industrial policy.

also favors voluntary restraints because they do not seem to impede multilateral negotiations to improve trade liberalization: the United States has been able to conclude seven rounds of GATT talks despite its widespread use of the restraints. Because voluntary restraints are also typically leaky arrangements—imports usually continue to increase rapidly—some price competition is often maintained. And finally, even though voluntary restraints have rarely provided long-term benefits for the industries they were designed to protect, they have historically appeased the demanders of protection, at least for a while.[43] Industries that have been offered voluntary restraints consider the potential increase in prices, even if they are only temporary, as better than potential results under the alternative of free trade.

An unforeseen consequence of procrastinating on protectionism and giving industries less than they want (and usually less than they need to make permanent adjustments to international competition) is that they continually request more assistance. When relatively few industries were requesting protection in the 1950s and 1960s, recidivism did not threaten the system. The textile industry, for instance, has repeated its requests to the government every two or three years since the early 1950s, but as long as the industry remained isolated, it could be bought off with a new, slightly tighter set of voluntary restraints. Potential problems have arisen, however, from a protectionist snowballing effect. Among larger industries, textiles was virtually the lone recidivist in the 1960s; by the mid-1970s it was joined by steel; by the late 1970s, TVs and footwear became repeat requesters. By 1985 more than sixty industry groups had filed repeat petitions. In fact, most of the increase in demand for protection during the Reagan administration can be traced to recidivists. The number of industries filing for protection for the first time has been relatively flat since 1979 (table 5). Even if one discounts the long-time activists—textiles and steel—the lion's share of growth in demand has come from recidivists.

The dangers of recidivism for the future of American trade policy and institutions are manyfold. Recidivists can and do use trade statutes to harass foreign competitors and overload the institutional mechanisms of the ITC and the Department of Commerce. By filing a dumping or countervailing suit under varying customs

43. See David B. Yoffie, "Orderly Marketing Agreements as an Industrial Policy: The Case of the Footwear Industry," Public Policy, vol. 29 (Winter 1981), pp. 93–119.

TABLE 5. *Recidivism of Industries Filing for Protection, 1979–85*[a]

Category	1979	1980	1981	1982	1983	1984	1985
Nonsteel, nontextile industries applying for protection	22	19	18	33	30	31	33
Industries filing for the first time	22	17	16	29	26	22	23
Industries filing repeat petitions (percent)	0	10.5	11.1	12.1	13.3	29.0	30.0

SOURCE: Calculated from Destler, *American Trade Politics*, pp. 223–334.

a. Includes escape clause, countervailing duty, and antidumping petitions. The number of industries filing petitions will not correlate with the total number of petitions. If an industry group filed multiple petitions in a year, it was scored as a single industry. Textiles and steel have been excluded because they have continually filed petitions for thirty years and twenty years respectively. Their inclusion would bias the figures upward and would not indicate a new trend.

definitions or against different countries, a domestic industry can increase a competitor's uncertainty and potentially reduce international trade. Even if duties are never imposed, the process of applying for protection or fighting a protectionist proposal is costly for domestic and foreign firms alike.

The political dangers of recidivism are even more worrisome. One of the primary purposes of the Reciprocal Trade Agreements Act and its implicit bargain between Congress and the executive was to divide and conquer protectionist interests by treating each industry individually. Textiles thus had few incentives to collaborate with steel, and neither had incentives to work with footwear. As a consequence, they rarely learned anything from each other. For instance, even though the textile industry had two decades of experience with protection under voluntary export restraints, by the time the footwear industry was given comparable protection in 1977, the footwear association had made virtually every mistake in seeking voluntary restraints that the textile industry had made in 1957.[44] The footwear industry agreed to protectionist arrangements that made no provision for cheating and defined categories so broadly that foreign circumvention was easy—problems the textile industry had been addressing for a decade.

Recidivism compromises this isolation. Recidivists tend to have strong common interests and common complaints: they all feel

44. Yoffie, *Power and Protectionism*, chap. 5.

that the existing system has not adequately protected them. More-over, unlike newcomers to Washington, recidivists are likely to know one another. They may have testified in front of the International Trade Commission a dozen times, used the same specialized Washington lawyers, or simply lobbied the same committees on Capitol Hill. As a result, industries are more likely to learn from each other and to become sophisticated in building coalitions.

Many of the changes in the laws governing countervailing and antidumping duties and the use of the escape clause can be traced to pressures from industries that at first failed to get a satisfactory judgment. If a firm or industry loses on a technicality in its initial suit, it lobbies Congress to make small technical changes in legislation that will allow it to win later. Gradually these revisions have produced changes in trade law significant enough to allow firms to misuse or abuse the system. For instance, even though imports were increasing and plants were closing, the ITC rejected the footwear industry's escape clause petition in 1984 because corporate profitability was greater than the average for all U.S. manufacturing. Footwear firms, much wiser eight years after their first successful petition, responded by convincing Congress to require the ITC to consider more than one criterion for rejecting a petition. The industry then reapplied a year later and won an affirmative ITC judgment, even though profitability remained strong.[45]

If the present demand for protection among recidivists is cyclical or a consequence of the previously overvalued dollar, the dangers of renewed logrolling in Congress and greater sophistication of protectionist interests should diminish with exchange rate adjustments. However, recidivism will probably not disappear. For industries that compete only against developing countries, exchange rate adjustments are irrelevant: most developing nations peg their currencies to the American dollar, and its depreciation will have no impact on price competition vis-à-vis those particular countries. Exchange rate adjustments could even make recidivism worse. The falling dollar will strengthen the competitive position of domestic industries that compete against countries with rising currencies, such as Germany, Japan, and to a lesser extent Taiwan and Korea.

45. Operating income as a percent of sales was 8.8 percent in 1983 when the industry's petition was rejected and 5.8 percent in 1984 when the petition was accepted under the new trade law. David B. Yoffie and Stewart Burton, "B-W Footwear," Harvard Business School case no. 9-387-022 (1986), p. 19.

However, without a technological revolution or an unthinkable exchange rate adjustment that would reduce relative American wage levels by 50 to 75 percent, industries such as apparel and footwear have little hope of regaining competitiveness. According to the Organization for Economic Cooperation and Development, the United States has lost comparative advantage to the newly industrializing countries in a wide range of manufactured products.[46] The increasing competitiveness of Taiwan, Korea, Hong Kong, and Singapore poses a challenge to intermediate-technology American industries that cannot be solved by standard macroeconomic measures. Thus a weaker dollar will not reduce the resolve of many recidivists. In fact, if a weak dollar modestly improves profits or cuts losses, it could have the paradoxical effect of funding recidivists' political activities.

Demands for Contingent Protection

Congress could resist growing protectionist demands in the late 1970s and early 1980s in part because of the antiprotectionist activities of multinational companies. Historically, most multinationals, especially those with extensive intrafirm trade flows and dependence on exports, advocated freer trade because domestic barriers could disrupt global production strategies, raise the costs of key materials, and provoke retaliation against highly exposed fixed assets overseas.[47] Multinationals did not consider foreign trade barriers an insurmountable problem because they did not feel threatened by foreign competitors and because they could usually break into closed foreign markets by direct investment. In the 1980s, however, access to foreign markets has often become as important as access to low-cost inputs. Especially for industries in which the sources of competitive advantage are economies of scale and learning by doing, American firms have found that inability to export to large foreign markets has given foreign rivals significant competitive advantages.[48] Where foreign governments have protected and

46. Organization for Economic Cooperation and Development, *The Impact of the Newly Industrialising Countries on Production and Trade in Manufactures* (Paris: OECD, 1979), pp. 32–36.

47. Milner, "Resisting the Protectionist Temptation."

48. In industries with high scale requirements, firms need very large sales volumes to realize a return on initial investments. If the home market is not large

subsidized their industries, multinational firms that formerly supported free trade unconditionally have advocated contingent protectionism: that is, they have been willing to support freer trade for the American market only if foreign markets are equally open to their products. Where foreign markets have remained closed and American firms have felt threatened by rivals from them, they have recommended that the U.S. government retaliate.

There is evidence of such behavior in three large industries: semiconductors, telecommunications, and mainframe aircraft.[49] Since the mid-1970s all three have become more scale-intensive, and their costs have declined sharply as they have accumulated production experience. In all three cases foreign governments have used protection or subsidies to create competitive advantages for their own firms. In reaction each U.S. industry abandoned unconditional support of free trade and began to advocate closing American markets if foreign practices could not be changed. These were not simply examples of disguised protectionism: all three industries were actively seeking to enter foreign markets and made their demands for protection contingent on changes in foreign behavior.

The demands for contingent protectionism may become more pervasive. The economic changes that partially motivated the alteration in trade strategies have become widely evident, and foreign government intervention in high-technology industries has been rising.[50] Increasing demand for contingent protectionism has also

---

enough to enable them to achieve the minimum scale necessary to break even, access to foreign markets becomes critical. Furthermore, if learning effects (that is, reduced costs of production due to greater experience and knowledge of the manufacturing process) are important, the first firm or national industry to build a large sales base will have lower costs that cannot be profitably replicated by competitors. Because these economic changes separately or collectively cause market entry to become more difficult, foreign protectionism or subsidies could give foreign competitors advantages. When the U.S. market is open and the foreign market is closed, foreign competitors can achieve more efficient scales and sales volumes through domestic and overseas sales, while U.S. competitors are squeezed into a portion of the domestic market, making them less efficient. Once firms fall behind in these types of industries, they cannot recover and retain their profitability. Under these conditions, access to foreign markets and control over the home market become a firm's top priorities. See Helen V. Milner and David B. Yoffie, "Between Free Trade and Protectionism: Strategic Trade Policy and a Theory of Corporate Trade Demand," *International Organization* (forthcoming, 1989).

49. Ibid.

50. On the growing prevalence of market imperfections, see Paul R. Krugman, "Introduction: New Thinking about Trade Policy," in Krugman, ed., *Strategic Trade*

inevitably weakened the antiprotectionist coalition that helped fight for trade liberalization in the late 1970s and early 1980s. While these industries may still favor liberalization, they are less likely to fight against protectionism aimed at particular foreign rivals. The semiconductor industry, for instance, unconditionally supported trade liberalization in the 1970s. But while it continued to recommend giving the president more authority to negotiate freer trade multilaterally during the debate over trade in 1987, it also joined coalitions that were seeking tighter rules for applying countervailing and antidumping duties.

Demands for contingent protectionism also challenge the traditional separation between free trade and protectionism. For most of the postwar period, protectionism was defined as tariffs and quotas that could be easily identified. Typically, basic industries advocated these restrictions while more dynamic, export-oriented ones advocated free trade. American trade policy was designed to reduce these obvious barriers while creating opportunities for free trade interests to balance protectionist interests. But when export-oriented industries begin asking for contingent protection, the old rules no longer apply. On the one hand, such demands are incongruent with the traditional strategy of providing protection only temporarily to industries in distress. On the other hand, the demands are targeted against "unfair" practices—closed markets and direct or indirect subsidies—that have long been recognized as legitimate reasons for intervention.

A political problem is created by this ambiguity. Requests for unconditional protection or countervailing or antidumping duties trigger decisions based on relatively explicit rules. But the government has not developed rules or even guidelines for coping with pressures for contingent protectionism. There is no confusion over authority: section 301 of the 1974 Trade Act gave the president virtually unlimited powers to retaliate against any foreign policy or practice that is inconsistent with a trade agreement or is "unjustifiable, unreasonable, or discriminatory and burdens or restricts U.S.

Policy and the New International Economics (MIT Press, 1986), chap. 1. For foreign intervention see Stephen Cohen and John Zysman, *Manufacturing Matters: The Myth of the Post-Industrial Economy* (Basic Books, 1987); and Bruce Scott and George Lodge, eds., *U.S. Competitiveness in the World Economy* (Harvard Business School Press, 1985).

TABLE 6. *Section 301 Cases, June 1985 to June 1987*[a]

Date	Country and industry	Result
June 14, 1985	Japan, semiconductors	United States negotiates settlement in July 1986. President determines in March 1987 that Japan has violated the agreement, and increases duties on $300 million worth of Japanese imports; $136 million duties are dropped given improved Japanese adherence to the original agreement
September 16, 1985	Brazil, informatics[b]	The president announces in November 1987 that the United States would impose punitive tariffs on $105 million worth of imports from Brazil. Brazil tightens up its software copyright laws but continues to restrict imports of microcomputers and microcomputer software products
September 16, 1985	Japan, tobacco products[b]	Japan agrees to eliminate cigarette tariff and discriminatory tax and distribution practices
September 16, 1985	Korea, insurance[b]	Korea agrees to allow U.S. firms to underwrite Korean insurance

commerce."[51] The president can "impose duties or other import restrictions and . . . take any other appropriate and feasible actions within his power."[52] To date, the greatest confusion has been conceptual. Should the president use this authority to assist large American industries to compete in world markets, or should he use it to buy off special interests and thus forestall protectionist legislation?

Presidential actions have reflected this confusion. Historically, petitions for protection under the provisions of section 301 were initiated by the industries claiming to suffer from unfair practices. In September 1985, however, the president began initiating such

51. *Economic Report of the President, 1987,* p. 131.
52. Commerce Department, *Business America* (December 8, 1986), p. 9.

TABLE 6 (continued)

Date	Country and industry	Result
November 4, 1985	Korea, intellectual property rights[b]	Korea agrees to improve copyright protection
April 4, 1986	Argentina, soybeans and soybean products	Argentina agrees to eliminate export taxes on soybeans which advantaged its soybean processors
March 31, 1986	European Community enlargement[b]	EC agrees to guarantee the United States a share of grain exports to Portugal and Spain and lowers levies on other U.S. exports to EC
April 1, 1986	Canada, fish	Pending
August 1, 1986	Taiwan, customs violation[b]	Taiwan agrees to abolish duty-paying schedule
October 27, 1986	Taiwan, beer, wine, tobacco[b]	Taiwan agrees to cease unfair distribution practices
December 30, 1986	Canada, softwood lumber[b]	Canada agrees to impose export surcharge of 15 percent
January 6, 1987	India, almonds	Pending

SOURCE: Office of the U.S. Trade Representative, "Section 301 Table of Cases" (January 1988).

a. Of the forty-three section 301 cases acted on from January 1975 to June 1987, twenty were resolved through negotiations and twelve produced retaliation. The others were suspended, withdrawn, or terminated for other reasons.

b. Initiated by the president.

petitions. The targets of these petitions were inconsistent. As table 6 shows, they have included developed and developing countries, and industries that were big (tobacco) and small (insurance in Korea), high-technology (informatics in Brazil) and basic (beer and wine in Taiwan), agricultural (oil seed exports to the European Communities) and services (insurance). The pattern of resolution, however, is clearer. The first preference has been to negotiate solutions. If that fails, the government has demonstrated a willingness to retaliate, but typically in symbolic ways or in ways that transfer the funds received from protection to the foreign producers. Thus, in 1986 the Commerce Department found that Canada subsidized softwood lumber exports, but rather than collect a duty for American taxpayers, in the name of improved foreign relations the department allowed Canada to collect the duty for its taxpayers. In 1987, in conjunction with a section 301 suit, the United States found that Japan was violating a bilateral agreement on semiconductors. Rather than coerce Japan into compliance with meaningful sanctions, the president retaliated against 0.33 percent of Japanese annual exports to the United States ($300 million).[53] When the government sought to open the multibillion dollar Japanese construction market in 1987–88, it promoted more headlines than sales. American construction firms had a competitive advantage in bidding for high-technology projects in Japan and little advantage in bidding on more labor-intensive jobs. But when the U.S. government signed an agreement to allow American firms to bid on $17 billion in contracts, the lion's share was for digging ditches and building roads. Lack of coordination with the industry and the Commerce Department's desire to claim a big victory for freer trade were cited as the reasons for the inept performance.[54]

The dilemma of rising demands for contingent protectionism is that without clear guidelines the president is damned if he meets the demands and damned if he does not. There is no explicit basis in law or policy to tell one interest group that it qualifies for government assistance and another that it does not. An aggressive policy of retaliating against almost any foreign competitor in industries of all sizes and shapes for virtually any offense aggravates foreign relations as well as stimulating more demands for action.[55] If the president retaliates against Japan on market access, Taiwan for its investment guidelines, and Brazil on intellectual property, then other industries might learn from the experience, thereby increasing the demand. Symbolic gestures toward contingent protectionism, however, pose the same danger as symbolic protectionism for declining industries: unless the gestures make U.S. indus-

53. David B. Yoffie and John Coleman, "The Semiconductor Industry Association and the Trade Dispute with Japan (A)," Harvard Business School case no. 9-387-205 (1987); and Clyde V. Prestowitz, Jr., *Trading Places: How We Allowed Japan to Take the Lead* (Basic Books, 1988), chap. 2.

54. Elisabeth Rubinfien, "In Construction Talks, U.S. Showed Japanese It Is Often Confused," *Wall Street Journal*, March 31, 1988.

55. For example, one industry may receive a favorable negotiated settlement in one country in year one, so it returns in year two with a petition against another country, in year three against a third country, and so on. Since there are no prohibitions against such filings, several industries have followed this pattern. The insurance industry filed section 301 petitions against the Soviet Union in 1978, Argentina in 1979, and Korea in 1985. Leather tanners filed against Japan in 1977 and Argentina in 1981, and soybean processors against Brazil in May 1983, Portugal in November 1983, Spain in December 1983, and Argentina in April 1986. Office of the U.S. Trade Representative, "Section 301 Table of Cases" (June 1987).

tries more competitive or profitable, even dynamic industries might become recidivists. Hence, without a clear strategy for accommodating these demands, trade policy could potentially become more ad hoc, less efficient, and more protectionist.

An Intellectual Challenge: Strategic Trade Policy Theory

The executive's ability to define clear rules for managing demands for protection has largely depended on a fifty-year consensus on the benefits of free trade. As one economist recently put it, "If there were an Economist's Creed, it would surely contain the affirmations, 'I understand the Principle of Comparative Advantage' and 'I advocate Free Trade.' " The defense of free trade is "as close to a sacred tenet as any idea in Economics."[56] This unwavering belief among economists and many politicians has reinforced the institutional resistance to trade barriers of any type.

Yet perhaps for the first time since David Ricardo published *Principles of Comparative Advantage* in 1817, the classical theory of international trade has been challenged by well-respected academic economists. The traditional model of comparative advantage postulated that trade patterns were determined by differences in taste, access to raw materials and other natural advantages, or technology and that free trade was the best policy for ensuring economic welfare.[57] The challenge to the traditional model has stemmed from the recognition in the past two decades that the Ricardian assumptions of constant returns to scale and perfect competition do not reflect actual conditions.[58] Mainstream trade

---

56. Paul R. Krugman, "Is Free Trade Passé?" *Economics Perspectives*, vol. 1 (Fall 1987), p. 131.

57. Ricardo argued that differences in tastes were critical, Eli Heckscher and Bertil Ohlin were proponents of factor endowments, and Raymond Vernon advocated technology as the driving force behind trade patterns. See David Ricardo, *The Principles of Political Economy and Taxation* (Totowa, N.J.: Biblio Distribution Center, 1978); Eli Heckscher, "The Effect of Foreign Trade on the Distribution of Income," reprinted in American Economic Association, *Readings in the Theory of International Trade* (Philadelphia: Blakiston, 1949), pp. 272–300; and Raymond Vernon, "International Investment and International Trade in the Product Cycle," *Quarterly Journal of Economics*, vol. 80 (May 1966), pp. 190–207.

58. Louis T. Wells, ed., *The Product Life Cycle and International Trade* (Harvard Business School Press, 1972); and Staffan Burenstam Linder, "Causes of Trade in Primary Products versus Manufactures," in Robert E. Baldwin and J. David

theory, however, continued to deny the value of alternative formulations because of their lack of rigor.

Not until the late 1970s did microeconomists specializing in industrial organization begin to devise more careful models of imperfect competition which suggested that gains from trade were not necessarily maximized by the free international exchange of goods and services.[59] In the mid-1980s theoretical research has hypothesized that patterns of international trade are no longer determined by comparative advantage but rather by economies of scale and government exploitation of market imperfections. Even though the models have not been very robust and most economists have been careful about generalizing from the research, a growing number of policy recommendations argue that free trade is no longer ideal under many conditions. Some economists have shown that limited forms of protection or subsidies can help raise a nation's welfare, although at the expense of other nations.[60] And subsidies or protection can also improve welfare when protected industries generate benefits for other industries.

Economists have been cautious about the political difficulties of implementing such measures in the United States. As one noted, "to exercise effective strategic direction over trade policy for imperfectly competitive firms would seem to require a corporate managerial style of government decisionmaking. Such managerial decisionmaking is typically hierarchical—not 'democratic,' 'representative,' 'participatory,' or 'multiagency.' "[61] One of the strongest critics of the classic trade model has similarly written that the results of attempting strategic trade policy can easily be "excessive or misguided intervention. . . . To ask the Commerce Department

Richardson, eds., *International Trade and Finance: Readings*, 2d ed. (Little, Brown, 1981), pp. 40–51.

59. This work was pioneered by Avinash K. Dixit and Joseph E. Stiglitz, "Monopolistic Competition and Optimum Product Diversity," *American Economic Review*, vol. 67 (June 1977), pp. 297–308; and Paul R. Krugman, "Increasing Returns, Monopolistic Competition, and International Trade," *Journal of International Economics*, vol. 9 (November 1979), pp. 469–79.

60. The pros and cons are laid out in Krugman, ed., *Strategic Trade Policy and the New International Economics*.

61. J. David Richardson, "Trade Policy Implications of 'Strategic' Economic Models," paper prepared for National Bureau of Economic Research conference, January 1986, p. 29.

to ignore special-interest politics while formulating detailed policy for many industries is not realistic."[62]

Yet despite the care with which economists have restricted their findings, the sudden existence of a potential justification for protection could have important implications. It may give politicians a new political weapon. A new president or policymaker within Congress or the executive branch could interpret this theory in such a way as to justify departures from the traditional liberal trade strategy. As has been shown in the case of fiscal deficits, presidents find it hard to make dramatic departures from long-standing national policies without a consistent intellectual grounding for them.[63] Just as President Reagan was able to use monetarists and supply-side theories to justify big changes in fiscal policy, the next president might find strategic trade policy a politically convenient vehicle for defending various forms of protection.

This possibility is all the greater because market imperfections described by the new trade theory may be partially responsible for the slow reduction in the trade deficit, despite exchange rate adjustments and other traditional macroeconomic solutions. Just as Keynesians were put on the defensive in the late 1970s by the combination of high unemployment and high inflation, advocates of free trade and comparative advantage would be put on the defensive if trade deficits continue to hover between $120 billion and $150 billion. Should the trade deficits decrease rapidly, the political viability of new trade theory could dissipate. If the deficits persist, it will become easier for people such as Congressman Richard Gephardt to use strategic trade theory to achieve political legitimacy.

IMPLICATIONS FOR AMERICAN TRADE POLICY AND INSTITUTIONS

The American strategy of liberalizing international commerce through multilateral negotiations has been under attack for some

---

62. Krugman, "Is Free Trade Passé?" p. 142.
63. Paul E. Peterson, "The New Politics of Deficits," in John E. Chubb and Paul E. Peterson, eds., *The New Direction in American Politics* (Brookings, 1985), p. 392.

time. Ever since the decline of the Bretton Woods agreement and Nixon's closing of the gold window in 1971, scholars of international political economy have been predicting that America's waning hegemony would tumble it into protectionism.[64] Other scholars have seen the cause of America's slide into protectionism as coming from a weakening in the institutional structure governing trade decisions.

The deterioration of hegemony and the undesirable changes in the way Congress and the president make trade policy have surely weakened America's commitment to liberal trade. The greater problem, however, is that the liberal strategy has nurtured the seeds of its own destruction. The symbolic compensation for those who have sought protection has produced repeated requests for more comprehensive barriers and raised the ugly specter of the kind of logrolling common at the time of the passage of the Smoot-Hawley Act. Even if one assumes that members of Congress want to be protected from such potentially harmful bargaining, free trade, which is by definition noninterventionist and passive, will not work. A liberal strategy providing minimal protection will no longer satisfy seasoned veterans of Capitol Hill lobbying.

Demands for contingent protectionism by former leaders of the free trade coalition similarly confuse and confound the government's ability to pursue a liberal trade strategy. Congress and the executive have always needed the corporate beneficiaries of free trade to help balance the pressures from protectionists. A weakening of these beneficiaries coupled with demands for contingent protection further undermines the political consensus favoring free trade. Even if simple advocacy of free trade were the best policy economically, it would be politically unstable.

Finally, rising demand for changes in trade policy and the new theories regarding the most effective use of protection could create

---

64. Bretton Woods was an international regime negotiated in 1944 that required participating countries to fix the price of their currencies to the U.S. dollar and called for the U.S. dollar to be convertible into a fixed price of gold. This regime ended in 1973. For predictions about the stability of U.S. trade policy, see Charles Kindleberger, *History of the World Economy in the 20th Century*, vol. 4: *The World in Depression, 1929–1939* (University of California Press, 1975); and Stephen D. Krasner, "State Power and the Structure of International Trade," *World Politics*, vol. 27 (April 1976), pp. 317–43. For an exception to these views, see Robert O. Keohane, *After Hegemony: Cooperation and Discord in the World Political Economy* (Princeton University Press, 1984).

a political opportunity for a new president or congressman to pursue a more activist trade policy. Under present institutional arrangements, however, the executive would be as likely to pursue such policies to appease Congress as to promote welfare and efficiency. Therefore, any effort to adopt strategic trade policy could easily turn into ad hoc protectionism.

It is important to emphasize that these political problems will not go away simply because the dollar has a lower value. Even if the trade deficit improves, a more expensive Japanese yen, deutsche mark, or Swiss franc will not reduce the political activities of recidivists like steel, textiles, and footwear. In addition, a cheaper dollar will not necessarily improve American high-technology firms' access to restricted foreign markets.

If we hope to solve these dilemmas, the first order of business has to be devising a new trade strategy. Since the problems described in this chapter are partly a function of the division of labor between Congress and the executive and partly a function of new political and economic conditions, just rearranging political institutions will not guarantee better trade performance. A stronger executive with greater authority over trade might improve coherence, but institutional change will be effective only if it is coupled with a new approach toward trade policy. Before politicians start reorganizing the trade bureaucracy or passing legislation to restructure trade decisionmaking, government should learn the lesson that business historian Alfred Chandler has been telling companies for twenty-five years: success usually comes about when structure follows strategy.[65] We need to know what we are going to do before we can decide how we are going to do it.

Because the current economics and politics of international trade are far more complicated than they were in 1934 or even in the 1950s, standard answers, such as recommendations to follow unconditional free trade and allow the market to correct itself through the exchange rate, are no longer sufficient. To prevent recidivism, the U.S. needs a more activist trade policy. Since there is no economic justification for providing continued protection for industries ranging from textiles and steel to mushrooms, the government must change the incentives for recidivists. This could be done

---

65. Alfred D. Chandler, *Strategy and Structure: Chapters in the History of American Industrial Enterprise* (MIT Press, 1962).

if Congress would abdicate significant trade responsibilities and allow the executive to resist all protectionist demands, or if Congress would give the executive the authority to use truly temporary protection to facilitate positive adjustment of recidivist industries.[66] However, Congress's ability to fend off recidivists has been decidedly limited. The passage in 1988 by the House and Senate of yet another bill to restrict imports of textiles, apparel, and footwear is a prime example of continued congressional susceptibility to recidivist pressures.

The strategic and institutional problems raised by the new theoretical developments in the international trade literature and the growing demands on trade policy from high-technology sectors are even more vexing. The best means to confront these issues would be to create a true "strategic" trade policy. While critics have rightly pointed out that any strategic trade policy for America would be difficult to devise and even harder to implement,[67] in theory a strategic trade policy could serve several political and economic objectives. Politically, the goal would be to manage the demands for contingent protectionism and prevent the new trade theory from turning into de facto protectionism; economically, the goal would be to increase efficiency in selected industries, which in turn would improve the national well-being of the United States. It is hypothetically possible that subsidies or trade restrictions in some special businesses could allow the United States to capture "rents" or profits that might otherwise accrue to a foreign country; in other industries, similar trade restrictions could give the United States the benefit of "external economies" or the gains from accruing knowledge in one sector that would help other sectors of American industry and society.

The enormous complexity of a strategic trade policy would put a strain on any political system. To be effective, government officials would need the capacity to identify industries with significant external economies or the potential for greatly increased profitability through trade intervention. Next, government would have to

66. The case of Harley Davidson may be significant. In 1982 the company became one of the few firms in recent memory to be awarded ITC tariff hikes up to 40 percent. With the added cash flow, Harley Davidson was able to restructure its product line and diversify its business. The company's revival was so successful that it requested the tariffs be lifted two years before their scheduled expiration.

67. Gene M. Grossman, "Strategic Export Promotion: A Critique," in Krugman, ed., *Strategic Trade Policy*, pp. 47–68.

choose the appropriate tool: export subsidies, domestic subsidies, or trade restrictions can have varying effects, depending on the industry's structure. For instance, a domestic subsidy might be more desirable than trade barriers in an intermediate product such as semiconductors, because trade restrictions could drive up prices to users while subsidies might ensure the requisite profitability or technological benefits. But in an industry where the key problem is foreign restrictions on American products, such as telecommunications, a tariff might be more sensible because it would deter foreign entry and could be easily withdrawn if foreign markets were to open.

A third, related requirement of strategic trade policy would be the government's ability to allocate resources to some sectors and not others, and then to monitor, adjust, and, when necessary, discontinue trade intervention. Finally, any policy of protection or subsidy that seeks to increase the U.S. national welfare at another country's expense would increase the probability of foreign retaliation. Therefore, a strategic trade policy would necessitate that a government possess brinkmanship skills in trade.

The institutional requirements for this type of strategy far exceed the present capacity of Congress or the executive. A strategic trade policy would require an institution with judgment, flexibility, expertise, and, last but not least, the incentive to employ these qualities in the national interest. Since the U.S. Congress, or any democratic legislature for that matter, could not legislate all possible contingencies for implementing a strategic trade policy, the country would need to rely more heavily on the executive than it has in recent years. In practical terms, this would entail a major expansion of the executive bureaucracy, increasing the inventory of industry-specific knowledge, and expanding the bureaucracy's capacity to coordinate business and trade interests closely.

In political terms, it would entail something more difficult. It would require a new institutional bargain between Congress and the president. Like the bargain of the 1930s, such a deal would have to increase the effective authority of the executive and weaken the programmatic powers of the Congress. But unlike the bargain of the 1930s, it would have to reverse a strong trend toward greater congressional trade influence that has been going on for two decades. To be sure, senators and representatives recognize that the president is more likely than Congress to implement trade policy in the overall interest of the nation. Yet there is no evidence in congressional action during the 1980s that Congress is willing to give the president the power to do so.

The 1988 trade bill is a case in point. The key trade provisions in the 1,000-page bill were further steps in the trends toward tying the president's hands in section 201 and 301 cases and tightening the antidumping and countervailing duty laws in ways that make it easier for firms to get relief. While the bill included some marginally positive measures, such as authority for trade liberalization and enhanced copyright protection, the likely effect of the trade bill on reducing the trade deficit or redefining the executive's trade strategy is minimal. Issues of recidivism were not addressed, and the added authority under section 301 has done little to build a capacity for strategic trade policy.

Although the United States faces a serious trade problem, the 1988 trade bill was the product of trade politics as usual. Of course history suggests that this should be so. After institutional arrangements have been in place for decades, a host of political interests in Congress, the bureaucracy, the presidency, and society at large inevitably develop a stake in their maintenance—even when their long-term effects are no longer widely beneficial. The last time U.S. trade institutions were restructured, it took the force of the Great Depression to push the old ones aside. In the more complicated and institutionalized world of today, it is difficult to imagine building new and effective institutions for managing a more strategic trade policy without a force of similar historic proportions.

Macroeconomic Policymaking: Who Is in Control?

PAUL E. PETERSON and MARK ROM

SOMETHING SEEMS amiss with the United States' economy. By virtually any standard, it is not performing as well as it did during the first few decades after World War II. Until the late 1960s the economy was growing at the rate of 3–4 percent a year, worker productivity was increasing at a rapid rate, and inflation was low and stable. Apart from brief recessionary periods, unemployment levels were acceptably low, worker earnings were on the rise, the United States regularly enjoyed a favorable balance of trade, and the national debt acquired during the depression and war years was gradually being retired.[1]

But by the end of the 1970s, the American economy seemed to be in serious trouble. Prices were rising at a faster pace. People who lost jobs had greater difficulty finding new ones. Interest rates rose to levels previously charged only by loan sharks. When presidential candidate Ronald Reagan asked the American voters in 1980 if they were better off than they had been four years earlier, he correctly expected them to blame Jimmy Carter and his party for a decade of slow growth, stagnant productivity, and rising rates of inflation. At first trends under Reagan worsened, as the country experienced the deepest recession of the postwar era. But since 1983 the triple threat of high inflation, high unemployment, and high interest rates has become a fading—though occasionally haunting—memory. By 1988 inflation had fallen to 4.0 percent, the

---

1. As a percentage of GNP, it declined from 130 percent in 1946 to 35 percent in the early 1970s. See Paul E. Peterson, "The New Politics of Deficits," in John E. Chubb and Paul E. Peterson, eds., *The New Direction in American Politics* (Brookings, 1985), p. 369.

unemployment rate was lower than it had been in thirteen years, and interest rates were less than half their peak.[2]

Many have suggested, however, that the recent prosperity has been purchased on credit. The federal government, by running budget deficits averaging $161 billion for the first six years of the 1980s, has been borrowing $1 for every $4 it actually collected in taxes.[3] At the same time, the United States started importing much more than it exported, pushing the annual trade deficit as high as $125 billion.[4] To satisfy the need for funds to finance the budget and trade deficits, the United States inhaled huge amounts of foreign capital. By 1986 it had become the world's largest debtor.

For a while, the triple deficits—budget, trade, global investment—seemed not to matter. The stock market, moved as much by investor psychology as by underlying economic trends, had more than tripled in value between 1982 and 1987. Then, on a quiet Monday morning in October 1987, with no economic news to speak of, Americans were reminded of how tenuous their newfound prosperity might be. Its most prominent indicator fell by over 500 points and the value of investments dropped by half a trillion dollars.[5] Although the causes of the crash could not be found in the news of that day, it revealed an underlying nervousness about an economic future resting on budget and trade deficits of unprecedented size. These difficulties may not have materialized into perceptible economic misfortunes during the Reagan years, but productivity gains remained modest, economic growth had not returned to the levels obtained just after World War II, and budget and trade deficits created an inextinguishable anxiety about what the economic future would hold.

Is There an Institutional Problem?

When problems occur, fingers naturally point at those who hold power. President Carter was accused of indecisiveness. President

2. *Economic Report of the President, February 1988*, pp. 317, 202; and *The Economist* (August 27, 1988), p. 53.

3. Paul E. Peterson and Mark Rom, "Lower Taxes, More Spending, and Budget Deficits," in Charles O. Jones, ed., *The Reagan Legacy* (Chatham House, 1988), p. 215.

4. *Economic Report of the President, February 1988*, p. 364.

5. Ibid., p. 40.

Reagan was blamed for his obstinate refusal to contemplate a tax increase needed to balance the budget. House Speaker Thomas P. (Tip) O'Neill was accused of letting social security and other entitlement costs mount unnecessarily. Federal Reserve Board Chairman Paul Volcker was attacked for his rigid adherence to a monetarist doctrine that generated both wide fluctuations in interest rates and the deepest recession of the postwar period.

As problems persist, however, critics, especially scholarly ones, look beyond personalities to the institutions they direct. These critics claim that institutional arrangements systematically produce ineffective policies by giving decisionmakers both the power and the incentive to err. Their mistakes are not simply due to temporary misunderstanding of economic relationships, weakness of character, faulty judgment, or unlucky circumstances. They are regular, recurring, and predictable, and in the absence of heroism or exceptional circumstances, likely to happen again.

Two broad arguments are used to attribute macroeconomic problems to institutional failure. First, a number of scholars have argued that presidents have the incentive to manipulate macroeconomic policy for political reasons. In order to help win reelection, presidents create a "political business cycle" in which the economy booms during election years.[6] Because these election year booms are unsustainable, the president will accept an economic slowdown after an election. It is also said that presidents create economic conditions that favor their particular electoral coalition. Because Democratic voters are at greater risk of unemployment, Democratic leaders are said to favor rapid growth even if it is inflationary, while Republicans are said to prefer price stability even if it causes higher unemployment rates.[7]

The second argument focuses not on presidents' incentives but

6. The theoretical rationale for a political business cycle was developed by William P. Nordhaus, "The Political Business Cycle," *Review of Economic Studies*, vol. 42 (April 1975), pp. 169–90. A concise presentation and review of the literature can be found in James E. Alt and K. Alec Chrystal, *Political Economics* (University of California Press, 1983). The latest review and empirical study in a continually growing collection is by Alberto Alesina and Jeffrey Sachs, "Political Parties and the Business Cycle in the United States, 1948–1984," *Journal of Money, Credit, and Banking*, vol. 20 (February 1988), pp. 63–82. Their sophisticated analysis, based on "rational expectations" assumptions, still presents only weak support for the theory.

7. The basic theoretical idea for class- and party-based differences in macroeconomic policymaking is developed by Michael Kalecki, "Political Aspects of Full Employment," *Political Quarterly*, vol. 14 (October–December 1943), pp. 322–31.

on the limits to their power. It is argued that policies are ineffective because the direction of macroeconomic policy is poorly coordinated. The two main levers of macroeconomic management—fiscal policy and monetary policy—are controlled by different institutions. The argument is that Congress makes the decisions to tax and spend that determine the nation's fiscal policies. The Federal Reserve, an independent agency within the government, largely determines the supply of money and the price at which it can be obtained. Both these institutions are said to operate independently of the White House,[8] and each of them, it is said, has the ability and motivation to pursue goals that may serve their particular organizational needs but are harmful to overall welfare. Congress's fiscal policy is said to tend toward excessively expansionary budgets (that is, recurring deficits), while the Federal Reserve's monetary policy is accused of encouraging high interest rates and contraction.[9]

These two broad lines of argument are contradictory. The first holds that the president has too much influence over macroeconomic policymaking and his political motivations lead to too much policy variability. The second maintains that the president has too little influence and that consequently fiscal and monetary policy are uncoordinated and frequently at odds. Although evidence can be gathered to support both arguments, we are not persuaded that either is correct. Both fail to consider carefully the tenuous powers and complex incentives possessed by the president, the Federal

8. Certainly there are those within the White House who complain about this independence. See, for example, Erwin C. Hargrove and Samuel A. Morley, eds., *The President and the Council of Economic Advisers: Interviews with CEA Chairmen* (Westview Press, 1984).

9. James M. Buchanan and Richard E. Wagner make the theoretical case for excessive congressional spending in *Democracy in Deficit: The Political Legacy of Lord Keynes* (Academic Press, 1977); see also Dennis S. Ippolito, *Congressional Spending: A Twentieth Century Fund Report* (Cornell University Press, 1981). The contractionary bias of the Federal Reserve is a common theme of muckrakers: see Maxwell Newton, *The Fed: Inside the Federal Reserve, the Secret Power Center that Controls the American Economy* (Times Books, 1983); and William Greider, *Secrets of the Temple: How the Federal Reserve Runs the Country* (Simon & Schuster, 1987). More balanced versions of the deflationary argument can be found Douglas A. Hibbs, Jr., "Inflation, Political Support, and Macroeconomic Policy," in Leon N. Lindberg and Charles S. Maier, eds., *The Politics of Inflation and Economic Stagnation: Theoretical Approaches and International Case Studies* (Brookings, 1985), pp. 175–95; and John T. Woolley, *Monetary Politics: The Federal Reserve and the Politics of Monetary Policy* (Cambridge University Press, 1984), especially pp. 69–87.

Reserve, and Congress, as well as the institutional relationships that, like the powerful forces within an atom, both bind them together and drive them apart.

In this essay we will try to show that these critics have neither presented convincing evidence that presidents systematically place their own political interests ahead of those of the country nor have shown that presidents are unable to coordinate macroeconomic policy. Although policymaking is frequently imperfect, the failures have mainly been due to faulty economic judgment, not politically inspired manipulation. Fiscal policy is another matter, but that has more to do with long-range considerations than short-term management of the economy. The difficulty with fiscal policy is not so much that presidents are unable to shape the overall tax and expenditure policies as that they no longer have the incentive to do so in a fiscally responsible way. As events have shown, fiscal policy is relatively unimportant for the stabilization of the economy over the short run. The political benefits of fiscal deficits to strong presidents with ambitious agendas now outweigh any short-term economic costs. Given this new political reality, and the fact that large fiscal deficits are damaging in the long run, a constitutionally mandated balanced budget merits consideration.

PRESIDENTIAL INCENTIVES

Theories about presidential incentives differ. Some analysts place primary emphasis on presidential strategies designed to appeal to the electorate as a whole, while others stress attempts to favor partisan bases of support. Both sets of theories give little credence to the idea that a president seeks to serve the public interest and govern effectively. Instead they portray a president primarily motivated by more narrow considerations.

Electoral Motivation

The theory of the political business cycle assumes that presidents have the incentive and ability to create a stop-and-go economy. It is based upon the idea that in the short run fiscal and monetary policy can produce rising growth, falling unemployment, and stable prices. Because voters react favorably to such conditions, presidents will pursue such policies immediately before elections. These booms are unsustainable, however. As an economy moves toward full employment, consumer demand cannot be accommodated by existing productive capacities. Inflation spirals higher as businesses bring into production less efficient facilities and agree to high wage settlements induced by shortages in the labor supply. To bring inflation under control, the government finds it necessary to slow down growth rates, causing unemployment to rise.

A political business cycle is possible because this trade-off between inflation and unemployment takes time. In general, the benefits of faster growth and lower unemployment come before the costs of rising inflation: on the way up, the good news arrives before the bad. The return trip is less pleasant. During the attempt to cut inflation, growth falters and unemployment rises before price increases are slowed very much. Thus a grateful electorate rewards a president (or his heir apparent) for preelection growth, suffers afterward (without recourse), and then enjoys renewed economic growth during the next campaign.[10]

The political business cycle theory has a certain surface plausibility. Federal Reserve Board members regularly report that they enter election years with trepidation, anticipating that they will be subjected to political pressure or accused of undue partisanship. And only once in the postwar period has the economy experienced a recession during a presidential election year. In the years since 1947 when the president himself has been running for reelection (1948, 1956, 1964, 1972, 1976, 1980, and 1984), economic growth has averaged 4.0 percent (compared with a nonelection year average of only 3.1 percent).[11]

But in spite of the superficial evidence in support of the theory, more careful analyses lead most scholars to reject it. For example, one rather complete test of the theory found no significant relationships in the postwar period between a presidential election year and unemployment rates, economic growth rates, growth in per-

---

10. As Barry puts it, this model of politics pictures "a collection of rogues competing for the favors of a larger collection of dupes." Brian Barry, "Does Democracy Cause Inflation? Political Ideas of Some Economists," in Lindberg and Maier, eds., *Politics of Inflation and Economic Stagnation*, pp. 280–317.

11. Data from *Economic Report of the President, February 1988*, table B.2.

sonal disposable income, money supply growth rates, or the rate of deficit spending. Nor does the hypothesis work any better if all election years are included in the analysis, or if the last two years of a presidential term are treated as the politically inspired period.[12]

Case studies of politically motivated economic recoveries are no more convincing than the statistical analysis. Eisenhower resisted political pressures to heat up the economy in 1960; and if the Johnsonian boom in 1964 was accelerated by an election-year tax cut, the cut itself had been proposed by John Kennedy in 1962. Neither Gerald Ford nor Jimmy Carter enjoyed an economic boom during their unsuccessful reelection campaigns, and economic trends in the 1980s seem to have been shaped more by Paul Volcker and his colleagues at the Federal Reserve than by any influence, overt or covert, exercised by Ronald Reagan.

The one president who seems to have carefully planned his economic program with the reelection year in mind was Richard Nixon.[13] Against the wishes of his economic advisers (but with the backing of politically astute Treasury Secretary John Connolly), Nixon imposed a wage and price freeze in 1971 to slow inflationary pressures. Once inflation had been frozen, Federal Reserve Chairman Arthur Burns, a staunch supporter of the Nixon administration, reduced interest rates, opening the way for a strong expansion in 1972. But if 1972 seems to be a classic example of the political business cycle, even the decisions of the Federal Reserve in that politically charged year have been defended as sound economic judgments, given the facts known at the time.[14]

The main reason the political business cycle has been difficult to identify empirically is that the theory on which it is based too narrowly construes presidential motivations. That presidents seek electoral success, and that economic conditions can affect success, are hardly contestable propositions. It is difficult to imagine how a modern president could reach the White House without more than the usual share of political ambition.[15] And a president's chances

12. Douglas A. Hibbs, Jr., *The American Political Economy: Macroeconomics and Electoral Politics* (Harvard University Press, 1987), pp. 260–61.

13. Edward R. Tufte, *Political Control of the Economy* (Princeton University Press, 1978), pp. 45–54.

14. Woolley, *Monetary Politics*, pp. 161–78.

15. Stephen Hess, " 'Why Great Men are Not Chosen Presidents': Lord Bryce Revisited," in A. James Reichley, ed., *Elections American Style* (Brookings, 1987), pp. 75–94.

for reelection are greatly enhanced if the economy is performing well in an election year. Even in midterm congressional elections, when the party of the president usually loses seats in both the House and the Senate, the losses are reduced if the economy is doing well. More generally, presidential popularity, as measured by public opinion polls, is significantly influenced by economic factors. Indeed, apart from the short-term effects of major foreign policy events, no single factor is nearly so powerful a determinant of presidential popularity as the overall economic health of the country.[16]

Prosperity has other effects on a president's capacity to govern. If his reelection chances are good and if his party gains seats in Congress, he can more easily persuade other policymakers to follow his lead. Economic prosperity provides greater material resources upon which to draw, reduces conflict among advisers and cabinet members, enhances his ability to convince congressional leaders of the merit of his programs, and strengthens his position in negotiations with foreign countries.

It appears from this that the president has ample incentive to attempt to boost the economy during election years. But this hardly means that he is willing to sacrifice prosperity in his first, second, or third year in office in order to be in a position to push the economy at full steam in the fourth year. Presidents know they must remain popular enough to accomplish their policy objectives. And sustaining presidential popularity, never easy, is especially hard for a president caught in an economic recession.[17] Given the close relationship between economic performance and presidential popularity, what president would willingly drive both down at any time during his term of office?[18]

16. See Alt and Chrystal, *Political Economics*; M. Stephen Weatherford, "Economic Determinants of Voting," in Samuel Long, ed., *Research in Micropolitics*, vol. 1: *Voting Behavior* (Greenwich, Conn.: JAI Press, 1986), pp. 219–69; and Kristen R. Monroe, *Presidential Popularity and the Economy* (Praeger, 1984).

17. Samuel Kernell, *Going Public: New Strategies of Presidential Leadership* (Washington, D.C.: CQ Press, 1986), pp. 201–03.

18. Insider accounts of the Reagan administration are especially revealing on this point. A number of high-ranking White House officials cared almost exclusively about Reagan's popularity and were unwilling to do anything to damage it. Stockman himself, who did have explicit policy goals, knew that they had to be pushed through very quickly after Reagan came into office, before the deteriorating economy made such attempts futile. David A. Stockman, *The Triumph of Politics: How the Reagan Revolution Failed* (Harper and Row, 1986).

The first year sets the tone for most presidential administrations, and few presidents are eager to place their political strength in jeopardy by plunging the nation into a recession as a manipulative move to allow preelection reflation. Since the midterm election, whose outcome affects the success of a presidency, is also influenced by economic factors, it, too, has to be taken into account in any political calculations made in the second year. A recession in the third year of a presidency is exceptionally dangerous, because that is the time that opposition candidates are assembling resources for the contest ahead. Also, if a third-year recession is mistimed, and slips into the fourth year, it could well mean political disaster. Since no president can take that chance, steady growth over the entire four-year period seems politically preferable to a manipulative approach.

Partisan Motivation

A less sinister, but still economically unsettling, model of presidential manipulation of the economy follows a partisan interpretation. In this model presidents choose policies that favor the dominant economic group within their party. Since the Democratic party has a primarily working-class constituency, which is vulnerable to unemployment, the Democrats are allegedly willing to sacrifice price stability for faster growth and more jobs. Republicans, who are more representative of the middle and upper classes, are seen as more concerned about stopping inflation, even if this requires slower growth and occasional recessions.

There is some evidence that Republican administrations on average produce less growth and higher unemployment rates than do Democratic ones.[19] However, these differences are not extreme and are "probably of trivial magnitude when measured against the public's threshold for learning about political issues."[20] Systematic

19. In the seventeen years since 1947 that a Democrat has been president, the average unemployment rate was 5.1 percent and GNP growth rate averaged 4.4 percent. During the twenty-three years a Republican was president (excluding 1988), unemployment averaged 6.1 percent and GNP growth averaged 2.4 percent. Calculated from data in *Economic Report of the President, February 1988*, pp. 255, 292. For a sophisticated analysis reaching a similar conclusion, see Hibbs, *American Political Economy*, pp. 224–32.

20. M. Stephen Weatherford, "Comparative Research on Presidential Leadership in Economic Policymaking" (National Science Foundation proposal, 1985),

partisan differences between administrations are dominated by the idiosyncracies of particular presidential terms.[21] Again, the weakness of the empirical results is related to the weakness of the theory's two main assumptions: that the differences on economic issues of the parties' core constituencies are politically important and that it is possible to implement sustainable policies that benefit these constituencies.

The constituencies of the two political parties do have different preferences as to the appropriate trade-off between inflation and unemployment. Compared with business and professional people, blue-collar workers are 5 to 18 percent less likely to be more concerned about inflation than unemployment, and the lowest-income people are 7 to 15 percent less likely to be more concerned about inflation than unemployment than is the highest-income group.[22] But these differences between social groups at any one time are dwarfed by the consensus of opinion among all groups over time. During the 1975 recession, majorities of all groups saw unemployment as a bigger problem than inflation. And as inflation climbed from 7.0 percent in 1975 to 12.4 percent in 1980, the concern about inflation among both the highest and lowest social classes climbed by about 20 percent.[23] Consequently, presidents of both parties place their popularity at risk if they either allow inflation to rise too much or tolerate long bouts of high unemployment. While Republicans are a shade more tolerant of unemployment and Democrats a touch easier on inflation, no president can safely choose one and ignore the other.

Furthermore, it is not at all clear that a president can select the trade-off between inflation and unemployment that favors his coalition and sustain it through his term in office. Although unex-

app. 1, p. 4; see also Paul Mosley, *The Making of Economic Policy: Theory and Empirical Evidence from Britain and the United States Since 1945* (St. Martin's, 1984).

21. Nathaniel Beck, "Parties, Administrations, and American Macroeconomic Outcomes," *American Political Science Review*, vol. 76 (March 1982), pp. 83–94; Beck, "Presidential Influence on the Federal Reserve in the 1970s," *American Journal of Political Science*, vol. 26 (August 1982), pp. 415–45; and Beck, "Domestic Political Sources of American Monetary Policy, 1955–1982," *Journal of Politics*, vol. 46 (August 1984), pp. 786–817.

22. Hibbs, *American Political Economy*, pp. 138–39. Also see Hibbs, "Political Parties and Macroeconomic Policy," *American Political Science Review*, vol. 71 (December 1977), pp. 1467–87.

23. Hibbs, *American Political Economy*, pp. 140–41; and *Economic Report of the President, February 1988*, p. 317.

pected inflation can lower unemployment and increase growth for short periods of time, once a certain level of inflation is anticipated, still higher levels of inflation are necessary to further reduce unemployment rates.[24] Were a Democratic president to use macroeconomic policies to lower the unemployment rate below its natural level, he would commit himself to a continuing inflationary spiral. On the other hand, attempts to eliminate inflation can ripple through the economy, provoking continually higher unemployment—and ultimately financial crisis—unless the government steps in to prevent this through reflation.[25] Were a Republican president to attempt to eliminate inflation, he would risk the Hooverian nightmare.

In sum, the president has little incentive to manipulate the economy for either electoral or partisan reasons. Deliberate attempts to move the economy away from steady, stable growth may occur for political reasons under some limited circumstances, but such attempts are unlikely to account for the weakening of the U.S. economy over the past two decades. On the whole, presidential policies (whether Democratic or Republican) are likely to be based upon the president's interest in a steady expansion of the economy that keeps unemployment rates at a minimum yet does not encourage inflation. A steady balance among objectives sustained over a prolonged period of time is more likely to help a president achieve his diverse objectives than any more manipulative approach to economic growth.

PRESIDENTIAL CONTROL

If deviations from stable growth are not due to a president's political interests, perhaps they occur because he cannot control the institutions that actually make macroeconomic policy. After all, the Federal Reserve has the responsibility for monetary policy and Congress the authoritative control of fiscal policy. The institutional

24. See, for example, Robert J. Gordon, *Macroeconomics*, 3d ed. (Little, Brown, 1984), p. 241.

25. For discussions of deflation, financial crises, and the importance of the government as lender of last resort, see Charles P. Kindleberger and Jean-Pierre Laffargue, eds., *Financial Crises: Theory, History, and Policy* (Cambridge University Press, 1982), especially the chapter by Hyman P. Minsky, "The Financial-Instability Hypothesis: Capitalist Processes and the Behavior of the Economy," pp. 13–39.

problem may arise not so much from the incentives of the White House as from the incentives of the equally powerful institutions that the president cannot control.

The Federal Reserve and Monetary Policy

The Federal Reserve, familiarly known as the "Fed," establishes the nation's monetary policy. It does this by controlling bank reserve requirements, setting the discount rate, and buying and selling government securities, the latter tool being the one most frequently used. Control over this activity is exercised not by the Federal Reserve itself, but by the twelve-member Federal Open Market Committee (FOMC).[26]

The Federal Open Market Committee

The title of this group is misleading in nearly every respect. It is not a "federal" mixture of national and state authority but is instead a blend of publicly appointed and privately elected officials. Although the Fed chairman also serves as chairman of the FOMC, and the other Fed governors are also members, the FOMC includes the presidents of the twelve regional Federal Reserve Banks as well. Five of them vote on a rotating basis.[27] The Reserve Bank presidents are neither appointed by the president nor confirmed by Congress. Instead, they are chosen by each bank's board of directors; a majority of these directors are elected by the member banks within that Reserve Bank's jurisdiction. Although the bank presidents' nomination must be approved by the Federal Reserve Board (whose members are appointed by the president), their experience and selection are rooted in the commercial banking community of which they are a part.

Neither are the meetings of the group "open." The FOMC meets every four to six weeks, but the group's decisions are announced thirty days after they have been taken (and, presumably, after their effect has been felt and new actions have been taken at

---

26. G. L. Bach, *Making Monetary and Fiscal Policy* (Brookings, 1971), pp. 34–35.

27. The president of the Reserve Bank in New York is always one of the five; the other seven bank presidents are ex officio members. The members of the Reserve Board provide the other seven voting members of the FOMC.

the next meeting).[28] The meetings themselves are held behind closed doors—a rarity among official decisionmaking bodies exercising national governmental authority.

It is almost as misleading to include "market" in its title. The FOMC does not operate as just another actor in a free market. By buying and selling government securities, it directly manipulates the supply of money and credit, which in turn has a powerful impact on the level of inflation and unemployment. Although the FOMC does not by any means have complete control over the money and credit markets, it is a powerful force in determining the performance of the economy. If the FOMC believes inflationary pressures are too strong or the dollar needs strengthening in the exchange markets, it sells securities, which pushes up interest rates. If it is concerned that economic growth is sluggish, unemployment rates are too high, or the dollar is overvalued in world markets, it buys securities, which pumps more money into the economy to bring growth back and unemployment down.

Nor is the FOMC a celebrated instance of John Stuart Mills's marketplace of ideas. Although there are outposts of economic dissent within the Federal Reserve System, the FOMC itself represents a narrow spectrum of opinion about appropriate policy.[29] When Nancy Teeter was appointed a board member in 1978, she wondered aloud how her economic liberalism would be accepted. Chairman Arthur Burns assured her, "Don't worry, Nancy. Within six months you will think just like a central banker."[30] One scholar's research shows that FOMC votes were either unanimous or resulted in only one dissent 86 percent of the time; as he puts it, "There is a strong tendency for policy debate . . . to be restricted to narrow technical issues."[31] A great premium is placed on unity and support for the chairman, and public disputes among members of the FOMC are almost unheard of.

Finally, the FOMC is not a "committee" if one means "a group

28. Woolley, *Monetary Politics*, pp. 3, 195.

29. For example, the St. Louis Reserve Bank is closely associated with monetarist theory, while the Minneapolis Fed is more supportive of "rational expectations" ideas. Greider, *Secrets of the Temple*, p. 97.

30. Ibid., p. 74.

31. Woolley, *Monetary Politics*, pp. 61, 88. Woolley's analysis covers the years 1965–81.

of equals." The chairman, with rare exception, greatly influences
FOMC decisionmaking. He is the Federal Reserve spokesman before the president, the Treasury, Congress, and the news media.
He has the most direct access to information gathered and interpreted by the professional staff. And the office has gained luster
from those who have held the position. Under its most prominent
leaders (such as Marriner S. Eccles, William McChesney Martin,
Jr., Arthur F. Burns, and Paul Volcker) the chairman's view was
seldom contradicted by the FOMC.[32] As in a parliamentary government, the chairman virtually never loses a policy vote. When he
does, as Volcker once did in 1986, "he talked about resigning immediately. He was the chairman, the man responsible for policy,
and the institution could not function otherwise."[33]

The Fed and the Financial Community

Because of the FOMC's secretive consensual decisionmaking
style, its independence from presidential authority, and its responsibility for maintaining the stability of the banking system, the
Federal Reserve is thought to be strongly influenced by the financial industry, to which it is closely tied historically, socially, and
professionally.[34] The banking community lobbies the White House
vigorously on all board appointments, and when the chair becomes vacant, the discussion can become quite intense. Newspapers speculate about the "soundness" and "acceptability" of various candidates, fluctuations in the bond and stock markets are
interpreted as signs of Wall Street nervousness over the impending
appointment, and presidents have never challenged Wall Street by
choosing a chair unacceptable to bankers. Carter selected Paul
Volcker, who had strong support from the financial community,
even though it was rumored that Volcker would not flinch from a
recession in an election year if he thought it necessary.[35] Reagan
reappointed Volcker even though he risked the same fate Carter
had suffered. In 1987 Reagan appointed Alan Greenspan, a cautious pragmatist well regarded by Wall Street professionals, in-

32. Michael D. Reagan, "The Political Structure of the Federal Reserve System,"
American Political Science Review, vol. 55 (March 1961), pp. 64–76; and Donald F. Kettl,
Leadership at the Fed (Yale University Press, 1986).

33. Greider, *Secrets of the Temple*, p. 700.

34. Richard H. Timberlake, *The Origins of Central Banking in the United States*
(Harvard University Press, 1978).

35. Greider, *Secrets of the Temple*, pp. 11–47.

stead of one of the administration's fervent monetarist or supply-side supporters.

Some have mistakenly jumped from the observation that the financial community influences the selection of Fed governors to the conclusion that the Fed pursues tight money policies to fulfill the financial community's desire for a high rate of return on investments.[36] According to those holding this view, the Fed protects asset holders—financial institutions and the wealthy—by keeping inflation (which erodes wealth) down and interest rates (which increase it) high.

The major defect in this argument is the assumption that lending institutions prefer high interest rates. Banks and other financiers are in fact generally indifferent to interest rate levels as long as they are stable. Profits depend on business volume and the size of the differential between the amount banks pay depositors and the amount they charge borrowers. The size of this differential is due in part to the fact that banks typically receive short-term deposits, which usually have a lower yield than the longer-term loans they make. As long as interest rates—and this differential—are relatively stable, banks can operate at low risk. In times of economic boom their volume increases, but the boom often causes short-term rates to rise, reducing the differential on outstanding loans. During recessions short-term rates fall, increasing the size of the differential on outstanding loans, but reducing the volume of new business. All in all, bankers "care relatively little about the ease or tightness of monetary policy so long as they are not caught by surprise by sudden shifts in policy."[37] The very phrase—"leaning against the wind"—that William Martin popularized during his fourteen-year stint as Fed chairman reflects the Fed's identification with the financial community's interest in stability and predictability.[38] If the

36. This is the standard populist critique. See Newton, *The Fed*.

37. Woolley, *Monetary Politics*, p. 72. See Edward J. Kane, "The Three Faces of Commercial Bank Liability Management," in Michael P. Dooley, Herbert M. Kaufman, and Raymond E. Lombra, eds., *The Political Economy of Policy Making* (Sage, 1979), pp. 149–74.

38. William Poole, "Benefits and Costs of Stable Monetary Growth," in Allan H. Meltzer and Karl Brunner, eds., *Institutional Arrangement and the Inflation Problem*, Carnegie Rochester Conference Series on Public Policy, vol. 3 (Amsterdam: North Holland, 1976), pp. 15–50. During the financially uncertain period of the early 1980s, Irving Kristol concluded that "anyone who actually spends time talking to living members of this financial community quickly finds out that fear of inflation is minimal as compared with fear of tighter money resulting from monetarist

economy begins to grow vigorously, slow it down. If signs of recession begin to emerge, speed the economy along. It is better to miss an exceptional opportunity than to incur an avoidable risk.

During the 1970s the Fed pursued a set of policies that were all too attached to the financial community's commitment to stable rates of interest. Although interest rates gradually rose in tandem with increases in the cost of living, they never seemed to climb quite fast enough to slow inflationary pressures. Long committed to a practice of making interest rate adjustments slowly and cautiously, taking into account the bankers' need for interest rate stability, the Fed never seemed able to catch up with inflation and bring it under control.

Banks run the greatest risk when interest rates fluctuate the most rapidly, as they did in 1979–80, the first year that Paul Volcker served as Fed chairman. Volcker convinced the board that inflation had been rising steadily because the Federal Reserve had been unwilling to let interest rates rise rapidly enough to choke off expansionary pressures. FOMC attention shifted away from interest rates to monetary aggregates. By urging that the Fed keep money growth stable, the chairman was able to put in place a policy that permitted rapid changes in interest rates, a policy quite out of keeping with Fed traditions.

Within months, short-term interest rates doubled from 10 to 20 percent, leaving banks and savings and loans that had made single-digit long-term loans greatly exposed. Just as suddenly, short-term rates fell back to their 10 percent level. Growth in the money supply had slowed unexpectedly, and the Fed feared a recession was at hand. But just as the banks had begun to sigh with relief, the money supply began to grow rapidly again, and the Fed, concerned about renewed inflation, allowed interest rates to shoot up toward 20 percent. This time interest rates remained very high, and the recession of 1981–83 began in earnest, ending only after the Fed abandoned its experiment with monetarism in the fall of 1982. In the meantime banks and other lending institutions suffered severe losses, a number went bankrupt, and the stability of the entire financial system was threatened. In subsequent years interest rates were adjusted slowly, and the Fed reassumed its emphasis on

---

policies." Kristol, "The Focus in on the Fed," *Wall Street Journal*, February 12, 1982, p. 28.

stability and predictability rather than the rapid growth that Reagan's supply-side advisers recommended.

The President and the Fed

If the Fed shares the cautious outlook of the financial community, that does not necessarily mean it is beyond White House control. The relationship between the president and the board seems so mutually satisfactory that some observers have concluded the president exercises de facto control over the de jure independent board. While we believe this overlooks the subtlety of the relationship between the Fed and the White House, it must be recognized that no Fed chairman, no matter how independent-minded, can safely ignore the vigorously expressed wishes of a strong president.

The president's formal powers are considerable. Although the Fed is an independent agency beyond the direct authority of the White House, the president appoints the members of the board and can designate which one shall hold the office of chairman. Moreover, a president's influence can be felt as much by board anticipation of what he wants as by any direct selection of board members. For one thing, the Fed fears overt politicization of its decisionmaking process.[39] It dislikes being the object of White House criticism or the butt of congressional investigation. The Fed knows that its statutory powers, with all the independence and autonomy they confer, can be altered at any time by new legislation. If a strong president, backed by loyal supporters on the Hill, wished to restructure the board, the Fed could not prevent him from doing so.

Nor does the chairman of the Fed often have to guess at what the administration wishes. Professional and social contacts frequently occur between the executive branch and the Fed. For example, the chairman has lunch at the Treasury every week, and there are frequent exchanges between the Fed's senior staff and the Office of Management and Budget (OMB) as well as the president's Council of Economic Advisers.[40] At times these meetings

39. A. Jerome Clifford, *The Independence of the Federal Reserve System* (University of Pennsylvania Press, 1965).

40. Thomas Havrilesky, "Monetary Policy Signaling from the Administration to the Federal Reserve," *Journal of Money, Credit, and Banking,* vol. 20 (February 1988), pp. 83–101; and Woolley, *Monetary Politics,* pp. 112–14. Havrilesky argues that the Fed

have been organized into a quasi-formal working group; other times the exchanges are conducted with less formality. But in either case both sides have plentiful opportunities to make their views known about the state of the economy and preferred monetary policies.[41] It is not easy to ascertain the direction of influence at such meetings, but Fed policy is usually quite consistent with administration policy and presidential disagreements with the Fed are usually marginal or short-lived. Eisenhower and Eccles had a close working relationship, Volcker was invited by Carter to participate in the administration's economic strategy sessions, and Reagan's Treasury Secretary, James Baker, worked closely with Volcker in formulating the U.S. bargaining position vis-à-vis its trading partners. Volcker did not want to restrict credit card purchases in 1980, but when Jimmy Carter insisted, he reluctantly agreed. As one careful observer has noted, "Much of the history of monetary policy can be explained just by noting who the President was when the policy under review was in effect."[42] Only a small handful of cases can be produced showing serious conflict between the president and the Fed.[43]

Political Autonomy

Fed responsiveness to political realities cannot be denied, but neither should it be exaggerated. Presidents may seldom be denied their strongly worded demands, but the Fed has political resources to resist claims it regards as egregious. The president appoints

---

is responding to signals from the administration, but his analysis is unable to disprove the equally plausible hypothesis that the White House asks the Fed to do what it knows (or expects) the Fed has already done.

41. Sometimes these meetings indicate the confusion existing within an administration regarding both conditions and cures. Greider describes a fascinating set of meetings between Volcker and various Reagan officials, each of whom presented Volcker with an almost entirely different reading about what was happening in the economy and what should be done about it. Greider, *Secrets of the Temple*, p. 477.

42. Robert E. Weintraub, "Congressional Supervision of Monetary Policy," *Journal of Monetary Economics*, vol. 4 (April 1978), p. 356. See also Woolley, *Monetary Politics*, pp. 108-30; Beck, "Presidential Influence on the Federal Reserve in the 1970s"; Beck, "Domestic Political Sources of American Monetary Policy"; Robert D. Auerback, "Politics and the Federal Reserve," *Contemporary Policy Issues*, vol. 3 (Fall 1985), pp. 43-58; and Milton Friedman, "Monetary Policy: Theory and Practice," *Journal of Money, Credit, and Banking*, vol. 14 (February 1982), pp. 98-118.

43. John T. Woolley, "Central Banks and Inflation: Influence and Independence," in Lindberg and Maier, eds., *The Politics of Inflation and Economic Stagnation*, pp. 318-48.

members of the board, but they do not serve at his pleasure. The chairman is not a member of the president's cabinet. The president cannot fire board members and their terms are far longer than his. He does not control their budget. He cannot veto their policies. Federal Reserve chairmen have made it very clear in their public statements that they do not consider themselves subordinate to the president and that they are willing to defend their autonomy.[44] In addition the Fed enjoys a staff whose technical expertise and cohesiveness is the envy of Washington.

The degree to which the Fed's staff is professionalized, aloof from Washington politics, removed from congressional oversight, and free of political appointments is, in fact, one of the agency's most distinctive characteristics. Most federal agencies are subject to ever-changing political currents and regulatory suggestions. Their budgets, proposals, and policies are reviewed by political appointees at the departmental level and then ruthlessly examined once again by an increasingly politicized OMB as well as a White House staff consisting of the president's key political lieutenants.[45] The agencies must also constantly adapt policies to congressional priorities, further frustrating agency capacity to develop consistent, long-term policies. Practices must be defended before House and Senate subcommittees that originate authorizing legislation and appropriate agency expenditures. Since still other congressional committees have a legitimate interest in agency operations, they subject civil servants to continuing scrutiny.

By comparison with most agencies, then, the Fed operates with extraordinary autonomy. Although it is an agency of the federal government, its procedures, staff salary schedules, and terms of appointment need not conform to the requirements of the Office of Personnel Management.[46] The Fed's budget is neither reviewed by the OMB nor approved by Congress. Instead the board keeps a

---

44. Kettl, *Leadership at the Fed*. This occurred in early 1988 when Chairman Alan Greenspan warned the Reagan administration that it should stop pressuring the Fed to lower interest rates or the Fed might tighten credit and raise rates, even if economic conditions did not warrant these policies, just to show its political independence. John M. Berry, "Greenspan Tells Administration to Stop Pressure," *Washington Post*, February 25, 1988, p. B1.

45. Terry M. Moe, "The Politicized Presidency," in Chubb and Peterson, eds., *New Direction in American Politics*, pp. 235–71.

46. The Federal Reserve has recently moved to have staff salaries set at rates prevailing in the private sector. Paul Blustein, "Pay at the Fed to Follow the Market," *Washington Post*, May 26, 1988, p. A19.

self-determined share (a small fraction of its income) of the interest it receives on the government securities it owns, returning to the Treasury the portion not required to pay its expenses.

Were the Fed subjected to the usual administrative politics of most executive agencies, it might have more difficulty in recruiting and retaining a talented staff. As it stands, the Fed's staff is unusually able and well educated. About half the top staff have a Ph.D. in economics from one of the top ten or eleven departments in the country. It has strengths "greatly exceeding the density of coverage of major topics that is possible even in the economics department of leading universities."[47] The Federal Reserve staff remains academically productive; over 8 percent of the articles published by a leading journal for monetary economics are contributions from Fed staff.[48] That the Fed can compete on even terms with academic appointments is evidence of its prestige. Few executive branch agencies can make a comparable claim.

These resources enable the Fed to act with an unusual independence. Even though it has frequent contact with the White House, the Fed can dominate the policy discussions through its expertise. When administration officials negotiate with the Fed, they must speak the language of money aggregates, discount rates, and bank reserves that the Fed understands so well and most politicians grasp only hazily. Whenever a president proposes a course of action with which a Fed chairman disagrees, the latter can give a sophisticated, technical answer that explains why the result will be exactly the opposite of what the president intends.

Cooperation

Some have seen the relationship between the president and the Federal Reserve as another case of symbolic politics, in which the key players in the drama play well-rehearsed roles.[49] They say that

47. Henry Wallach, quoted in Woolley, *Monetary Politics*, p. 98.

48. Woolley, *Monetary Politics*, pp. 60–61. The Federal Reserve has so many Ph.D.s on its staff that honorifics are not used: Chairman Alan Greenspan has said "We don't 'doctor' anybody." "The Fed Prescribes an Ounce of Prevention," *Business Week*, May 23, 1988, p. 54.

49. Murray Edelman develops this idea in *The Symbolic Uses of Politics* (University of Illinois Press, 1964). Kane sees the relationship between the president and the Federal Reserve basically in these terms. See Edward J. Kane, "External Pressure and the Operation of the Fed," in Raymond E. Lombra and Willard E. Witte, eds., *Political Economy of International and Domestic Monetary Relations* (Iowa State Univer-

the Fed values the appearance of autonomy because it brings prestige and other bureaucratic perquisites. But in order to maintain the illusion of autonomy, they argue, it must in fact do what the president wants. If the Fed does not follow the president, he has the political resources to bring it under control. Meanwhile, the president can direct the Fed to pursue policies he wants, but he also wants this to be little known to outsiders so that he can blame someone for unpopular economic policies. Critics point out that a nominally independent central bank is the perfect scapegoat. Like actors, both the president and the Fed are able to fool the public while at the same time drawing applause from it.

Without denying that theatrics is often smart politics, this convoluted theory of presidential-Fed relations is not altogether convincing. For one thing, it is difficult to fool inquisitive journalists and informed observers indefinitely. Also, the public holds the president responsible for the state of the economy, no matter how much he may try to hide behind his Federal Reserve Board. One needs to look beyond a strategy of public deception to account for Fed-presidential relations.

The institutional relationship that allows independence without conflict and consensus with minimal coordination arises because both the president and the Federal Reserve have similar goals. Both want policies that promote stable economic growth. The Federal Reserve knows that the president wants policies that will produce these conditions and that the surest way for the Fed to lose its autonomy is to do otherwise. The president needs an institutional arrangement that can assemble the best information and expertise for making policy decisions. He can obtain this from a central bank removed from direct political control, which has considerable latitude in recruiting, retaining, and rewarding a highly professional staff. In essence, the Federal Reserve produces skillfully the kind of policies the administration wants but is unable to provide itself. In this presidents are like Ulysses, who commanded that he be tied to the mast so he would not steer toward the Sirens.[50] A president may face temptations to direct the economy that are against its

---

sity Press, 1982), pp. 211–32; and Kane, "Politics and Fed Policymaking: The More Things Change, the More They Remain the Same," *Journal of Monetary Economics*, vol. 6 (April 1980), pp. 199–211.

50. Jon Elster, *Ulysses and the Sirens: Studies in Rationality and Irrationality* (Cambridge University Press, 1979).

(and his) long-term interests. To keep himself from listening and following, he sensibly delegates the responsibility to the independent Federal Reserve, which can be trusted to steer between the reefs.

Arguing that the Fed chooses policies to promote stable growth does not simply reassert the traditional claim that the Fed is a wholly neutral economic agency platonically selecting the one best policy. The political fact that the president needs a healthy economy is essential for understanding the latitude given to the Fed. The Fed's task is in part a technical one, but where technique is not enough—as is inevitably the case in the complex world of macroeconomic policymaking—the board is asked to reach a judgment. In general its judgment will differ only marginally from that of White House staff and the banking community and the broad policymaking consensus that shapes macroeconomic policymaking.[51] Of course, consensus does not imply unanimity; occasionally there is high-pitched public debate about the correct monetary policy. But in most cases this debate is over rather narrow differences in opinion rather than wide gaps in understanding.

Congress and the Federal Reserve

In contrast with the Federal Reserve's complex, subtle relationship with the White House, its contacts with Capitol Hill are more symbolic than substantive. The Federal Reserve is, of course, a creature of Congress, the product of a statute originally passed in 1914, and thus technically subject to congressional control. Congress likes to remind the Fed of this fact: one congressman asked Chairman William McChesney Martin to tape a slip of paper reading "the Federal Reserve is an agency of Congress" to his mirror where he could see it while shaving each morning.[52] The Senate approves nominations of board members, and both houses regularly have the Fed chairman testify before them. Congress can at any time pass new legislation changing the Fed's terms of reference, and in virtually all sessions of Congress legislation is introduced that would have exactly that effect. In 1971 Congress gave the president the authority to regulate interest rates whenever he

51. Alberta M. Sbragia, "Monetary Policy and Monetary Theory: The Poverty of Choice," in James P. Pfiffner, ed., *The President and Economic Policy* (Philadelphia: Institute for the Study of Human Issues, 1986), p. 230.

52. Clifford, *Independence of the Federal Reserve System*, p. 330.

instituted wage and price controls. In 1975 it required the chairman to report quarterly to Congress on current Federal Reserve policy. In 1977 it required Senate confirmation of presidential nominations for the board's chair and vice-chair.[53]

But if Congress potentially has the authority to restructure the Fed, only minor changes in its operating procedures have had any realistic chance of congressional passage. The Fed has the prestige that comes with the responsibility of managing the national economy. Its pronouncements draw upon an arcane language mysterious to many members of Congress, and it enjoys the support of the thousands of its member banks located in every congressional district in the country. Any major alteration in the workings of the Fed would require vigorous presidential support. Lacking that, most efforts to limit the authority of the Fed or reorganize its operating procedures fail to negotiate the complex congressional maze.

The Federal Reserve also escapes most normal congressional oversight. Congress does not appropriate an annual budget for the Fed; instead, the Fed returns its profits to the Treasury. Nor does Congress authorize new programmatic authority for the Fed every four or five years; the statutory provisions under which it operates are indefinite. Congress's evaluative arm, the General Accounting Office, has only limited authority over Fed operations. It can audit the Fed's administrative practices but not its monetary policies. And when Congress passed the Freedom of Information Act requiring all government agencies to make public transcripts of formal meetings, Fed Chairman Arthur Burns simply decided to stop recording complete minutes of FOMC meetings to protect its debates from public scrutiny.[54]

Congress's original intention in requiring Fed chairmen to testify before the Joint Economic Committee was to obtain specific information on the Fed's monetary policy objectives. By requiring that the hearings be held quarterly, Congress hoped to hold the Fed responsible for achieving the objectives it had stated in prior testimony. Fed chairmen have proved to be adept politicians, however. Statements of objectives are generally couched in broad

53. Weintraub, "Congressional Supervision of Monetary Policy"; and James L. Pierce, "The Myth of Congressional Supervision of Monetary Policy," *Journal of Monetary Economics*, vol. 4 (April 1978), pp. 363–70.

54. "No other agency of government, not even the Central Intelligence Agency, enjoyed such privacy." Greider, *Secrets of the Temple*, pp. 54–55.

terms, leaving a good deal of room to maneuver. The occasion gives members of the Joint Economic Committee an opportunity to articulate their own growth strategies and to browbeat the Fed for any presumed errors of judgment it may have made. But the committee hearings lack bite, mainly because there is nothing for Congress to do—no money to appropriate, no legislation to pass—once the hearings have been adjourned.

Sensing that he has the upper hand in these hearings, the Fed chairman typically takes this opportunity to criticize fiscal policy, for which he holds Congress responsible. The economic situation is delicate, the chairman regularly reports. It could improve, but it might worsen. The most urgent policy issue is the deficit, the chairman typically observes. Immediate action on this question will greatly relieve the pressure on the Fed. The Fed chairman seems to take this position whether deficits are large or small, whether the economy is growing or a recession is deepening, whether he is appointed by a Republican or Democratic president, and whether he is holding to a Keynesian philosophy that treats budget deficits as determinants of short-term economic trends or he professes monetarism, which treats fiscal policy as irrelevant to the management of the economy.

It is probably not surprising that in March 1988, when the economy was nearing full employment and deficits remained near their all-time high, Alan Greenspan warned of inflation and urged fiscal constraint: "There are risks in delaying or retreating, even a little, on an issue of such great importance. It is urgent that the Congress fully implement the deficit-reduction measures agreed to in December and continue to consider additional measures."[55] But his call for fiscal restraint differs hardly at all from the one enunciated by Arthur Burns in January 1975, when the country was in the depths of a recession: "I would . . . urge Congress to scrutinize federal expenditures with special care and to look for ways to hold federal spending well below the levels projected in the President's state of the union message."[56] Seven years later in the midst of another recession, Paul Volcker, who at the time was choosing

55. Statement by Alan Greenspan before the Joint Economic Committee, March 15, 1988, printed in *Federal Reserve Bulletin*, vol. 74 (May 1988), p. 303.

56. Statement by Arthur F. Burns before the House Committee on Ways and Means, January 30, 1975, printed in *Federal Reserve Bulletin*, vol. 61 (February 1975), p. 62.

policies as prescribed by monetarist doctrine, expressed much the same concern: "Paradoxical as it may seem, action by the administration and the Congress to bring spending and our revenue potential into closer balance—and ultimately into balance and surplus—as the economy expands can be a major element . . . in promoting recovery. . . . The need for disciplined financial policies to carry throughout the anti-inflation effort is not lessened by the current recession."[57]

Each of these chairmen may have strongly believed that deficits were adversely affecting the economic well-being of the country. But quite apart from his sense of the economic situation, each chairman had good political reasons for emphasizing budget deficits in his congressional testimony. If deficits were the problem, the responsibility for solving it was located not at the Federal Reserve, but on Capitol Hill. His congressional questioners may or may not have agreed with him, but only the most daring were willing to claim publicly that fiscal deficits were of no consequence. The Fed chairman thus regularly took the high ground in his congressional testimony, leaving his legislative critics without much of a political leg to stand on.

Congress and Fiscal Policy

The chairman of the Federal Reserve is not alone in blaming Congress for incurring fiscal deficits damaging to the economic health of the nation. The standard criticism of Congress is that it cannot keep its fiscal house in order. The story is that Congress loves to spend and hates to tax, so government programs continually grow, revenues do not, and deficits become ever larger. Congress is a decentralized institution that makes its decisions through committees and subcommittees that have a vested interest in the expansion of the programs that they supervise. Since members of Congress tend to join committees in which their constituents have a special interest, they become advocates, not critics, of the agencies they supervise. As each program expands in size, overall governmental expenditures steadily climb. But revenues do not keep pace with increases in expenditure growth because politicians do

57. Statement by Paul A. Volcker before the Joint Economic Committee, January 26, 1982, printed in *Federal Reserve Bulletin*, vol. 68 (February 1982), p. 90.

not wish to incur blame for tax increases. Because spending provides immediate, clear benefits, taxes impose visible costs, and deficits seem more abstract, Congress tolerates deficits.

We have three difficulties with the argument that Congress is largely responsible for the country's economic problems because of its mismanagement of fiscal policy. First, it blames Congress for lacking self-discipline, disregarding the institutional mechanisms Congress has created to control its committees. Second, it blames Congress for ignoring the president's budget, not recognizing that Congress follows the president's budget recommendations fairly closely. And, third, it blames the deficit for short-term economic problems, giving fiscal policy undue significance for the macroeconomy.

Institutional Mechanisms for Fiscal Control

Although most members of Congress concentrate considerable attention on parochial concerns of special interest to their state or district, they have, as a group, established a set of institutional constraints that limit their particularistic behavior.[58] In the 1950s the appropriations committees were the major institutional vehicle performing this function. They consisted of senior members from fairly safe districts who gained prestige by becoming subject specialists and assumed a skeptical stance toward agency requests for additional funds. Appropriations not only were kept well below the amount authorized by the more constituency-oriented substantive committees, but they also were regularly reduced below the level recommended to Congress by the executive branch. As long as the president's budgetary requests made macroeconomic sense, this congressional procedure ensured that outcomes would be just as sound.

The success of the procedure depended upon recruitment to the appropriations committees of members willing to play the budget-cutting role. This became increasingly difficult after 1958, when the northern wing of the Democratic party gained increasing ascendancy within Congress. Gradually, advocates of program expansion won positions on key appropriations subcommittees. In response to these congressional developments, the executive branch became a more vigorous advocate of fiscal constraint. And as presidential

58. See Kenneth Shepsle's "The Changing Textbook Congress" in this volume.

opposition to favorite congressional programs increased, subcommittees of the appropriations committees became even more intensely committed to programmatic objectives instead of budgetary ones.

The increasingly bitter struggle over budget recommendations, rescissions and impoundments during the Nixon years provoked a series of court suits and ultimately culminated in procedural reform initiated by Congress. Congress decided to limit both presidential authority to impound funds and congressional capacity to enact legislation without taking into account its effect on the budget. The result was a set of new institutions—the budget committees and the Congressional Budget Office (CBO)—that were given the formal responsibility to do what had been achieved informally by the old appropriations process.[59] Procedural changes were also introduced that forced both houses of Congress to make a clear determination as to what the overall level of spending would be.

Initially the budget reform was thought to be of little consequence. Early research tended to find only modest adjustments in congressional behavior.[60] Although the CBO had become a respected, independent source of information on the federal budget and its relation to the national economy, the new budget committees had not usurped the authority of the appropriations committees, and they were unable to impose their policy vision on Congress as a whole.

The enduring effect of new organizational arrangements seldom becomes immediately apparent.[61] Participants are still accustomed to old patterns, the new institutions are treated with suspicion, and misunderstandings are most likely to occur. It was thus not until the 1980s that the consequences of the budgetary reform of 1974 became fully evident. In this era of high deficits and domestic

59. Aaron Wildavsky, *Politics of the Budgetary Process*, 4th ed. (Little, Brown, 1984), pp. 222–51.

60. John W. Ellwood and James A. Thurber, "The New Congressional Budget Process Reexamined," in Lawrence C. Dodd and Bruce I. Oppenheimer, eds., *Congress Reconsidered*, 2d ed. (Washington, D.C.: Congressional Quarterly Press, 1981), p. 246; and Allen Schick, *Congress and Money: Budgeting, Spending and Taxing* (Washington, D.C.: Urban Institute, 1980).

61. Although most studies of institutional change are conducted soon after the innovations are put into place (that is when the topic is most likely to engage foundation support and the attention of scholar-entrepreneurs), the findings tend to underestimate the significance of the change.

expenditure reductions, Congress postponed decisions until just before (or after) the new fiscal year was to begin. Nearly all major policy decisions were combined into a few pieces of omnibus legislation that set tax policy, domestic expenditure levels, and defense appropriations. Since all decisions affected the deficit, none could be taken without regard to its effect on the others. In this context, power shifted from the authorizing and appropriating subcommittees to party leaders who negotiated compromises with the White House, factions within their parties, and each other. The terms of the compromise were heavily influenced by the data, analyses, and recommendations of the budget committees.[62]

Congressional Deference to Presidents

More centralized and more partisan decisionmaking did not prevent deficits from occurring, but Congress did not increase deficits above levels proposed by the president. When congressional tax changes and appropriations are compared with presidential tax proposals and budgetary requests for each administration in the postwar era, the data reveal that Congress has appropriated almost exactly the same amount as presidents have recommended, differing on average by less than $1 billion each year over the last four decades. Even during the Carter administration—when, surprisingly enough, the fiscal differences between the executive and legislative branches were the largest—congressional appropriations differed from presidential requests by less than 0.7 percent of GNP.[63]

The finding that Congress follows the president on spending totals, while shifting particular spending priorities, can be easily explained by considering the incentives legislators face. Like the president, their electoral prospects are enhanced by economic prosperity.[64] Because they face elections both frequently (at least in the House of Representatives) and indefinitely (unlike the president, they have no constitutional limits to the number of terms they can serve), they have even more reason to support macroeco-

62. Peterson and Rom, "Lower Taxes, More Spending, and Budget Deficits."

63. Peterson, "The New Politics of Deficits," pp. 365–98. See especially p. 375 (table 13-1) and p. 381 (table 13-2).

64. Gary C. Jacobson, *The Politics of Congressional Elections*, 2d ed. (Little, Brown, 1987), pp. 142–48.

nomic policies that produce stable long-term growth. The effect of the economy on congressional elections, however, is considerably less than its effect on presidential elections.[65] Congress benefits from prosperity, but the president benefits even more. Congress therefore has little reason to second-guess the president's judgments. Although in recent years Congress has significantly boosted its own technical fiscal expertise (through the Congressional Budget Office), in general its overall spending recommendations will tend to be similar to the president's for much the same reasons that the president's monetary objectives will coincide with the Federal Reserve's. On fiscal policy legislators are in the same boat as the president.

The electoral incentives of the president and Congress differ, however, in that legislators face particular—and much smaller—sets of constituents than the national electorate. For individual congressional districts, certain governmental programs can be extremely important.[66] Legislators are unlikely to want to make local sacrifices to accomplish national fiscal goals and so will strongly resist any presidential attempts to shortchange programs dear to their hearts. They do this not so much by changing the president's fiscal policy as by rearranging spending within its overall limits.

Congress also prefers to make only marginal changes in spending decisions. For example, Congress tends to pass smaller defense appropriations than Republican presidents want and to grant less in nondefense spending than Democratic presidents propose.[67] This occurs because the congressional budgeting system is (or at least was until the 1980s) built on longstanding relationships between committees, constituencies, and agencies, and it relies on previous decisions as a guide to future policy. The spending decisions of these budgetary triangles are not easily overruled by a newly elected president who claims a mandate to alter budget priorities. Admittedly, these budgetary triangles lost influence in the 1980s, as conflict became more centralized with each party

65. D. Roderick Kiewiet, *Macroeconomics and Micropolitics: The Electoral Effects of Economic Issues* (University of Chicago Press, 1983).

66. R. Douglas Arnold, "The Local Roots of Domestic Policy," in Thomas E. Mann and Norman J. Ornstein, eds., *The New Congress* (Washington, D.C.: American Enterprise Institute for Public Policy Research, 1981), pp. 250–87.

67. Peterson, "The New Politics of Deficits."

seeking to protect its favorite programs in a fiscal climate shaped by large deficits.[68] But once again the partisan fight was more over the allocation of funds than about the overall spending levels.

Fiscal Policy and Economic Stabilization

In assessing the congressional role in managing the macro-economy, one needs, finally, to consider whether fiscal policy significantly affects in the short run such factors as inflation, unemployment, and economic growth. It has been standard wisdom that fiscal policy has a large, immediate effect on these outcomes. Thus not only Fed chairmen, but many economists and policy analysts as well, have urged Congress to take steps quickly to reduce the large fiscal deficits of the 1980s. But these recommendations have lost much of their political force because there has been no obvious connection between deficits and economic stability. The political debate over the deficits, it seems to us, would have been a good deal less murky if the effect of fiscal and monetary policy on both temporary and long-term conditions had been better understood.

The debate over the effect of fiscal policy on economic performance was a major dispute between Keynesians and monetarists. Central to their dispute is a disagreement over the inherent capacity of the government to stabilize the macroeconomy. Keynesians assumed that discretionary changes in both fiscal and monetary policy could be used to counter the effects of the business cycle; monetarists argued that neither could be effectively controlled. Neither theory paid much attention to the actual characteristics of political institutions in any given country. In the United States Keynesians are correct about institutions governing monetary policy, while monetarists are correct about fiscal institutions.

To show the crucial role that assumptions about governmental effectiveness play in the Keynesian-monetarist debate, we must first contrast their general understandings of the way in which the macroeconomy works. Keynes argued that economic downturns were not necessarily self-correcting, because demand could fall so low during a depression that firms would have no incentive to increase their production, even though sources of supply were inexpensive. Falling interest rates would not stimulate new de-

---

68. Peterson and Rom, "Lower Taxes, More Spending, and Budget Deficits."

mand for credit if businesses lacked a market for the goods this credit would help finance. Only the government could reignite the economy by running deficits, which would put money into the hands of consumers to provide them additional purchasing power the economy needed.[69] In a deep recession monetary policy by itself might be impotent.

In the postwar period Keynes's ideas were expanded: if government could pull an economy out of recession with fiscal policy, why couldn't these same policies be used to push the economy into faster growth all the time? If the economy was growing too rapidly (that is, if inflation was becoming a real problem), the government could reverse the process by creating budget surpluses— taking money out of the hands of consumers through taxes, which would reduce total consumer demand. While Keynesians also gradually came to add money and credit to their analyses, fiscal policy remained the sun, while monetary policy was but a distant star.[70] In applying fiscal and monetary tools to economic problems, Keynesians also have tended to emphasize the present: if macroeconomic policies can improve conditions now, use them. For Keynesians, the right long-term policy is to pick the correct short-term measures.

Keynes's ideas were sharply criticized in the 1970s by an emerging group of economists known as monetarists, who revived a number of classical, pre-Keynesian economic principles.[71] According to monetarist theory, fiscal deficits cannot be used to stimulate the rate of economic growth. Even during the 1930s fiscal policy had little short-term effect on the course of the depression.[72] The stimulative value of the expenditure is offset by the withdrawal of an equal amount of money from private circulation borrowed to finance the deficit. Instead, deficits cause some combination of inflation, as the government covers its debts by printing money;

69. John Maynard Keynes, *The General Theory of Employment, Interest, and Money* (Harcourt, Brace and Company, 1936).

70. Leading Keynesian scholar Franco Modigliani formally introduced monetary policy into the Keynesian analysis in his 1944 article, "Liquidity Preference and the Theory of Interest and Money," *Econometrica*, vol. 12 (January 1944), pp. 45–88.

71. See Harry G. Johnson, "The Keynesian Revolution and the Monetarist Counter-Revolution," *American Economic Review*, vol. 61 (May 1971, *Papers and Proceedings, 1970*), pp. 1–14.

72. Milton Friedman and Anna J. Schwartz, *A Monetary History of the United States, 1867–1960* (Princeton University Press, 1963).

"crowding out," as government borrowing shrinks the amount of funds available for private investment; and rising exchange rates, as foreign investors take advantage of higher interest rates caused by the growth in public debt. Not only are there no stabilizing effects of deficits, but they also produce long-term damage: inflation, falling investment, and trade deficits all discourage sustainable growth.

It is monetary policy that has the most decisive effects on economic stability, monetarists continue. If the money supply grows faster than real growth rates, inflation will occur. This may temporarily stimulate the economy, but cause longer-term economic distortions. If the Federal Reserve attempts to restrain inflation by restraining monetary growth while the rest of the government is running budget deficits, it faces the unpleasant alternatives of retarding domestic investment as the government soaks up available savings and curtailing current production by making imports cheaper and exports more costly. Though monetarists do not think that "only money matters," they emphasize that "money matters more" than fiscal policy.[73] In contrast to the Keynesians, the monetarists believe that the best short-term policy is to use the correct long-term strategy: keep monetary growth stable.

The Keynesian-monetarist debate is thus mainly a dispute about the nature of political power and the capacity the government has for effective action. Monetarists are quite pessimistic. Given the option of manipulating fiscal policy, elected politicians will normally shoot for more growth, incurring even larger deficits. Given the opportunity to regulate the money supply, policymakers will generally err on the side of excessive growth, thereby encouraging inflation. This will be offset by occasional—but excessive—inflation infighting that will plunge the nation into a recession by contracting the money supply too strictly. Consequently, monetarists have recommended that macroeconomic policy be conducted by a simple rule: keep the money supply growing at a constant rate. This will also keep fiscal policy sensible, as budget deficits will no longer provide stimulus. Unfortunately, creating and sustaining a simple monetary rule is no simple matter. It implies that government can be conducted by a giant computer that analyzes the

73. In 1966 monetarist Milton Friedman accepted the notion that "fiscal policy could affect real output in the short run and the price level in the long run." Gordon, *Macroeconomics*, p. 398.

money supply and calculates the changes necessary to keep its growth constant. But how is money supply to be measured? What if the velocity with which money is circulating should change? What if the system sustains an external shock? In short, how is the computer to be programmed: The monetarist engineers may be comforted to know that Hal is in charge, but is he really as dependable as they claim?[74]

The more optimistic Keynesians believe that discretionary macroeconomic policy is not only necessary to avoid wide fluctuations in the real economy, but is also within the reach of modern governments. Unfortunately, their political theory assumes the presence of a wise and beneficent sovereign who can make fine adjustments in fiscal and monetary policies whenever necessary. The applicability of the theory is particularly suspect when it comes to the making of fiscal policy. Fiscal policy is controlled not by a wise sovereign nor by technically sophisticated economists, but is negotiated by a Congress and a president. It is true that some automatic stabilizers have (accidentally) been built into federal statutes—in times of recession, unemployment and welfare benefits rise while tax revenues fall—but these cannot be counted on to make the necessary fiscal adjustment. The remaining adjustments can be made only after prolonged political deliberation. Changes in tax policy may take two or more years to resolve. Appropriations are typically made nine or more months after the president makes his initial recommendation. Even after legislation is signed into law, it can take years before appropriations are actually expended. These policy and expenditure decisions are made, moreover, for many reasons besides their effects on the macroeconomy. Policy innovations may have been promised to politically powerful constituents. The president may propose tax cuts out of a philosophical conviction that government has grown too large, or he may propose increased defense expenditures to meet the threat of foreign ag-

---

74. "The rules-versus-discretion debate has been raging for more than fifty years now—with no end in sight." Alan S. Blinder, "The Rules-versus-Discretion Debate in the Light of Recent Experience," *Weltwirtschaftliches Archiv (Review of World Economics)*, vol. 123, no. 3 (1987), pp. 399–413. Blinder opposes the notion of monetary rules. The most consistent advocate of a simple, unchanging monetary rule continues to be Milton Friedman. See his "The Case for Overhauling the Federal Reserve," *Challenge*, vol. 28 (July–August 1985), pp. 4–12. An excellent explanation of the issues involved in creating a monetary rule can be found in Ralph C. Bryant, *Controlling Money: The Federal Reserve and Its Critics* (Brookings, 1983).

gression. The fiscal price may have to be paid even if economic circumstances are not optimum.

If the responsibility for fiscal policy is divided among too many institutions, there is more hope for monetary policy, which is decided by a relatively able and disinterested Federal Reserve. It seldom takes decisive action, to be sure. The board contains no Prince Hamlets strutting across the domestic policy stage. It looks more like J. Alfred Prufrock, whose decisions and revisions are slight adjustments on the margin that are sometimes denied even as they are being made. But the board nonetheless has many of the advantages of a sovereign. It can act quickly, silently, and, in the short run, contrary to public opinion. From 1979 to 1982 the Federal Reserve toyed with the possibility of giving up much of its royal prerogative when it decided to forgo direct management of the economy in favor of the monetarist strategy of keeping money growth steady. When the experiment failed, the Fed eagerly resumed its royal mantle.

The monetarists may have lost the war, but they nonetheless destroyed one of the Keynesians' leading offensive weapons: the use of fiscal policy as a tool for macroeconomic stabilization. The monetarists had long questioned the theoretical basis for a centrally managed fiscal policy. President Reagan put the theory to its stiffest empirical test: the government incurred its largest and most sustained peacetime fiscal deficits. Those who expected deficits of this magnitude to stimulate spectacular growth or inflation were sorely disappointed.[75] Instead, the country experienced a deep recession from 1981 to the spring of 1983, followed by one year of steep growth and then a gradual, modest, but prolonged recovery. Inflation fell from the double-digit levels of the 1970s to an average of 4 percent. Deficits were irrelevant to stabilizing the ups and downs of the business cycle as long as they were offset by monetary policy set by the Fed.

The deficits of the Reagan era also dramatized the government's incapacity to use the fiscal tool. There had been hints that fiscal policy was an ineffective macroeconomic tool in prior administrations. John F. Kennedy proposed a tax cut in 1962, but it did not pass until after his assassination unblocked the legislative logjam.

---

75. Blinder noted that those who thought the deficits would lead to explosive inflation "quickly looked silly." Alan S. Blinder, "The Policy Mix: Lessons from the Recent Past," *Economic Outlook USA* (First Quarter 1986), pp. 3–8.

Economic advisers urged Lyndon B. Johnson to propose a tax increase to offset the inflationary pressures of the Vietnam War, but he resisted such an unpopular move until 1967, and Congress did not enact his recommended surtax until 1968, well after price levels had begun to rise. Although these early attempts cast doubt on Keynesians' implicit political theory, the coup de grace came with the deficits of the 1980s. If the President and Congress could not agree on mechanisms for reducing deficits approaching 20 percent of the national fisc, how could deficits be modulated from quarter to quarter with each change in the American economy?

Keynesians defended their theory by insisting that the Federal Reserve had drawn monetary policy so tightly that it more than offset the expansionary thrust of the deficits. But such a rebuttal only confirmed the political reality that monetary policy will necessarily dominate fiscal policy as long as U.S. governmental arrangements remain as they are. Fiscal policy evolves slowly and ineptly; monetary policy is deftly managed by politically knowledgeable technical experts.

THE FUTURE OF ECONOMIC POLICYMAKING

In more innocent times, it might have seemed pedestrian to conclude optimistically that the president has both the incentive and the capacity to promote stable economic growth. But the point carries more bite in an age when sophisticated cynics have regularly claimed that presidents induced business cycles for their own election purposes, or jerked the economy around to meet the needs of their partisan supporters, or succumbed to the demands of the financial community on the Federal Reserve, or were unable to keep Congress from pursuing ruinous fiscal policies. Each of these charges has some plausibility, but none has the clarity of reasoning or weight of evidence necessary to sustain close examination. The evidence on the other side is that since 1951, when presidents began relying on the Federal Reserve as their key to economic stabilization, the United States has experienced more rapid economic growth and less extreme swings in the business cycle than in earlier decades.[76] Although avoidable recessions have

76. Hibbs, *American Political Economy,* pp. 13–42.

occurred and unnecessary inflation has been tolerated, these errors seem modest by comparison with the earlier erratic performance of the U.S. economy.

Has the Economy Gone Awry?

The deterioration in the U.S. economy during the 1970s and 1980s described in the opening paragraphs of this chapter is real and significant when the immediate postwar period is taken as the reference point. But it must also be recognized that the country enjoyed remarkably favorable economic circumstances in the years immediately following World War II. The United States was the one major industrial power whose economy had not been damaged by the war. The military superiority of the United States enabled it to virtually dictate the terms of international trade. Those who disagreed (such as the Soviet Union and China) had to create their own autarchic economies. U.S. producers dominated growing, increasingly open, foreign markets. They had little to fear from a competition weakened by wartime dislocation and destruction.

Postwar military power did not automatically translate into extraordinary economic growth, of course. U.S. policymakers succeeded only by exercising unusual restraint toward the defeated countries. Neither Germany nor Japan was to be punished or exploited in the way the central powers had been after World War I. Instead, they were to be incorporated into an increasingly integrated set of worldwide economic and political institutions that would help create a global economy and contain communist influence emanating from the Soviet Union. The milestones in this process are well known: Bretton Woods, the United Nations, the Marshall Plan, Japanese reconstruction, the General Agreement on Trade and Tariffs, and the European Economic Community (EEC).

Many of these steps involved a degree of financial sacrifice on the part of the United States. It financed economic development in Europe and Asia, lowered its tariffs more quickly and completely than did other nations, subsidized the United Nations, and tolerated an external tariff imposed by the EEC. As long as it was the dominant superpower, it could accept these costs in exchange for the major gains in international trade and comity.

Only later would the size of these self-imposed costs become apparent. As other nations regained their economic prowess, Bretton-Wood exchange rates overvalued the dollar and gave foreign countries ready access to U.S. markets. Differential trade barrier practices placed U.S. producers at a further disadvantage. Inexorably, the U.S. position shifted from dominance to first among equals.

Although the exact ways in which this change in the international position of the United States affected its growth and productivity are difficult to trace, some of the elements are well known. The Bretton-Woods agreement broke down, and the world entered an era of uncertain, constantly fluctuating, rates of exchange. An oil cartel increased the price of oil by eightfold on two separate occasions, plunging the United States into two recessions. When oil and commodity prices plummeted in the 1980s, the international economy was destabilized once again. As debt-ridden developing nations lurched toward bankruptcy, investors chose the United States as one of the safest harbors for their funds. The investments proved to be a mixed blessing, however. Although they financed rising budgetary deficits, the dollar escalated upward and U.S. manufacturers found it difficult to market their products in the face of stiffened foreign competition.

In retrospect the postwar era begins to appear to have been unusually conducive to economic growth not only in the United States, but throughout the world. Although this decade's rate of growth in GNP is only one-half of that of the decades immediately following World War II, it is still very close to the average U.S. growth since 1890. In addition, the growth in recent years has been fairly stable, quite unlike the extraordinary vacillation in economic conditions that marked earlier decades. Severe recessions on the order of those occurring in 1892, 1907, 1920, and 1929 have not occurred since the Federal Reserve has been given the authority to stabilize the economy. Eliminating such instability could not guarantee better than 3 percent growth in a period when the United States was no longer an overwhelmingly dominant superpower. But the record even in the last eighteen years is more than respectable once a longer time horizon is taken into account.

Do Deficits Matter?

The optimistic conclusion that the Fed can stabilize the macroeconomy rests on a controversial claim, however: namely, that fiscal and monetary policy can be divorced from one another. The mechanisms for administering monetary policy are amazingly supple. The FOMC frequently decides whether to buy or sell government securities so as to ease or tighten credit conditions. It can move to accommodate or frustrate changes in fiscal policy. It can act simultaneously with congressional legislation, after changes in revenue or expenditure have occurred, or in anticipation of their fiscal effects. The FOMC, moreover, has direct access to the latest information on both fiscal policy and the state of the macroeconomy. Its members have the training, experience, and inclination necessary to take into account the macroeconomic consequences of their decisions. Apart from a certain bankers' caution, its deliberations and judgments are usually shaped almost entirely by these considerations.

If for no reasons other than political ones, monetary policy dominates fiscal policy. Unless the Fed chooses to let a fiscal stimulus affect the macroeconomy by keeping interest rates low in the presence of heavy new government borrowing, the stimulus will be offset by the higher interest rate generated by the increased demand for money. Congress can hardly be blamed for macroeconomic conditions when its policies can be completely offset by the actions of another institutional participant perfectly capable of anticipating and overriding any fiscal decisions. Even if Keynesians are correct in saying that fiscal policy has short-term effects, Congress and the presidency, as institutions, cannot make the deft maneuvers in the coordinated manner that Keynesian theory requires. Many Keynesians claim that this institutional reality poses a central problem of governance, but inasmuch as the same (or indeed, superior) economic effects can be achieved through appropriate management of monetary policy, the governmental arrangements for short-term management of the economy are quite satisfactory as they are.

Once it is recognized that the management of the economy is essentially a matter of monetary policy, the makers of fiscal policy no longer need be concerned about its short-term macroeconomic effects. This lesson already seems well known to policymakers. Recent efforts to reduce the size of the deficit have not varied with fluctuations in the national economy. Calls for fiscal responsibility were as widespread during the depths of the 1982 recession as in the growth spurt of 1984. And when the stock market crashed in

1987, the pressure for fiscal responsibility only increased (though Keynesian doctrine would have suggested that Congress take an opposite course of action). Congress has even passed legislation (Gramm-Rudman-Hollings) that mandates regular reductions in the size of the budget deficit, almost without regard to the state of the economy. Although the deficit still is considered a potential economic problem, Wall Street analysts and Washington policymakers now look to the Fed for managing the economy.

Although this lesson seems to be recognized by policymakers, it has yet to be clearly articulated. Politicians cannot afford to say publicly that deficits do not matter. The Republican president blames a Democratic Congress for uncontrolled spending. Congress blames the president for refusing to present a responsible set of budget proposals. The chairman of the Federal Reserve has a vested organizational interest in identifying the budget deficit as the most urgent economic issue. Keynesians have treated the budget as a key macroeconomic tool for so many decades that they cannot easily assume a contrary stance.

Appearances and reality often have little to do with one another in the game of politics. It is important to all participants in the policymaking game that they appear to take the short-term effects of budget deficits seriously. It would seem irresponsible of them to say otherwise. In reality the annual deficits of more than $150 billion continue from year to year without any immediate economic consequences. As that reality refuses to go away, political gamesmanship becomes increasingly evident.

If the lesson that fiscal policy cannot be used to stabilize the economy were clearly articulated, then perhaps attention could be focused on the genuine issues posed by the large deficits of the 1980s: they have added to the economic difficulties the United States has encountered as a result of its relative decline in the world economy. At the very time when world competition was increasing, U.S. deficits reduced the national savings rate, encouraged increased foreign investment in the United States, and raised the value of the dollar to the point that U.S. firms could not sell their products in foreign markets (while foreign competitors were lured into the United States). As one group of analysts observed, "Large continuing deficits in times of prosperity are costly because they reduce national saving and the future returns to that saving. The reduction in saving either forces a reduction in investment in the United States or finances that investment with funds from abroad. Either effect reduces the growth of income for residents of the United States."[77]

Since persistent deficits pose a long-term problem for the U.S. economy, it is worth considering whether the deficits of the 1980s are institutionally rooted or simply the product of the unusual politics of the Reagan era. If they are a deviant practice, then institutional solutions would seem to be inappropriate, perhaps even counterproductive. But if they are more than simply the peculiarity of one administration, then it may be necessary to introduce an institutional innovation such as a constitutional amendment requiring a balanced budget.

The main institutional problem identified by many of those proposing such an amendment is the congressional propensity to favor expenditures over taxes. Congress is organized, it is said, in such a way as to maximize the reelection chances of its members, and these members profit politically from spend now, pay later policies. On the one hand, this argument, as we have seen, ignores both the fact that until 1980 the public debt as a percentage of GNP fell steadily throughout the postwar period and the fact that Congress seldom increases expenditures or cuts taxes much beyond what the president proposes. Deficits have not been endemic to American politics, nor are these deficits caused mainly by congressional procedures. On the other hand, it can hardly be said that Congress fights vigorously for fiscal responsibility on those occasions when a president does not. At best it follows presidential leadership.

Others identify the separation of powers as the main institutional cause of deficits.[78] During the Reagan era, the president wanted to increase defense expenditures while cutting both taxes and domestic spending. Congress wanted to extend entitlement programs and keep cuts in other federal activities to a minimum. Because neither president nor Congress had full responsibility for fiscal policy, compromises were found at the lowest common political denominator: increases in defense, tax cuts, continuation of entitlement and other politically popular programs, and reductions

---

77. Henry J. Aaron and others, *Economic Choices 1987* (Brookings, 1986), p. 22.

78. James L. Sundquist, *Constitutional Reform and Effective Government* (Brookings, 1986).

only in programs that constituted too small a proportion of the budget to bring it into balance. As a result, deficits and the cost of financing them climbed steadily.

The contrast to Margaret Thatcher's policies in Britain are instructive, these commentators point out. No less conservative than Ronald Reagan, Thatcher cut taxes only by an amount comparable to the expenditure reductions the government was prepared to carry out. The fact that the Conservative party had full control of Parliament as well as the cabinet precluded Thatcher from pursuing a potentially more popular course of proposing large deficit-producing tax cuts while blaming Parliament for any failure to cut expenditures by a comparable amount. If this argument still does not quite take into account the fact that Congress has generally followed the president's lead on overall tax and expenditure policies, it does highlight the fact that the president and Congress can blame each other for deficits: Congress criticizes the president for proposing imbalanced budgets, and the president accuses Congress of passing them. This ability to shift the blame is all the more disturbing, given the fact that deficit politics has proven to be a winning strategy for two popular presidents, both of whom had controversial agendas that shifted American policy in a new direction.

Franklin Delano Roosevelt was the first to seize upon this strategy as a way of financing his Works Progress Administration, Public Works Administration, Farm Security Administration, Tennessee Valley Authority, and a host of other New Deal programs. Undoubtedly, the popularity of these programs was enhanced not only by the fact that they put people to work, but also by the fact that their costs were to be paid later. Forty percent of the federal budget between 1933 and 1939 was paid for by deficit financing, an average annual amount that was 3.2 percent of GNP.[79]

At the time deficits were being incurred, Roosevelt was being solidly, if fruitlessly, denounced by Republicans for his unprecedented irresponsibility. But Keynes's claim that deficit financing could be used to stimulate a depressed economy has been used by historians to excuse Roosevelt's profligate policies. But whatever benefits deficits might have had, they were more than offset by the

---

79. U.S. Bureau of the Census, *Historical Statistics of the United States, Colonial Times to 1970* (Government Printing Office, 1975), pt. 1, p. 224; pt. 2, p. 1105.

excessively restrictive policies of an inexperienced Federal Reserve Board; indeed, the depression worsened in 1938, a time when deficit spending reached its peak.[80]

It is probably no accident that Ronald Reagan, the next president to recommend to Congress budgets with fiscal deficits of comparable size, was a self-described admirer of Franklin Roosevelt. Like FDR, Reagan wanted to change dramatically the policies of the federal government. If the content of Reagan's policies was quite different—Reagan wanted his increases in spending to be concentrated on defense—their political needs were similar. Both had large objectives, wanted to act quickly and decisively, faced considerable opposition, needed (after the first one hundred days) to bring a reluctant Congress along, and so appealed above the Washington establishment to the country at large. Once Reagan had cut taxes in 1981, he could no more afford to ask for an increase in subsequent years than FDR could have asked for a tax increase during the depths of the depression. It is true that Reagan accepted modest tax increases in 1982 and 1984 (mainly rescissions of tax cuts promised in 1981 that had yet to go into effect), but even then he only acquiesced to a congressionally led initiative. But, overall, deficit politics became a vital component of the two strongest, most dramatic presidencies of the twentieth century.

A number of economic and political conditions make it extraordinarily difficult to eliminate the deficits of the 1980s. Interest on the national debt has grown rapidly during the 1980s and now requires a large portion of the federal budget; this part of the federal budget is truly "untouchable," in that it cannot be reduced unless the government defaults on its obligations. But other parts of the budget are also difficult to change. Indexation of income taxes (included in the 1981 tax bill) means that the government no longer automatically increases its claim on GNP as incomes rise (and individuals are pushed into higher tax brackets by inflation). Indexation of entitlements, meanwhile, has caused the bill for these programs to increase steadily as the cost of living climbs. Indexing taxes and entitlements has also altered the political calculus: raising taxes or lowering benefits no longer occurs automatically, but only by explicit legislation.

It is possible that these economic and political changes are not so

80. Friedman and Schwartz, *Monetary History of the United States.*

great that they require changes in the nation's institutional arrangements. If so, one does not need an institutional reform to solve a large but infrequent problem. Instead, one should learn from the political solutions devised for two other thorny issues of the 1980s: social security reform and tax simplification.[81] In each case it was widely seen that the government's policies were severely flawed: social security was going broke, and the tax system appeared ready to collapse of its own weight. In each case most observers believed that the political system made it virtually impossible to take sensible and effective steps to solve the problem. In each case, any solution called for a significant amount of pain to be allocated to each party, both branches of government, and a variety of powerful interest groups.

Yet, both times a successful compromise was crafted between the political parties and between Congress and the president because they were determined to solve the problems. Although the budget deficit cannot be resolved simply by trying to repeat the process used for social security and tax reform (idiosyncratic problems cannot be resolved by routine means), resolution does require small, private, face-to-face meetings between the president (or select aides) and congressional leaders from both sides of the aisle to build and enforce acceptable solutions based on shared sacrifices. If these conditions are met, solving the large deficit problem is possible. Without them, no amount of institutional change will work.

Although this kind of solution is possible, there remains the fact that deficits have contributed to successful presidencies. When Roosevelt experimented with large peacetime deficits, there was a chance that these policies would be regarded as a depression-induced aberration. Now that the experiment has been repeated during a decade of moderate economic growth—with equal political success—the chances of deficit politics becoming a frequently repeated, if not entrenched, part of the American political system are that much greater. There is some possibility that the reserves that are building up in the social security trust fund will eventually help offset the deficits in the operating part of the budget. It is also

81. See especially Paul Light, *Artful Work: The Politics of Social Security Reform* (Random House, 1985); and Jeffrey H. Birnbaum and Alan S. Murray, *Showdown at Gucci Gulch: Lawmakers, Lobbyists, and the Unlikely Triumph of Tax Reform* (Random House, 1987).

possible that the less heroic, but more responsible, presidents who follow Reagan will encourage Congress to move in a more frugal direction. But it is also possible that presidents of the future will notice the political success that accompanied both Roosevelt's and Reagan's deficits. Thus one cannot count on the energetic presidential leadership that is necessary to keep the deficits of the 1980s from continuing on into the twenty-first century.

We began this essay by emphasizing the stake that presidents have in stabilizing economic growth for the four to eight years they are in office. We end by noting that presidents can enjoy stable growth over their terms of office even while running deficits amounting to 20 percent of the federal budget. It is for this reason that serious thought should be given to a constitutional amendment requiring that presidents submit—and Congresses enact—a balanced budget.

The defects of such an amendment are well known. It can be evaded by including certain expenditures as off-budget items. It can be dodged by misestimating growth, inflation rates, outlays, and entitlement costs. It does not require that government run a surplus during the years the social security trust fund needs to accumulate resources necessary to pay the high retirement costs of the mid-twenty-first century. It is no substitute for the willingness to compromise political differences that was finally evident in the debates over social security and tax reform. But even though the amendment cannot ensure more sensible fiscal policies in the future, it can at least place profligate presidents—and the Congresses who support them—at risk of being charged with unconstitutional action, both by other politicians and by the courts. Since it has not been shown that peacetime deficits have lasting value—and the costs of continuous large peacetime deficits are serious—such an amendment imposes few risks and may well constrain future presidents and Congresses from abusing the public fisc for short-term political profit. It might even provide a new structural incentive that will help obtain the deficit-eliminating political compromises that have been so elusive in recent years.

Part II
Institutions and Governance

The Evolution of
the White House Staff

SAMUEL KERNELL

THE SUCCESSES and failures of presidents have been increasingly attributed to the performances of their staffs. After the Iran-contra scandal broke, a special commission headed by former Senator John G. Tower examined the staffing system that yielded such ill-advised schemes as the exchange of missiles for hostages and the diversion of funds to the Nicaraguan contras. The commission faulted many on the White House staff, as well as the president, but the first political casualty was Chief of Staff Donald Regan, whose replacement was announced before he had a chance to resign. According to the Tower commission, Regan did not adequately inquire about the actions of others once news of irregularities began to appear in the press. These charges rang true to many Washingtonians. When he took over the staff early in the president's second term, Regan sharply cut the number of senior staff and installed a pyramidal White House organization with himself at the apex. As a result, President Reagan came to depend on his chief more than he had on any individual during his first term, and when his chief failed to perform, the president was left uninformed in the midst of a crisis.

The Iran-contra scandal has begged for explanation because it contrasted so starkly with the president's first-term successes. Students of the presidency, including Garry Trudeau, the cartoonist of "Doonesbury," had noted Reagan's lacadaisical work habits and heavy reliance on staff. But the president's remarkable legislative successes in forcing a Democratic House to accept sharp reductions in social programs, equally sharp hikes in defense spending, and a major tax cut had transformed this potential weakness into a strength. (One liberal Democratic congressman confided in 1982 that the president's example had persuaded him to delegate more

185

responsibility to his office staff.) Kudos were heaped on James Baker for organizing Reagan's legislative strategies and Michael Deaver for keeping his public image well burnished. Independent of the individual staff members, the triumvirate that governed the early Reagan White House—Baker, Deaver, and Edwin Meese—was widely complimented as an ideal form of organization.

If awareness of the importance of presidential staffing peaked under Reagan, it certainly did not begin with him. Carter's micro-management style overloaded the president and prevented him from developing priorities. Nixon's oversized staff of loyalists headed by H. R. Haldeman and John Ehrlichman was widely judged to have contributed to the misdeeds of Watergate. Every president's organization, in fact, has received a measure of credit or blame for the president's performance. But with the president's performance so dependent on the workings of his staff, and the staff's performance apparently dependent on its organization, what accounts for the structure of the modern White House Office?

The conventional scholarly answer is that the organization of the White House staff reflects the style and work habits of the incumbent president.[1] Staffing arrangements have been as individual and as variable as the men who occupied the office. Thus former General Dwight D. Eisenhower rejected Harry Truman's informal staff system and installed an orderly chain of command headed by a chief of staff. John Kennedy, self-assured and charismatic, replaced Ike's structure with an entourage of close advisers who, with himself as team leader, managed the White House informally. Similar personalized arrangements can be observed for each successor. The history of the modern White House Office can be recounted in terms of highly individualistic, four-to-eight-year bundles of organizational reformulations.

Not only does the conventional wisdom hold that presidents distinctively mold their staffs, it also strongly endorses this influence. Writing in the 1960s, one leading presidential scholar concluded that the president requires "the utmost flexibility in the choice, number, characteristics, and deployment of his staff."[2] This highly personalized view of staff structure appears to leave little to

1. James D. Barber, *The Presidential Character: Predicting Performance in the White House* (Prentice-Hall, 1972).

2. Aaron Wildavsky, "Salvation by Staff: Reform and the Presidential Office," in Wildavsky, ed., *The Presidency* (Little, Brown, 1969), p. 700.

be explained. But appearances are deceptive. Any number of organizational arrangements might satisfy a given president's needs. From all accounts, President Reagan found Donald Regan's strong-chief approach to White House management as congenial as the more open and less hierarchical staff administration of the first-term troika. And when Regan left, his successor, Howard Baker, set up a completely different operation, again without apparent discomfort to the president.

Also, critics have complained, the White House staff has become a separate entity, frequently working at cross purposes with the intent and needs of the president. Increasingly, presidential lapses in judgment and policy appear to reflect failed staff work. The White House Office is clearly far different from what it once was. No longer just the president's entourage of cronies and campaign staff, it appears to have been shaped by more significant and more stable forces than can be found in the comings and goings of presidents.

DEVELOPMENT OF
THE MODERN WHITE HOUSE

Unlike the other presidential agencies created in the Reorganization Act of 1939, or those introduced subsequently, the White House Office was not intended to participate in administration. Instead, its attentions were to be devoted exclusively to the incidental needs of the president, to be, as Roosevelt said, his legs. Consequently, it was no slight to the office or the presidency that the staff was initially kept small and free of statutory responsibilities. These men and women were expected to be factotums.

Shortly after entering office in 1933, Franklin Roosevelt assembled a dozen or so assistants to help plan his assault on the Great Depression. He had also inherited roughly fifty clerks and secretaries from the outgoing Hoover administration.[3] As with his predecessors, many of these were on loan from various agencies, which presumably saw some advantage in having their people stationed close to the president. Precise figures on the total staff are unavailable, since the White House Office was not created until the Reor-

3. Transcript, William Hopkins oral history interview, pp. 2–4, Harry S. Truman Library.

FIGURE 1.   *Growth of the White House Staff, 1935–85*

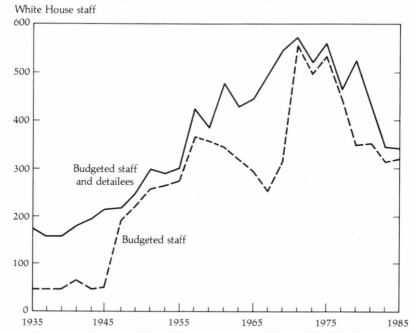

White House staff

SOURCE: Samuel Kernell and Samuel L. Popkin, eds., *Chief of Staff: Twenty-five Years of Managing the Presidency* (University of California Press, 1986), p. 201. Number of detailees for 1981 unavailable.

ganization Act allowed a modest professional staff of six newly created assistants to the president.

When James Rowe, the first of these assistants, returned from World War II, he called a friend in the Truman White House to ask how things had changed. He recalled later that they had "nine people doing what I used to do," and guessed that "nowadays they must have 300 or 400 doing what I used to do."[4] Figure 1 supports Rowe's impression. Until the aftermath of Watergate reversed the trend, the president's staff grew about 5 percent a year.[5]

4. Katie Louchheim, ed., *The Making of the New Deal: The Insiders Speak* (Harvard University Press, 1983), p. 285.

5. The totals in figure 1 are estimates based on research undertaken in 1978 by the Office of Personnel Management at the request of Congress. Note that there are alternative ways of calculating staff size, depending on whether recently created agencies such as the Office of Policy Development are included. For more information on the difficulties of measuring the size of the staff, see John Hart, *The Presidential Branch* (Pergamon Press, 1987), pp. 97–109.

Although there seem to have been few constraints on growth, the aggregate numbers imply that presidents have avoided formal increases in staff. Until 1979 they were not required to report to Congress the number of aides loaned to the White House from the agencies, and they clearly preferred this inconspicuous, informal way of expanding. Gradually the number of detailees grew in relation to budgeted staff, until a new president would clean up the bookkeeping by including the positions in the White House Office budget.

Watergate and the subsequent criminal convictions of Richard Nixon's aides drew attention to the president's staff as no event had before or has since. An obvious way for Nixon's successors to dissociate themselves from the stigma of the imperial presidency was to trim personnel. In 1976 Jimmy Carter assured the American people that pruning the staff would be one of the first items of business in his new administration. The trend continued with Ronald Reagan, although some members of Congress charged that he misrepresented the number of detailees working in the White House.[6] While such borrowing makes firm estimates elusive, the White House Office seems to have leveled off at about 400 people.

Although organizational manuals for each White House do not exist, the increase in size seems to have been paralleled by an increase in complexity. As the number and variety of tasks multiplied, duties were divided and eventually parceled among subunits. The formal designation of roles became more common and so did organization charts.

The development of specialization and chains of command has proceeded with seeming inevitability. Reviewing an early draft of his administrative reform plan, Roosevelt told its author, Louis Brownlow, that he did not want his assistants consigned to "little boxes." Nonetheless, he did make two formal assignments. Aggravated with the tardiness of legal advice from the Justice Department, he created the White House Special Counsel's Office. The counsel, Samuel I. Rosenman, however, spent more time writing speeches than advising on legal matters. Roosevelt also designated

6. Personnel detailed to the White House for less than six months are exempted from reporting to the department that pays them. The Reagan administration interpreted this rule as allowing persons to be detailed indefinitely as long as they change positions in the departments within a six-month period. Judith Havemann, "How White House Beefed Up Staff," *Washington Post*, July 22, 1987, p. A17.

the first press secretary, Stephen Early, although previous presidents had informally assigned aides to tend to Washington correspondents.

Even in hindsight, Roosevelt's staff arrangements resist classification. Thomas Corcoran and Harry Hopkins, arguably the most valued aides, were never members of the White House Office. And those who were rarely interacted: the president's personal and appointments secretaries were located in the west wing of the White House, and his new assistants across the street. "Not much of a presence," William Hopkins, veteran executive clerk of the White House Office, summed up this first official staff.[7]

Early in Truman's first term, when long-time personal friend Ed McKim tried to assert management control and began drafting an organization chart, the president promoted him to another job away from the White House. Other efforts to assign fellow staffers to organizational niches were no more successful.[8] Reflecting his military experience, Dwight Eisenhower introduced fixed assignments and a chain of command for the White House staff. But he did so without formal titles, organization charts, or other appurtenances of bureaucracy.

Presidents Kennedy and Johnson restored more informal relations and more fluid assignments, but the staff's greater size and responsibilities meant that they could not return to Roosevelt's desultory management style. Periodically, Lyndon Johnson would become frustrated with his loose staff structure and, in the words of Bill Moyers, get in one of his "organizational moods."[9] Over the years at least five senior aides were assigned, on arriving at the White House, the job of charting a formal staff structure. Since there was little formal division of labor among Johnson's staff, the attempt was doomed. Johnson would look at each effort, wad it up and throw it away, and instruct the now wary aide to try again. Eventually, the president would let the matter drop until some energetic recruit would rekindle his enthusiasm.[10]

7. Interview with William Hopkins, April 1, 1988, Silver Spring, Maryland. In searching through the Roosevelt archives, I turned up only one staff memo, to assistants telling them not to bother the president before 11:30. By the Nixon administration, such notes would become a standard way of coordinating staff activities.

8. George J. Schoeneman to Raymond R. Zimmerman, January 4, 1946, Truman Library.

9. Bill Moyers to Bob Kintner, May 5, 1966, Lyndon B. Johnson Library.

10. By the time Robert Kintner joined the staff in 1966 and was promptly given

No subsequent president has had to suffer Johnson's frustrations. All worked within the confines of formal organizational designations for each staff member. Richard Nixon's White House staff underwent two major reorganizations, and the finishing touches were being given to a third when Watergate struck. Organizational charts identified the implications of proposed changes.[11] Similarly, Presidents Ford and Carter employed charts and formal titles as a way of understanding and at times reorganizing the staff.

According to one account, when Edwin Meese, the head of Reagan's transition team, asked to see what the White House Office looked like, the Carter people produced an elaborate chart that located more than 400 budgeted staff among the twenty or so sub-units of the White House Office. Meese accepted it matter of factly. Some changes were made, of course. James Baker had agreed to assume day-to-day management responsibilities as chief of staff, while Meese would take charge of policy planning in his position as counselor, and offices were shuffled accordingly. Some offices, such as Communications under David Gergen, became more important; others, including that of the national security adviser, less. But no major functions or organizational divisions were deleted or added by the new administration.

Both the number of formal subunits and levels of hierarchy have steadily increased, from one level and eleven subunits under Eisenhower to four levels and twenty-nine subunits under Reagan.[12] These increases in size and complexity have transformed a small group closely attentive and responsive to the president into a larger, more formal organization governed by rules and procedures, and have given it the appearance of a steadily institutional-

---

this assignment, the other aides had become jaded and perhaps in a few instances opposed to the prospect of organizing Johnson. As Kintner made his rounds researching the different duties of staff members, they would pointedly explain to him the futility of trying to organize the Johnson White House Office. See ibid. The tenor of comments to and about Kintner's efforts suggest that by that late date some aides may have feared reorganization would have removed them from direct access to the president.

11. For example, see John Dean, "Methods for Reorganizing the Executive Branch," January 2, 1973, Richard M. Nixon collection, National Archives.

12. Eisenhower figures are from "Staff Work for the President and the Executive Branch," Legislative Background Collection, Johnson Library, n.d. For Reagan's White House structure, see Samuel Kernell and Samuel L. Popkin, eds., *Chief of Staff: Twenty-five Years of Managing the Presidency* (University of California Press, 1986), p. 202.

izing organization rather than one remade in each new president's image. The continuity in the organization of Carter's and Reagan's staff further undermines the idea that staff organization merely reflects each president's style.

The decisions of presidents and senior aides provide more direct evidence. In many instances, they appear to have been engaged in a rear-guard action to prevent bureaucratization rather than an expansionist venture. During the transition in 1968, President Nixon's chief, H. R. Haldeman, summoned the new White House aides and read to them Brownlow's principles for assistants, emphasizing the passage instructing aides to cultivate a "passion for anonymity."[13] At some moment in each of their terms, presidents from Johnson to Carter inveighed against large staffs and occasionally ordered cutbacks.[14] One of the ironies of Watergate is that by late 1972 President Nixon had decided that his staff had "grown like Topsy" and directed a disbelieving aide to come up with a plan to cut it by half early in the second term.[15] If neither presidents nor their aides have wanted larger, more complex staffs, why has the White House developed the way it has?

TOWARD AN EXPLANATION OF WHITE HOUSE DEVELOPMENT

One answer is that while the upper reaches of the staff system may have been distinctively shaped by each president, its overall size and complexity have been dictated by the growth of the national government, particularly the president's increased responsibilities since World War II.[16] Or as Donald Rumsfeld, Gerald Ford's chief of staff, commented, "You have all these threads, and the White House staff's function is to see that those threads get through the needle's eye in a reasonably coherent way."[17] In this

13. See William Safire, *Before the Fall: An Inside View of the Pre-Watergate White House* (Doubleday, 1975), p. 116.

14. *A Discussion with Gerald R. Ford: The American Presidency* (Washington, D.C.: American Enterprise Institute for Public Policy Research, 1977); and Jimmy Carter, *Keeping Faith: Memoirs of a President* (Bantam, 1982).

15. Richard P. Nathan, *The Plot That Failed: Nixon and the Administrative Presidency* (John Wiley, 1975), p. 53.

16. Hart, *Presidential Branch*, p. 114.

17. Kernell and Popkin, eds., *Chief of Staff*, p. 112.

regard the president's staff is unexceptional; the senior civil service and congressional staffs may have grown and professionalized even faster.[18] According to this argument, work load drives development more than presidential proclivities do.

A variant of this argument claims that the growth of responsibilities has induced a profound transformation. "Whatever his particular policy objectives, whatever his personality and style, the modern president is driven by . . . formidable expectations to seek control over the structures and processes of government . . . [to create] an institutional system responsive to his needs as a political leader."[19] This desire for responsiveness has prompted presidents to centralize decisionmaking in the White House and to politicize the bureaucracy.[20] The size and complexity of the modern office are the products of this centralization.

Clearly, this explanation elucidates one motivating force of presidential behavior. To gain the cooperation he felt he deserved from others, every president has tried to extend his control into the jurisdictions of others. But insufficient responsiveness has less to do with the increasing volume of demands than with the structure of American politics. Suspicious of the conservative sympathies of the old line departments, Franklin Roosevelt located many of the New Deal agencies under his direct supervision. Each subsequent president has followed his lead because, although some may have been more disposed to assert unilateral authority than others, the search for greater responsiveness inheres in the predicament of the office, in the clash of expectations of presidential leadership with a system of separated powers. The search is neither more nor less than the pursuit of power in a system all presidents come to feel has dealt them too little.[21] When Truman remarked of Eisenhower,

18. Congressional staffs increased from 3,556 in 1957 to 11,432 in 1981; the number of committee staffers rose from 715 in 1955 to 2,865 in 1981. Norman J. Ornstein and others, *Vital Statistics on Congress, 1984–1985* (Washington, D.C.: American Enterprise Institute for Public Policy Research, 1984), pp. 121, 124.

19. Terry M. Moe, "The Politicized Presidency," in John E. Chubb and Paul E. Peterson, eds., *The New Direction in American Politics* (Brookings, 1985), p. 239.

20. Hugh Heclo, *A Government of Strangers: Executive Politics in Washington* (Brookings, 1977), pp. 71–75; and Margaret J. Wyzomirski, "The De-Institutionalization of Presidential Staff Agencies," *Public Administration Review*, vol. 42 (September–October 1982), pp. 448–58.

21. Thirty-five years ago, Robert A. Dahl and Charles E. Lindblom made precisely this point: "If presidential politicians could be given 'sufficient' *power* over the bureaucracies, the bureaucracies would be *responsive* to presidential politicians—

"He'll sit here and he'll say, 'Do this! Do that!' *And nothing will happen,*" he was talking as much about the office as about his successor.[22] Since every president, most of the time, has wished for greater responsiveness, its ever-present pursuit cannot alone explain the modern evolution of the office.

The argument does, however, identify vital features of presidential leadership. Presidents are constantly probing the boundaries of their control, and where they meet little resistance, new authority can be established. Each successive decision becomes marginally less costly as accommodation becomes unnecessary and the president's options less confined by other Washingtonians' prerogatives. The growing size and complexity of the White House Office offers indirect evidence of the steady successes of postwar presidents in poaching in the domains of others.

The interests of presidents and their fellow Washingtonians have been diverging for a long time, and in ways that could not always be reconciled through negotiation and reciprocity. The president, unlike other politicians, has the nation as his constituency. He may at times find a tactical advantage in cultivating support among particular segments of the population, but such concerns are clearly secondary. By contrast, members of Congress represent local constituencies. However interested a congressman or senator may be in a national policy, his or her job requires servicing the district or state first. Similarly, when party leaders were still consequential political figures, they considered their responsibilities to be little more than collecting the claims of state party organizations and presenting them to the White House for action. In both instances, insatiable particularism frequently conflicted with the president's notion of the national interest. It still does.

The conventional view is that these differing perspectives provided the basis of reciprocity, and generally they did. Presidents swapped specific jobs and projects for support for their programs so routinely that expectations sometimes became institutionalized in such informal rules as senatorial courtesy. But in many

---

a neat tautology." (Emphasis added.) *Politics, Economics, and Welfare: Planning and Politico-Economic Systems Resolved into Basic Social Processes* (Harper and Row, 1953), p. 351.

22. Quoted in Richard E. Neustadt, *Presidential Power: The Politics of Leadership from FDR to Carter* (John Wiley, 1980), p. 9.

instances, such exchanges compromised the president's goals. Evidence in the historical record shows that on these occasions, presidents sought to skirt traditional rules. Even Franklin Roosevelt—considered a paragon of the bargaining president—at times chose strategies that undermined the political order founded on reciprocity. He did so when he allowed the Internal Revenue Service to expose corruption among Democratic machines and send the leaders to prison. He did so when he directed Harry Hopkins to create a federal administration for delivering relief programs instead of turning them over to expectant Democratic organizations skilled in the efficient distribution of patronage. And he did so when he resisted the patronage claims of senators who wanted their nominees rather than New Deal professionals to run federal relief and public works programs in their states.[23] These actions reaped political ill will, but they preserved the president's national policy objectives. Well before presidents became habituated to centralization, their preoccupation with the needs of the national constituency sometimes led them to resist arrangements among community members predicated on the axiom that a collective good was the simple sum of highly divisible parts.

Presidents' concern with providing collective goods may explain their preoccupation with other politicians' insufficient responsiveness and their efforts to extend presidential authority. To explain their success, however, one must investigate the weakening of the forces that once contained them and kept political relations in a state of mutual dependency. The evolution of the White House staff is as much a result of the transformation of American politics beyond the Oval Office as of the efforts of presidents searching for responsiveness.

Today's Washington is not the one that greeted President

23. Perhaps the most famous and well-documented instance of exposing a Democratic machine under FDR is the dismantling of Tom Pendergast's Kansas City organization. See Lyle W. Dorsett, *The Pendergast Machine* (Oxford University Press, 1968). Roosevelt did not rebuke all machine claims for control of federal relief programs. Hopkins turned over most of the Chicago operations of the WPA to Ed Kelly's organization. Lyle Dorsett describes this exceptional arrangement and more typical patterns in *Franklin D. Roosevelt and the City Bosses* (Port Washington, N.Y.: Kennikat Press, 1977). An example of conflict between senatorial claims of patronage and the president's program can be found in Senator Ellender's insistent appeals for appointments for federal administrative posts in Louisiana. See James Rowe, "Memorandum for the President," May 19, 1939, Rowe papers, Franklin D. Roosevelt Library.

Roosevelt in 1933. Gone are the national party committees that represented state and local party organizations whose interests had to be attended to by elected politicians. The national apparatus was especially important to the president because it ran his campaign and, after the victory, served as a clearinghouse for the distribution of federal patronage. Gone too is the power of the national party chairman. Although the chairman was always subordinate to the president, that did not keep James Farley from openly courting Democratic delegates for the 1940 nomination or deter him and his successor Ed Flynn from openly feuding with the White House staff.[24] National party chairmen could be disregarded only at the risk of alienating state party organizations.

The stature of congressional leaders has also diminished. When Roosevelt took office, they spoke with such authority that they could cut a deal with the president and return to their committees in the full expectation of being able to implement it. Had the president created an in-house congressional liaison office, as was occasionally recommended, he would have been tacitly challenging the position of the Big Four legislative leaders with whom he lunched each week to plan legislative strategy. Such a tactic would have inevitably redounded to his disadvantage, which, of course, is why Roosevelt spurned such advice. But today the president can no longer rely on the floor leaders, and the congressional liaison office is a necessity.

The limiting power of the press has also changed.[25] In 1933 a comparatively small, homogeneous band of Washington newspaper correspondents controlled the president's access to the citizenry, and to court their favor he obligingly conducted "family gatherings" with them twice a week. For Roosevelt to have avoided the press conference would have been tantamount to surrendering the national stage to his adversaries. He did contemplate more frequent fireside radio chats, but until the war he resisted

24. The relationship between president and national party apparatus since Roosevelt is discussed by Lester G. Seligman, "The Presidential Office and the President as Party Leader (with a Postscript on the Kennedy-Nixon Era)," in Jeff Fishel, ed., *Parties and Elections in an Anti-Party Age: American Politics and the Crisis of Confidence* (Indiana University Press, 1978), pp. 295-302.

25. For a fuller account of this transformation, see Samuel Kernell, *Going Public: New Strategies of Presidential Leadership* (CQ Press, 1986), pp. 51-81.

having more than an average of two a year because he did not want to dilute their effect. Such dedicated presidential courtship of White House correspondents became more desultory, however, as television deprived them of their near monopoly. Before long, broadcast journalists had reduced them to second-class citizenship, and recent presidents have decided that the fewer press conferences the better.

All these evolving political relations are rooted in forces well beyond the control of politicians. Ultimately, the arrival of broadcast technology, especially television, ended the grip of print journalists on political communication from Washington and thereby weakened their leverage at the White House. This does not mean that presidents, the political system's most resourceful participants, merely acquiesced to the new limits and opportunities presented by political evolution; when it served their purposes, they became agents of change. President Kennedy, concerned that the press would turn against him sooner or later, confided to a friend that he adopted televised press conferences to communicate directly to the American people.[26]

To summarize, the modern White House staff is the cumulative product of presidents' strategic adaptations to an evolving political community. Presidents seeking responsiveness probe for new power. Other participants in the political process, because of their own deteriorating power, have found themselves at times unable to resist. The cumulative result of presidential encroachment has been the steady centralization of policymaking within the White House. Internally, it has taken the form of increased work, which in turn has stimulated the growth of staff and the subdivision of work into more specialized tasks. This sequence by which presidential strategy has begotten staff structure can be confirmed in the history of the White House Office as an organization. One finds it in the character of new staff work and the timing of its introduction, in its subsequent routinization as resistance from outsiders weakens, and ultimately, in the efforts required of modern presidents and their senior staff aides to harness their staff's disparate activities to achieve coherent leadership.

26. Blaire Atherton French, *The Presidential Press Conference* (University Press of America, 1982), p. 13.

A HISTORY OF WHITE HOUSE ORGANIZATION

The modern White House staff is a two-tiered organization. The lower tier consists of such line units responsible for conducting the president's external relations as the press secretary, the congressional liaison staff, the secretary to the cabinet, and the speechwriters. The upper tier comprises staff who are primarily responsible for planning and internal maintenance of the organization. While such a distinction is not applicable to the early staffs, it is essential for understanding the evolution of the modern White House. Even President Truman, who was his own office manager, had aides such as John Steelman, Clark Clifford, and Charles Murphy to help supervise the activities of others. More recently, formal offices such as the chief of staff have been created for this purpose. Whether or not such offices are present, however, a half dozen or so senior aides who work directly with the president will assume some management control.

These two domains of activity place their members in different settings. As the number and variety of routine external tasks increase, layers of specialized subunits proliferate to handle them. On-the-job training and selective recruitment results in a cadre of experts. How well an aide works the Hill, monitors public opinion, analyzes diplomatic messages, or performs other specialized tasks determines his worth to the organization and relationship to the president. Only as the president requires a particular expertise will an aide be asked to write a memo or be summoned to the Oval Office. The rest of the aide's time, which is most of the time, will be spent on routine relations.

Those charged with planning and coordinating the affairs of the line staff, by contrast, remain generalists, working closely with the president on a wide range of issues. They confront the world outside the White House the same way the president does, not as matters requiring routine relations but as exigencies that demand presidential action. Because their job is to help the president do his job, they must be responsive to his personal style and work habits.

And yet the imperatives of size and complexity are no different for the president's senior staff than for the managers of any other organization. Beneath the surface idiosyncrasy of personalities, predictable organizational trends toward rationalization prevail here as well. Presidents, ill disposed to work within formal structures, may resist such bureaucratization, but they do so at the risk of leaving line staff insufficiently supervised, resulting in such pathologies as presidential overload, aides' interpreting for themselves what actions are in the best interest of the president, and fights among subunits for influence over policy. A history of presidential staffing must take into account the development of each tier of White House organization.

The Development of White House Line Staff

Were the White House Office an ordinary organization, it would have a manual listing dozens of tasks from coordinating foreign policy to answering the president's mail. Most of these routines have evolved from incidental activities that proved so valuable they began to require special resources. Others were once prerogatives shared with, if not wholly controlled by, other politicians. Underlying each loss of prerogative is a story of political transformation. Why did a particular authority or responsibility become the president's and how did it affect the organization of the staff?

To answer, I have chosen to examine the way the White House staff has made political appointments and managed public relations. These activities epitomize recent trends in presidential leadership over time. Through his early successes President Reagan, more than any of his predecessors, demonstrated that by assiduously recruiting loyalists the president can take control of the bureaucracy and by rallying public support he can gain leverage with fellow politicians. But neither Reagan's personnel strategy nor his communications strategy was altogether novel. Each adapted practices that can be traced back decades. In this respect they parallel histories of other staff routines. Similar stories could be told for the development of congressional liaison activities, White House responsibility for making domestic and national security policy, interest group staff work, and many others.

The Appointment Process

The Constitution gives the chief executive the power to appoint government workers, except as the power is limited by Congress. In the nineteenth century, dispensing patronage jobs helped the president cement relations with his party in Congress and the states. The steady expansion of the civil service during the twentieth century has removed most lower-grade positions from presidential control, but the numbers of political executives in Washington have grown dramatically, and presidential appointments have gained in importance what they have lost in overall extent. Today most of the appointments are for the several thousand or so political executive positions responsible for running the federal bureaucracy, the regulatory agencies, and the federal judiciary.[27]

Although Roosevelt distributed five or six times as many patronage positions as Ronald Reagan, no one on his staff in his first term had any special responsibility for screening and recommending appointments. Many people, of course, volunteered advice. Harry Hopkins, the czar of relief programs, helped deal with patronage matters, and Felix Frankfurter and Thomas Corcoran identified personnel for critical administrative positions.[28] But not until 1939, when James Rowe became the first assistant to the president, did Roosevelt assign an aide to be routinely responsible for presidential appointments. And Rowe's involvement was neither comprehensive nor exclusive.

Part of the reason is that many of Roosevelt's appointments were his in name only. The departments usually consulted directly with Democrats in Congress to award the least important positions. Professional positions, such as commissioners of the regulatory agencies, district attorneys, and state administrators of federal programs, required complex negotiations among the department with the position, the Democratic National Committee, senators from the state affected, and, frequently, interest groups. The president made the final decision, but these others created the short list and, for certain positions, exercised a veto. Roosevelt's mandate to Rowe was as much to adjudicate the frequent disputes as to advance the president's interest. When the principals agreed, the White House staff simply reported the result to the president for endorsement.

Rowe's contribution was to preserve for the president a more than pro forma role in appointments. He and other aides resisted the efforts of the Democratic National Committee to make the

27. Heclo, *A Government of Strangers*, pp. 58–67.

28. Dorsett, *Franklin D. Roosevelt and the City Bosses*; and Steven P. Erie, *Rainbow's End: Irish-Americans and the Dilemmas of Urban Machine Politics, 1840–1985* (University of California Press, 1988), pp. 128–39.

short list rather than merely to give political clearance to the president's tentative choices. They also forwarded irreconcilable appointment fights to the president and occasionally alerted him to agency choices of persons known to be unsympathetic to him. Frequently Rowe's efforts made him unpopular with politicians jealous of their long-held prerogatives.[29] Since many of them wielded enough clout to get into the Oval Office more easily than the White House assistants, they could often undo his efforts.

Neither Rowe nor Marvin McIntyre, a White House aide who joined him in clearing appointments in 1941, nor any other staffer routinely became involved in appointments of upper-level administrative executives (principally assistant and under secretaries) in the departments. This remained the preserve of the cabinet secretaries in private consultation with the president. Roosevelt valued Rowe's counsel and often acted on his advice, but the president's calculated disorderliness precluded all but the most desultory efforts at White House coordination of personnel recruitment. And although Roosevelt wanted to make the most of the political capital to be earned through smart appointments, any effort to give the president greater control over appointments would have been strenuously opposed within his party in Congress and around the country.

Harry Truman practiced more orderly administration than Roosevelt, which finally implemented the White House staff's original mandate to manage the flow of people and messages to and from the president. Truman's administrative style shows clearly in his designating assistant Donald Dawson an informal clearinghouse for political appointments. According to Dawson, even cabinet secretaries submitted the names of candidates for senior department appointments to him for political vetting before introducing them to Truman.[30] And while Appointments Secretary Matthew Connelly occasionally represented the patronage interest of the Democratic machines, presidential patronage and administrative appointments generally passed across Dawson's desk.

This arrangement appears to have worked well and certainly

29. DNC chairman Ed Flynn opposed Rowe's appointment as assistant attorney general in charge of patronage and legislative affairs for the Department of Justice. Rowe to Franklin D. Roosevelt, October 20, 1941, and Rowe to Flynn, October 25, 1941, Roosevelt Library.

30. Interview with Donald Dawson, March 30, 1988, Washington, D.C.

avoided the rivalry and rancor that had plagued Roosevelt's appointments. There are several reasons for this. The expansion of the civil service reduced the number of patronage appointments the White House could make. Politicians also appear to have been less persistent in pursuing appointments. DNC chairmen Robert Hannegan, Howard McGrath, and Bob Boyle did not press the party's interest over that of congressmen or the agencies as aggressively as did James Farley and Ed Flynn. And perhaps the party's naturally subordinate role to Congress and a rapidly professionalizing social service bureaucracy had preempted many of the patronage games popular in the 1930s.

At least as important, however, was the president's commitment to Dawson. Truman consistently turned direct appeals over to him, and the members of Congress, the national party, and even department secretaries came to appreciate that Dawson's recommendation carried great weight with the president. Significantly, Dawson and not the DNC kept the book that logged the patronage appointments granted to Democratic representatives and senators.[31]

Thus if Roosevelt frequently nurtured contention among competing claimants so that he could control the final decision and extract political advantage, Truman surrendered many of the potential political gains in favor of a more orderly process. While the president continued to make important appointments and could be acutely attentive to their political ramifications, the lesser but more voluminous choices were resolved through Dawson's recommendations.

This arrangement made the White House Office the forum where the patronage barons of the Democratic party played appointment politics. But valuable as Dawson's skills as an arbiter were, he did not attempt to promote the president's programs through political appointments. Procedures remained relatively primitive, mostly because the administration had no overarching selection policy, nor could it.[32] The arena may have shifted to the White House, but the appointments game remained largely in the hands of Democratic politicians in Congress and the party organizations.

31. Ibid.
32. G. Calvin Mackenzie, *The Politics of Presidential Appointments* (Free Press, 1981) p. 14.

Dawson wished otherwise, and he organized a task force that produced a book-length report, "The Best Brains," which proposed that the president create a data bank of talented potential appointees. The project was abandoned, however, when, under Truman's instruction, Dawson realized that the White House "had to be practical about presidential appointees. Use them for political advantage, use them to get the best people of your own party persuasion . . . and build up the party. And get people that were loyal—that was the first qualification; ability was second."[33]

Dwight Eisenhower's administration also maintained the status quo, even though the campaign had promised to end cronyism and streamline government. After twenty years in the wilderness, the Republican party now controlled federal patronage, and Congress and the state organizations wanted to cleanse the bureaucracy of Democrats and reward those who had been steadfast. Although Eisenhower at first appeared insensitive to these pent-up demands, after consulting with Senator Robert Taft and others he agreed to follow tradition.

Others on Eisenhower's staff had a more sophisticated appreciation of the political advantages that controlling appointments conferred. During the transition, Herbert Brownell, former chairman of the Republican National Committee and subsequently Eisenhower's attorney general, made strategic appointments to incorporate the Dewey wing of the party into the administration. Once the term began, Charles F. Willis, Jr., assistant to Chief of Staff Sherman Adams, handled both political executive and patronage appointments. Although Willis and his staff occupied a lofty position in the White House Office, they did little more than quench the Republican congressmen's thirst for patronage. Systematic recruitment of loyalists was tried, but Operation People's Mandate, as the effort was called, aroused such controversy when it began tampering with the independence of civil service positions that the enterprise was quickly abandoned.[34] By the end of the administration, staff clearance of appointments had settled into an established, perfunctory routine.

Inclined neither to seize control of appointments nor to exploit Republican politicians' claims to the president's advantage, the

33. Dawson interview.

34. Laurin L. Henry, *Presidential Transitions* (Brookings, 1960), pp. 676–80.

Eisenhower White House did little more than formalize further the traditional process. Requests were submitted and proposed appointments were cleared by means of orderly, well-delineated guidelines.[35] Eisenhower appears rarely to have become involved in appointments.

The vision of Dawson's "Best Brains" entered presidential practice in John Kennedy's administration. For such a consequential innovation, staff responsibility for identifying candidates occurred casually, even inadvertently. It was not born of dissatisfaction with the service the president was receiving from his political executives, although Kennedy was no different from any other president in complaining about the unresponsiveness in the departments. Nor is there any evidence that the White House was trying to wrest control of appointments from party or Congress. Instead, the president was cultivating the goodwill of congressional Democrats and working harmoniously with the national party apparatus. In fact, the reform appears to have arisen more as an afterthought.

Six months into Kennedy's term, the White House senior staff realized that filling vacancies would be a continuing activity. Because no one was much interested in clearing appointments, Ralph Dungan, who had informally taken on the responsibility, recruited Harvard professor Dan Fenn to set up an office for selection. "We started with nothing really," Fenn recalled, "no charter, no discussions with [Kenneth] O'Donnell or Dungan or with the President about what this thing was supposed to do or how it was supposed to function. . . . They just wanted some recruiting done."[36] Given a free hand, and unsophisticated in Washington ways, Fenn developed a plan for the staff to identify candidates who had the technical expertise rather than political assets. Instead of state parties and congressional staffs, the hunting grounds became universities, think tanks, and the career federal service. The staff's function was clearly important: one study found that more than half of Kennedy's appointees were initially contacted by someone in the White

35. For example, whereas Truman's staff informally solicited the FBI to provide security clearances, Eisenhower's staff made such clearances standard procedure. Mackenzie, *Politics of Presidential Appointments*, pp. 14–21.

36. National Academy of Public Administration, "Recruiting Presidential Appointees: A Conference of Former Presidential Personnel Assistants" (Washington, D.C.: NAPA, 1985), p. 3.

House Office, compared with fewer than a quarter for Kennedy's predecessors.[37]

Why this expansion of the president's authority did not generate howls of protest from Congress and the Democratic party is not altogether clear. Fenn's low profile and his standard reassurance to outsiders that his was not a "job shop" may have initially allayed suspicions. He also began work after the transition appointments had been made and the Democratic faithful had recaptured most of the plums in the executive agencies. Then too, the demand for positions may have been at a low ebb during the early 1960s: few field offices remained exempt from civil service, and these jobs had traditionally been more valued for sustaining the local party than those located in Washington. Dungan and Fenn also limited White House involvement to the most important executive appointments, and because these were fewer than they would be after the creation of the Senior Executive Service in the late 1970s, Kennedy's staff may have received fewer candidates than their counterparts in subsequent administrations. These reasons aside, this innovation would never have been tolerated had patronage not lost its value as the currency of support.

Clearly, Fenn's operation set important precedents. Limited in scope and staff and lacking grand aspirations, however, its innovations were more procedural than substantive. The full transformation of personnel selection from an appurtenance of party politics to a centralized management device was left for subsequent presidents to discover.

After his election in 1964, Lyndon Johnson faced a recruitment task comparable to that of a new president. Many holdovers from the Kennedy administration were anxious to leave, and others were deemed less necessary to the president now that he had been elected in his own right. Johnson also knew that he would soon need special recruits to implement the Great Society programs. Rather than return to arrangements that placed a premium on political accommodation, he expanded Kennedy's personnel operation. He enlisted John Macy, the head of the Civil Service Commission, to oversee White House recruitment and directed him to canvass universities and the career government service for the ex-

37. Dean E. Mann and Jameson W. Doig, *The Assistant Secretaries: Problems and Processes of Appointment* (Brookings, 1965).

perts he needed. "Do not worry about politics," he instructed Macy; others in the White House would concern themselves with those matters. Thus began the most comprehensive presidential talent search to date. Within a year or so, Macy had accumulated more than 30,000 names of potential appointees for about 600 offices.[38]

Johnson invested more than his predecessors in establishing personnel recruitment as a White House routine. He insisted that nominations for all but the highest positions pass through Macy's office.[39] He also insulated Macy from political pressure by having him run the operation from his office at the Civil Service Commission. The system seemed to work, although from time to time assistants who had to clear Macy's recommendations with party politicians would carp about his political naiveté or what they viewed as his meddling in politically sensitive matters. Macy recalled White House staffers in less than nostalgic terms: "Each one of those power-seekers really feels he's in charge of getting the people in his particular program area."[40] The creation of a formal White House unit for presidential appointments would await the Nixon administration. Johnson prepared the way, however, by recruiting a professional, insulating him from intrusion by others on the staff, and elevating his work to central importance in staffing the administration.

Richard Nixon began without a personnel strategy, and in an early cabinet meeting, becoming caught up in his own rhetoric, he ceded to his secretaries the prerogative to fill their departmental positions. Ability, not loyalty to the administration, he advised them, should be the primary criterion in hiring. But by the time the meeting was over he confided to an aide, "I have just made a big mistake."[41]

In the absence of a plan that would quickly correct this error, the White House staff was relegated to processing a deluge of nominees from Congress and the bureaucracy. Peter Flanigan and his

38. Transcript, John W. Macy oral history interview, tape 3, pp. 8–14, Johnson Library.

39. Richard L. Schott and Dagmar S. Hamilton, *People, Positions, and Power: The Political Appointments of Lyndon Johnson* (University of Chicago Press, 1983), pp. 22–26.

40. NAPA, "Recruiting Presidential Appointees," p. 42.

41. Rowland Evans, Jr., and Robert D. Novak, *Nixon in the White House: The Frustration of Power* (Random House, 1971), p. 66.

assistant, Harry Fleming, went through the motions of assembling a talent bank, but under these arrangements, it had little purpose. Clearance rather than recruitment became the order of the day.

Within six months, the president and his senior aides had become frustrated with the White House's limited role. They frequently found themselves having to spend time to prevent some appointments, such as those opposed by an important constituency that appealed directly to the White House. In the fall of 1970 Chief of Staff H. R. Haldeman invited Frederic Malek, who as undersecretary at Health, Education, and Welfare had helped purge administrators unsympathetic to the president's social policies, to propose alternative arrangements. After several months Malek presented a highly critical report, charging that "Presidential directives have not been carried out, and counter-productive efforts have taken place within a number of Departments."[42] He proposed creating a multidivisional White House personnel office that would have exclusive jurisdiction over appointments. Nixon liked his ideas, and by year's end Malek had moved into the White House.

Within his new office Malek established subunits responsible for recruiting and for drafting procedures to evaluate management. The recruiting unit was divided into one group charged with identifying and clearing the best political appointments and a second that searched for talent loyal to the president. Frequently these groups conducted searches for the same slot and forwarded their recommendations to the president.[43] Malek also brought in private management consultants, one of whom, Pendleton James, would later head Reagan's personnel operation. Within a short time about thirty staff members had created an office that "was more specialized, more centralized, and more professional than any of its predecessors."[44]

For all it sought, the Personnel Office initially stayed clear of two politically sensitive activities: appointments to supergrade and

42. "Management of Non-Career Personnel: Recommendations for Improvement" (December 18, 1970), pp. 30–31, cited in Mackenzie, *Politics of Presidential Appointments*, p. 53.

43. Malek added that generally the substantive nominee got the appointment, but frequently when a strong political appointment was identified, he would be checked out and approved by those recruiters concerned exclusively with professional standards. NAPA, "Recruiting Presidential Appointees," pp. 9–10.

44. Mackenzie, *Politics of Presidential Appointments*, pp. 49–50.

similarly exempted positions and a purge of current appointees selected under the earlier system. Both were first orders of business to be taken up in the second term. Within days of Nixon's reelection, the office sent out evaluation forms for all presidential appointees, putting them on notice that they might be asked to resign. This was the first phase of a strategy to take control of the departments through recruitment, retention, and promotion. These unprecedented efforts took staff; by the end of 1972 the personnel staff reached fifty-two and would grow yet larger. The second phase was to be a year-long effort to centralize recruitment of lower-level executives and establish control over agencies by placing Nixon loyalists in their personnel offices and at other pressure points. The third phase, to begin in 1974, was to consolidate control and to place people who had been politically helpful.[45]

Execution fell far short of White House expectations, however, because the president's goals were contrary to those of the bureaucracy, the congressional committees that oversaw it, and clientele groups that had been achieving representation in the agencies. Overly aggressive staff generated bad publicity when they ran afoul of civil service regulations or appeared callous about careers. Then the distractions of Watergate ended any designs for running the bureaucracy from the White House. Still, presidential appointments that had once been determined through negotiating among fragmented institutions had now become a resource that a president could use unilaterally to expand his control over the operations of government.

In the aftermath of Watergate, Presidents Ford and Carter assumed less aggressive postures, but, significantly, neither wholly abandoned Nixon's innovations. Ford pared the personnel staff to thirty-five people and renamed the office. Outside recruiters were replaced by those with government experience who would presumably be more politically sensitive. The administration also invited representatives from the agencies to join White House staff in interviewing potential appointees. But if the Ford White House lowered its sights, it did not surrender the president's prerogative to recruit loyalists. This was left to Jimmy Carter.

Despite auspicious signs—the staff had started to inventory talent before the election—the Carter administration never ade-

45. Memo, Jerry Jones to H. R. Haldeman, March 7, 1973, Nixon collection, National Archives.

quately outlined a White House role in presidential appointments. An early jurisdictional battle among the senior staff sidetracked advanced planning for a comprehensive talent search. The White House was also unprepared for the volume of requests from the Democrats in Congress, who had been denied access to federal appointments for eight years. Neither problem would have been too serious had President Carter been committed to a centralized personnel strategy. But he was not. Indeed, within weeks after the inauguration, Washington insiders realized that the president did not much care who occupied the agency posts. One tell-tale sign was that when the White House staff and a cabinet secretary disagreed over a particular appointment, the secretary usually prevailed. Each loss, of course, only emboldened the cabinet secretaries and reduced the staff's importance.

The result was reminiscent of Nixon's inadvertent early abandonment of the presidential prerogative.[46] Like Nixon, by midterm Carter had become disillusioned with the results. In 1978 Arnie Miller joined the president's staff to ensure a stronger presidential hand in appointments. Miller compiled a data bank of potential appointees, hired one of Malek's assistants, and borrowed elements of Nixon's controversial personnel policies.[47]

Ronald Reagan's transition team behaved as though it had learned from the mistakes of the Nixon and Carter administrations. Although Reagan gave lip service to the tradition of cabinet government, he abandoned any pretense of returning to it well before the inauguration. The transition staff decided at the outset that appointments would be a jealously guarded prerogative of the White House Office, and that meant for the first time appointments at every rank, from the cabinet secretary down to the 2,500 schedule C and other noncareer administrative positions. Even the

46. So too was Stuart Eizenstat's remark, "That's the whole ball game." James P. Pfiffner, *The Strategic Presidency: Hitting the Ground Running* (Chicago: Dorsey Press, 1988), p. 83. Personnel director Arnie Miller concurs that Carter's early approach was a failure. "He tried to decentralize personnel. He tried to cut back on the size of the Presidential Personnel Office staff. He bumbled it. Midway through his presidency, he suddenly realized that he had given away the store." Miller then reflected, "The expectations are still there on a President." NAPA, "Recruiting Presidential Appointees," p. 39.

47. But gaining control over the process proved difficult. "Even in our own office," Miller recalled, "someone else was calling with a Schedule C recommendation who had no business making that recommendation. It jeopardized our own credibility." NAPA, "Recruiting Presidential Appointees," p. 10.

selection of federal appeals court judges, traditionally the responsibility of the Justice Department, was moved into the White House. According to Pendleton James, Reagan's first personnel director,

> the Cabinet officers and major agency heads were advised prior to their accepting the position . . . that there would be an organization in the White House that would make its voice heard on the appointments and, if you had somebody that you wanted in an office, it would have to go through the White House Presidential Personnel Office because everything in the appointment process went into the Oval Office through the Presidential Personnel Office. We clearly established control at the beginning.[48]

Not surprisingly, given the new mandate, the size of the personnel office more than doubled. But as important as these resources were, they would have counted for little had President Reagan not consistently displayed a keen interest in his staff's progress toward filling key department positions. By appointing James to the highest staff rank, assistant to the president, and moving the personnel office into the west wing of the White House, the president strengthened his personnel director's hand in dealing with the departments.

James generally followed Malek's lead and later credited him with making the breakthrough in organizing recruitment. While hiring loyalist managers was the most important responsibility, political approval was required. But, in a new twist, political clearance now was achieved within the White House. The Congressional Liaison Office, the domestic policy adviser, the national security adviser, and the Political Affairs Office, as well as each of the governing troika of James Baker, Michael Deaver, and Edwin Meese, were given an opportunity to approve candidates. These offices certainly checked with politicians whose opinions needed to be taken into account, but the White House staff now firmly controlled the process.

President Reagan's innovation did not require a dramatic departure from past personnel practices. He could enlist the White House staff because Truman had made political clearance a task of his staff and because Kennedy's staff had focused on recruitment

---

48. Ibid., p. 11.

instead of clearance. Johnson too had contributed by employing Macy's office to identify nominees who would not be beholden to other politicians. And Nixon allocated a sizable staff and created the White House Personnel Office to supervise selection. Reagan's innovations were but the culminating increments of an evolution long under way.

The Growth of Communications

Because cultivating popular support for the president's programs is fundamental to democratic leadership, every president's staff has at some point been put to work making phone calls to friendly journalists, doing advance work for presidential travel, writing speeches, monitoring public opinion polls, or performing the myriad other activities designed to bolster the president's image with the American public. Historically, in-house public relations arose as the president turned his attention to winning reelection. Only in the past two decades, however, have presidents employed professionals in the White House to pursue public relations campaigns to promote their policies in Washington.

For many years some public relations work was performed by the presidential press secretary. Early in the twentieth century, the president discovered that if he wanted to speak to the American public, he would have to do so through correspondents based in Washington.[49] To help attend to their needs, Franklin Roosevelt designated Stephen Early as the first press secretary. Since then the press secretary's office has expanded at a faster pace than the overall staff. One obvious reason has been the emergence of radio and television. Cozy, unrecorded press conferences with give and take between the president and the reporters and casual background briefings by the press secretary were the daily bread of print journalists. They did not, however, nourish broadcast journalists, who worked to a different deadline and needed live feeds or film. These different needs and the new opportunities provided presidents by television led to the creation of a second White House media office in the late 1960s.

Before then there were occasional glimpses of the future. Harry Truman wanted to appoint a radio executive as his press secretary

49. This is described more fully in Kernell, *Going Public,* pp. 55–68. Also see Leo Rosten, *The Washington Correspondents* (Harcourt Brace Jovanovich, 1937); and James E. Pollard, *The Presidents and the Press* (Macmillan, 1947).

after Early's departure, but the uproar from correspondents quickly changed his mind. Eisenhower's press secretary James Hagerty had once waxed enthusiastically of having a weekly television show for President Eisenhower, but slowly the idea fell by the wayside.[50] His understandable preoccupation with the White House press corps, however, did not prevent him from keeping close tabs on Howard Pyle, who had been brought into the administration to help with publicity.[51] Clearly, direct nationwide public relations remained subordinate to press relations within Washington. Bill Moyers, who served as Johnson's press secretary from 1965 until 1967, wrote numerous proposals outlining how the administration could use public relations to counter an increasingly hostile press treatment of the president's Vietnam policies. His ideas included many of those that would be implemented in the next administration.[52]

Suffering from a credibility gap, Johnson is known to have wanted the help of some "public relations genius." When longtime journalist and NBC executive Robert Kintner joined the White House staff, many thought this would be his job. He advised the president on how to handle columnists, periodically urged him to change his media strategy, and made some modest revisions in the flow of public relations activities out of the White House.[53] But despite propitious circumstances, splitting public relations from press relations was apparently never seriously contemplated. Perhaps Kintner was no match for Moyers. Or perhaps, as Joseph Laitin, a former Johnson aide, has suggested, the president trusted none of his aides sufficiently to enshrine one as public relations czar.[54]

After experimenting briefly with the arrangements of his predecessors, President Nixon decided that the press secretary was so busy responding to the Washington press corps that he could not

50. James C. Hagerty, *The Diary of James C. Hagerty: Eisenhower in Mid-Course, 1954–1955,* ed. Robert H. Ferrell (Indiana University Press, 1983).

51. Michael B. Grossman and Martha J. Kumar, *Portraying the President: The White House and the News Media* (John Hopkins University Press, 1981), p. 97.

52. Bill Moyers to President Johnson, June 6, 1966, Johnson Library.

53. Instances are reported by Larry Berman in "Johnson and the White House Staff," in Robert A. Divine, ed., *The Johnson Years, Volume One: Foreign Policy, The Great Society, and the White House* (University Press of Kansas, 1981), pp. 187–213. Also see Robert Kintner to Bill Moyers, April 8, 1966, Johnson Library.

54. Grossman and Kumar, *Portraying the President,* p. 97.

help the president attract more sympathetic coverage in the rest of the country. Nixon needed an adviser who commanded a broader view of his publicity needs and someone who had ties with the non-Washington press. So in 1969 he hired Herbert Klein, director of the American Society of Newspaper Editors, to head a new Office of Communications.

Early in his tenure, Klein proposed several ways his office could make a special contribution. It could "develop the means of depicting pictorially the programs of the Administration as seen on television." Radio, he noted, was an "almost untouched area . . . which has a growing audience particularly in news." He also believed the office could arrange more briefing sessions for broadcast journalists, as well as newspaper editors in "key areas across the country" and could "work with each of the departments of government in coordinating and augmenting their public relations efforts."[55] Subsequent administrations have weighted these activities differently and have added others, but Klein had clearly identified what would become the primary missions of the office.

Although a long-time friend of Nixon, Klein was an outsider to the senior aides. Known for his close ties to the newspaper industry, he was never fully accepted into Nixon's inner circle. And perhaps worse, he had an insufficiently low regard for the press. He actually set up the office to help journalists and increase the quality of information about the administration disseminated to the news media around the country.[56] He refused to send out stories he considered propaganda, and when the administration's press relations deteriorated, he refused to break off his contacts.

Suspicious of Klein's loyalties, Haldeman appointed his own aide, Jeb Stuart Magruder, as assistant communications director. Thus began a rivalry so antagonistic that it continued after the men left office. While Klein sought to coordinate news releases from the agencies, Magruder orchestrated their public statements to boost the administration. While Klein tried to cooperate with the press, Magruder devised plans to discredit NBC's David Brinkley. Only when Charles Colson attempted to take over the Communications Office as a post from which he could bash the press did the two

55. Herbert G. Klein, Memorandum for the President, October 9, 1969, Nixon collection, National Archives.

56. For instance, he helped journalists file requests under the Freedom of Information Act. Herbert G. Klein, *Making it Perfectly Clear* (Doubleday, 1980), p. 186.

cooperate.[57] But in the end, the hardliners won out. Klein "became a virtual figurehead. Magruder—dutifully taking his cues from Haldeman—was the de facto director." In 1973 Klein left and was replaced by fellow staff member Ken Clawson, "a hardliner himself, who took his cues from Colson."[58]

This internal combat and its subsequent association with Watergate rocked the office to its foundation. Yet in one guise or another, every subsequent president has found it necessary to designate someone to perform the kinds of services described in Klein's memo. President Ford dismissed Clawson and subordinated the office to the Press Secretary's Office under Ron Nessen. Gerald Warren, assistant press secretary in the Nixon White House, was selected to head the unit, and to avoid the politically charged title of communications director, he was given the convoluted one of deputy press secretary for information liaison. For the next two years the office limited itself to low-profile activities such as feeding stories to the non-Washington press and arranging interviews between correspondents and administration officials.

In 1976 Ford's chief of staff, Richard Cheney, rejuvenated the Communications Office to put the White House on a campaign footing. Speechwriter David Gergen was appointed head of an informal communications group to coordinate the statements of the various White House units and presidential agencies and to promote favorable images of the president. The separate Office of Communications was restored and incorporated speechwriting, research, and a television office. Cheney, like Haldeman before him, used the office to control the flow of information from the White House.[59]

The Carter administration rechristened the Office of Communications the Media Liaison Office and subordinated it once again to the press secretary's office. But in 1978, with his public and congressional support in disarray, Carter recruited his former campaign adviser, Gerald Rafshoon, to solve his communication problems. Media Liaison remained under the press secretary, but a new

57. Klein, *Making it Perfectly Clear*; and Jeb Stuart Magruder, *An American Life: One Man's Road to Watergate* (Antheneum, 1974).

58. John A. Maltese, "The Office of Communications: Its Functional Evolution (1969–1974)" (Master's thesis, Johns Hopkins University, 1985).

59. John A. Maltese, "The White House Office of Communication: Channeling Information in the Executive Branch," paper prepared for the 1988 Midwestern Political Science Association meeting, p. 34.

Communications Office was quickly assembled from existing units to oversee speechwriting and media advance work. As a long-standing confidant of the president, Rafshoon wielded the authority necessary to make coordination work. Working closely with Press Secretary Jody Powell, he succeeded more than any of his predecessors in orchestrating the administration's public relations.[60]

With the arrival of Ronald Reagan, the "Great Communicator," the office's position became secure. James Baker's staff director, David Gergen, was appointed assistant to the president for communications, thus allowing the heads of speechwriting, the press office, and communications to report directly to the same person. Reflecting its importance to Reagan, the Communications Office was subdivided into a White House television office for arranging the president's television appearances, a speaker's bureau for scheduling appearances of administration officials, and a research and writing section for preparing fact sheets and briefing the president for press conferences.[61] In a repetition of the emerging pattern, control of communications gradually gravitated to the senior staff. In early 1984, with the election approaching, Gergen resigned and troika member Mike Deaver assumed full operational control of the White House's public relations.

The importance of public relations was confirmed in that each of the four chiefs of staff who served Reagan picked his own director of communications. One of Donald Regan's first acts was to appoint Patrick Buchanan. Where Gergen and his boss Baker had viewed the office's duties as coordinating public activities and generating goodwill within the news industry, Buchanan made it a focal point and ultimately a lightning rod for the administration. "Let Reagan be Reagan," was to be the leitmotif of this second, more conservative Reagan regime, and Buchanan sounded the theme as loudly as anyone. The directorship was being transformed from an administrative to a policymaking position. Within a brief time, he emerged as the administration's spokesman for the conservative movement. Eventually, Buchanan's ambitions outgrew the office, and in the spring of 1987 he resigned, saying that he could better promote conservative causes from outside the

---

60. Grossman and Kumar, *Portraying the President,* pp. 98–99.

61. Dom Bonafede, "The Selling of the Executive Branch—Public Information or Promotion?" *National Journal,* vol. 13 (June 27, 1981), pp. 1153–57.

White House, and began taking soundings of his support for the Republican nomination for the presidency.[62]

Reagan's third chief, Howard Baker, immediately chose former Senate aide Thomas Griscom as the new communications director.[63] Together they took on the task of conciliating Congress and others about the involvement of Reagan and his staff in the Iran-contra scandal. Griscom returned the position to its managerial function. Still, the directorship retained its importance. When, in Reagan's words, "rhetoric is policy," the aide who controls the flow of presidential messages to the country shapes the course of policy discussion.

Both Johnson's reluctance to entrust public relations to an aide and the subsequent politicization of the communications director's role illustrate how vital this activity has become to modern presidential leadership. Its policy implications are too important for it to be consigned to the lower reaches of the line staff, and yet it is a job that requires a great deal of routine work performed with a high level of competence. The communications director should both understand the techniques of public relations and appreciate the needs and practices of those in the media whose favor the president seeks to curry. Moreover, the communications director must frequently coordinate the activities of other administration officials in the White House and in the executive departments. They will naturally be inclined to view him as overstepping his authority. To succeed, then, the director needs the level of support from the president that is normally associated with being a member of the upper-tier senior staff. Thus the communications director occupies an ambivalent status in the White House Office. He needs to be firmly footed on both tiers of the organization and as a consequence sometimes finds himself on shaky ground on one or the other.

While the rising importance of public relations politicized the role of the director within the staff, it guaranteed that the routines

62. On the disagreement between Regan and Buchanan, see "Reagan's Speechwriter Says He Was Dismissed in Dispute," *New York Times*, June 10, 1986, p. A20. Buchanan's resignation is reported in James R. Dickenson, "White House Communications Aide Buchanan Resigns," *Washington Post*, February 4, 1987, p. A8.

63. The rising status of the communications director is indicated by Griscom's willingness to accept the post when the position he wanted, deputy chief of staff, had been offered to someone else. Steven V. Roberts, "President Names Tennessean as Director of Communications," *New York Times*, April 2, 1987, p. B10.

of communications would continue to flourish. In 1969, Klein had begun modestly with four aides and an ill-defined mandate to cultivate the non-Washington press. By 1988, the office contained a sizable staff supervising five other units, two of which did not even exist in the highly rationalized Nixon White House Office.[64]

Commonalities of Line Staff Development

In the Reagan administration, personnel and public relations became fully developed operations and were widely predicted to become models for his successors. Each began years earlier as incidental activities of a few aides and subsequently showed the same development tendencies. As centralized personnel selection and communications became more important to their leadership, presidents recruited people with backgrounds in these fields. In neither cases did the first expert brought into the White House—Truman's Dawson in personnel and Johnson's Kintner in communications—occupy a fully specialized role. The first two aides to be given fixed responsibilities were John Macy in personnel and Herbert Klein in communications. Under President Nixon, both these line activities were for the first time formally designated as separate organizational subunits of the White House Office. Since then, they have steadily expanded in size and function to the extent that the senior aides who preside over the personnel and communications offices are commonly referred to as czars.

A superficial reading of these histories might suggest that the emergence of routines has less to do with the leadership strategies of presidents than with the steady expansion of function and accretion of structure that typify growth within organizations. The incremental development of staff structure should not conceal its true cause: the strategic behavior of presidents. A principle of political physics is at work. The more aggressively a president probes the frontier of his control, the greater the resistance he encounters. Those politicians whose prerogatives are threatened may themselves react aggressively and seek to pare back the president's authority. Minor departures from current baselines that are consis-

---

64. They are the Office of Media Relations and the Office of Public Affairs. The other three offices under the Communications umbrella are speechwriting, scheduling, and advance planning. Maltese, "White House Office of Communications," app.

tent with precedents may, by contrast, accomplish the same purposes without triggering resistance.

The comparative advantage of incrementalist strategies can be found in the history of staff development. When presidents have sought new institutional resources requiring statutory authority, they have frequently been rebuffed.[65] Chilly congressional receptions met proposals by various task forces and commissions to strengthen presidential staff. But until recent times, by contrast, the ancient practice of detailing went almost unnoticed.

One finds incrementalism as well in advances in presidential public relations. President-elect Kennedy announced that he would conduct live televised news conferences and thereby gained a means for speaking directly to the American public. While seeming to preserve the special access of Washington correspondents to the president, he transformed the press conference.[66] When presidents have sought to increase dramatically their access to prime-time television, they have occasionally been challenged by network executives.[67] Similarly, when the national networks denied airtime to President Reagan in 1987, chief of staff Howard Baker argued vigorously that the denial violated previous understandings about the president's access to television.[68]

Instances of building on precedents to increase the president's control over personnel recruitment are also plentiful. When Nix-

65. A Democratic Congress refused to go along with the Brownlow commission's recommendations that the Civil Service Commission be installed in the new Executive Office of the President. For the congressional politics of the enactment of the Brownlow proposals, see Peri E. Arnold, *Making the Managerial Presidency: Comprehensive Reorganization Planning, 1905–1980* (Princeton University Press, 1986), pp. 107–15. A decade later, President Truman had designs on converting the Office of War Mobilization and Reconversion to a national planning agency, but when he was advised that the new Republican Congress would never agree, he quietly moved its director John Steelman and much of his staff into the White House. Herman Miles Somers, *Presidential Agency, OWMR: The Office of War Mobilization and Reconversion* (Harvard University Press, 1950), pp. 95–101.

66. Kernell, *Going Public*, pp. 104–05.

67. When this happened to the Nixon White House, it responded by arguing that its requests were not out of line with the time the networks had given its predecessors. Ibid., pp. 102–04.

68. The networks responded that the president had not submitted a formal request but had simply announced he would be speaking on contra aid "if cameras wanted to attend." James Gerstenzang and Josh Getlin, "Reagan Offers New Contra Aid Compromise," *Los Angeles Times*, February 3, 1988; and Eleanor Randolph, "Reagan's Preemptive Strikeout," *Washington Post*, February 3, 1988, p. C1.

on's staff codified recruitment procedures in a White House manual for political executives early in the president's second term, every technique, including those for circumventing civil service rules, cited as precedent the practices of past presidents. Yet never before had these practices been formed into a code of conduct sanctioned by the White House. The difference between Nixon's operation and what had preceded it was the difference between "organized and unorganized crime."[69]

Expanding the base and enlisting precedents are venerable strategies to allow the president to reach some new point without disrupting current sensibilities or arousing opposition. But they do so by encouraging presidential self-restraint. The result is what I have described in the case studies: the gradual, nearly continuous expansion of staff responsibilities and institutional resources—strategically inspired and environmentally conditioned.

Incrementalism may have provided the tactics of change, but to understand the motivation and direction, one must delve elsewhere. Presidents have chosen to centralize functions in the White House because the resources (potential benefits) and leverage (potential costs) of those politicians whose compliance the president traditionally needed have eroded. For example, when Dawson proposed the concept of a talent bank to Truman, the benefits of patronage and the costs of violating other politicians' expectations made it an impractical idea. Truman felt he could not afford to upset politicians whose support was needed.[70]

Lyndon Johnson decided differently, but he appears to have arrived at his choice employing much the same calculus: balancing the loyalty of executives with few political assets versus the resourcefulness but independence of those with strong political connections. Johnson emphasized to Macy that he wanted loyalty most, and that career civil servants and university professors, rather than local politicians or congressional staffs, were to be the source, because whatever advantage to be had from appointing Washington politicians would be outweighed by the costs of their divided loyalties.[71] So Johnson, the protegé of Franklin Roosevelt

69. Heclo, *Government of Strangers*, p. 74.

70. Dawson interview.

71. And in many instances civil servants and academics had the technical competence he wanted for his Great Society programs. Interview with John Macy, July 27, 1983, Washington, D.C.

and as politically acute, made a decision his mentor would have shunned.[72]

What about politics had altered the strategy for making appointments? First, appointments had declined as the currency of politics. The continued extension of the civil service had greatly depleted the availability of lower-level patronage positions. And although the emergence of a large bureaucracy administering federal social policies had generated many more executive positions in Washington, these offices were less valuable to congressmen trying to shore up local campaign organizations and demanded a level of technical or managerial competence that was exceptional for the political appointments of an earlier era.

Second, the traditional claimants had either disappeared or their needs had changed in ways that made patronage less important. The state and national party apparatus had so atrophied that it played little part in identifying or clearing appointments. With great effort James Rowe fended off assertions of rights by DNC chairmen James Farley and Ed Flynn to preserve an independent role for President Roosevelt. But now presidents occasionally explore ways to invigorate the formal party apparatus in an effort to rekindle a party feeling on which they might then draw.

Members of Congress no longer need patronage the way they once did. In an age of television advertising, professional phone banks, and targeted mail, campaigns are less labor intensive. Money suffices. And staffs have grown to such an extent that congressman have been able to outfit a permanent campaign organization under the guise of district offices.

These and other changes, gradual as they have been, have given presidents the latitude to select political executives according to their technical expertise and loyalty. The evolution of the White House staff's role in recruitment reflects this transformation of the political landscape.

The same holds true for White House communications. More

72. Symbolic of the political transformation were the efforts of James Rowe to educate John Macy in the kinds of men and women who would serve the president well. Good Democrats, particularly Washington lawyers with strong associations throughout the party, were being overlooked in favor of bureaucrats. How, Rowe questioned at one point, would they help Johnson pull the party together for the 1968 election? Exasperated, Rowe finally turned to his friend Johnson who told him to "lay off Macy." His talent search was going precisely the way he wanted. Macy interview.

than any other president, Ronald Reagan sought to mobilize public support for himself and his policies in Washington; and his success was unparalleled. But his record was the culmination of a long process; every president since Hoover has incorporated ever greater doses of public relations into his leadership strategy. However measured—political travel outside of Washington, speeches to particular constituencies, appearances at photogenic gatherings—presidents have increasingly resorted to public relations to improve their chances of success in Washington.[73]

The growth of these public activities was made possible by technological advances. Instead of arduous treks across America by rail, such as President Wilson's ill-fated attempt to generate popular support for joining the League of Nations, air travel allows the president to deliver an address to an important constituency in Los Angeles and return to Washington the same day. Presidents are more inclined to take their case to the people because it is much easier to do so. Again, before radio, presidents could appeal to the country only through highly mediated news reporting and movie newsreels. Not until Franklin Roosevelt delivered his famous fireside chats was any president able fully to convert his status as a national representative into a compelling resource for pressuring Congress and the bureaucracy. The omnipresence of television has made "going public" a vital ingredient in modern presidential leadership.

Technological advances are, however, only half the story. For the increased use of technology to be worthwhile, those whom the president seeks to influence must be vulnerable to appeals for public support. If leadership could be maintained only through bargaining and compromise, a public appeal would be harmful. A public relations campaign introduces an element of pressure when negotiators are supposed to be searching for mutual accommodation. It commits the president to a position, making it awkward for him to come away from the bargaining table with less than he wanted. Finally, by appealing to the public to call, write and send Mailgrams, the president undermines other politicians' claims to represent the interests of their constituencies. Consider the bemusement of a congressional leader who returns to the Hill after a strategy lunch at the White House, only to hear the president on

73. On each dimension, a steady growth rate has been under way since Hoover. See Kernell, *Going Public*, pp. 83–110, especially pp. 86, 94, 97.

the radio exhorting the American public to pressure their representatives to accept his legislative program. When Roosevelt actually did something like that in attempting to push his plans for expanding the Supreme Court, he suffered the worst legislative defeat of his thirteen years in the White House.

Washington is a more individualistic community today than in Roosevelt's time.[74] The growth of the modern welfare state has created larger, more diverse constituencies that are highly attuned to and represented in Washington decisionmaking. Modern communications has made ordinary citizens more familiar with the actions of their representatives, and has made the representatives more sensitive to the opinions of their voters. Consequently, the media has become a far more prominent force in Washington politics, especially as political parties have lost their importance in guiding voters and aggregating disparate constituency interests.

These long-term trends have created Washington politicians who are less willing to subordinate individual prerogatives to the collective needs of their institutions. They are more short-sighted, less willing to defer immediate benefits for long-term investments in coalition building. One result is that would-be leaders have greater difficulty attracting followers. Presidents find fewer politicians who will serve as potential coalition partners. In the absence of leaders, presidents have to engage many more trading partners, unsure as they do so that these politicians can or will deliver their end of the bargain. Weakening party ties have further eroded the affinities that traditionally made bargaining easier and occasionally unnecessary. Increasingly presidents have found comparative economy in giving up bargaining and working instead on politicians' preferences en masse. Public relations then substitutes for negotiation with political leaders.

The Emergence of White House Managers

The White House is the president's workplace. Some presidents work well with many assistants; others prefer to work intimately with only two or three. Some prefer formal and highly structured

74. For a good impression of the changing political relations in Washington, compare Douglass Cater, *Power in Washington: A Critical Look at Today's Struggle to Govern the Nation's Capital* (Random House, 1964); and Hedrick Smith, *The Power Game: How Washington Works* (Random House, 1988).

staffs; others like to mix up assignments and have no fixed schedule for staff meetings. These work habits largely determine the organization and responsibilities of the senior staff, the White House managers.

Yet the special demands on coordination made by the growing size and complexity of the White House staff suggest that the president's choices in these matters will not be totally free.[75] What are the implications for the senior staff of the presidential strategy of centralization and the structure it begets? Coping with a large, complex organization involves more than fine tuning for maximum efficiency. In the absence of coordination, not only will some tasks fail to be performed while others will be unnecessarily duplicated, but also the organization will be rife with personal disputes and battles over jurisdiction.

Organizations need policing. The more complex the organization, the greater the problem posed by the cover of anonymity. And staffs with high turnover, such as the president's, will have the most serious problems, since its members have little stake in the integrity of procedures but may have a great stake in policy decisions. Hence they find themselves exploiting or even sacrificing procedural integrity to advocate certain policies. This divergence of interests is one reason the White House Office has become so notorious for the leaks and infighting that frustrate the best efforts of every president.

Much of the work senior managers do is to relieve the president from coordination qua policing. President Ford's first chief of staff, Donald Rumsfeld, commented that the chief of staff was always "heaving his body" between White House groups to make sure that the process worked.[76] Similarly, Michael Deaver, one of Ronald Reagan's first-term senior managers, described his role as the "protector" of the president. "Everybody who runs a department within the White House has a constituency," he explained. "And they . . . want to get those people off their backs, so they dump them on us in the scheduling office in hopes that the president will take care of it."[77]

75. Herbert A. Simon, *Administrative Behavior: A Study of Decision-making Processes in Administrative Organizations*, 2d ed. (Macmillan, 1957), pp. 26–28.

76. Kernell and Popkin, eds., *Chief of Staff*, pp. 172–73.

77. Colin Campbell, personal interview with Mike Deaver, May 3, 1983, Washington, D.C.

Such stratagems have a purpose. It is not writer's block that makes the speechwriters chronically tardy in turning in drafts for review. They simply do not want the text changed. Lower-level employees leak embarrassing information about their colleagues to gain an advantage as the moment of decision approaches. They push decisions onto the president to avoid blame if things go badly and to show their influence if they go well. Size and complexity imply more than the need for managers to make sure the organizational parts mesh. They must also contain the competition for influence and channel it in constructive ways.[78] As the White House becomes more complex, so too do these management problems. Presidents who manage their own offices will increasingly risk being overwhelmed with police work.

In the early days, senior aides were a president's trusted advisers, and chief executives could mold staffs to their liking without creating a crisis. The experience of Roosevelt, Truman, and Eisenhower suggested that the White House staff could and should be organized however the president wanted. Yet even during these presidencies, elements of organizational imperative were emerging, so that now the question of how to organize the staff has become a paramount concern of those who study and advise presidents.

One can discern the consequences of size and complexity for senior aides in the ways presidents have used their assistants. To illustrate the trend, I shall inspect three presidents' approaches to their senior staffs. Presidents Truman and Reagan represent endpoints of both the chronology and a continuum of staff responsibility. President Johnson is a transitional figure, a self-manager struggling at times with a gangly staff structure.

Harry Truman: Hands-on Management

Truman began his tenure in the Oval Office more dependent on his staff than Roosevelt had ever been. A fair reading of the record indicates he got off to a poor start, having trouble recruiting the right talent and creating the kind of White House organization he needed.[79] These problems soon reflected on the man, and observ-

78. Lou Cannon provides a typical example in "Writing Reagan's Final Scenes," *Washington Post*, July 27, 1987, p. A1.

79. "Joint Oral History Interview: The Truman White House," February 20, 1980, Truman Library.

ers found him failing to measure up to the job.[80] Much to his displeasure, Truman was soon besieged by offers of help in straightening out the disarray of his White House.[81] By late 1946, however, he had achieved the type of organization he would employ for the remainder of his presidency. The turnaround was dramatic. Looking back, William Hopkins, who served in every White House from Roosevelt through Nixon—most of the time as its executive clerk—found more favor with Truman's approach than with any of the others.

President Truman was more orderly than his predecessor, more informal than his successor, and more egalitarian than either. He diligently ran his own staff, largely through a regular morning meeting in which ten to fifteen aides would report and be given assignments. A few, such as Donald Dawson, had more or less fixed duties. At one time or another, all were pressed into service as troubleshooters.

Among these regular attendees, two were more senior than the others. John Steelman, who retained nearly a dozen of his staff from the dismantled Office of War Mobilization and Reconversion, was principally charged with conducting the president's day-to-day business. He also was the administration's chief labor negotiator during a time when labor unrest was a major issue facing the country. Clark Clifford, who served as special counsel, presided over a group of speechwriters and idea men. Reflecting the informal partitioning of staff, lower-level aides who worked for either of these men were unfamiliar with the daily duties of their counterparts who worked for the others.[82]

80. See, for example, Walter Lippmann's syndicated column, "Today and Tomorrow," January 5, 1946. Lippmann stressed that the presidency "is not just a man with some secretaries and clerks. It is the central department of Government where all other departments meet, and have to be guided, corrected, superintended, and made a team. . . . [Truman] did not see that he needed . . . to make the White House itself an efficient department."

81. See various entries in the Harold Smith Papers, particularly those for May 4 and August 10, 1945, and February 8 and 28, 1946. See also Truman's penciled remarks on his appointments schedule of March 23, 1946: DNC Chairman and Postmaster General Robert Hannegan "is most anxious to control my staff—nothing doing. I wouldn't let my wife or mother do that . . . my personal staff are responsible to me." Truman Library.

82. One indicator of incipient partitioning of work is that no one clearly remembered what others did. "I don't know what Steelman did with all his staff" and "Connelly ran patronage and political travel and we stayed out of it" characterize recollections in oral history interviews.

Politics reinforced the division of labor. As union leaders came to recognize the comparative advantage of working with the White House rather than through their traditional representative, the secretary of labor, Steelman became organized labor's unofficial contact with the president. Occasionally, this brought him into disagreement with Clifford, who, concerned with burnishing the president's leadership image, would counsel Truman to take a tough line with striking unions while Steelman was urging conciliation. The two differed on other issues as well, with Clifford generally taking the more liberal position. After the disastrous 1946 midterm elections, Clifford joined a small, informal weekly discussion group of administration liberals to ponder ideas that might save the president in the next election. Through him, many of this group's proposals reached Truman. He adopted some, including the creation of a permanent Fair Employment Practices Commission, the recognition of Israel, and the decision in the summer of 1948 to call the Republican Congress back into a special session to create issues for the fall's campaign.[83] President Truman tolerated competition among his staff with the proviso that his aides not publicly criticize one another. By running the staff personally, he could take advantage of its independent thinking while containing some of its internal tensions.

Truman succeeded because his staff remained small. Most of the growth in routines and complexity during his tenure occurred among other presidential agencies. The new Council of Economic Advisers and National Security Council had not yet assumed major responsibilities, but the rejuvenated Bureau of the Budget under James Webb took over preparation of Truman's legislative program and helped write his State of the Union addresses. This reduced the pressure for diversification and growth within the White House staff and gave the president the flexibility of choosing his advice from among the departments and presidential agencies.

Lyndon Johnson: The Struggle With Hands-on Management

The daily White House activities under LBJ were more presidentially centered than they had been for any president since Franklin

83. One of the best accounts of Clifford's role is Patrick Anderson's *The President's Men: White House Assistants of Franklin D. Roosevelt, Harry S. Truman, Dwight D. Eisenhower, John F. Kennedy, and Lyndon B. Johnson* (Doubleday, 1969), pp. 113–32. After his departure from the White House staff, Clifford's position was filled by Charles Murphy.

Roosevelt. As one aide observed, "Johnson didn't compartmental-ize his mind, and therefore he didn't subdivide the work in the office that way."[84] The randomness of presidential needs was re-flected in staff assignments, and there was no John Steelman, much less Eisenhower's Sherman Adams, to impose order. Indica-tive of this, Jack Valenti, who served as the staff's de facto ring leader, had, among other duties, editing drafts of speeches, main-taining close relations with Senate Minority Leader Everett Dirk-sen, keeping tabs on the bureaucracy, and "telling important peo-ple things they did not want to hear."[85] Bill Moyers described the staff structure as "like the spokes of a wheel radiating out from a hub. Each person has a special relationship to the President and does what the President needs done."[86]

Johnson may have been temperamentally disposed to emulate Roosevelt by keeping staff relations fluid. But with three times the White House personnel, there were simply more people who re-quired guidance and more specialized units that required coordina-tion, including adjudication of internal policy and jurisdictional disputes. Moyers's spokes to the Oval Office were neither the same thickness or length. Nor, according to scholars of the Johnson presidency, were they "unsegmented hierarchically," and "king-pins" emerged to serve as "centers of integration."[87] When Joseph Califano joined the staff in 1965 and took over the task forces, for example, he coordinated the activities of domestic policy staff and fashioned dozens of task force reports into a coherent legislative program.

Still, frequent instances of confusion, contradictory assign-ments, and abrasive relations among aides spilled into the press,[88]

---

84. Jake Jacobsen oral history interview, May 27, 1969, tape 3, p. 16, Johnson Library.

85. Eric F. Goldman, *The Tragedy of Lyndon Johnson* (Knopf, 1969), p. 117.

86. Moyers continued, "You can define very briefly what each man does, but it is impossible to catch the full scope of his duties." Memo, Moyers to Kintner, May 5, 1966, Johnson Library.

87. Emmette S. Redford and Richard T. McCulley, *White House Operations: The Johnson Presidency* (University of Texas Press, 1986), pp. 52-53.

88. Press attention to disputes among the White House staff was a regular irritant to President Johnson. He could be heard complaining "you never hear of Harold Ickes and Harry Hopkins fist-fighting in the Rose Garden in [Roosevelt's] administration." Berman, "Johnson and the White House Staff," p. 191. Such incidents inspired a seasoned veteran of staff competition, George E. Reedy, to write *The Twilight of the Presidency* (New American Library, 1970).

and numerous staff memos over the years advised Johnson of the external liabilities created by the absence of coherent management. Johnson's own periodic search for someone who could draw up an organization chart reflected his yearnings for a solution to the management problems. But the president was ambivalent, as Robert Kintner's unhappy experiences indicated. Of the senior staff, Kintner alone was recruited principally to help coordinate staff activities. One of his innovations that at least survived throughout his fourteen-month tenure was a weekly staff meeting in which senior and second-tier aides heard reports from their colleagues on what the rest of the White House was doing. Initially, Johnson supported these meetings and attended at least one, expressing his satisfaction with it to Kintner. But as membership grew to nearly thirty aides and press leaks became a serious problem, the president became suspicious of the gatherings. As Johnson's enthusiasm waned, so did that of his senior advisers. Attendance fell off; only the second-tier staff, who had few other avenues of acquiring information, remained enthusiastic.

Despite his frustration, then, Johnson was ultimately unwilling to turn management responsibility over to his senior staff. And without his backing, efforts at systematic coordination became no more than false starts. Perhaps only someone with Johnson's "herculean readiness to take on any task at any time" could at this late date of staff development attempt to cope largely on his own.[89] In fact, all of his successors have delegated management duties to senior aides and eventually appointed someone to be chief of staff. Still, Johnson's attempt underscores that the incumbent president retains the prerogative to try to do it himself.

Ronald Reagan: The Staff Takes Over

The organizational history of the Reagan White House must center on its four chiefs of staff. More than for any other president, Reagan's assistants established the management philosophy of the White House Office. That they differed dramatically in their concepts of organization illustrates the ways the backgrounds and personal preferences of senior aides can be as important as those of the president in organizing the staff; it certainly cautions us from facilely taking the measure of the president by studying his work-

89. Goldman, *Tragedy of Lyndon Johnson*, p. 102.

place. And yet in the welter of administrative styles, Reagan's approach to the office is evident. The president's general lack of interest in details and, collaterally, his insistence on delegating routine planning and administration characterized his leadership with each chief. The latitude he gave senior advisers is what allowed their styles to come to the fore. Donald Regan reported that when he took over the White House Office, the president's only advice was to be sure he received all points of view on an issue before making a decision.[90]

Under Reagan, the individuality of the White House organization usually attributed directly to presidential style became a reflection of the styles of his senior staff: James Baker, the skilled strategist who sought to moderate the conservative arguments the president had always found so persuasive; Donald Regan, the corporate chief executive officer from Merrill Lynch, who considered the staff implementers rather than creators of policies; Howard Baker, the Senate minority leader, who had spent his career helping assemble governing coalitions among people with disparate political viewpoints; and Kenneth Duberstein, the manager whose quiet diplomacy and attention to detail had served him well in the White House and given him a good reputation on Capitol Hill. The style of each is evident in the teams he assembled and in the top-level organization he created. But amid the diversity of management styles, is there any evidence of continuity in the architecture of the upper strata of the staff system that reflects the constraining influence of institutional forces?

The answer must be yes. The size and complexity of the modern White House Office dictates that whoever manages the staff, even if it is the president, must solve the puzzle of coordination. This is where the variety of Reagan's advisory systems becomes instructive. The architecture of the White House Office is not fixed by its broad foundation of line offices in the organization. Reagan's first-term troika of James Baker, Edwin Meese, and Michael Deaver (later expanded when William Clark became national security adviser) and the second-term, strong-chief system under Donald Re-

90. Donald T. Regan, *For the Record: From Wall Street to Washington* (Harcourt Brace Jovanovich, 1988). For an overview of Reagan's staffing arrangements, see Bert A. Rockman, "The Style and Organization of the Reagan Presidency," in Charles O. Jones, ed., *The Reagan Legacy: Promise and Performance* (Chatham, N.J.: Chatham House, 1988), pp. 3–29.

gan represent distinctive approaches to solving this puzzle. The troika has generally been judged a success, the latter a disaster.

The collective management of the first term involved teams. A coterie of senior aides under Meese planned the president's domestic policies. The aides of Chief of Staff Baker ran operations. Deaver's small group oversaw scheduling and public relations; and Clark (later Robert McFarlane), ran the National Security Council's staff. Most line units within the White House Office were fairly separate from each other and directly responsible to one of these management teams. And these lower-tier offices kept abreast of the others' activities through regularly scheduled meetings. This horizontal character of the staff organization was extended into the upper reaches of the bureaucracy by the creation of cabinet councils and subcabinet working groups. The relative absence of hierarchy is evidenced by the large number of people holding titles of assistant or deputy assistant to the president.

Whatever its advantages in assuring Reagan a variety of opinions—and compared with what followed, these were considerable—the presence of four hubs posed some distinct problems. The organization could be cumbersome and could fuel conflict, especially when the four disagreed strongly on policy recommendations or when the agenda became congested. Hammered-out consensus rather than deference and reciprocity was the normal resolution. Such practices can be taxing, however, which was why David Gergen demurred from recommending the system to future presidents. Michael Deaver attributed much of its viability to the special esprit generated after the assassination attempt early in the term as personnel were learning to work together.[91] Having the line staff bunched around multiple hubs also risked having too many people involved in planning the president's program. The nearly exclusive access of Baker, Clark, Deaver, and Meese, however, prevented Reagan from being overrun with importunities. Beyond this, the senior staff devised the Legislative Strategy Group, an ad hoc committee whose membership would be limited to a half dozen and changed according to whom the senior men thought needed to be involved in a decision.

From his vantage in the Treasury Department, Secretary Donald Regan saw much in the first-term performance of the president's

91. Colin Campbell, interviews with David Gergen, January 11, 1983, Washington, D.C., and Michael Deaver, May 3, 1983, Washington, D.C.

staff that grated on his sensibilities. The staff spoke with too many voices; leaks were so common as to be unexceptional; some of the staff, particularly Deaver, were too absorbed with preserving the president's public image and were too easily distracted by current opinion in Washington. Most distasteful of all to Regan, many aides enjoyed friendly relations with Washingtonians normally numbered among the president's adversaries, including liberal Democrats and White House correspondents. "Reagan was continuously being pressured to compromise in ways that preserved the influence and the policies of the defeated opposition," Regan complains in his memoirs.[92] All this he set out to change. The White House would be the president's command post.

Because most of the first-term senior staff had departed and the president had given him a free hand, Regan set out to redesign the administrative system along a strict hierarchy with himself as a strong chief of staff. He pared the top-heavy organization, reducing the number of assistants to the president from eighteen to eleven.[93] He consolidated or gutted offices, especially those that mostly cultivated relations with outside groups: the staff of the Public Liaison Office, for example, was halved.[94] He scaled back the Personnel Office, moved it out of the west wing of the White House, and demoted its new director. Regan consolidated most responsibilities of the triumvirate in his office. The resulting centralization was profound. The Domestic Council was brought under the direct supervision of the chief of staff's office, and the number of cabinet councils that had mostly been staffed by the Domestic Council was reduced from seven to two.

The one office upgraded was Communications; it was now to enjoy a more prominent place in the constellation of line offices. As part of Regan's strategy for the administration to speak with a single voice, Patrick Buchanan, the new communications director, was given control over the speechwriters and Public Liaison Office.

By the end of summer, many of the first-term lieutenants had either made peace with their reduced status or had departed. Regan's pyramid was in place. Internal communication was to flow

92. Regan, *For the Record*, p. 245.

93. Dick Kirschten, "It's Crowded at Top of Regan's Command . . . Causing a Case of West Wing Job Jitters," *National Journal*, vol. 17 (February 23, 1985), pp. 434–35.

94. Jane Mayer and Doyle McManus, *Landslide: The Unmaking of the President, 1984–1988* (Houghton Mifflin, 1988), p. 40.

mostly down the organization in an orderly fashion and with minimum leakage. Messages for external consumption were to go up the ladder to designated senior aides for dissemination to the press.

At least, that was the plan. But Regan's reorganization mostly managed to create friction, ill will, and open infighting. From his post at the much-reduced Political Affairs Office, Ed Rollins warred with Buchanan over the latter's desire to have the president campaign vigorously for aid to the Nicaraguan rebels; by October Rollins was gone. Frustrated with being unable to get through to the president, Max Friedersdorf, head of congressional liaison, left the next month. Eventually, Buchanan left after Regan vetoed his nominee for new head of the speechwriters' group. Aside from Nancy Reagan's east wing office, the only unit that escaped Regan's control was McFarlane's National Security Council. Worn down by continuous bickering with Regan, difficulty in getting access to the president, and rumors and innuendos planted in gossip columns, McFarlane too resigned in late November.

So Donald Regan's orderly system in which the heads of the lower-tier offices took orders from the senior staff failed. Perhaps someone with more political sensitivity and more active backing from the president could have better succeeded. The tale is, however, a caution for White House managers who would trust in hierarchy to coordinate the staff. Under threat, the second-tier units emerged as "rival baronies" warring with one another and the chief's office. And leaks to the press became "part of the job" as all quarters of the administration sought to "aggrandize their own roles."[95]

The first two staff organizations under Reagan's presidency thus represent very different approaches to management. While the cabinet councils and the operation of the domestic and national security offices were part of the White House staff's effort to administer the executive branch, much of their work and the rest of the apparatus described here concerned management of the staff system. The brilliant successes of the first term and the debilitating failure of staff work that led to the Iran-contra scandal in the second suggest that the recondite issues of internal staff management have important implications for presidential leadership.

95. Mayer and McManus, *Landslide*, p. 186.

The varieties of top-level organization, indeed the variety of styles among recent chiefs of staff, indicate that the way the president and his senior advisers approach the job is a matter of choice. Yet undeniably, the development of a large, specialized line staff within the White House places a heavy burden of administration on the president. Aside from the purely organizational matter of integrating the activities of compartmentalized units, there is the centrifugal pull from the clienteles of line staff, which must be checked by the president or those who work closely with him. These organizational and internal political dynamics create strong pressure for the president to centralize management of his staff. From Roosevelt through Johnson, only Eisenhower resorted to a system based on a chief of staff. After Johnson, only Carter failed to do so, and he changed his mind later in his term. The role of senior staff as White House managers is now well established.

GOVERNABILITY AND THE MODERN WHITE HOUSE

A partial list of the responsibilities of the modern White House Office includes managing the executive branch, tending to the political needs of Washington politicians, planning the president's program, and generating support for him in Congress and across the nation. Such services are now routinely performed by a staff that was originally mandated to do little more than coordinate the flow of people and messages to and from the White House. Expanded work has produced a bureaucracy comprising hundreds of specialists. Presidential aides who deal on an equal footing with other government leaders hold positions created fifty years earlier for half a dozen self-effacing, circumambient White House assistants. Discussions of the nation's governability now invariably turn to the emergence of these aides who have great power and little legitimacy.

Critics complain that the White House staff meddles in affairs best left to others, and the performances of recent aides offer them outstanding justification. Failing to obtain cooperation from the FBI in investigating Daniel Ellsberg, Egil Krogh, a second-tier staffer in the Nixon White House, organized the "White House plumbers" to break into the office of Ellsberg's doctor in hope of discovering incriminating evidence. A decade later, Oliver North, from his NSC office, diverted funds from the sale of missiles to Iran to aid the contras in Nicaragua. Both men had seen their president frustrated in trying to accomplish his goals through legitimate channels. Zealous loyalty inspired each to undertake illegal actions that ultimately undermined the president they were so eager to serve. Such responsiveness presidents do not need.

Critics also charge that large staffs insulate presidents, preventing them from acquiring political information essential for building a governing coalition in a fragmented governmental system.[96] The vantage of White House aides is, or soon becomes, too parochial for its exclusive counsel to be sufficient. Only by understanding other politicians who view policy choices from different perspectives can a president assess the likely responses of those whose cooperation he ultimately needs. Despite protests from his secretaries of state and defense, President Reagan remained convinced that politicians and the American public would view his dealings with the ayatollah as something other than trading arms for hostages. Had he brought key senators into his confidence, he probably would not have continued to harbor such a naive view. Moreover, less self-reliance at the outset would have subsequently allowed him to avoid bearing the full brunt of responsibility for failed policies.

If somehow the growth and activities of the White House staff had been arrested at a more modest level, these critics charge, presidents and the nation would be a lot better off. For them, the staff is the problem, and pruning it is the solution. "Rigorous efforts should be made to keep this staff small," was the first guideline offered Reagan's transition team by the National Academy of Public Administration in 1980.[97] Presumably, if there were fewer Egil Kroghs or Oliver Norths in the White House, there would be fewer opportunities for staff to run wild.

Yet causality runs primarily in the other direction. The modern White House Office is the cumulative result of the ways presidents have engaged an evolving political community. Had the web of

96. "Suffocation" is the way Richard E. Neustadt, writing long before the White House staff reached its current size, characterized the ill effects of large staffs; see "Presidency and Legislation: Planning the President's Program," *American Political Science Review*, vol. 49 (December 1955), pp. 1020–21.

97. National Academy of Public Administration, *A Presidency for the 1980s* (Washington, D.C.: NAPA, 1980), p. 17.

mutual dependency that obliged presidents to work closely with fellow Washingtonians not weakened, the size of their staffs would have remained inconsequential to leadership, and therefore would not have grown so. As presidents grew self-reliant and they centralized their leadership, however, they began to outfit themselves with the necessary resources. Consequently, each president, liberal Democrat and conservative Republican alike, has broadened the mandate of his staff as he sought to take on certain activities that his predecessors had relied on others to do. To assume that the governability of the modern presidency simply required reducing the staff and returning it to its original size and importance would be to ignore the pervasive environmental forces that have transformed presidential leadership. To try to remove surgically the problems that attend large organization would only succeed in leaving the president an invalid, as self-reliant as ever, yet incapacitated.

Half a century ago, Louis Brownlow proclaimed, "The President needs help." The president still does, but now it is ironically in figuring out how best to use Brownlow's unintended progeny, the White House staff. Instead of trying to wish it away, the presence of a large, complex staff must be accepted as a given and its problems addressed forthrightly. The president's aides must be recognized for what they are—his agents, routinely representing his interest in their dealings with Capitol Hill and the permanent government. Their value derives from taking those actions the president would if he were undertaking the task himself. The White House staff offers the president economy, but it is not a free ride. The president must give the staff clear direction and vigilantly oversee its performance. Presidents who did so, such as Truman and Johnson, rarely had problems resulting from overly aggressive aides. In the absence of presidential guidance, aides can compromise the presidency and the country. Oliver North, who was identified early as someone who needed to be kept on a "very short leash" but was not, devised and executed his own version of America's foreign policy and very nearly brought down the president.[98] One of the major challenges to the president in staffing and organizing his office is to keep his agents on course, neither shirking their duty nor arrogating to themselves presidential decisions.

98. Mayer and McManus, *Landslide*, p. 81.

The other principal problem of modern presidential staffing is that layers of organization overly filter the president's contact with the outside community, preventing him from receiving advice from other political leaders. Much of the criticism of this problem should be directed toward the strategy of centralization that has removed presidents from the daily transactions of other politicians.

The president will be no more captive to staff than he allows. Yet the concern with suffocation by staff is a legitimate one. Beyond his daily reciting a mantra to remind himself of this, a president can do much to mold the White House staff into a creative force rather than allow it to become a retinue of sycophants.

The raw material for such shaping can be found in the pluralistic character of the modern White House staff. Its division of labor and recruitment of experts with varying backgrounds will create differing opinions about the president's priorities and interests. Moreover, outside pressures for representation on the White House staff are great. Presidents tacitly acknowledge this when they appoint aides from competing wings of their political party. And special groups and constituencies are diligent in trying to infiltrate the staff with one of their number and in cultivating contacts with presidential assistants.

None of these dynamics is peculiar to the modern White House. Each was present in the organization and politics of Truman's staff. But as decisions have steadily shifted to the White House, the forces promoting pluralism have intensified, making staffs more difficult to manage. Uncontrolled, the president's staff becomes a cacophony of voices, leaving outsiders wondering if anyone is in charge at the White House. And yet the political diversity of the modern White House offers an invaluable source of second opinions and new ideas.

The challenge facing modern presidents is to create staff structures that supervise without stultifying. Platitudes are easy; practice promises to be more difficult, for the task involves nothing less than balancing order and creativity. Procedures designed to keep the president's agents well tethered are apt to be enlisted by senior aides to suppress dissent from below. Also, the competition of political interests rarely conforms to the requirements of orderly administration. Protracted disputes among staff members may lead one faction to decide it can do better by disrupting established procedures it sees favoring its adversary. Senior aides bent on order and maintaining the integrity of their administrative apparatus may be quick to enlist hierarchical controls. But these methods easily become oversubscribed. Suppressing dissent only guarantees that competition will be vented in a more virulent form through leaks and personal attacks in the press. The hammered-out consensus of Reagan's first-term staff may have been taxing on its participants, but it unquestionably served him better than the pyramidal management system that replaced it.

Future presidents must better appreciate that the modern White House Office has evolved into more than their personal entourage of legislative or campaign aides. They may be present as the inner circle, but the legacy of centralization is a larger, more inclusive staff whose routine activities are increasingly important to, and to a degree responsive to, the outside political community. And while the president can fairly insist on and expect staff loyalty, he must recognize that as his agents, this staff will daily make choices that affect his welfare. The moral of recent presidential failures—Watergate, the Iran-contra scandal, and the many pratfalls—reinforces the implication of the evolution of presidential staff. Managing the White House has become an essential feature of presidential leadership.

The Changing Textbook Congress

KENNETH A. SHEPSLE

WHEN SCHOLARS talk about Congress to one another, their students, or the public, they often have a stylized version in mind, a textbook Congress characterized by a few main tendencies and described in broad terms. This is not to say that they are incapable of filling in fine-grained detail, making distinctions, or describing change. But at the core of their descriptions and distinctions are approximations, caricatures, and generalities. They are always incomplete and somewhat inaccurate, but still they consist of robust regularities. This textbook Congress is a specification of equilibrium practices and tendencies; the portrait endures as long as the generalities on which it is based hold true. Major revisions in the textbooks occur when events and practices change the equilibrium and some scholars offer a new vision that more nearly resembles current practice. The new textbook description becomes persuasive when things settle into a new pattern.

The textbook Congress I have in mind is the one that emerged from World War II and the Legislative Reorganization Act of 1946. Its main features persisted until the mid-1960s; its images remained in writings on Congress well into the 1970s. Scholarship on Congress during this period was widely influenced by the behavioral revolution in political science and, more particularly, by the Study of Congress project. Sponsored by the American Political Science Association, the Social Science Research Council, and several other foundations, the project produced a number of descriptive studies that formed the core understanding of the textbook Congress.

To illuminate the institutional dynamics of the past forty years, this chapter describes some early signs of change in the textbook Congress in the 1950s, suggests how events of the 1960s and 1970s disrupted the equilibrium, and looks at some of the emerging features of a new textbook Congress, though I am not convinced that

238

a new equilibrium has yet been established. The story I develop here is not a historical tour d'horizon. Rather it addresses theoretical issues of institutional development involving the capacity of Congress and its members to represent their constituencies, to make national policy, and to balance the intrinsic tensions between these tasks.

Let me preview my argument. The tensions between constituency representation and national policymaking derive from three competing imperatives—geographical, jurisdictional, and partisan. Put differently and more alliteratively, Congress is an arena for constituencies, committees, and coalitions. The textbook Congress of the 1950s represented an equilibrium among these imperatives involving an institutional bargain that gave prominence to committees and the jurisdictional imperative. During these years Congress was a quintessential example of a division of labor. Committees provided a structure for members to realize their ambitions, on the one hand, and poured content into partisan vessels, on the other.

Beginning with the 1958 elections, shocks destroyed this committee-based equilibrium. Members began to give increased attention to their respective geographic constituencies, firming up their electoral bases by redeploying institutional resources to individual electoral purposes. It was during this period that an "incumbency advantage" first began to take on significant proportions.

Tensions between representation and policymaking emerged as the now electorally more secure members sought to have greater effect on policymaking inside the legislature. These tensions erupted in a fit of institutional reform during the 1970s. Throughout this entire period, parties inside the legislature assumed a residual function while rank-and-file members and committee barons, like two sumo wrestlers, fought for control of the legislature's machinery for setting agendas and making decisions.

As committees were weakened by decentralizing reform, coordination suffered. In response, beginning in the late 1970s and continuing into the 1980s, centralized party institutions were strengthened—the result of increased demand for coordination to fill the void left by the committees and an increased willingness by Democratic politicians to grant partisan institutions the authority to provide this coordination.

The 1950s committee-based legislative equilibrium has thus been radically transformed. The jurisdictional imperative of committees has given way to the imperatives of geography and party. A tenuous balance has been established among legislators with enhanced capabilities, a decentralized subcommittee system, and a recentralized and reinvigorated set of partisan institutions. Is this the new textbook Congress? Before speculating, I think it best to fill in some details.

THE TEXTBOOK CONGRESS: THE LATE 1940S TO THE MID-1960S

Any portrait of Congress after World War II must begin with the member and, in a popular phrase of the time, "his work as he sees it."[1] Then, as now, legislators divided their time between Washington and home, the relative proportions slowly changing in favor of Washington during the 1950s.[2] In Washington they divided their time between chamber, committee, and personal office; all three demands grew from the 1940s to the 1960s as chamber work load, committee activity, and constituency demands increased.

In 1947, just after passage of the Legislative Reorganization Act, the average House member had three staff assistants and the average senator six.[3] Because even these modest averages would be the envy of a contemporary member of the British Parliament or of most state legislatures, they indicate that by midcentury the American national legislature was a highly professional place. Nevertheless, by the mid-1960s congressional staffs had swelled even further: a typical House member now had twelve assistants and a typical senator eighteen. Committee staffs, too, grew dramatically from an average of ten to nearly thirty in the House and from fifteen to more than thirty in the Senate. These numbers do not include the substantial staffs of the nearly 400 offices of institutional leaders, informal groups, and legislative support agencies.[4]

1. Charles L. Clapp, *The Congressman: His Work As He Sees It* (Brookings, 1963).

2. In the Eightieth Congress (1947–48) the House was in session for 254 days, and sessions remained about the same length throughout the 1950s. Since 1960 the average has been 321. See Norman J. Ornstein and others, *Vital Statistics on Congress, 1984–1985* (Washington, D.C.: American Enterprise Institute for Public Policy Research, 1984), table 6-1. Senate sessions have been longer and have also been lengthening.

3. Ibid., table 5-2.

4. Robert H. Salisbury and Kenneth A. Shepsle, "U.S. Congressman as Enterprise," *Legislative Studies Quarterly*, vol. 6 (November 1981), pp. 559–76.

Since most committee staffers during these twenty years were in fact under the control of committee chairmen, some of the more senior legislators came to head sizable organizations. Indeed, if most legislators in the Eightieth Congress could be said to have headed mom 'n pop businesses with a handful of clerks and assistants, by the mid-1960s they had come to oversee major modern enterprises with secretaries, receptionists, interns, and a variety of legislative, administrative, and political professionals (typically lawyers).[5] A committee chair or ranking minority member, a Warren Magnuson or a Jacob Javits, who might also head a couple of subcommittees or party committees, might have a staff exceeding one hundred.

This growth transformed legislative life and work. In the 1940s the House had its norms and the Senate its folkways, perhaps even an inner club.[6] Hard work, long apprenticeship, restrained participation of younger members, specialization (particularly in the House), courtesy, reciprocity, and institutional loyalty characterized daily life in each chamber. Even if these norms of behavior were only suggestions, frequent contact among colleagues made them a reality.[7] Undoubtedly, members who were neighbors in the same office building, who shared a committee assignment, or who traveled back and forth to Washington from the same state or region came to know each other exceedingly well. But even more distant relationships were based on familiarity and frequent formal or informal meeting.[8]

5. Ibid; and Burdett A. Loomis, "The Congressional Office as a Small (?) Business: New Members Set Up Shop," *Publius*, vol. 9 (Summer 1979), pp. 35–55.

6. Richard F. Fenno, *The Power of the Purse* (Little, Brown, 1966); Clapp, *The Congressman*; William S. White, *Citadel: The Story of the United States Senate* (Harper and Brothers, 1957); Ralph K. Huitt, "Democratic Party Leadership in the Senate," *American Political Science Review*, vol. 55 (June 1961), pp. 333–44; Ralph K. Huitt, "The Outsider in the Senate: An Alternative Role," *American Political Science Review*, vol. 55 (September 1961), pp. 566–75; Donald R. Matthews, *U.S. Senators and Their World* (University of North Carolina Press, 1960); and Nelson W. Polsby, "Goodbye to the Inner Club," *Washington Monthly* (August 1969), pp. 30–34.

7. Herbert B. Asher, "The Learning of Legislative Norms," *American Political Science Review*, vol. 67 (June 1973), pp. 499–513; and Steven S. Smith, "Going to the Floor: Changing Patterns of Participation in the U.S. House of Representatives, 1955–86," Governmental Studies discussion paper 13 (Brookings, 1987).

8. In his classic on congressional committees, written before the turn of the century, Lauros G. McConachie wrote in his delightfully purple prose, "Small committees are not debating, but working, societies. While the distracting passions of the Committee of the Whole helped to rend the Union asunder, bright friendships, resulting between men of widely separated regions and vitally antagonistic

By the mid-1960s this had all changed. The rubbing of elbows was replaced by liaisons between legislative corporate enterprises, typically at the staff level. Surrounded or protected by a bevy of clerks and assistants, members met other members only occasionally and briefly on the chamber floor or in committee meetings. And many of the norms supporting work and specialization eroded.[9]

With limited time and resources, legislators of the 1940s and 1950s concentrated on only a few activities. They simply did not have the staffs or money to be able to involve themselves in a wide range of policy issues, manage a network of ombudsman activities back home, raise campaign finances, or intercede broadly and frequently in the executive branch's administration of programs. Rather, they picked their spots selectively and depended on jurisdictional decentralization and reciprocity among committees to divide the legislative labor, on the legislative party for voting cues inside the chamber, and on local party organizations for campaign resources and electioneering.[10]

During the 1960s, as congressional offices gained staff and funding, members began to take on many new activities. Larger staffs in district offices, trips home, and franking privileges enabled them to develop a personal presence before their constituencies. This permitted them to orchestrate electioneering, polling, voter mobilization, and campaign finance activities themselves. They grew less dependent on organizations outside their own enterprises—local parties, for example—which previously performed such functions. The geographic constituency had, of course, always been impor-

---

parties from the touch of elbows around a standing committee table, have gone far to remove those misunderstandings and heal those discords which were cause and effect of the Civil War." *Congressional Committees* (Crowell, 1898), p. 146.

9. Asher, "Learning of Legislative Norms"; and David W. Rohde, Norman Ornstein, and Robert L. Peabody, "Political Change and Legislative Norms in the U.S. Senate, 1957–1974," in Glenn R. Parker, ed., *Studies of Congress* (CQ Press, 1985), pp. 147–88. It is perhaps surprising that, especially in the Senate, a number of norms for the "general benefit," such as courtesy and institutional loyalty, survive. They seem to have fared less well in the House.

10. Keith Krehbiel has brought to my attention the point that the congressional norms of the 1950s evolved as part of the equilibrium arrangement of the textbook Congress, and they began to erode as other pieces of the equilibrium arrangement changed. The limited resources of members encouraged deference, reciprocity, and specialization; the rationale for these norms became weaker as members began to have access to increased resources.

tant, but it had often been mediated by party, both local and national. By the mid-1960s the members' relationships with their constituencies were growing increasingly unmediated (just as the relationships between members were growing increasingly mediated). They were constant presences in their districts, had begun to develop personal followings, and consequently achieved a certain independence from their parties (and hence some insulation from party fortunes). As members made more trips home and allocated more staff to district offices and more Washington staff to constituency service and constituency-oriented legislation, calculations of how they would present themselves to the folks back home and explain their Washington activities took on added importance.[11] Constituents' needs (the geographic imperative) began to compete with party as a guide to behavior.[12]

Personal and institutional arrangements in Washington also changed. In the 1950s members, especially in the House, limited themselves to work on a few issues, determined to a considerable extent by their places in the committee system. Most members were able to land assignments to committees that were directly relevant to their constituencies.[13] Much of their time, energy, and limited staff resources were devoted to work inside these little legislatures. By partitioning policy into committee jurisdictions, and matching member interests with those jurisdictions, legislative arrangements permitted members to get the most out of their limited resources.[14] Aside from those with institutional ambitions, who hoped one day to be appointed to the Appropriations, Rules, or Ways and Means committees (Appropriations, Finance, Foreign

11. Richard F. Fenno, Jr., *Homestyle: House Members in Their Districts* (Little, Brown, 1978).

12. The literature on incumbency, constituency attentiveness, money, and party decline is immense. A good sampling may be acquired from John A. Ferejohn and Morris P. Fiorina, "Incumbency and Realignment in Congressional Elections," in John E. Chubb and Paul E. Peterson, eds., *The New Direction in American Politics* (Brookings, 1985), pp. 91–115; Gary C. Jacobson, *Money in Congressional Elections* (Yale University Press, 1980); Gary C. Jacobson and Samuel Kernell, *Strategy and Choice in Congressional Elections* (Yale University Press, 1981); and Gary C. Jacobson, *The Politics of Congressional Elections*, 2d ed. (Little, Brown, 1987).

13. Nicholas A. Masters, "Committee Assignments in the House of Representatives," *American Political Science Review*, vol. 55 (June 1961), pp. 345–57; and Kenneth A. Shepsle, *The Giant Jigsaw Puzzle: Democratic Committee Assignments in the Modern House* (University of Chicago Press, 1978).

14. The division of labor, and the consequent specialization it entails, has always been more important in the House than in the Senate. This is discussed below.

Relations, or Armed Services in the Senate), most members had only limited incentives to become actively involved in policy areas outside their own assignments and were content to serve on legislative committees that had jurisdiction over the issues of central importance to their constituents. Thus, with limited means and incentives, members sustained a system of deference and reciprocity as part of the 1950s equilibrium, especially in the House.

Because of the growth of resources within their own enterprises in the 1960s, members began to acquire enhanced in-house capabilities. Deference to expert committee judgments on policy outside the jurisdiction of committees on which a member served was no longer so necessary. Members could now afford to assign some of their staff to track developments in other policy areas. The charge to the staffer became "Find something of interest for the boss, something that will help the district." Members were also no longer so dependent on party signals; with greater resources they were better able to determine their interests. In short, greater resources led to vertical integration—the absorption into the member enterprise of activities formerly conducted outside it—and with that, to member independence. Consequently, the relationship in which jurisdiction constrained both interest and activism began to fray as the 1960s came to an end.

Incentives for members to break away from the institutional niches in which they found themselves also multiplied. In both the 1960s and the 1970s, reapportionments, along with economic and demographic changes, produced congressional districts that were neither so purely rural nor so purely urban as they had been. Increasingly, the districts were mixed, often including a major city and a number of towns, as well as perhaps some rural areas. Member interests began to reflect this heterogeneity. Issues were also evolving in ways that cut across existing interest-group configurations and committee jurisdictions. Except in a few cases, one or two major committee jurisdictions could no longer encompass the interests of a district. Members thus had to diversify their portfolios of legislative activities. And this meant less specialization, less deference, less reciprocity.

Thus the limited resources and truncated policy interests characteristic of House members and to a lesser extent members of the Senate in the 1940s and 1950s began to give way in the 1960s and 1970s. Increased member resources and more diverse constituencies provided both the means and the incentives for members to break out of a now restrictive division and specialization of labor. Geographic imperatives were beginning to supersede considerations of party and seniority to become the principal basis on which members defined their responsibilities and work habits. Geography was also beginning to threaten jurisdiction as the principal basis on which the House organized its business.

These changes were less dramatic in the Senate only because it had traditionally been a much less specialized institution. Resources were more plentiful and constituencies more heterogeneous than in the House. And because the Senate was smaller, members had to have more diverse activities and interests. Yet even in the Senate the pressure toward less specialization was growing. Entire states were becoming more heterogeneous as a result of the industrialization of the South, the switch to a service economy in the North, and the nationalization of financial matters (so that even South Dakota could become a center for credit activities). And senators, like their House counterparts, were expanding their enterprises. By the end of the period the Senate, though less dramatically than the House, was also a less specialized place.

The argument I am making here is that geography, jurisdiction, and party hang together in a sort of equilibrium.[15] The 1940s and 1950s represented one such equilibrium in which local parties helped the members get elected and legislative parties loosely coordinated committee activity. But the division of labor and committee dominance of jurisdiction were the central features of the textbook Congress. Committees both accommodated member needs and controlled agendas and decisionmaking. This arrangement "advantaged senior members, committees, and the majority party, with the chairmen of the standing committees sitting at the intersection of these groups."[16] More heterogeneous constituencies and increased member resources upset this textbook equilibrium. Members have adapted by voting themselves even more resources and expanding their activities. By the 1970s parties both inside and outside the legislature had become considerably more submissive

15. For a similar perspective, see Bruce Cain, John A. Ferejohn, and Morris Fiorina, *The Personal Vote: Constituency Service and Electoral Independence* (Harvard University Press, 1987).

16. Smith, "Going to the Floor," p. 1.

holding companies for member enterprises than had earlier been the case. Committees, too, had changed character.

Before turning to these developments, however, it is useful to ask about the effects of institutional arrangements on policy. How did politics and policy interact in the textbook Congress of the 1940s and 1950s? And, how did the interaction change in the 1960s?

Congressional politics of the 1940s and 1950s was principally committee politics. Three foundations sustained this arrangement, especially in the House. First, the revolt against Speaker Joe Cannon in 1910–11 had so weakened central party organs and had so strengthened seniority as a basis for power that, despite the respect for and skill of party leaders like Sam Rayburn and Lyndon Johnson, parties at best coordinated legislative activity rather than coerced it. Party leaders were agents for, rather than superiors to, committee leaders and members of the inner club. Second, the Legislative Reorganization Act of 1946 had rationalized committee jurisdictions so that, once members had been allocated appropriate committee berths, committee life came to define their activities. Finally, norms and folkways rewarded committee activity. Apprenticeship, hard work, and specialization—workhorse rather than showhorse activity—provided a foundation that inspired confidence and trust in committees. Although there was certainly a partisan and ideological overlay to activities in the 1950s—the congressional Democrats were the national party and the conservative coalition was alive and well—the autonomy of committees in policymaking was only partially restrained.[17]

In terms of making policy, committee politics provided fertile soil for interest group liberalism, policy whirlpools, cozy little triangles, and unholy trinities. Policy was incubated and crafted by interested members who monopolized the berths on committees important to their constituents' concerns. Proposed legislation attracted few amendments on the floor because political conflicts were resolved inside committees, the legislators most interested were already on them, and those not on a given committee had little expertise and few resources to mobilize against committee recommendations. For all these reasons, deference to the committees' positions became the norm. Thus a gigantic institutional logroll sanctified the division of labor that permitted policymaking by

17. The principal arena for both partisanship and ideological influences was the House Rules Committee.

subgovernments—congressional committees, interest groups, and governmental agencies—an equilibrium emphasized in the scholarship of the 1950s and 1960s.[18]

In some respects this pattern was amplified because so little was at stake. The 1950s never witnessed the burst of legislative activity that was to mark the early and middle 1960s. Divided government and "that man in the White House" wielding the veto permitted few departures from the status quo. In some areas such as civil rights there were efforts to alter the system, but even here the committee structure kept activities in check and controlled change. The House Rules Committee, especially, was a conservative force, collaborating with senior committee leaders who were also conservative.

This committee-based leadership in policymaking, a bias toward incremental change, and quid pro quo politics in which committee members traded influence in other policy areas for dominance in their own persisted into the 1960s. Although the 1958 elections brought a large contingent of northern liberal Democrats into both House and Senate, creating considerable tension between an increasingly liberal floor and increasingly conservative committee barons, practices remained essentially unscathed. Neither Rayburn nor Johnson was prepared to lead an attack on the committees, especially since any legislative activism that might be unleashed would ultimately be frustrated by President Eisenhower.

But after the election of John Kennedy in 1960, his assassination in 1963, and especially after Lyndon Johnson's landslide election in 1964, the engines of legislative activism accelerated. Mostly this occurred because Democrats now had larger, more liberal majorities in each chamber committed to social legislation that had languished during the 1950s, and they no longer needed to fear a veto-wielding executive. Some structural and procedural changes came to reflect this situation. The expansion of the Rules Committee and the temporary use of the twenty-one-day rule in the House reduced the capacity of committees to bottle up legislation and keep it from the floor. The change in rule 22 in the Senate restricted individual senators' filibuster right by making it easier for the Senate to bring closure to debate. For the most part, however, it was

18. J. Leiper Freeman, *The Political Process: Executive Bureau-Legislative Committee Relations* (Doubleday, 1955); David B. Truman, *The Governmental Process* (Knopf, 1951); and Theodore J. Lowi, *The End of Liberalism* (Norton, 1969).

business as usual. Although a political awakening outside the leg-islature—in civil rights, women's rights, the environmental move-ment, the consumer movement, and the antiwar movement—picked up steam, such activism was reflected mainly in what temporarily oversized coalitions could accomplish. It left only a slight institutional residue, and the textbook Congress remained essentially intact. Temporary majorities did occasionally institu-tionalize their more activist preferences, as when Speaker Rayburn led the assault on the Rules Committee in 1961 and, by a 217–212 vote, managed to increase its size, thereby breaking a conservative stranglehold on legislation. If anything, however, this change lib-erated committees in their policymaking even more.

Beginning with the 1958 elections, however, and continuing throughout the 1960s, a new breed of legislator was coming to Washington, one more committed to legislative activism and policy entrepreneurship than in the past, one beginning to reflect demo-graphic changes, and, most important, one that found ways to stay in office.[19] By the early 1970s these legislators had accumulated considerable seniority. Thus the old equilibrium was disrupted and the stage set for institutional developments that would strike at the heart of the textbook Congress.

THE CHANGING TEXTBOOK CONGRESS: THE 1970S AND 1980S

An idiosyncratic historical factor had an important bearing on the institutional reforms of the 1970s that undermined the textbook Congress. For much of the twentieth century the Democratic party in Congress spoke with a heavy southern accent. In 1948, for exam-ple, more than 53 percent of the Democrats in the House and nearly 56 percent of those in the Senate came from the eleven Confederate states and five border states (Kentucky, Maryland, Missouri, Okla-homa, and West Virginia). These states accounted for only a third of all House and Senate seats.[20] Beginning with the 1958 landslide,

19. John S. Saloma III, *Congress and the New Politics* (Little, Brown, 1969); and Charles S. Bullock III and Burdett A. Loomis, "The Changing Congressional Ca-reer," in Lawrence C. Dodd and Bruce I. Oppenheimer, eds., *Congress Reconsidered*, 3d ed. (CQ Press, 1985), pp. 65–85. See also the references in note 12.

20. Ornstein and others, *Vital Statistics*, tables 1-1, 1-3, 1-5.

however, this distribution changed. In 1960 the same sixteen states accounted for just under 50 percent of Democratically held House seats and 43 percent of Democratically held Senate seats. By 1982 the numbers had fallen to 40 percent and 39 percent respectively, and have held at that level in the One-hundredth Congress. Increasingly, Democrats were winning and holding seats in the North and West and, to a somewhat lesser extent, Republicans were becoming competitive in the South.

The nationalization of the Democratic coalition in Congress, however, was reflected far more slowly at the top of the seniority ladder. Although between 1955 and 1967 the proportion of southern Democrats (border states excluded) in the House had dropped from 43 percent to 35 percent (46 percent to 28 percent in the Senate), the proportion of House committee chairs held by southerners fell from 63 percent to 50 percent, and rose from 53 percent to 56 percent in the Senate. Southerners held two of the three exclusive committee chairs in the House and two of the four in the Senate in 1955; in 1967 they held all of them.

The tension between liberal rank-and-file legislators and conservative southern committee chairs was important in the 1960s but had few institutional repercussions. True, Judge Howard Smith (Democrat of Virginia), the tyrannical chairman of the House Rules Committee, lost in a classic power struggle with Speaker Rayburn in 1961. But the defeat should not be exaggerated. Committees and their chairs maintained both the power to propose legislation and the power to block it in their respective jurisdictions. In 1967 southern Democrats George H. Mahon of Texas, William M. Colmer of Mississippi, and Wilbur D. Mills of Arkansas chaired the Appropriations, Rules, and Ways and Means committees, respectively, in a manner not very different from that of the incumbents a decade earlier. Although the massive legislative productivity of the Eighty-ninth Congress (1965–66) did much to relieve this tension, it relieved it not so much by changing legislative institutions as by managing to mobilize very large liberal majorities. After the 1966 elections, and with the Vietnam War consuming more and more resources and attention, the Eighty-ninth Congress increasingly seemed like a brief interlude in the committee dominance that stretched back to World War II, if not earlier.

By the end of the 1960s a Democratic president had been chased from office, and the 1968 Democratic convention revealed the tensions created by the war in Vietnam and disagreements over a range of domestic issues. Despite a Democratic landslide in 1964, Republican gains for the decade amounted to thirty-eight seats in the House and eight in the Senate, further accentuating the liberal cast of the Democratic rank and file in Congress.[21] As the 1970s opened, then, liberal Democratic majorities in each chamber confronted a conservative president, conservative Republican minorities in each chamber, and often conservative southern committee chairmen of their own party who together blocked many of their legislative initiatives.[22] The liberals thus turned inward, using the Democratic Caucus to effect dramatic changes in institutional practices, especially in the House.[23]

The Age of Reform

Despite the tensions it caused, the mature committee system had many advantages.[24] The division of labor in the House not only allowed for decisions based on expertise, but perhaps more important, it sorted out and routinized congressional careers. Committees provided opportunities for political ambitions to be realized, and they did so in a manner that encouraged members to invest in committee careers. In an undifferentiated legislature, or in a committee-based legislature in which the durability of a committee career or the prospects for a committee leadership post depended on the wishes and whims of powerful party leaders (for example, the Speaker in the nineteenth century House), individual legislators have less incentive to invest effort in committee activi-

21. Ibid., table 2-3.

22. Actually, this is not entirely accurate. Despite its conservative credentials, the Nixon presidency was marked by a liberalization on many foreign policy fronts and a substantial increase in the creation of regulatory institutions and in domestic spending generally.

23. To avoid continually repeating "except in the Senate," "to a lesser extent in the Senate," or "especially in the House," I shall from this point on focus on developments in the House.

24. For a more detailed discussion, see Kenneth A. Shepsle, "Representation and Governance: The Great Legislative Tradeoff," *Political Science Quarterly*, vol. 103 (Fall 1988), pp. 461–85. Also see Lawrence C. Dodd and Richard L. Schott, *Congress and the Administrative State*, 2d ed. (Macmillan, 1986); and Lawrence C. Dodd, "The Rise of the Technocratic Congress: Congressional Reform in the 1970s," in Richard A. Harris and Sidney M. Milkis, eds., *Remaking American Politics* (Westview, forthcoming).

ties. Such investments are put at risk every time the political environment changes. Specialization and careerism are encouraged, however, when rewards depend primarily on individual effort (and luck), and not on the interventions and patronage of others. An important by-product is the encouragement given talented men and women to come to the legislature and to remain there. The slow predictability of career development under a seniority system may repel the impatient, but its inexorability places limits on risks by reducing a member's dependence on arbitrary power and unexpected events.

Even Voltaire's optimistic Dr. Pangloss, however, would recognize another side to this coin. When a committee system that links geography and jurisdiction through the assignment process is combined with an institutional bargain producing deference and reciprocity, it provides the foundation for the distributive politics of interest-group liberalism. But there are no guarantees of success. The legislative process is full of hurdles and veto groups, and occasionally they restrain legislative activism enough to stimulate a reaction. Thus in the 1950s, authorizing committees, frustrated by a stingy House Appropriations Committee, created entitlements as a means of circumventing the normal appropriations process. In the 1960s the Rules Committee became the major obstacle and it, too, was tamed. In the 1970s the Ways and Means Committee, which lacked an internal division of labor through subcommittees, bottled up many significant legislative proposals; it was dealt with by the Subcommittee Bill of Rights and the Committee Reform Amendments of 1974. The solution in the 1950s had no effect on legislative arrangements. The solution in the 1960s entailed modest structural reform that directly affected only one committee. In the 1970s, however, the committee system itself became the object of tinkering.

The decade of the 1970s was truly an age of legislative reform. In effect, it witnessed a representational revolt against a system that dramatically skewed rewards toward the old and senior who were often out of step with fellow partisans. It is a long story, admirably told in detail elsewhere.[25] Here I shall focus on the way reforms

25. Roger H. Davidson and Walter J. Oleszek, *Congress Against Itself* (Indiana University Press, 1977); Leroy N. Rieselbach, *Congressional Reform: The Policy Impact* (Lexington, 1978); Leroy N. Rieselbach, *Congressional Reform* (CQ Press, 1986); Lawrence C. Dodd and Bruce I. Oppenheimer, "The House in Transition: Partisanship and Opposition," in Dodd and Oppenheimer, eds., *Congress Reconsidered*, 3d ed.,

enabled the rise of four power centers that competed, and continue to compete, with the standing committees for political influence.

First, full committees and their chairs steadily lost power to their subcommittees. At least since the Legislative Reorganization Act of 1946, subcommittees have been a significant structural element of the committee system in the House. However, until the 1970s they were principally a tool of senior committee members, especially committee chairmen, who typically determined subcommittee structure, named members, assigned bills, allocated staff resources, and orchestrated the timing and sequence in which the full committee would take up their proposals and forward them to the floor. Because the structures were determined idiosyncratically by individual chairmen, committees could be very different. Ways and Means had no subcommittees. Armed Services had numbered subcommittees with no fixed jurisdictions. Appropriations had rigidly arranged subcommittees. In almost all cases the chairman called the tune, despite an occasional committee revolt.[26]

During the 1970s a series of reforms whittled away at the powers of the committee chairmen. In 1970 chairmen began to lose some control of their agendas. They could no longer refuse to call meetings; a committee majority could vote to meet anyway with the ranking majority member presiding. Once a rule had been granted for floor consideration of a bill, the chairman could not delay consideration for more than a week; after seven days, a committee majority could move floor consideration.

In 1973 the Democratic members of a House committee were designated as the committee caucus and empowered to choose subcommittee chairs and set subcommittee budgets. During the next two years, committees developed a procedure that allowed members, in order of committee seniority, to bid for subcommittee chairmanships. Also in 1973 the Democratic Caucus passed the Subcommittee Bill of Rights, which mandated that legislation be referred to subcommittees, that subcommittees have full control over their own agendas, and that they be provided with adequate

---

pp. 34–64; and James L. Sundquist, *The Decline and Resurgence of Congress* (Brookings, 1981).

26. In the 1960s there were revolts against the chairmen of the Interior and the Post Office committees, and against two separate chairmen of Education and Labor.

staff and budget.[27] In 1974 the Committee Reform Amendments required that full committees (Budget and Rules excepted) establish at least four subcommittees, an implicit strike against the undifferentiated structure of Ways and Means. In 1976 committee caucuses were given the authority to determine the number of subcommittees and their respective jurisdictions. Finally, in 1977 the selection procedure for committee chairs was changed, allowing the party caucus to elect them by secret ballot.

Full committees and their chairs thus had had their wings clipped. A chair was now beholden to the committee caucus, power had devolved upon subcommittees, and standing committees were rapidly becoming holding companies for their subunits.

Another center of power was created by the growth of member resources. Through House Resolution 5 and Senate Resolution 60, members were able to tap into committee and subcommittee budgets to hire staff to conduct their committee work. Additional resources were available for travel and office support. Budgets for congressional support agencies such as the General Accounting Office, the Congressional Research Service, and the Office of Technology Assessment, which individual members could employ for specific projects, also increased enormously. In short, member enterprises were becoming increasingly self-sufficient.

Committee power was also compromised by increased voting and amendment activity on the floor. The early 1970s marked the virtual end to anonymous floor votes. The secret ballot was never used in floor votes in the House, but voice votes, division votes, and unrecorded teller votes had allowed tallies to be detached from the identity of individual members. This changed as it became increasingly easy to demand a public roll call, a demand greatly facilitated by the advent of electronic voting in 1973.[28] Roll call votes in turn stimulated amendment activity on the floor.[29] In effect, full

27. David W. Rohde, "Committee Reform in the House of Representatives and the Subcommittee Bill of Rights," in Norman J. Ornstein, ed., *Changing Congress: The Committee System* (Philadelphia: American Academy of Political and Social Science, 1974), pp. 39–47.

28. Smith, "Going to the Floor."

29. Stanley Bach, "Representatives and Committees on the Floor: Amendments to Appropriations Bills in the House of Representatives, 1963–1982," *Congress and the Presidency*, vol. 13 (Spring 1986), pp. 1–58; and Steven S. Smith, "Revolution in the

committees and their chairs, robbed of some of their control of agendas by subcommittees, were now robbed of more control by this change in floor procedure.

Floor activity was further stimulated by the declining frequency with which the Rules Committee was permitted to issue closed rules, which barred floor amendments to legislation. The specific occasion for this change was the debate on retaining the oil depletion allowance. Because this tax break was protected by the Ways and Means Committee, on which the oil-producing states were well represented, efforts to change the policy could only come about through floor amendments. But Ways and Means bills traditionally were protected by a closed rule. The Democratic Caucus devised a policy in which a caucus majority could instruct its members on the Rules Committee to vote specific amendments in order. Applying this strategy to the oil depletion allowance, the caucus in effect ended the tradition of closed-rule protection of committee bills. This encouraged floor amendments and at the same time reduced committee control over final legislation. It also encouraged committees to anticipate floor behavior more carefully when they marked up a bill.[30]

Finally, committee dominance was challenged by the increased power of the Democratic Caucus and the Speaker. For all the delegation of committee operations to subcommittees and individual members, the changes in the congressional landscape were not all of one piece. In particular, before the 1970s the Democratic Caucus was a moribund organization primarily concerned with electing officers and attending to the final stages of committee assignments. After these activities were completed in the first few days of a new Congress, the caucus was rarely heard from. In the 1970s, however, as committees and chairmen were being undermined by subcommittees, there was a parallel movement to strengthen central party leadership and rank-and-file participation.

The first breach came in the seniority system. In 1971 the Democratic Caucus relieved its Committee on Committees—the Democratic members of the Ways and Means Committee—of having to

House: Why Don't We Do It on the Floor?'' Governmental Studies discussion paper 5 (Brookings, 1986).

30. Barry R. Weingast, "Floor Behavior in Congress: Committee Power Under the Open Rule," paper prepared for the 1987 annual meeting of the American Political Science Association.

rely on seniority in nominating committee chairs. This had the effect of putting sitting chairs on notice, although none was threatened at the time. In 1974 it became possible for a small number of caucus members to force individual votes on nominees for chairs and later to vote by secret ballot. In 1975 the caucus took upon itself the right to vote on subcommittee chairs of the Appropriations Committee. In that same year three incumbent chairmen were denied reelection to their posts (a fourth, Wilbur Mills, resigned under pressure).

Next came the democratizing reforms. Members were limited in the number of committee and subcommittee berths they could occupy and the number they could chair. As the constraints became more binding, it was necessary to move further down the ladder of seniority to fill positions. Power thus became more broadly distributed.

But perhaps the most significant reforms were those that strengthened the Speaker and made the position accountable to the caucus. In 1973 House party leaders (Speaker, majority leader, and whip) were included on the Committee on Committees, giving them an increased say in committee assignments. The caucus also established the Steering and Policy Committee with the Speaker as chair. In 1974 Democratic committee assignments were taken away from the party's complement on Ways and Means and given to the new committee. In addition, the Speaker was given the power to appoint and remove a majority of the members of the committee and the Democratic members of the Rules Committee. In 1974 the Speaker also was empowered to refer bills simultaneously or sequentially to several committees, to create ad hoc committees, and, in 1977, to set time limits for their deliberations. Finally, in 1977 Speaker Thomas P. O'Neill started employing task forces to develop and manage particular policy issues. These task forces overlapped but were not coincident with the committees of jurisdiction and, most significant, they were appointed by the Speaker.[31]

The caucus itself became more powerful. As mentioned, caucus majorities could instruct the Rules Committee and elect committee chairs and Appropriations subcommittee chairs. Caucus meetings could be called easily, requiring only a small number of signatories to a request, so that party matters could be thoroughly aired. In

31. Barbara Sinclair, "The Speaker's Task Force in the Post-Reform House of Representatives," *American Political Science Review*, vol. 75 (June 1981), pp. 397–410.

effect, the caucus became a substitute arena for both the floor and the committee rooms in which issues could be joined and majorities mobilized.

The revolt of the 1970s thus strengthened four power centers. It liberated members and subcommittees, restored to the Speakership an authority it had not known since the days of Joe Cannon, and invigorated the party caucus. Some of the reforms had a decentralizing effect, some a recentralizing effect. Standing committees and their chairs were caught in the middle. Geography and party benefited; the division-of-labor jurisdictions were its victims.

The Northernization of the South

Reform was not the only broad change taking place during the 1970s, though its effects were perhaps the most immediately visible. Changes in the electorate and in the economy were also having legislative repercussions.

Although the Democratic party in Congress was heavily southern in the 1940s and 1950s, in the ensuing decades the party became more thoroughly national, and the influence of its southern wing declined markedly. In this regard, not only did southern representation among Democrats decline numerically, but also the behavior of southern legislators became less distinctively southern.

The Voting Rights Act of 1965 was something of a watershed in this respect.[32] By the 1970s southern electorates began to show the effects of tremendous increases in black voter registration. Not only did the number of local black officeholders increase, but more important, white politicians began to take account of black voters in their electoral calculus. In district after district and state after state, blacks constituted a growing bloc of voters, especially in the Democratic primary. At the same time, there were indications of some white flight toward the Republicans.

The South also experienced rapid population growth as the outmigration, especially of blacks, that characterized the period of the textbook Congress was reversed and the inmigration of northerners increased. A revitalized Republican party benefited from this northern influx as well as from changes in the party loyalty of

32. Abigail M. Thernstrom, *Whose Votes Count? Affirmative Action and Minority Voting Rights* (Harvard University Press, 1987).

indigenous white southerners. More generally, the inmigration was accompanied by increased industrialization and urbanization, giving the South a demographic and socioeconomic profile more like the North than was true a generation before.

Throughout the 1970s popular writers, seduced by these changes, hailed the dawn of a new era, one of southern strategies and electoral realignments. They were half-right—the South was up for grabs at the presidential level (though this had been true for some time), and it has become routine to assume that southern electoral votes will most likely find their way into the Republican column, barring a Charles Robb, Sam Nunn, Albert Gore, or other native son candidacy for the Democrats. Elections for Congress and for state offices have been less reliably Republican, but the number of Republican governors and senators has increased. A realignment, however, has not transpired. Republicans have made only minor dents in the overwhelmingly Democratic flavor of local officeholders and congressmen.[33]

The mistake made by the pundits was to assume static behavior on the part of southern congressmen. But like good Downsian politicians, members of the House adapted to changes in their constituencies or were replaced by those who could adapt.

David Rohde has thoroughly analyzed the changing behavior of southern Democratic congressmen relative to their northern partisan colleagues.[34] Consider first their party loyalty. Between 1969 and 1973 the average difference between northern and southern Democrats on *Congressional Quarterly* party unity scores was 36 percentage points; northerners voted with the Democratic majority 84 percent of the time, southerners 48 percent of the time. Between 1975 and 1979 the difference shrank to 27 points and between 1981 and 1985 to 21 points; the difference fell to 14 points in 1986, when southern Democrats voted with their party 76 percent of the time. Between 1969 and 1986 southern party loyalty had increased 34 percentage points, whereas the northern increase was only 5 points.

Alternatively, consider the frequency of party voting. Between 1969 and 1973 a majority of northern and southern Democrats voted

33. Ferejohn and Fiorina, "Incumbency and Realignment."
34. David W. Rohde, "Something's Happening Here; What It Is Ain't Exactly Clear: Southern Democrats in the House of Representatives," paper prepared for the Conference in Honor of Richard Fenno, 1986.

together against a majority of Republicans on about one-third of all roll calls. By 1978 the proportion had risen to 38 percent, by 1983 to 43 percent, and in 1984–85, the last two years that Rohde reports, to 54 percent (the percentage is only slightly lower if the large number of roll calls concerning a disputed election result in Indiana is eliminated).

The argument these numbers support is that demographic and political change in the South has homogenized the Democratic party in the House. While this was not anticipated by the pundits, neither was it particularly apparent to the politicians. Indeed, the Reagan election in 1980 threw quite a scare into southern Democratic officeholders who often provided the margin of victory for David Stockman and company in 1981–82 (remember the Boll Weevils?) because they feared what the pundits hailed: a realignment that would reach all the way down to congressional districts. When the realignment failed to materialize in the 1982 elections, southern Democrats realized they could vote with their northern colleagues—for which they would be rewarded by their increasingly black and liberal primary-election constituencies—without being penalized in a general election. At the congressional district level, the Republicans were paper tigers.

The increasing homogeneity of the Democrats in Congress should probably not be attributed exclusively to southern changes of behavior. Northern districts and northern congressional behavior surely changed as well. But more important, the agenda of issues has changed to one which allows greater homogeneity in the behavior of the two regional wings of the Democratic party. While one might argue that the agenda is endogenous, reflecting the preferences of now more homogeneous Democrats, it has probably also been affected by the exogenous decline of race as an issue. For most of the 1940s and 1950s, race was the most divisive issue among Democrats. With the civil rights revolution of the 1960s and the adaptations to it of the 1970s, that is no longer so.

How has the northernization of the South affected the textbook Congress? The increasing homogenization within parties, and conflict between them, holds the key to the answer.[35] A party's ability

35. David W. Rohde and Kenneth A. Shepsle, "Leaders and Followers in the House of Representatives: Reflections on Woodrow Wilson's *Congressional Government*," *Congress and the Presidency*, vol. 14 (Autumn 1987), pp. 111–33; and Joseph

to operate coherently depends on how well its members agree on the substance of policy. When parties are holding companies for disparate views, members are unlikely to delegate power to centralized party institutions. Indeed, this seems to have been the case during the 1950s, when a heterogeneous decentralized Democratic party operated with weak party institutions and a Speaker who was at best a well-liked first among equals. Power emanated from senior members and committee chairmen. The party's growing homogeneity in the past twenty years has been accompanied by growing centralization—the rise of the caucus and the strengthening of the Speaker—that has occurred at the expense of committees and committee leaders.

The Fiscalization of Politics

The policy agenda was influenced not only by changing demographic factors in the mid-1970s but also by economic developments that were beginning to affect the way Congress went about its business.

The election of a Democratic president in 1960 liberated policy activists who had begun to fill the ranks of the Democratic party in Congress. Trying to finance a war and a number of new domestic programs at the same time, these Democratic majorities taxed and taxed, spent and spent (and elected and elected). They were certain they saw the "light at the end of the tunnel" in Vietnam and thus could finance their appetite for domestic social programs. During the Nixon presidency the spending and regulating continued. When President Nixon impounded funds to try to control the growth, he invoked a precedent that he claimed stretched back to Thomas Jefferson's administration. This situation encouraged a full-scale congressional consideration of taxing and spending arrangements in the early 1970s. As inflation and deficits mounted, reformers sought to restructure the ways expenditures and revenue raising were considered. The result was the Congressional Budget and Impoundment Control Act of 1974, which created two

Cooper and David W. Brady, "Institutional Context and Leadership Style: The House from Cannon to Rayburn," *American Political Science Review*, vol. 75 (June 1981), pp. 411–25.

budget committees and established the congressional budget process.[36]

Since then, analyzing the budget process has become an academic light industry.[37] I will focus on several aspects of the growing salience of fiscal matters that have affected the way Congress went about its business.

The most significant consequence of the Budget Act has been that Congress has had little time to consider anything else. Assessing the various budget resolutions, reconciliation acts, and proposals for deferrals and rescissions, and coordinating these moves with authorizing, appropriating, and revenue-raising actions, has stretched Congress's capacity to act. In fact, Congress often fails to complete its work and is forced to resort to such stop-gap, jerry-built schemes as continuing resolutions and other omnibus vehicles. By almost any measure the congressional work load has increased, yet the number of bills introduced and the proportion of those passed have declined precipitously. Congress, in short, has been enmeshed in its own procedures.

This impotence has been made worse by the growing dominance of entitlements in spending. As discretionary spending has been squeezed by a conservative administration and the discipline of the budget process, entitlements (of which most new ones were halted by the Budget Act of 1974) have come to dominate domestic spending. At the height of the Vietnam War, "uncontrollable" spending represented less than 60 percent of total spending. After the end of the war and the passage of the Budget Act, spending for entitlements jumped to 70 percent, and today it constitutes 75 percent of all spending.[38] Thus when Congress is not consumed by Budget Act requirements, appropriations bills, or supplemental

36. Allen Schick, *Congress and Money* (Washington, D.C.: Urban Institute, 1980); and Dennis S. Ippolito, *Congressional Spending* (Cornell University Press, 1981).

37. Schick, *Congress and Money*; Allen Schick, ed., *Making Economic Policy in Congress* (Washington, D.C.: American Enterprise Institute for Public Policy Research, 1983); Ippolito, *Congressional Spending*; Dennis S. Ippolito, *Hidden Spending* (University of North Carolina Press, 1984); Rudolph G. Penner, ed., *The Congressional Budget Process After Five Years* (Washington, D.C.: American Enterprise Institute for Public Policy Research, 1981); W. Thomas Wander, F. Ted Hebert, and Gary W. Copeland, eds., *Congressional Budgeting: Politics, Process, and the Power* (Johns Hopkins University Press, 1984); Howard E. Shuman, *Politics and the Budget* (Prentice-Hall, 1984); and G. Lowell Harriss, ed., *Control of Federal Spending* (New York: Academy of Political Science, 1985).

38. Ornstein and others, *Vital Statistics*, table 7-4.

appropriations, it spends most of its time renewing and revising measures about to expire; many of these involve entitlements. As a legislative body, Congress no longer does much legislating. No wonder the constant refrain on the Hill is "nothing gets done around here."[39]

The tempo of legislative activity is also increasingly dictated by the Budget committees, and this has generated a good deal of animosity toward them. When I was completing my study of committee assignments, which ended with the Ninety-fourth Congress (1974–75), the House Budget Committee was not a particularly popular committee to request.[40] By the 1980s, competition for berths had risen to a level seen only for the exclusive committees (and perhaps the Commerce Committee) in the past. Substantive legislative committees, as well as Appropriations and Ways and Means, often take considerable umbrage at having to conform their legislative processes to constraints imposed by the Budget committees.

Perhaps of greatest theoretical relevance, congressional activities today are considerably more interdependent than before the Budget Act, another indication that the division of labor that characterized the textbook Congress has eroded. The fiscalization of politics has compounded the effects of the representational revolt of the 1970s. It has diminished the stature of standing committees, encouraged members to become generalists rather than specialists,

---

39. It is reasonable to ask why Congress has permitted this situation to persist. If entitlement legislation has contributed to legislative logjams and the squeezing of domestic discretionary spending, why doesn't Congress change it? The answer has two parts. First, the aim of an entitlement strategy is precisely to prevent future Congresses from easily enacting changes opposed by program proponents. Dating back at least to Franklin Roosevelt's formulation of social security legislation, program advocates have realized that the only way to reduce spending on an entitlement activity (since it does not pass through the ordinary appropriations process) is to change the definition of eligibility and other program parameters. To do this under normal procedures requires the acquiescence of the congressional committees with legislative jurisdiction, since they must bring forth a bill containing proposed statutory changes. However, given the accommodating nature of the committee assignment process, these committees are typically stacked with program supporters. Consequently, they are in a position to veto adverse changes. Second, however, changes have been effected in entitlement programs through "abnormal" procedures. This was the genius of David Stockman's strategy in using the reconciliation procedure (a part of the budget process created by the Budget Act) to force committees to weigh trade-offs between entitlement spending and discretionary spending in the 1981 Gramm-Latta maneuvers.

40. Shepsle, *The Giant Jigsaw Puzzle*.

ceded political advantage to those in party leadership positions, and put a premium on coordination among policy areas.

The Reagan years have witnessed the continuation of this trend. The decline in revenues caused by the Economic Recovery Tax Act of 1981, combined with the substantial growth in military discretionary spending that began in the Carter administration, squeezed domestic discretionary spending and caused deficits to surge. While Democrats in Congress employ the rhetoric of fiscal responsibility, some of them continue to urge new domestic programs in a way reminiscent of the late 1950s. But the legislative demands now confront the reality of incentives for less specialization, less activism, and more centrally orchestrated coordination.

In the 1970s and 1980s, then, the postwar textbook portrait of congressional politics has been increasingly wide of the mark. The division-of-labor committee system, while still an important feature of Congress, is not what it once was; nor are the chairmen of standing committees the powers they once were. The power centers of the textbook Congress—the Rules, Ways and Means, and Appropriations committees and the committee chairmen—have been replaced by other power centers—the member enterprises, the Budget committees, the party caucus, central party leaders, and subcommittee chairmen. Demographic and economic changes have further eroded the broad contours of the textbook Congress, replacing the deep partisan divisions in the Democratic party in the 1950s with greater homogeneity in and distinctiveness between the parties. The fiscalization of politics has maintained the momentum, set into motion by the reforms of the 1970s, toward recentralization, interdependence among policy areas, and a growing premium placed on political skill on the floor and coordination of committees' activities.

A NEW TEXTBOOK CONGRESS?

The textbook Congress of the 1940s and 1950s reflected an equilibrium of sorts among institutional structure, partisan alignments, and electoral forces. There was a "conspiracy" between jurisdiction and geography. Congressional institutions were organized around policy jurisdictions, and geographic forces were accommodated through an assignment process that ensured representatives would land berths on committees important to their constituents. Reciprocity and deference sealed the bargain. Committees controlled policy formation in their respective jurisdictions. Floor activity was generally dominated by members from the committee of jurisdiction. Members' resources were sufficiently modest that they were devoted chiefly to committee-related activities. Constituencies were sufficiently homogeneous that this limitation did not, for most members, impose much hardship. Coordination was accomplished by senior committee members, each minding his own store. This system was supported by a structure that rewarded specialization, hard work, and waiting one's turn in the queue. Parties hovered in the background as the institutional means for organizing each chamber and electing leaders. Occasionally they would serve to mobilize majorities for partisan objectives, but these occasions were rare. The parties, especially the Democrats, were heterogeneous holding companies, incapable of cohering around specific policy directions except under unusual circumstances and therefore unwilling to empower their respective leaders or caucuses.

Something happened in the 1960s. The election of an executive and a congressional majority from the same party certainly was one important feature. Policy activism, restrained since the end of World War II, was encouraged. This exacerbated some divisions inside the Democratic coalition, leading to piecemeal institutional tinkering such as the expansion of the Rules Committee and the circumvention of the Appropriations Committee. At the same time the Voting Rights Act, occasioned by the temporarily oversized condition of the majority party in the Eighty-ninth Congress, set into motion political events that, together with demographic and economic trends, altered political alignments in the South. By the 1980s, Democrats from the North and the South were coming into greater agreement on matters of policy.

Thus the underlying conditions supporting the equilibrium among geographical, jurisdictional, and partisan imperatives were overwhelmed during the 1960s. The 1970s witnessed adjustments to these changed conditions that transformed the textbook Congress. Institutional reform was initiated by the Democratic Caucus. Demographic, generational, and political trends, frustrated by the inexorable workings of the seniority system, sought an alternative mode of expression. Majorities in the caucus remade the committee system. With this victimization came less emphasis on specialization, less deference toward committees as the floor became a genuine forum for policy formulation, and a general fraying of the division of labor.

One trend began with the Legislative Reorganization Act of 1946 itself. In the past forty years members have gradually acquired the resources to free themselves from other institutional players. The condition of the contemporary member of Congress has been described as "atomistic individualism" and the members themselves have been called "enterprises."[41] The slow accretion of resources permitted members to respond to the changes in their home districts and encouraged them to cross the boundaries of specialization. These developments began to erode the reciprocity, deference, and division of labor that defined the textbook Congress.

The old equilibrium between geography and jurisdiction, with party hovering in the background, has changed. Geography (as represented by resource-rich member enterprises) has undermined the strictures of jurisdiction. But has the new order liberated party from its former holding-company status? In terms of political power the Democratic Caucus has reached new heights in the past decade. Party leaders have not had so many institutional tools and resources since the days of Boss Cannon. Committee leaders have never in the modern era been weaker or more beholden to party institutions. And, in terms of voting behavior, Democrats and Republicans have not exhibited as much internal cohesion in a good long while. Party, it would seem, is on the rise. But so, too, are the member enterprises.

What, then, has grown up in the vacuum created by the demise of the textbook Congress? I am not convinced that relationships have settled into a regular pattern in anything like the way they were institutionalized in the textbook Congress.

First, too many members of Congress remain too dissatisfied. The aggressive moves by Jim Wright to redefine the Speaker's role are a partial response to this circumstance.[42] Prospective changes in the Senate majority party leadership alignment in the 101st Congress convey a similar signal. The issue at stake is whether central

41. Samuel Kernell, *Going Public: New Strategies of Presidential Leadership* (CQ Press, 1986); and Salisbury and Shepsle, "Congressman as Enterprise."

42. Janet Hook, "Jim Wright: Taking Big Risks to Amass Power," *Congressional Quarterly Weekly Report*, vol. 46 (March 12, 1988), pp. 623–26.

party organs can credibly coordinate activities in Congress, thereby damping the centrifugal tendencies of resource-rich members, or whether leaders will remain, in one scholar's words, "janitors for an untidy chamber."[43]

One possible equilibrium of a new textbook Congress, therefore, would have member enterprises balanced off against party leaders; committees and other manifestations of a specialized division of labor would be relegated to the background. Coordination, formerly achieved in a piecemeal, decentralized fashion by the committee system, would fall heavily on party leaders and their institutional allies, the Rules and Budget committees and the party caucuses. However, unless party leaders can construct a solution to the budgetary mess in Congress—a solution that will entail revising the budget process—the burden of coordination will be more than the leaders can bear.[44] Government by continuing resolutions, reconciliation proposals, and other omnibus mechanisms forms an unstable fulcrum for institutional equilibrium.

Second, any success from the continued strengthening of leadership resources and institutions is highly contingent on the support of the members. Strong leadership institutions have to be seen by the rank and file as solutions to institutional problems. This requires a consensus among majority party members both on the nature of the problems and the desirability of the solutions. A consensus of sorts has existed for several years: demographic and other trends have homogenized the priorities of Democrats; experience with the spate of reforms in the 1970s has convinced many that decentralized ways of doing things severely tax the capacity of Congress to act; and, since 1982, the Reagan presidency has provided a unifying target.

But what happens if the bases for consensus erode? A major issue—trade and currency problems, for instance, or war in Central America or the Middle East—could set region against region within the majority party and reverse the trend toward consensus. Alternatively, the election of a Democratic president could redefine the roles of legislative leaders, possibly pitting congressional and pres-

43. Roger H. Davidson, "Senate Leaders: Janitors for an Untidy Chamber?" in Dodd and Oppenheimer, *Congress Reconsidered*, 3d ed., pp. 225–52.

44. Kenneth A. Shepsle, "The Congressional Budget Process: Diagnosis, Prescription, Prognosis," in Wander, Hebert, and Copeland, *Congressional Budgeting*, pp. 190–217.

idential factions against one another in a battle for partisan leadership.[45] The point here is that the equilibrium between strong leaders and strong members is vulnerable to perturbations in the circumstances supporting it.

The next few years will be an institutionally messy period during which Speaker Wright and whoever succeeds Senate Majority Leader Robert Byrd have some time to solidify the coordinating power of the central leadership. I would be surprised if the power survived without some major institutional reorganization, perhaps the restoration of some power to committee chairs or the renovation of the budget process. The member enterprises, however, will not go away. Members will never again be as specialized, as deferential, as willing "to go along to get along" as in the textbook Congress of the 1950s. For better or worse, we are stuck with full-service members of Congress. They are incredibly competent at representing the diverse interests that geographic representation has given them. But can they pass a bill or mobilize a coalition? Can they govern?

45. Might this be reminiscent of the late nineteenth century conflict, when "party government" in the legislature was at something of a high-water mark, between Republican President William McKinley and Republican Speaker Thomas Reed, not over the issue of party government, but rather over the location of party leadership—White House or Speaker's chair? The conflict ended with Reed's resignation from the Speakership. A classic treatment of conflict between presidential and congressional wings of American parties is James MacGregor Burns, *The Deadlock of Democracy* (Prentice-Hall, 1963).

The Politics of Bureaucratic Structure

TERRY M. MOE

AMERICAN PUBLIC bureaucracy is not designed to be effective. The bureaucracy arises out of politics, and its design reflects the interests, strategies, and compromises of those who exercise political power.

This politicized notion of bureaucracy has never appealed to most academics or reformers. They accept it—indeed, they adamantly argue its truth—and the social science of public bureaucracy is a decidedly political body of work as a result. Yet, for the most part, those who study and practice public administration have a thinly veiled disdain for politics, and they want it kept out of bureaucracy as much as possible. They want presidents to stop politicizing the departments and bureaus. They want Congress to stop its incessant meddling in bureaucratic affairs. They want all politicians to respect bureaucratic autonomy, expertise, and professionalism.[1]

The bureaucracy's defenders are not apologists. Problems of capture, inertia, parochialism, fragmentation, and imperialism are familiar grounds for criticism. And there is lots of criticism. But once the subversive influence of politics is mentally factored out, these bureaucratic problems are understood to have bureaucratic solutions—new mandates, new rules and procedures, new personnel systems, better training and management, better people. These are the quintessential reforms that politicians are urged to adopt to bring about effective bureaucracy. The goal at all times is the greater good: "In designing any political structure, whether it be

I want to extend special thanks to Gary J. Miller for his valuable collaboration during the early stages of this project.

1. Harold Seidman and Robert Gilmour, *Politics, Position, and Power: From the Positive to the Regulatory State*, 4th ed. (Oxford University Press, 1986); and Frederick C. Mosher, *Democracy and the Public Service*, 2d ed. (Oxford University Press, 1982).

the Congress, the executive branch, or the judiciary, it is important to build arrangements that weigh the scale in favor of those advocating the national interest."[2]

The hitch is that those in positions of power are not necessarily motivated by the national interest. They have their own interests to pursue in politics—the interests of southwest Pennsylvania or cotton farmers or the maritime industry—and they exercise their power in ways conducive to those interests. Moreover, choices about bureaucratic structure are not matters that can be separated off from all this, to be guided by technical criteria of efficiency and effectiveness. Structural choices have important consequences for the content and direction of policy, and political actors know it. When they make choices about structure, they are implicitly making choices about policy. And precisely because this is so, issues of structure are inevitably caught up in the larger political struggle. Any notion that political actors might confine their attention to policymaking and turn organizational design over to neutral criteria or efficiency experts denies the realities of politics.

This essay is an effort to understand bureaucracy by understanding its foundation in political choice and self-interest. The central question boils down to this: what sorts of structures do the various political actors—interest groups, presidents, members of Congress, bureaucrats—find conducive to their own interests, and what kind of bureaucracy is therefore likely to emerge from their efforts to exercise political power? In other words, why do they build the bureaucracy they do?

The analysis is divided into two parts. The first outlines a theoretical perspective on the politics of structural choice. The second puts this perspective to use in exploring the structural politics of three modern bureaucracies: the Consumer Product Safety Commission, the Occupational Safety and Health Administration, and the Environmental Protection Agency.

A PERSPECTIVE ON STRUCTURAL POLITICS

Most citizens do not get terribly excited about the arcane details of public administration. When they choose among candidates in

2. Seidman and Gilmour, *Politics, Position, and Power*, p. 330.

elections, they pay attention to such things as party or image or stands on policy. If pressed, the candidates would probably have views or even voting records on structural issues—for example, whether the Occupational Safety and Health Administration should be required to carry out cost-benefit analysis before proposing a formal rule or whether the Consumer Product Safety Commission should be moved into the Commerce Department—but this is hardly the stuff that political campaigns are made of. People just do not know or care much about these sorts of things.

Organized interest groups are another matter. They are active, informed participants in their specialized issue areas, and they know that their policy goals are crucially dependent on precisely those fine details of administrative structure that cause voters' eyes to glaze over. Structure is valuable to them, and they have every incentive to mobilize their political resources to get what they want. As a result, they are normally the only source of political pressure when structural issues are at stake. Structural politics is interest group politics.

Interest Groups: The Technical Problem of Structural Choice

Most accounts of structural politics pay attention to interest groups, but their analytical focus is on the politicians who exercise public authority and make the final choices. This tends to be misleading. It is well known that politicians, even legislators from safe districts, are extraordinarily concerned about their electoral popularity and, for that reason, are highly responsive to their constituencies.[3] To the extent this holds true, their positions on issues are not really their own, but are induced by the positions of others. If one seeks to understand why structural choices turn out as they do, then, it does not make much sense to start with politicians. The more fundamental questions have to do with how interest groups decide what kinds of structures they want politicians to provide. This is the place to start.

In approaching these questions about interest groups, it is useful to begin with an extreme case. Suppose that, in a given issue

3. David R. Mayhew, *Congress: The Electoral Connection* (Yale University Press, 1974); and Morris P. Fiorina, *Representatives, Roll Calls, and Constituencies* (Lexington Books, 1974).

area, there is a single dominant group (or coalition) with a reasonably complex problem—pollution, poverty, job safety, health—it seeks to address through governmental action, and that the group is so powerful that politicians will enact virtually any proposal the group offers, subject to reasonable budget constraints. In effect, the group is able to exercise public authority on its own by writing legislation that is binding on everyone and enforceable in the courts.

The dominant group is an instructive case because, as it makes choices about structure, it faces no political problems. It need not worry about losing its grip on public authority or about the influence of its political opponents—considerations which, as I will later show, would otherwise weigh heavily in its calculations. Without the usual uncertainties and constraints of politics, the group has the luxury of concerning itself entirely with the technical requirements of effective organization. Its job is to identify those structural arrangements that best realize its policy goals.[4]

It is perhaps natural to think that, since a dominant group can have anything it wants, it would proceed by figuring out what types of behaviors are called for by what types of people under what types of conditions and by writing legislation spelling all this out in the minutest detail. If an administrative agency were necessary to perform services, process applications, or inspect business operations, the jobs of bureaucrats could be specified with such precision that they would have little choice but to do the group's bidding.

For simple policy goals—requiring, say, little more than transfer payments—these strategies would be attractive. But they are quite unsuited to policy problems of any complexity. The reason is that, although the group has the political power to impose its will on everyone, it almost surely lacks the knowledge to do it well. It does not know what to tell people to do.

In part, this is an expertise problem. Society as a whole simply

---

4. The reasoning in this section follows that of recent work on contingent-claims contracting, agency theory, and other components of the "new economics of organization." For an extensive but accessible treatment of the broader literature, see Oliver E. Williamson, *The Economic Institutions of Capitalism: Firms, Markets, Relational Contracting* (Free Press, 1985); Terry M. Moe, "The New Economics of Organization," *American Journal of Political Science*, vol. 28 (November 1984), pp. 739–77; and David M. Kreps, "Corporate Culture and Economic Theory" (Stanford University Graduate School of Business, 1984).

has not developed sufficient knowledge to determine the causes of or solutions for most social problems; and the group typically knows much less than society does, even when it hires experts of its own. These knowledge problems are compounded by uncertainty about the future. The world is subject to unpredictable changes over time, and some will call for specific policy adjustments if the group's interests are to be pursued effectively. The group could attempt to specify all future contingencies in the current legislation and, through continuous monitoring and intervention, update it over time. But the knowledge requirements of a halfway decent job would prove enormously costly, cumbersome, and time-consuming.

A group with the political power to tell everyone what to do, then, will typically not find it worthwhile to try. A more attractive option is to write legislation in general terms, put experts on the public payroll, and grant them the authority to "fill in the details" and make whatever adjustments are necessary over time. This compensates nicely for the group's formidable knowledge problems, allowing it to pursue its own interests without knowing exactly how to implement its policies and without having to grapple with future contingencies. The experts do what the group is unable to do for itself. And because they are public officials on the public payroll, the arrangement economizes greatly on the group's resources and time.

It does, however, raise a new worry: there is no guarantee the experts will always act in the group's best interests. Experts have their own interests—in career, in autonomy—that may conflict with those of the group. And, due largely to experts' specialized knowledge and the often intangible nature of their outputs, the group cannot know exactly what its expert agents are doing or why. These are problems of conflict of interest and asymmetric information, and they are unavoidable. Because of them, control will be imperfect.

When the group's political power is assured, as we assume it is here, these control problems are at the heart of structural choice. The most direct approach is for the group to impose a set of rules to constrain bureaucratic behavior. Among other things, these rules might specify the criteria and procedures bureaucrats are to use in making decisions; shape incentives by specifying how bureaucrats are to be evaluated, rewarded, and sanctioned; require them to collect and report certain kinds of information on their internal operations; and set up oversight procedures by which their activities can be monitored. These are basic components of bureaucratic structure.

But some slippage will remain. The group's knowledge problems, combined with the experts' will and capacity to resist (at least at the margins), make perfect control impossible. Fortunately, though, the group can do more than impose a set of rules on its agents. It also has the power to choose who its agents will be—and wise use of this power could make the extensive use of rules unnecessary.

The key here is reputation.[5] Most individuals in the expert market come with reputations that speak to their job-relevant traits: expertise, intelligence, honesty, loyalty, policy preferences, ideology. "Good" reputations provide reliable information. The reason is that individuals value good reputations, they invest in them—by behaving honestly, for instance, even when they could realize short-term gains through cheating—and, having built up reputations, they have strong incentives to maintain them through consistent behavior. To the group, therefore, reputation is of enormous value because it allows predictability in an uncertain world. And predictability facilitates control.

To see more concretely how this works, consider an important reputational syndrome: professionalism. If individuals are known to be accountants or securities lawyers or highway engineers, the group will immediately know a great deal about their "type." They will be experts in certain issues. They will have specialized educations and occupational experiences. They will analyze issues, collect data, and propose solutions in characteristic ways. They will hew to the norms of their professional communities. Particularly when professionalism is combined with reputational information of a more personal nature, the behavior of these experts will be highly predictable.

The link between predictability and control would seem especially troublesome in this case, since professionals are widely known to demand autonomy in their work. And, as far as restrictive rules and hierarchical directives are concerned, their demand for autonomy does indeed pose problems. But the group is forced

5. On the rationality and consequences of reputations, see especially Kreps, "Corporate Culture and Economic Theory."

to grant experts discretion anyway, owing to its knowledge problems. What professionalism does—via reputation—is allow the group to anticipate how expert discretion will be exercised under various conditions; it can then plan accordingly as it designs a structure that takes best advantage of their expertise. In the extreme, one might think of professionals as automatons, programmed to behave in specific ways. Knowing how they are programmed, the group can select those with the desired programs, place them in a structure designed to accommodate them, and turn them loose to exercise free choice. The professionals would see themselves as independent decisionmakers. The group would see them as under control. And both would be right.[6]

The purpose of this illustration is not to emphasize professionalism per se, but to clarify a general point about the technical requirements of organizational design. A politically powerful group, acting under uncertainty and concerned with solving a complex policy problem, is normally best off if it resists using its power to tell bureaucrats exactly what to do. It can use its power more productively by selecting the right types of bureaucrats and designing a structure that affords them reasonable autonomy. Through the judicious allocation of bureaucratic roles and responsibilities, incentive systems, and structural checks on bureaucratic choice, a select set of bureaucrats can be unleashed to follow their expert judgment, free from detailed formal instructions.

Interest Groups: The Political Problem of Structural Choice

Political dominance is an extreme case for purposes of illustration. In the real world of democratic politics, interest groups cannot lay claim to unchallenged legal authority. Because this is so, they face two fundamental problems that a dominant group does not. The first I will call political uncertainty, the second political compromise. Both have enormous consequences for the strategic design of public bureaucracy—consequences that entail substantial departures from effective organization.

Political uncertainty is inherent in democratic government. No

6. For an illustration of how this happens in political practice, see Terry M. Moe, "Interests, Institutions, and Positive Theory: The Politics of the NLRB," *Studies in American Political Development*, vol. 2 (1987), pp. 236–99.

one has a perpetual hold on public authority nor, therefore, a perpetual right to control public agencies. An interest group may be powerful enough to exercise public authority today, but tomorrow its power may ebb, and its right to exercise public authority may then be usurped by its political opponents. Should this occur, they would become the new "owners" of whatever the group had created, and they could use their authority to destroy—quite legitimately—everything the group had worked so hard to achieve.

A group that is currently advantaged, then, must anticipate all this. Precisely because its own authority is not guaranteed, it cannot afford to focus entirely on technical issues of effective organization. It must also design its creations so that they have the capacity to pursue its policy goals in a world in which its enemies may achieve the right to govern. The group's task in the current period, then, is to build agencies that are difficult for its opponents to gain control over later. Given the way authority is allocated and exercised in a democracy, this will often mean building agencies that are insulated from public authority in general—and thus insulated from formal control by the group itself.

There are various structural means by which the group can try to protect and nurture its bureaucratic agents. They include the following.

—It can write detailed legislation that imposes rigid constraints on the agency's mandate and decision procedures. While these constraints will tend to be flawed, cumbersome, and costly, they serve to remove important types of decisions from future political control. The reason they are so attractive is rooted in the American separation-of-powers system, which sets up obstacles that make formal legislation extremely difficult to achieve—and, if achieved, extremely difficult to overturn. Should the group's opponents gain in political power, there is a good chance they would still not be able to pass corrective legislation of their own.

—It can place even greater emphasis on professionalism than is technically justified, since professionals will generally act to protect their own autonomy and resist political interference. For similar reasons, the group can be a strong supporter of the career civil service and other personnel systems that insulate bureaucratic jobs, promotion, and pay from political intervention. And it can try to minimize the power and number of political appointees, since these too are routes by which opponents may exercise influence.

—It can oppose formal provisions that enhance political oversight and involvement. The legislative veto, for example, is bad because it gives opponents a direct mechanism for reversing agency decisions. Sunset provisions, which require reauthorization of the agency after some period of time, are also dangerous because they give opponents opportunities to overturn the group's legislative achievements.

—It can see that the agency is given a safe location in the scheme of government. Most obviously, it might try to place the agency in a friendly executive department, where it can be sheltered by the group's allies. Or it may favor formal independence, which provides special protection from presidential removal and managerial powers.

—It can favor judicialization of agency decisionmaking as a way of insulating policy choices from outside interference. It can also favor making various types of agency actions—or inactions—appealable to the courts. It must take care to design these procedures and checks, however, so that they disproportionately favor the group over its opponents.

The driving force of political uncertainty, then, causes the winning group to favor structural designs it would never favor on technical grounds alone: designs that place detailed formal restrictions on bureaucratic discretion, impose complex procedures for agency decisionmaking, minimize opportunities for oversight, and otherwise insulate the agency from politics. The group has to protect itself and its agency from the dangers of democracy, and it does so by imposing structures that appear strange and incongruous indeed when judged by almost any reasonable standards of what an effective organization ought to look like.

But this is only part of the story. The departure from technical rationality is still greater because of a second basic feature of American democratic politics: legislative victory of any consequence almost always requires compromise. This means that opposing groups will have a direct say in how the agency and its mandate are constructed. One form that this can take, of course, is the classic compromise over policy that is written about endlessly in textbooks and newspapers. But there is no real disjunction between policy and structure, and many of the opponents' interests will also be pursued through demands for structural concessions. What sorts of arrangements should they tend to favor?

—Opponents want structures that work against effective performance. They fear strong, coherent, centralized organization. They like fragmented authority, decentralization, federalism, checks and balances, and other structural means of promoting weakness, confusion, and delay.

—They want structures that allow politicians to get at the agency. They do not want to see the agency placed within a friendly department, nor do they favor formal independence. They are enthusiastic supporters of legislative veto and reauthorization provisions. They favor onerous requirements for the collection and reporting of information, the monitoring of agency operations, and the review of agency decisions—thus laying the basis for active, interventionist oversight by politicians.

—They want appointment and personnel arrangements that allow for political direction of the agency. They also want more active and influential roles for political appointees and less extensive reliance on professionalism and the civil service.

—They favor agency decisionmaking procedures that allow them to participate, to present evidence and arguments, to appeal adverse agency decisions, to delay, and, in general, to protect their own interests and inhibit effective agency action through formal, legally sanctioned rules. This means that they will tend to push for cumbersome, heavily judicialized decision processes, and that they will favor an active, easily triggered role for the courts in reviewing agency decisions.

—They want agency decisions to be accompanied by, and partially justified in terms of, "objective" assessments of their consequences: environmental impact statements, inflation impact statements, cost-benefit analysis. These are costly, time-consuming, and disruptive. Even better, their methods and conclusions can be challenged in the courts, providing new opportunities for delaying or quashing agency decisions.

Political compromise ushers the fox into the chicken coop. Opposing groups are dedicated to crippling the bureaucracy and gaining control over its decisions, and they will pressure for fragmented authority, labyrinthine procedures, mechanisms of political intervention, and other structures that subvert the bureaucracy's performance and open it up to attack. In the politics of structural choice, the inevitability of compromise means that agencies will be burdened with structures fully intended to cause their failure.

In short, democratic government gives rise to two major forces that cause the structure of public bureaucracy to depart from technical rationality. First, those currently in a position to exercise public authority will often face uncertainty about their own grip on political power in the years ahead, and this will prompt them to favor structures that insulate their achievements from politics. Second, opponents will also tend to have a say in structural design, and, to the degree they do, they will impose structures that subvert effective performance and politicize agency decisions.

Legislators and Structural Choice

If politicians were nothing more than conduits for political pressures, structural choice could be understood without paying much attention to them. But politicians, especially presidents, do sometimes have preferences about the structure of government that are not simple reflections of what the groups want. And when this is so, they can use their control of public authority to make their preferences felt in structural outcomes.

The conduit notion is not so wide of the mark for legislators, owing to their almost paranoid concern for reelection. In structural politics, well-informed interest groups make demands, observe legislators' responses, and accurately assign credit and blame as decisions are made and consequences realized. Legislators therefore have strong incentives to do what groups want—and, even in the absence of explicit demands, to take entrepreneurial action in actively representing group interests. They cannot satisfy groups with empty position taking. Nor can they costlessly "shift the responsibility" by delegating tough decisions to the bureaucracy.[7] Interest groups, unlike voters, are not easily fooled.

7. For a perspective on delegation that centers on the calculus of legislators rather than interest groups—and that leads, as a result, to very different conclusions about the politics of structural choice—see Morris P. Fiorina, "Legislative Choice of Regulatory Forms: Legal Process or Administrative Process?" *Public Choice*, vol. 39 (September 1982), pp. 33–66; "Group Concentration and the Delegation of Legislative Authority," in Roger G. Noll, ed., *Regulatory Policy and the Social Sciences* (University of California Press, 1982), pp. 175–97; and "Legislator Uncertainty, Legislative

This does not mean that legislators always do what groups demand of them. Autonomous behavior can arise even among legislators who are motivated by nothing other than reelection. This happens because politicians, like groups, recognize that their current choices are not just means of responding to current pressures, but are also means of imposing structure on their political lives. This will sometimes lead them to make unpopular choices today in order to reap political rewards later on.[8]

It is not quite right, moreover, to suggest that legislators have no interest of their own in controlling the bureaucracy. The more control legislators are able to exercise, the more groups will depend on them to get what they want; and this, in itself, makes control electorally attractive. But the attractiveness of control is diluted by other factors. First, the winning group—the more powerful side—will pressure to have its victories removed from political influence. Second, the capacity for control can be a curse for legislators in later conflict, since both sides will descend on them repeatedly. Third, oversight for purposes of serious policy control is time-consuming, costly, and difficult to do well; legislators typically have much more productive ways to spend their scarce resources.[9]

The result is that legislators tend not to invest in general policy control. Instead, they value "particularized" control: they want to be able to intervene quickly, inexpensively, and in ad hoc ways to protect or advance the interests of particular clients in particular matters.[10] This sort of control can be managed by an individual legislator without collective action; it has direct payoffs; it will generally be carried out behind the scenes; and it does not involve or provoke conflict. It generates political benefits without political costs. Moreover, it fits in quite nicely with a bureaucratic structure designed for conflict avoidance: an agency that is highly autonomous in the realm of policy yet highly constrained by complex

---

Control, and the Delegation of Legislative Power," *Journal of Law, Economics, and Organization*, vol. 2 (Spring 1986), pp. 33–51.

8. For a more extensive discussion of this point and its relation to both conflict avoidance and the "shift the responsibility" phenomenon, see Terry M. Moe, "The Politics of Structural Choice: Toward a Theory of Public Bureaucracy," paper prepared for the 1988 annual meeting of the American Political Science Association.

9. Lawrence C. Dodd and Richard L. Schott, *Congress and the Administrative State*, 2d ed. (Macmillan, 1986).

10. Mayhew, *Congress: The Electoral Connection*.

procedural requirements will offer all sorts of opportunities for particularistic interventions.

The more general point is that legislators, by and large, can be expected either to respond to group demands in structural politics or to take entrepreneurial action in trying to please them. They will not be given to flights of autonomous action or statesmanship.

Presidents and Structural Choice

Presidents are motivated differently. Governance is the driving force behind the modern presidency. All presidents, regardless of party, are expected to govern effectively and are held responsible for taking action on virtually the full range of problems facing society. To be judged successful in the eyes of history—arguably the single most important motivator for presidents—they must appear to be strong leaders. They need to achieve their policy initiatives, their initiatives must be regarded as socially valuable, and the structures for attaining them must appear to work.[11]

This raises two basic problems for interest groups. The first is that presidents are not very susceptible to the appeals of special interests. They want to make groups happy, to be sure, and sometimes responding to group demands will contribute nicely to governance. But this is often not so. In general, presidents have incentives to think in grander terms about what is best for society as a whole, or at least broad chunks of it, and they have their own agendas that may depart substantially from what even their more prominent group supporters might want. Even when they are simply responding to group pressures—which is more likely, of course, during their first term—the size and heterogeneity of their support coalitions tend to promote moderation, compromise, opposition to capture, and concern for social efficiency.

The second problem is that presidents want to control the bureaucracy. While legislators eagerly delegate their powers to administrative agencies, presidents are driven to take charge. They do not care about all agencies equally, of course. Some agencies are especially important because their programs are priority items on

11. Terry M. Moe, "The Politicized Presidency," in John E. Chubb and Paul E. Peterson, eds., *The New Direction in American Politics* (Brookings, 1985), pp. 235–71.

the presidential agenda. Others are important because they deal with sensitive issues that can become political bombshells if something goes wrong. But most all agencies impinge in one way or another on larger presidential responsibilities—for the budget, for the economy, for national defense—and presidents must have the capacity to direct and constrain agency behavior in basic respects if these larger responsibilities are to be handled successfully. They may often choose not to use their capacity for administrative control; they may even let favored groups use it when it suits their purposes. But the capacity must be there when they need it.

Presidents therefore have a unique role to play in the politics of structural choice. They are the only participants who are directly concerned with how the bureaucracy as a whole should be organized. And they are the only ones who actually want to run it through hands-on management and control. Their ideal is a rational, coherent, centrally directed bureaucracy that strongly resembles popular textbook notions of what an effective bureaucracy, public or private, ought to look like.

In general, presidents favor placing agencies within executive departments and subordinating them to hierarchical authority. They want to see important oversight, budget, and policy coordination functions given to department superiors—and, above them, to the Office of Management and Budget and other presidential management agencies—so that the bureaucracy can be brought under unified direction. While they value professionalism and civil service for their contributions to expertise, continuity, and impartiality, they want authority in the hands of their own political appointees—and they want to choose appointees whose types appear most conducive to presidential leadership.

This is just what the winning group and its legislative allies do not want. They want to protect their agencies and policy achievements by insulating them from politics, and presidents threaten to ruin everything by trying to control these agencies from above. The opposing groups are delighted with this, but they cannot always take comfort in the presidential approach to bureaucracy either. For presidents will tend to resist complex procedural protections, excessive judicial review, legislative veto provisions, and many other means by which the losers try to protect themselves and cripple bureaucratic performance. Presidents want agencies to have discretion, flexibility, and the capacity to take direction. They do not want agencies to be hamstrung by rules and regulations—unless, of course, they are presidential rules and regulations designed to enhance presidential control.

Legislators, Presidents, and Interest Groups

Obviously, presidents and legislators have very different orientations to the politics of structural choice. Interest groups can be expected to anticipate these differences from the outset and devise their own strategies accordingly.

Generally speaking, groups on both sides will find Congress a comfortable place in which to do business. Legislators are not bound by any overarching notion of what the bureaucracy as a whole ought to look like. They are not intrinsically motivated by effectiveness or efficiency or coordination or management or any other design criteria that might limit the kind of bureaucracy they are willing to create. They do not even want to retain political control for themselves.

The key thing about Congress is that it is open and responsive to what the groups want. It willingly builds, piece by piece—however grotesque the pieces, however inconsistent with one another—the kind of bureaucracy interest groups incrementally demand in their structural battles over time. This "congressional bureaucracy" is not supposed to function as a coherent whole, nor even to constitute one. Only the pieces are important. That is the way groups want it.

Presidents, of course, do not want it that way. Interest groups may find them attractive allies on occasion, especially when their interests and the presidential agenda coincide. But, in general, presidents are a fearsome presence on the political scene. Their broad support coalitions, their grand perspective on public policy, and their fundamental concern for a coherent, centrally controlled bureaucracy combine to make them maverick players in the game of structural politics. They want a "presidential bureaucracy" that is fundamentally at odds with the congressional bureaucracy everyone else is busily trying to create.

To the winning group, presidents are a major source of political uncertainty over and above the risks associated with the future power of the group's opponents. This gives it even greater incentives to pressure for structures that are insulated from politics—and, when possible, disproportionately insulated from presidential politics. Because of the seriousness of the presidency's threat, the winning group will place special emphasis on limiting the powers and numbers of political appointees, locating effective authority in the agency and its career personnel, and opposing new hierarchical powers—of review, coordination, veto—for units in the Executive Office or even the departments.

The losing side is much more pragmatic. Presidents offer important opportunities for expanding the scope of conflict, imposing new procedural constraints on agency action, and appealing unfavorable decisions. Especially if presidents are not entirely sympathetic to the agency and its mission, the losing side may actively support all the trappings of presidential bureaucracy—but only, of course, for the particular case at hand. Thus, while presidents may oppose group efforts to cripple the agency through congressional bureaucracy, groups may be able to achieve much the same end through presidential bureaucracy. The risk, however, is that the next president could turn out to be an avid supporter of the agency, in which case presidential bureaucracy might be targeted to quite different ends indeed. If there is a choice, sinking formal restrictions into legislative concrete offers a much more secure and permanent fix.

Bureaucracy

Bureaucratic structure emerges as a jerry-built fusion of congressional and presidential forms, their relative roles and particular features determined by the powers, priorities, and strategies of the various designers. The result is that each agency cannot help but begin life as a unique structural reflection of its own politics.

Once an agency is created, the political world becomes a different place. Agency bureaucrats are now political actors in their own right. They have career and institutional interests that may not be entirely congruent with their formal missions, and they have powerful resources—expertise and delegated authority—that might be employed toward these selfish ends. They are new players whose interests and resources alter the political game.

It is useful to think in terms of two basic types of bureaucratic players: political appointees and careerists. Careerists are the pure bureaucrats. As they carry out their jobs, they will be concerned with the technical requirements of effective organization, but they will also face the same problem that all other political actors face: political uncertainty. Changes in group power, committee composition, and presidential administration represent serious threats to things that bureaucrats hold dear. Their mandates could be restricted, their budgets cut, their discretion curtailed, their reputations blemished. Like groups and politicians, bureaucrats cannot afford to concern themselves solely with technical matters. They must take action to reduce their political uncertainty.

One attractive strategy is to nurture mutually beneficial relationships with groups and politicians whose political support the agency needs. If these are to provide real security, they must be more than isolated quid pro quos; they must be part of an ongoing stream of exchanges that give all participants expectations of future gain and thus incentives to resist short-term opportunities to profit at one another's expense. This is most easily done with the agency's initial supporters. Over time, however, the agency will be driven to broaden its support base, and it may move away from some of its creators—as regulatory agencies sometimes have, for example, in currying favor with the business interests they are supposed to be regulating.[12] All agencies will have a tendency to move away from presidents, who, as temporary players, are inherently unsuited to participation in stable, long-term relationships.

Political appointees are also unattractive allies. They are not long-term participants, and no one will treat them as though they are. They have no concrete basis for participating in the exchange relationships of benefit to careerists. Indeed, they may not want to, for they have incentives to pay special attention to White House policy, and they will try to forge alliances that further those ends. Their focus is on short-term presidential victories, and relationships that stabilize politics for the agency may get in the way and have to be challenged.

As this begins to suggest, the strategy of building supportive relationships is inherently limited. In the end, much of the environment remains out of control. This prompts careerists to rely on a second, complementary strategy of uncertainty avoidance: insu-

12. Marver H. Bernstein, *Regulating Business by Independent Commission* (Princeton University Press, 1955).

lation. If they cannot control the environment, they can try to shut themselves off from it in various ways. They can promote further professionalization and more extensive reliance on civil service. They can formalize and judicialize their decision procedures. They can base decisions on technical expertise, operational experience, and precedent, thus making them "objective" and agency-centered. They can try to monopolize the information necessary for effective political oversight. These insulating strategies are designed, moreover, not simply to shield the agency from its political environment, but also to shield it from the very appointees who are formally in charge.

All of this raises an obvious question: why can't groups and politicians anticipate the agency's alliance and insulationist strategies and design a structure ex ante that adjusts for them? The answer, of course, is that they can. Presidents may push for stronger hierarchical controls and greater formal power for appointees than they otherwise would. Group opponents may place even greater emphasis on opening the agency up to political oversight. And so on. The agency's design, therefore, should from the beginning incorporate everyone's anticipations about its incentives to form alliances and promote its own autonomy.

Thus, however active the agency is in forming alliances, insulating itself from politics, and otherwise shaping political outcomes, it would be a mistake to regard the agency as a truly independent force. It is literally manufactured by the other players as a vehicle for advancing and protecting their own interests, and their structural designs are premised on anticipations about the roles the agency and its bureaucrats will play in future politics. The whole point of structural choice is to anticipate, program, and engineer bureaucratic behavior. Although groups and politicians cannot do this perfectly, the agency is fundamentally a product of their designs, and so is the way it plays the political game. That is why, in our attempt to understand the structure and politics of bureaucracy, we turn to bureaucrats last rather than first.

Structural Choice as a Perpetual Process

The game of structural politics never ends. An agency is created and given a mandate, but, in principle at least, all of the choices that have been made in the formative round of decisionmaking can be reversed or modified later.

As the politics of structural choice unfolds over time, three basic forces supply its dynamics. First, group opponents will constantly be on the lookout for opportunities to impose structures of their own that will inhibit the agency's performance and open it up to external control. Second, the winning group must constantly be ready to defend its agency from attack—but it may also have attacks of its own to launch. The prime reason is poor performance: because the agency is burdened from the beginning with a structure unsuited to the lofty goals it is supposed to achieve, the supporting group is likely to be dissatisfied and to push for more productive structural arrangements. Third, the president will try to ensure that agency behavior is consistent with broader presidential priorities, and he will take action to impose his own structures on top of those already put in place by Congress. He may also act to impose structures on purely political grounds in response to the interests of either the winning or opposing group.

All of this is going on all the time, generating pressures for structural change that find expression in both the legislative and executive processes. These are potentially of great importance for bureaucracy and policy, and all the relevant participants are intensely aware of it. However, the choices about structure that are made in the first period, when the agency is designed and empowered with a mandate, are normally far more enduring and consequential than those that will be made later. They constitute an institutional base that is protected by all the impediments to new legislation inherent in separation of powers, as well as by the political clout of the agency's supporters. Most of the pushing and hauling in subsequent years is likely to produce only incremental change. This, obviously, is very much on everyone's minds in the first period.

SELF-INTEREST AND THE NEW SOCIAL REGULATION

I now want to make the argument a bit more concrete by exploring several interesting cases in American structural politics. I cannot, as a practical matter, entertain the full range of issues that the theory touches upon, nor, in any rigorous sense, test its validity. My intention is simply to help illustrate, clarify, and lend plausibility to what it has to say about structural choice.

It is widely remarked that one of the most fundamental—and welcome—of recent developments in American bureaucracy is the shift from "old-style" forms of regulatory organization to the innovative forms characteristic of the "new social regulation."[13] The stereotypical old-style agencies were the independent regulatory commissions set up during the New Deal. They were staffed by experts who presumably knew best how to deal with complex, specialized problems of particular industries; they were granted substantial discretion via broad, vague mandates to regulate in the public interest; and yet, over time, they appeared to use their discretion to serve the interests of the regulated sector. Independent agencies with vague mandates came to represent a formula for regulatory capture by business.[14]

By the late 1960s, much of the scholarly debate centered not on whether the independent commissions tended to become captured, but on why. Marver Bernstein popularized the argument that independence and vague mandates contribute to a regulatory life-cycle, in which youthful vigor gives way over time to capture.[15] For Bernstein, independence cuts the agencies off from important sources of political support and invigoration, and vagueness gives agency officials the discretion to serve regulated interests. For other scholars, notably Theodore J. Lowi and Kenneth Culp Davis, independence is perhaps less worrisome than broad delegations of legislative authority: bureaucrats who have substantial discretion tend to fall under the influence of their organized clienteles.[16]

13. Walter Lilley III and James C. Miller III, "The New 'Social Regulation,' " *The Public Interest*, no. 47 (Spring 1977), pp. 49–61; Paul H. Weaver, "Regulation, Social Policy, and Class Conflict," *The Public Interest*, no. 50 (Winter 1978), pp. 45–63; and David Vogel, "The 'New' Social Regulation in Historical and Comparative Perspective," in Thomas K. McGraw, ed., *Regulation in Perspective: Historical Essays* (Harvard University Press, 1981), pp. 155–85.

14. Bruce A. Ackerman and William T. Hassler, *Clean Coal/Dirty Air* (Yale University Press, 1981); and R. Shep Melnick, *Regulation and the Courts: The Case of the Clean Air Act* (Brookings, 1983).

15. Bernstein, *Regulating Business by Independent Commission*.

16. Theodore J. Lowi, *The End of Liberalism: The Second Republic of the United States*, 2d ed. (Norton, 1979); Kenneth Culp Davis, *Administrative Law Treatise*, 2d ed. (San Diego: K. C. Davis, 1978); and Davis, *Discretionary Justice: A Preliminary Inquiry* (University of Illinois Press, 1971).

But while explanations differed, there was almost universal agreement that something was wrong with the way Congress designed its bureaucratic creations. As an influential Brookings study put it, the regulatory agencies were "established through bad legislation."[17] Something clearly needed to be done about it. In almost all cases, the proposed remedies amounted to prescriptions for "good" legislation. Members of Congress were exhorted to be leery of the independent commission, to specify agency mandates and decision procedures in great detail, and, in general, to recognize that it must create regulatory forms that inhibit capture.

The prevailing view is that this body of research had a major influence on the design of American bureaucracy. Congress learned its lesson.

> The authors of the regulatory statutes passed in the late 1960s and 1970s attempted to meet criticisms aimed at traditional regulation and to instill in regulators an enduring sense of mission. Lectured incessantly about its failure to provide regulators with specific standards, Congress wrote lengthy statutes that did far more than tell administrators to grant licenses "in the public interest" or to guarantee "fair and reasonable rates." Many of the laws passed during this period included relatively specific standards, deadlines, and procedures. . . . To increase the efficiency with which administrators carry out these statutory mandates, Congress and the president usually created single-headed agencies located squarely within the executive branch rather than multimember independent commissions.[18]

This account implicitly takes politicians, particularly members of Congress, as public-spirited prime movers who are free to make whatever decisions they like about the structure of government. Convinced by academic research that they mistakenly made "bad" choices in the past, legislators acted upon a new theory that promised to create better bureaucracy. The modern agencies of the 1970s are accordingly different in conception from the traditional agencies of the 1930s, so the story goes, and they have to be explained and understood differently.

17. Roger G. Noll, *Reforming Regulation: An Evaluation of the Ash Council Proposals* (Brookings, 1971).
18. Melnick, *Regulation and the Courts*, pp. 7–8.

My own view is that the explanation is fundamentally the same for both. Congress did not make horrible mistakes in creating the New Deal commissions. Nor were its structural choices motivated by grandiose theories about how government is best designed. Nor were legislators really free to act on such theories. They were politicians sensitive to the interests of powerful groups, and their structural choices were shaped by what those groups wanted.

Consider the Civil Aeronautics Board (CAB), created in 1938 with the passage of the Civil Aeronautics Act. The purpose of this legislation was to set up a structural framework to protect, nurture, and regulate the nation's fledgling airline industry. The bill was unabashedly designed to serve the best interests of the airlines, and, as Bradley Behrman notes in his historical assessment of the CAB, "There was little the airlines wanted to have in the new legislation but did not get."[19] It was actually drafted in rooms 212 and 214 of the Carlton Hotel in Washington, D.C., by lawyers representing the Air Transport Association and five of the trunk airlines.[20]

So what kind of agency did they design for themselves and induce Congress to legislate on their behalf? An independent commission with a broad, vague mandate. This was not a "bad" choice on the part of Congress. It was a politically astute choice. Nor, of course, was it a "bad" choice for the airlines. They chose structural features that would keep politicians and potential enemies at arm's length, ensuring that the agency they were creating would stay theirs. And for the next forty years it did.

Independent commissions, vague mandates, and capture by business were not the product of poor choices. They were symptomatic of very smart ones. In the CAB's case, certainly, they were also symptomatic of something more fundamental: an unbalanced interest group system in which the industry group went largely unopposed in the politics of structural choice. The dominant group simply exercised public authority to put its creation out of reach. Independence and vagueness were not the causes of regulatory capture. It was the industry's desire to capture the agency that

19. Bradley Behrman, "Civil Aeronautics Board," in James Q. Wilson, ed., *The Politics of Regulation* (Basic Books, 1980), p. 84.

20. Joseph C. Goulden, *The Superlawyers: The Small and Powerful World of the Great Washington Law Firms* (Weybright and Talley, 1972), p. 34.

prompted them to opt for independence and vagueness in the first place.

The relevant players and the underlying balance of power may vary from agency to agency, but the driving force of their politics is the same: players try to impose structures that will protect and advance their own best interests. And what was true during the New Deal is just as true in more recent times. The "innovative" bureaucratic designs of the new social regulation are due not to some abstract theory of good government, but to changes in the distribution of political power that have thrust new players and interests into prominent roles in the the politics of structural choice.

To suggest what the substance of all this looks like, and, more generally, how well it seems to fit with the broader theory I elaborated earlier, I will now take a brief look at three agencies paradigmatic of the new social regulation: the Consumer Product Safety Commission (CPSC), the Occupational Safety and Health Administration (OSHA), and the Environmental Protection Agency (EPA).[21]

The Consumer Product Safety Commission

When Richard Nixon assumed the presidency in 1969, consumerism was a political power of the first magnitude, and all politicians were scrambling to convince voters that they were champions of the consumer cause. The new president was slow to jump on the bandwagon. During his first several months in office, he failed to appoint a consumer adviser within the White House and had no announced intention of presenting a consumer message to Congress. But when roundly criticized for these shortcomings, Nixon the pragmatic politician joined the scramble.[22]

By 1971 it was clear to political insiders that some sort of legislation on product safety was in the cards. A special commission on

---

21. I deal with the three agencies in this order, rather than (say) according to their "importance" or the chronology of their creation, because it allows me to proceed from reasonably simple cases in the politics of structural choice, the CPSC and OSHA, to one that is complex indeed, the EPA.

22. Mark V. Nadel, *The Politics of Consumer Protection* (Bobbs-Merrill, 1971).

product safety had recently focused public attention on the issue, calling for comprehensive national regulation and the creation of a new agency to set and enforce standards. This was popular stuff that no politician could resist. As a result, the policy issue— whether the federal government should regulate consumer products—was not the subject of controversy. However, it was also symbolic and quite devoid of meaningful content, for, depending on the structural choices that attached to the policy, regulation might run the gamut from vigorously strict to hopelessly ineffective. The real political battle took place over structure.

In his 1971 consumer address to Congress, Nixon championed the consumer cause by making a showy appeal for product safety legislation. His structural proposals, however, were clearly not designed to provide for vigorous regulation. They reflected the underlying interests of business and the institutional presidency. What business wanted was a weak, ineffective agency—although, for the public record, they too "supported" the idea of product safety regulation. What the president wanted, aside from making business happy, was to enhance his managerial capacity through presidential bureaucracy.

Among other things, the administration proposal called for a new Consumer Safety Administration to be located within the Department of Health, Education, and Welfare (HEW), with authority not only for product safety but also for food and drugs. The Food and Drug Administration would be dismantled, its personnel and functions transferred to the new agency. The agency's powers would be weak. Standard setting would give primacy to voluntary codes developed by industries and independent standard-setting organizations. The agency would be dependent on the Justice Department for its enforcement actions.[23]

In Congress, consumer groups were dominant. Business groups, always a powerful force, were strong enough to put up a stiff fight. But consumers largely had their way. What they wanted, above all else, was for their agency to be insulated from politics. Their strategy was to opt for the classic, allegedly much-despised form of regulatory organization: the independent regulatory commission. In the words of the Consumer Federation of

---

23. "Product Safety: Stricter Law in Congressional Mill," *Congressional Quarterly Weekly Report*, vol. 29 (December 18, 1971), pp. 2627–29.

America's Martha Robinson, "Independent structure lessens the possibility of political interference."[24] So much for the capture theory and academic ruminations on the independent commission.[25]

The battle in Congress centered on agency independence. Consumer groups firmly rejected the notion that their new agency should be placed within HEW and thus within the hierarchy of presidential authority. They also feared merger with the FDA, which had a reputation for excessive sensitivity to industry. In the end, consumerists got everything they wanted in these respects. The new Consumer Product Safety Commission was made formally independent, its five commissioners appointed for fixed, staggered, seven-year terms. The president would designate the chair, as he does for all the independent commissions, but consumerists were able to win an "innovative" twist to enhance agency autonomy: the chair would not serve in that position at the president's discretion, but would remain chair throughout his entire term as commissioner. Consumer groups tried to distance the agency still further from presidential control by directing it to submit its budget proposals simultaneously to both the OMB and Congress.

In addition, they were able to scuttle all attempts to merge components of the FDA into the new agency. The CPSC was kept pristine—and totally theirs. All presidential concerns for consolidation and coordination of governmental functions—concerns that were genuine, not just facades for business influence—were given short shrift. No one but the president cared in the slightest about these sorts of administrative niceties. The consumerists did not want their agency integrated into the organization of government. They were doing precisely what the airlines had done in designing the CAB. They were trying to build an agency that would stay theirs.

Independence was crucial, but it was only the beginning; for

24. "Consumer Product Safety Agency Created in 1972," *Congressional Quarterly Almanac*, vol. 28 (1972), p. 145.

25. The account that follows is taken from "Product Safety: Stricter Law in Congressional Mill"; "Senate Approves Independent Product Safety Agency," *Congressional Quarterly Weekly Report*, vol. 30 (July 1, 1972), pp. 1614–17; "Product Safety," *Congressional Quarterly Weekly Report*, vol. 30 (October 28, 1972), pp. 2850–51; "Consumer Product Safety Agency Created in 1972"; and Gary C. Bryner, *Bureaucratic Discretion: Law and Policy in Federal Regulatory Agencies* (Pergamon Press, 1987), especially chap. 7.

consumerists could not assume that even a pristine, well-insulated agency would aggressively pursue its mandate. Their task was to design and impose a set of structural constraints to ensure that bureaucrats would do what they were supposed to do. In practice, this concern led them to favor specific limitations on bureaucratic discretion, time requirements for agency action, procedural requirements, massive opportunities for consumer participation and input, and judicial checks on agency misbehavior. In these regards, too, they largely dominated the political struggle with business. Among their more notable achievements were the following.

—Rulemaking for the purpose of developing a product safety standard would be initiated by petitions from any interested individual or group, with the agency required to respond within 120 days. Petitioners whose petitions were rejected could seek review in federal district court.

—The CPSC was not simply to develop standards on its own, but to rely instead on the "offeror" process, whereby outside groups could offer to develop standards in regard to a certain product and the commission would consider the resulting proposals.

—Private parties were permitted to go to court to enforce safety standards if the agency did not enforce them. They were also permitted to sue for damages when injured by products not meeting safety standards—another form of enforcement. Any person affected by a commission rule was granted standing.

Business participation in agency proceedings was a fact of life, since regulated firms and industries would inevitably have opportunities—and strong incentives—to make arguments, present evidence, provide information and technical advice, and appeal agency decisions to the courts. Consumerists tried to counter this by imposing a set of rules that would guarantee active, influential participation by consumer groups as well. The petition and offeror processes guaranteed them roles in the development of standards, and provision for legal suits by private parties ensured that agency misbehavior or lax enforcement could be countered in the courts.

Business groups were not entirely shut out. They got the usual procedural protections—the right to judicial review, for instance. And they, along with the president, won the important battle over agency enforcement: the CPSC had to rely upon the Justice Department for virtually all of its legal actions against violators of its standards. In addition, it received only a three-year authorization, rather than the open-ended authorization bestowed upon virtually all the other regulatory agencies. This guaranteed that, just three years later, business would have an opportunity to launch a new political attack on the agency.

Consumer groups therefore had two basic problems. First, the fight was not really over; and, since it was unclear how long consumer dominance was going to last, the next fight might well come out differently. Second, precisely because they anticipated this, they loaded the agency down with cumbersome procedural requirements and checks on its behavior and discretion. These structural choices made it difficult for the agency to do anything very effectively. Political uncertainty—and political fear—drove them to do this. To protect themselves, they created a structure that did not work very well. It was, however, theirs.

When the CPSC came up for reauthorization in 1975, business was still out to cripple the agency by any means available. But consumers were unhappy too. Their agency was doing a frustratingly poor job, and they wanted some statutory changes that would beef up its capacity for effective action. They also wanted to insulate it further from presidential control. Thus the battle lines were drawn. The CPSC, however, was no longer anyone's darling. Even its ostensive supporters had lots of critical things to say about it.[26]

The House and Senate Commerce committees reported bills that were strongly proconsumer, imposing several important structural changes on the agency. They granted it substantial independence from the Justice Department in enforcing injunctions and conducting its own civil actions generally. They also stipulated that top commission staff could not be appointed subject to White House or executive branch approval, contravening a practice that had developed under Nixon.

The House bill was ambushed on the floor by business and its legislative allies, the Republicans and southern Democrats. The major proconsumer changes were defeated in close votes. In their

---

26. For accounts of the 1975–76 legislative struggle, see Prudence Crewdson, "House Votes Curbs on Consumer Commission," *Congressional Quarterly Weekly Report*, vol. 33 (November 1, 1975), pp. 2321–24; "Consumer Product Safety," *Congressional Quarterly Almanac*, vol. 31 (1975), pp. 565–73; and "Product Safety Commission Bill Cleared," *Congressional Quarterly Almanac*, vol. 32 (1976), pp. 441–43.

place was added a legislative veto of commission rules, the point of which, of course, was to politicize agency rulemaking and give business an open shot at every major decision the CPSC might take. It is worth emphasizing, given the way the legislative veto tends to be characterized in the academic literature, that this veto provision had nothing to do with a post-Watergate resurgent Congress flexing its muscles in opposition to the imperial presidency, nor did it reflect a partisan battle between a Democratically controlled Congress and a Republican president. The legislators imposing the veto provision were allies of the president on most issues, including the CPSC battle, and most were members of his own party. The veto was nothing more than another structural means of getting at an agency belonging to the other side. Conservatives and liberals alike have incentives to use the legislative veto. It all depends on whose ox is being gored.

In the end, the Senate and consumer groups won almost total victory in conference, a testament to the power of authorizing committees in ultimately having their way over insurgents from the floor. All the original structural changes were enacted. The House revolt produced one significant compromise: although the legislative veto provision was dropped in the final bill, the CPSC was hereafter required to submit all its proposed rules to Congress thirty days before adopting them, thus giving business and its allies a chance to respond. All in all, however, consumers came out of the 1975 battle with notable victories under their belts.

But from this point on, things began to fall apart. President Ford and the Appropriations committees kept the CPSC's budgets well below the levels authorized by the supportive Commerce committees. And President Carter, an ally of consumer causes, did not turn matters around—indeed, he seriously considered abolishing the agency, for two reasons.[27] First, not only did consumers continue to be dissatisfied, but separate studies by the General Accounting Office, the House Commerce Committee, the Civil Service Commission, and even a task force within the CPSC itself had suggested that dissatisfaction was amply justified by the facts.[28]

27. "Abolition of Consumer Product Agency Considered," *National Journal*, vol. 10 (March 4, 1978), p. 359.

28. For a brief review of their findings, see "Product Safety Agency," *Congressional Quarterly Almanac*, vol. 34 (1978), pp. 525–28. This same source provides background on the 1978 CPSC reauthorization.

The second reason for abolishing the CPSC was entirely presidential: its formal independence was inconsistent with the president's managerial responsibilities.

Carter ultimately sided with the moderate views of his consumer adviser, Esther Peterson. For the 1978 CPSC reauthorization, he requested several changes in agency procedures, but his major request was that the commission chair serve at the pleasure of the president. This then became the major bone of contention in congressional debate over CPSC reauthorization. Consumer advocates, dedicated as always to the political insulation of their agency, succeeded in having this provision deleted in the House bill, but not in the Senate version. The Senate—and the administration and business—won in conference. Consumerists now found themselves looking ahead to a future of more defeats and more structural changes designed to take their agency away from them.

Granted only a three-year authorization, the CPSC had the misfortune in early 1981 to be the first major regulatory agency to come up for reauthorization during the Reagan presidency. The new administration, dedicated to deregulation, cuts in government expenditures, and the causes of business, went for the throat. Initially, the administration wanted the CPSC abolished. When this appeared infeasible, it recommended that the agency be placed in the Commerce Department and its budget be cut by 30 percent from the Carter estimate. If successful, this would subject the agency to presidential authority, surround it with bureaucratic and legislative enemies, and destroy its resource base.[29]

With Congress more conservative since the 1980 election and Republicans in control of the Senate, business had its best chance ever to gut the commission. Since abolition was not likely, business and its legislative allies went on record as being supportive of the general policy of consumer product safety. The battle, once again, was fought over structure, and this time business groups very nearly pulled off a massive victory. But they were a few votes

---

29. For accounts of the 1981 battle over the CPSC, see Judy Sarasohn, "Product Safety Board Faces Agency Transfer, Fund Cuts," *Congressional Quarterly Weekly Report*, vol. 39 (May 16, 1981), pp. 846–47; Sarasohn, "CPSC Independence Saved But Staff Layoffs Are Likely," *Congressional Quarterly Weekly Report*, vol. 39 (August 1, 1981), p. 1384; "Congress Votes to Retain Consumer Safety Board As An Independent Agency," *Congressional Quarterly Weekly Report*, vol. 39 (August 15, 1981), p. 1479; "CPSC Authorization," *Congressional Quarterly Almanac*, vol. 37 (1981), pp. 572–73; and Bryner, *Bureaucratic Discretion*.

short. The Senate Consumer Subcommittee, under the probusiness leadership of Republican Robert Kasten, could not quite muster the support for a bill transferring the agency to the Commerce
Department; it also tried and failed to impose a one-year authorization. The House subcommittee, led by staunchly proconsumer
Democrat Henry Waxman, deadlocked 10-10 on these issues; and,
because conservatives claimed to have the votes in full committee,
Waxman refused to allow the full committee to consider the bill at
all. The CPSC would lose its independence, he claimed, "over my
dead body."[30] Ultimately, he succeeded in getting his subcommittee's legislation past the House by means of a crafty parliamentary
maneuver: he managed to have it incorporated in a reconciliation
bill.

The compromise legislation to come out of this, however, was a
major defeat for consumers. Far-reaching structural changes that
business had been demanding for many years were imposed on
the CPSC.

—All CPSC rules were now subject to congressional veto.

—The agency was directed to give precedence to voluntary over
mandatory standards when the former would adequately reduce
the risk of injury and when substantial compliance could be expected.

—The agency was required to issue standards in terms of performance requirements rather than product design (or other) requirements, leaving the means of compliance, therefore, up to business.

—Strict new guidelines for rulemaking were imposed. In developing rules, the agency was required to invite proposals for voluntary standards, which, if shown to be acceptable, must put an end
to the rulemaking. Three findings were required for the issuance of
a rule: any existing voluntary standards must be inadequate, benefits must bear a reasonable relationship to costs, and the rule must
impose the least burdensome requirement on business.

These structural changes redirected CPSC regulation toward
voluntary standards, made rulemaking more complex and time-
consuming, and opened the agency up to political intervention by
its enemies. In addition, business and the Reagan administration
won a 25 percent reduction from the Carter budget request and a
mere two-year authorization. After its restructuring of 1981, the

30. Bryner, *Bureaucratic Discretion*, p. 172.

CPSC swung into a Reagan-era equilibrium of meager budgets, spartan staffing, "unenlightened" appointees, poor performance, and voluntarism. Political battles continued in subsequent years without significant alteration of the structural status quo.

The CPSC is still a young agency, but it never really had a chance to perform effectively. It was not designed to be effective. Consumers were concerned with the technical requirements of effective performance, but their organizational designs were driven in large part by political uncertainty: they had to protect themselves and their agency from business. This explains why they so strongly favored an independent regulatory commission and why they imposed restrictive procedures, criteria, and time limits that weighed the agency down. Meanwhile, business was strong enough to lay claim to some portion of public authority, and it too was able to participate in structuring the agency—except that it was dedicated to crippling its capacity for effective performance. At its birth and throughout its life, then, the CPSC was a structural reflection of competitive politics. Structure was not a means to effective pursuit of the symbolic mandate. It was a means of political attack and defense.

Occupational Safety and Health Administration

Until the creation of OSHA, federal regulation of occupational safety and health amounted to little more than an uncoordinated patchwork of laws dealing with special problems in particular industries. For the AFL-CIO and most unions, it had never been a priority item, and politicians therefore had little incentive to pursue it.

This began to change in the late 1960s, when the surging popularity of the consumer and environmental movements imparted a new symbolic significance to the protection of workers from hazards in the workplace. Lyndon Johnson, looking ahead to the 1968 election, packaged it as a "quality of life" issue, which, like pollution control, automobile safety, and consumer product safety, signaled his commitment to the new reformist movements. Despite the AFL-CIO's lack of enthusiasm at the outset, a broad coalition of labor, consumer, and environmental groups eventually formed behind a strong administration proposal that concentrated new standard-setting and enforcement powers in the Department of Labor. This first major effort at federal regulation stimulated fierce opposition from business groups and their legislative allies, however, and it died in the House.[31]

By 1969 the political context was much more favorable. During Richard Nixon's first year in office, the consumer and environmental movements continued to amass political power, and the new president sought not only to gain their support, but also to broaden his and the Republican party's electoral coalitions by appealing to blue-collar workers. Occupational safety and health regulation was a natural under these conditions, and some sort of regulatory program was inevitable. Business groups, seeing the writing on the wall, announced that a policy of federal safety and health regulation was a good idea. Privately, they worked with the Nixon administration to design a bureaucratic structure that would make effective regulation impossible.[32]

In this case, unlike that of the CPSC, Nixon was in a bind in seeking a compromise between presidential bureaucracy and the demands of business. If a new agency were to be neatly fitted into the executive hierarchy, then it would clearly belong in the Department of Labor. But that, of course, was the last place business wanted the agency to be, since the department was traditionally a bastion of union control. Forced to choose, Nixon threw his lot in with business.

The administration proposed to delegate standard-setting authority to an independent five-member board, which was encouraged to adopt "national consensus standards" (standards devised within the private sector). The secretary of labor would have limited enforcement authority: he would encourage voluntary compliance with the board's standards and, upon evidence of noncompli-

31. For background on the history and politics of occupational safety and health regulation, see Charles Noble, *Liberalism at Work: The Rise and Fall of OSHA* (Temple University Press, 1986). My account of the structural politics of OSHA from 1970 to the present draws generally on Noble's book; on John Mendeloff, *Regulating Safety: An Economic and Political Analysis of Occupational Safety and Health Policy* (MIT Press, 1979); and on Bryner, *Bureaucratic Discretion*, especially chap. 6. Regarding the Johnson proposal in particular, see also "Occupational Safety," *Congressional Quarterly Almanac*, vol. 24 (1968), pp. 675–78.

32. On the Nixon plan, see "Occupational Safety," *Congressional Quarterly Weekly Report*, vol. 27 (November 7, 1969), p. 2204; "Occupational Safety," *Congressional Quarterly Weekly Report*, vol. 27 (November 28, 1969), p. 2402; and "Occupational Safety," *Congressional Quarterly Almanac*, vol. 25 (1969), pp. 568–70.

ance, could bring a complaint to the board. The board, if convinced of a violation, would then order compliance, which would be enforced through court action. The states would be encouraged to submit their own regulatory plans, and, if acceptable, their programs would preempt federal regulation within their own borders. HEW would have authority to carry out research and training.

While this had the appearance of a systematic attack on the problem, in fact it was an administrative nightmare that did a thorough job of protecting business's interests. Authority was divided among an independent board, the secretary of labor, the states, HEW, and the courts. This would create confusion, lack of coordination, and multiple veto points. No one was in charge, and the secretary of labor, in particular, was kept weak. In addition, the notion that standards should be set by an independent, professionally oriented board, which evoked the usual paeans to "good government," disguised the fact that almost all the relevant professionals were employed by business and sympathetic to its interests.[33]

Labor did not need to be told all this. What it wanted, ideally, was a strong, centralized regulatory program over which it could exercise control. In practice, it might have favored an all-powerful independent agency, trading a measure of control in return for protection from business and the president. But instead, it gambled that such a trade-off was unnecessary. Extrapolating from past experience, its leaders figured that any agency located within the Department of Labor would be subject to their exclusive control. This view was bolstered by a crucial fact of life in Congress: the AFL-CIO had a virtual stranglehold on the House and Senate Labor committees, which had jurisdiction over legislation and oversight for agencies within the department.

The political battle was fought out in 1970. Within Congress, labor's allies on the committees dutifully fashioned legislation that, among other things, placed the new agency within the Department of Labor and concentrated standard-setting and enforcement powers in the secretary of labor. Business's allies proposed structures much along the lines of the Nixon plan. Floor fights raged in

33. Note that neither business (as an opposing group) nor the president would normally be in favor of formal independence. Here it serves their purposes by providing an alternative to placement in the Department of Labor and by helping to fragment the regulatory structure.

both houses, and the committees lost control. In the House, conservatives won a major victory. They voted to exclude the secretary of labor completely from both the setting and enforcement of standards by creating two separate independent agencies, one to develop standards and one to enforce them. This was the ultimate in fragmentation and labor weakness, a business dream come true.[34]

A similar bill was narrowly voted down in the Senate, leading to a compromise offered by Jacob Javits: the secretary of labor would have the authority to set standards, but enforcement power would be delegated to a three-member independent commission. This was similar to the fragmented scheme proposed by Nixon, but the functions were reversed—Nixon had wanted a commission to set standards and the secretary to enforce. Although the Javits compromise was hardly ideal from the unions' standpoint, its way of fragmenting authority was certainly preferable to Nixon's, and they had little choice but to accept it. In the subsequent House-Senate conference, the Senate mostly had its way, and the Javits compromise became law, adding yet another bizarre bureaucratic arrangement to the structure of American government.

The Occupational Safety and Health Act was a multidimensional compromise. On many issues, labor got what it wanted. OSHA would set standards and be located within the Department of Labor. Uncertainty about how the new agency would behave, given the dangers of everyday contact with regulated firms as well as the business orientation of safety professionals, was countered in various ways. On important matters, agency discretion was virtually eliminated: OSHA was required to promulgate consensus standards within two years; it was required to respond to employee petitions for inspections; its inspectors were forced to issue citations and penalties for violations; and it had to follow certain procedures, criteria, and time requirements in developing standards. Also, the decisionmaking and appeals processes were designed to ensure that the creators—workers, unions, and their allies—could participate and impose checks on agency behavior, ensuring that OSHA could not settle into a cozy relationship with the firms it was to regulate.

34. For accounts of the 1970 legislative battles, see "Senate Passes Stringent Job Health and Safety Bill," *Congressional Quarterly Weekly Report*, vol. 28 (November 20, 1970), pp. 2813–14; and "Passage of Job Safety Bill Ends Three-Year Dispute," *Congressional Quarterly Almanac*, vol. 26 (1970), pp. 675–82.

Labor also won a big victory on the issue of whether economic costs should be a criterion in the formulation of rules. The statute vaguely required only that OSHA's rules be "feasible," leaving the term undefined. This might appear to be a textbook example of congressional unwillingness to face up to difficult decisions: seeking to avoid conflict, Congress shifted the responsibility by delegating the tough choices to the agency and the courts. But this is not what happened. Organized labor wanted nothing in the act that could be construed as requiring some sort of cost-benefit calculation. Business strongly demanded that cost be included as an explicit criterion of choice. The result was a compromise heavily weighted in favor of the unions. As Mendeloff observes, "a sufficient explanation for the absence of any mention of costs was that organized labor did not want any."[35]

Business did win a few battles. It succeeded in imposing a fragmented structure that labor had staunchly resisted from the beginning. While the secretary did get the authority to set standards, he was hemmed about by other players with important roles to play. The Occupational Safety and Health Review Commission made final decisions on enforcement actions (subject to court appeal)— and, in practice, it would later reverse or reduce a large percentage of penalties assessed by OSHA against business. The National Institute for Occupational Safety and Health (NIOSH), located within HEW, was to carry out research, survey the professional literature, and provide the "criteria documents" on which OSHA standard development was to be based. OSHA and the secretary of labor could not control NIOSH, and its delays, research interests, and very different political concerns would later cause many problems for them. The courts would also become actively involved, as business exercised its statutory rights to challenge virtually every decision OSHA made.

Business was also successful in securing a major role for the states, which were encouraged to submit regulatory plans that would preempt federal regulation by OSHA. This, of course, was not just a way of returning democracy to the people. It was a potent means of fragmenting government regulation. It was also a means of ensuring that regulatory decisions would be made in

---

35. Mendeloff, *Regulating Safety*, p. 21. For further details on the politics surrounding the "feasibility" language, see Noble, *Liberalism at Work*, p. 96 and note 53.

arenas more sympathetic to business interests, since business has historically done well at the state level. Labor knew all this and fought against "cooperative federalism" as it applied to OSHA. And after the act went into effect, labor continued to resist state regulation by pressuring governors and state legislatures not to participate. Many of these battles were lost, as about half of the states eventually submitted acceptable regulatory plans, leaving OSHA with only the remaining states.

The regulatory scheme that labor did "win," then, left much to be desired. OSHA itself was burdened with all sorts of structural constraints imposed by friend and foe alike, and, to make matters worse, the agency was but one component of a vast, byzantine structure, much of which was designed to ensure that the regulatory policy everyone agreed upon in principle would be a miserable failure in practice. And so it was.[36]

The troubles started right away. True to its agency-forcing mandate, OSHA immediately acted to promulgate over 4,000 consensus standards as mandatory rules—many of them later turning out to be trivial, absurd, or hopelessly complex. Small business, especially, became apoplectic as thousands of penalties were issued by discretionless inspectors compelled to enforce a ridiculous body of rules. OSHA tried to develop its own standards, but the procedural and research requirements slowed the process down to a snail's pace. Health regulation, far more complex and technically demanding than safety regulation, seemed to be going nowhere. The states were biting off bigger and bigger chunks of OSHA's jurisdiction—prodded by the Nixon administration, which, through its appointees in the Department of Labor, acted to weaken and decentralize OSHA's regulatory capacity. This was a problem labor had not seriously anticipated from its own department. It did not take long before the unions began training political fire on their own bureaucratic creation. OSHA found itself under attack from both sides.

36. On OSHA procedures and performance, see Charles Culhane, "Administration Works to Shift Safety, Health Programs to States Despite Labor Criticism," *National Journal*, vol. 4 (June 24, 1972), pp. 1041–59; Culhane, "Labor, Business Press Administration to Change Safety and Health Program," *National Journal*, vol. 4 (July 1, 1972), pp. 1093–1102; Linda E. Demkovich, "OSHA Launches Dual Effort to Reduce Job Health Hazards," *National Journal*, vol. 6 (December 7, 1974), pp. 1831–39; and "Occupational Safety: How Much Is Enough?" *Congressional Quarterly Weekly Report*, vol. 32 (August 24, 1974), pp. 2286–92.

Labor held one crucial card. By placing OSHA in the Department of Labor, it guaranteed a virtual monopoly of political jurisdiction for the Labor committees, which it dominated. This did not allow labor to make the kinds of changes it thought necessary for truly effective regulation, since the committees tended to lose control of legislation on the floor. But it did allow labor to throttle any business attempts to change the act. It could even prevent public hearings for debates about change. And, over the years, this negative power has worked like a charm. To date, there has not been a single major change in the act.

This did not put an end to OSHA politics. Efforts to shape the direction and efficacy of OSHA regulation were forced into other channels.[37] Since OSHA's creation, it has become an annual tradition for business to try to limit OSHA's powers by attaching riders to appropriations bills. Now and then, business has done the same with legislation coming out of the Small Business committees. These guerrilla attacks have sometimes been successful, and they are constant thorns in the sides of OSHA and organized labor. But they have not resulted in permanent changes of real consequence in the structure of the agency.

Far and away the most important channel of business influence has been presidential bureaucracy. This has occurred not simply because presidents have been responsive to business, although Republican presidents clearly have, but because all presidents since OSHA's creation have pursued larger goals and strategies that have dovetailed nicely with business's attack on OSHA. Throughout the 1970s the continuing problem of inflation, aggravated by the energy crisis, drove presidents to attach increasing importance to the scrutiny and control of agency rulemaking processes, particularly when they entailed decisions with far-reaching consequences for the economy.[38]

The institutionalization of a review capacity in the OMB began in the Nixon administration and developed steadily over the ensu-

37. Efforts of various sorts occur every year and are described in the annual *Congressional Quarterly Almanacs*, 1974 to the present.

38. The most detailed treatment of presidential control of OSHA can be found in Noble, *Liberalism at Work*. For overviews of presidential control of the regulatory agencies more generally, see George C. Eads and Michael Fix, eds., *The Reagan Regulatory Strategy: An Assessment* (Washington, D.C.: Urban Institute, 1984); Michael D. Reagan, *Regulation: The Politics of Policy* (Little, Brown, 1987); and Bryner, *Bureaucratic Discretion*, chap. 4.

ing years. Meanwhile, the OMB's efforts were supplemented by other managerial mechanisms that were created to respond quickly and flexibly to presidential needs. In 1974 the Council on Wage and Price Stability (COWPS) was created to ride herd on the anti-inflation effort, and Ford issued an executive order requiring all agencies to submit inflation impact statements along with their proposed rules to the OMB for review. The OMB and COWPS monitored and assessed agency compliance with the new requirements, and COWPS's formal comments became part of agency rulemaking processes. Carter continued along similar lines. He created the Regulatory Analysis Review Group and, through executive order, required agencies to submit economic impact statements that provided comprehensive analytical arguments for regulatory rules.

Because OSHA was widely regarded as a major offender in the imposition of costly, unreasonable rules on business, there was no escape. All of this had pervasive consequences for OSHA's rulemaking processes—complicating and encumbering them, introducing new external controls and veto points, and forcing OSHA to take economic costs and consequences into account as decision criteria. This was true even under a Democratic president concerned about maintaining strong ties with labor, consumer, and environmental groups.

But this was nothing compared with what happened during the Reagan years. Regulatory review was centralized in the OMB, which exercised close, comprehensive control over agency rulemaking. In his now-famous Executive Order 12291, Reagan required all agencies to submit regulatory impact analyses along with their proposed rules to the OMB. The new requirements, which included strict new criteria and procedures for cost-benefit analysis, imposed onerous constraints on rulemaking and, by forcing agencies to get OMB approval before publishing proposed rules, gave the administration an effective veto. The impact on OSHA was magnified by sagacious use of the presidential appointment power. Reagan appointed Thorne Auchter, a construction industry executive, as the assistant secretary in charge of OSHA. Under his leadership, the agency pursued a policy of voluntary compliance, cooperation with business, and—despite the wording of the act—rulemaking processes that attached primary salience to economic costs.

Business could not have hoped for a better outcome. Denied access to congressional Labor committees and forced to snipe at OSHA from the legislative fringes, it found a powerful ally in presidents of both parties who, driven by strong, institutionally based incentives of their own to control the regulatory process, imposed massive structural and policy changes through presidential bureaucracy.

The larger point, however, is that OSHA was a victim of American democracy—just as the CPSC was. The politics of structural choice endowed them both with organizational designs entirely ill suited to the effective pursuit of their policy goals. The specifics of their stories are different, but the consequences for public bureaucracy are essentially the same.

Consumer groups, driven by political uncertainty and forced to compromise with business, created an independent commission with limited enforcement powers and hemmed about by a variety of agency-forcing rules and procedures. They also lacked an iron grip on the relevant congressional committees, and, as the political struggle continued over the years, business was able to impose new structural burdens through formal legislation. Presidents did not play major roles, in part because the CPSC's independent status placed legal restrictions on the use of presidential management and appointment powers and in part because CPSC rules were not of sufficient economic consequence to merit aggressive presidential action. The CPSC's structural incapacities were legislative in origin, a reflection of political uncertainty and political compromise.

OSHA was burdened at the outset with awkward agency-forcing mechanisms imposed by labor in response to political uncertainty, as well as by an ingeniously fragmented set of bureaucratic arrangements imposed by business through political compromise. In subsequent years, it was successfully insulated from its enemies in Congress, thanks to union dominance of the House and Senate Labor committees. But it was not safe from presidents. Because OSHA's activities were of great economic consequence and because it was squarely located in the executive branch, presidents had strong incentives and ample opportunities to get at it—and they got at it with a vengeance. So, as a result, did business, whose priorities were nicely furthered through presidential bureaucracy.

Neither OSHA nor the CPSC was ever designed to do its job.

And things went from bad to worse over time as presidents and business opponents found ways of imposing bureaucratic arrangements that suited their own rather than the legislated purposes.

The Environmental Protection Agency

The EPA is often held up as the quintessential agency of the new social regulation. But its case is far more complex than those of OSHA or the CPSC, and in important respects it is unusual. In the first place, the EPA did not emerge from the legislative process, as major agencies within government typically do. It was created through presidential reorganization. During the year of its creation, 1970, the politics of structural choice focused not on what kind of agency was to be created or where it was to be located, but on the bureaucratic powers, procedures, restrictions, and deadlines that would be written into the Clean Air Act.

The reason for this points to the fundamental distinguishing feature of the EPA's story: the federal government had been addressing the problems of water and air pollution on a nationwide basis for some twenty years before the EPA's creation, and, in the process, had created, funded, and overseen a rich network of bureaucratic institutions to administer its antipollution policies. By 1970 these institutions were widely criticized for being cumbersome and ineffective, but they were also deeply entrenched and politically protected. This ensured that the politics of structural choice would not be a struggle over the design of entirely new institutions, as it had been for OSHA and the CPSC. It would be a struggle over adjustments to existing arrangements—and thus, for environmentalists, a struggle to impose mechanisms that might force these holdover institutions into doing what they wanted them to do.

The EPA's Institutional Heritage

In gaining perspective on the EPA's institutional heritage, it is important to realize that environmental groups were not the driving force behind early federal legislation in this area. Until environmentalism caught on among the public during the mid-1960s, these groups—the Sierra Club, the Izaak Walton League, the Wildlife Management Institute, and others—were neither very active nor very powerful. The compelling pressure for governmental action came instead from organizations representing state and local government—the American Municipal Association (later the National League of Cities), the Conference of Mayors, and myriad professional associations (state health officials, sanitary engineers). These interest groups, their appetites whetted by New Deal public works assistance for the construction of waste treatment plants, lobbied Congress hard for larger, more permanent infusions of federal funds and for antipollution programs that the states and localities could operate and control.[39]

The opponents were business groups, particularly those representing industries that did most of the polluting. They feared vigorous enforcement of strict pollution standards. Yet they had little to fear from toothless regulatory schemes, and they often had much to gain from the construction grant programs. As a result, business had a good deal in common with the state and local interest groups that largely dominated the proregulation side of the political struggle. The state and local groups were not zealots intent on cleaning up the environment at any price. They wanted to build political economies attractive to industry. They resisted strict, nondiscretionary enforcement, particularly if federal in origin. They sought regulation that would be sensitive to local conditions. And this, by and large, is what business wanted.

This happy confluence of interests was strongest in the formative period, which began with the Water Pollution Control Act of 1948. But as pollution began to attract more public attention and as new research began to shed troubling light on its severity, environmental groups slowly gained clout in the political process. With the balance of power shifting incrementally in their favor, they were better able to pressure for the kind of regulatory scheme they wanted: a politically autonomous agency, a strong, centralizing

39. My account of the early politics and institutions of environmental regulation is largely drawn from J. Clarence Davies III and Barbara S. Davies, *The Politics of Pollution*, 2d ed. (Bobbs-Merrill, 1975); Charles O. Jones, *Clean Air: The Policies and Politics of Pollution Control* (University of Pittsburgh Press, 1975); Randall B. Ripley, "Congress and Clean Air: The Issue of Enforcement, 1963," in Frederic N. Cleaveland and associates, eds., *Congress and Urban Problems: A Casebook on the Legislative Process* (Brookings, 1969), pp. 224–78; M. Kent Jennings, "Legislative Politics and Water Pollution Control, 1956–61," in ibid., pp. 72–109; "Anti-Water Pollution Law Strengthened," *Congressional Quarterly Almanac*, vol. 21 (1965), pp. 743–50; and "Congress Strengthens Air Pollution Control Powers," *Congressional Quarterly Almanac*, vol. 23 (1967), pp. 875–87.

role for the federal government, rigorous national standards, strict and swift enforcement. Environmental forces won concessions with each modification of the water and air pollution acts throughout the 1950s and 1960s. But as their power increased, the institutions of pollution control—designed, for the most part, by other groups with quite different interests—became increasingly entrenched. The environmentalists were never in a position to design their own arrangements.

Consider the institutions for water pollution control. The 1948 act authorized money for research, loans for construction, and federal enforcement powers so weak and procedure-bound that they were never exercised. Water pollution was defined as a health problem and assigned to the Public Health Service, which was run by medical professionals with no interest in economic regulation. Their approach to water pollution was to study it and to work cooperatively with state health agencies in discovering and implementing solutions. This was consistent with the designers' intent.

When the act came up for renewal in 1956, it was beefed up considerably. Two innovations were to leave an indelible mark on future regulation. First, the federal government would now provide grants to local communities for the construction of waste treatment plants. This strategic wedding of pollution control to pork barrel politics was enormously popular with groups and politicians of all kinds—except President Eisenhower, who opposed it on budgetary grounds (and as a threat to independent local government). From this point on, the grant program would make water pollution policy a universal favorite among members of Congress. It would also constrain the path of institutional development by anchoring federal regulation in local agencies and decisionmaking.

The second innovation took the form of stronger federal enforcement powers and new, less cumbersome procedures for taking action against polluters. These procedures, however, were designed to protect the interests of business and state and local governments—and, not surprisingly, they proved so unwieldy and complex that enforcement was virtually impossible. Despite this, or presumably because of it, they provided the basic procedural framework for water pollution regulation for many years. Moreover, because similar group forces were at work in the politics of air pollution, this same framework served as a model for that area as well.

As environmentalism grew rapidly in public support, politicians of all stripes grew increasingly sensitive to its concerns and those in positions of decisionmaking power began to endorse bolder policies in support of the environmental cause. Throughout the 1960s, however, much of this was symbolic. When it came to the crucial structural choices, choices of little salience to the broader public, politicians were not nearly so bold.

The environmentalists' organizational options were severely limited. State and local agencies were dug in. This was destined to be a federal-state-local "cooperative" effort no matter what. One goal within the realm of feasibility, however, was to push for more suitable bureaucratic arrangements at the national level. Historically, water and air pollution programs had been assigned to agencies buried deep within the Public Health Service, one of many units reporting to the secretary of health, education, and welfare. The environmentalists had no hope whatever of killing these agencies, creating new ones in some other location, and laying exclusive claim to them. But they could at least try to release them from the PHS, whose medical orientation and preference for state-local cooperation were most unwanted. They could also try to lift these agencies out of bureaucratic obscurity into a place of greater prominence and perhaps consolidate antipollution programs into one organization. Even these limited objectives, however, met with pervasive resistance.

Before 1970, progress on reorganization was limited and haphazard. In the 1965 Water Quality Act, environmentalists succeeded in lifting the water pollution agency out of PHS and making it a separate entity reporting to the secretary of HEW. In 1966, however, President Johnson transferred the Federal Water Pollution Control Agency (FWPCA), as it was called, out of HEW and into the Interior Department. This move was greeted with skepticism by environmentalists, who feared placing the FWPCA in a department with responsibilities for natural resource development. But the administration persisted, driven by characteristic concerns of presidential bureaucracy: President Johnson wanted to pull together the various federal water programs into one department, and Interior, with its already substantial responsibilities for water resources, was the logical candidate. From a purely organizational standpoint, HEW never should have had them in the first place.

Environmentalists' success in relocating the air pollution agency was even less noteworthy. While its name was changed several times, winding up as the impressive-sounding National Air Pollution Control Administration (NAPCA), and while its status was upgraded a bit within HEW when the department was reorganized in 1968, NAPCA remained a part of the Public Health Service until the EPA was created.

The EPA and Its Agency-forcing Mandate

By 1970, things were ripe for major reform. The popularity of environmental issues was at an all-time high, having jumped dramatically in the space of just a year or two. Environmentalists had virtually laid claim to the Democratic party, whose leaders in Congress "pledged a costly all-out assault on pollution problems and chided the Republicans for inaction."[40] Republicans looked for ways to jump on the bandwagon, and President Nixon, slow to take the bait, was now clearly intent on demonstrating his commitment to the environmental cause. His motivation was heightened considerably by the looming electoral contest in 1972: his Democratic challenger would most likely be "Mr. Environment," Edmund Muskie, chair of the Senate Subcommittee on Air and Water Pollution. Nixon and Muskie both knew that this was to be a showdown of enormous political consequence for their political futures.

The opportunities for action were obvious enough. The 1967 Clean Air Act was due to be reauthorized in 1970, and, as its institutions were widely regarded as failures, this was the occasion for major overhaul. Analogous circumstances obtained in the area of water pollution. A fascinating series of moves and countermoves, sparked by intense competition and one-upmanship between President Nixon and Senator Muskie, ultimately led to the Clean Air Amendments of 1970, the Federal Water Pollution Control Act Amendments of 1972, and the creation of the Environmental Protection Agency. Structural choices proceeded along two paths, one legislative and the other executive. The legislative process dealt sequentially with the air and water pollution laws, taking up the Clean Air Act first. The Muskie subcommittee, which

40. "Pollution: Will Man Succeed in Destroying Himself?" *Congressional Quarterly Weekly Report*, vol. 28 (January 30, 1970), p. 280.

assumed the congressional lead in all this, could not handle both at the same time owing to the formidable complexity of the issues. The executive process occurred within the larger framework of the President's Advisory Council on Executive Organization, known popularly as the Ash Council, which was set up by Nixon to devise a plan for reorganizing the entire federal bureaucracy. The EPA emerged from this executive process.

Nixon's grand reorganization project was the ultimate exercise in presidential bureaucracy. Federal agencies and even whole departments were to be shuffled and rationalized to produce a hierarchy conducive to effective presidential management and the comprehensive, coordinated administration of federal programs. Task forces were set up to study various parts of the problem and make recommendations. One such group had responsibility for considering how the various environmental programs and agencies should be fitted into a larger department pulling together all the government's natural resource functions.[41]

The people involved in this White House group were quite responsive to environmental concerns. At this stage of the game, this was the way Nixon wanted it. They sought to give the president a capacity for taking a systematic, comprehensive approach to the nation's environmental and natural resource problems. But, like the environmentalists, they feared putting environmental agencies into a department that also had responsibilities for resource development programs and was likely to be responsive to progrowth, probusiness interests. They concluded, accordingly, that the government's far-flung environmental programs should be brought together within an independent organization, the Environmental Protection Agency. It should be headed by a single administrator, appointable and removable by the president and directly subordinate to him in the bureaucratic hierarchy.

41. On the creation of the EPA within the executive, see Alfred A. Marcus, *Promise and Performance: Choosing and Implementing an Environmental Policy* (Westport, Conn.: Greenwood Press, 1980); John C. Whitaker, *Striking a Balance: Environment and Natural Resources Policy in the Nixon-Ford Years* (Washington, D.C.: American Enterprise Institute for Public Policy Research, 1976); John Quarles, *Cleaning Up America: An Insider's View of the Environmental Protection Agency* (Houghton-Mifflin, 1976); Richard Corrigan, "Nixon, Democrats, Agencies Rush to Take Up New Environment Cause," *National Journal*, vol. 2 (January 31, 1970), pp. 206–10; and Corrigan, "Pollution, Oceanography Reorganizations Leave Interior Department Biggest Loser," *National Journal*, vol. 2 (June 20, 1970), pp. 1316–18.

Their recommendation artfully furthered both presidential and environmental interests. The president got comprehensiveness, coordination, and control—presidential bureaucracy. The environmentalists, who had consistently run up against stone walls in trying to reorganize environmental institutions, were suddenly the recipients of a tremendous windfall: a single agency, high in status and visibility, distanced from competing and hostile interests, with comprehensive responsibility for a full range of environmental programs. The proposed EPA was not ideal. It was subject to presidential control, as all executive agencies were, and, for the time being, the programmatic structures it inherited were placed side by side rather than integrated. But, even so, it was the nearest thing to an answer to environmentalists' prayers.

With politicians of both parties predisposed to favor environmental reforms, the administration's reorganization plan was submitted to Congress on July 9, 1970, and sailed through with no concerted opposition. Business, in fact, had actually warmed to the idea after years of frustration with the hodgepodge of state regulations, which were gradually becoming strict enough to cause problems and confusion. If regulation was unavoidable, better for it to be comprehensive and consistent.[42]

Within Congress, environmental action centered on the Clean Air Act.[43] In late 1969 and early 1970, it appeared that the 1967 arrangements would be streamlined and beefed up to enhance their effectiveness, but that they would basically be left intact. This was Muskie's original intention. He had a stake in demonstrating that it could work, and he seemed unwilling to provoke a political fight by pushing for more. His bill maintained the 1967 act's regional standards rather than asking for national standards, required that standards be economically feasible, and kept the basic

42. Richard Corrigan, "Tough Local Actions on Air Quality Boost Nixon's National Standards Plan," *National Journal*, vol. 2 (May 9, 1970), pp. 968–70; and Corrigan, "Pollution, Oceanography Reorganizations."

43. On the politics of the Clean Air Act of 1970, see Marcus, *Promise and Performance*, pp. 121–39; Jones, *Clean Air*; Davies and Davies, *The Politics of Pollution*; Melnick, *Regulation and the Courts*; "Pollution: Will Man Succeed in Destroying Himself?"; "Clean Air Bill Cleared with Auto Emission Deadline," *Congressional Quarterly Almanac*, vol. 26 (1970), pp. 472–86; Corrigan, "Nixon, Democrats, Agencies Rush to Take Up New Environment Cause"; Corrigan, "Nixon's Antipollution Plan Seeks Federal Standards, Enforcement," *National Journal*, vol. 2 (February 14, 1970), pp. 326–28; and Corrigan, "Muskie Plays Dominant Role in Writing Tough New Air Pollution Law," *National Journal*, vol. 3 (January 2, 1971), pp. 25–33.

federal-state framework for standard setting and enforcement. Environmentalists were not impressed.

Then two things happened that changed the course of political events. On February 10, 1970, Nixon presented his environmental message to Congress in which he outlined his own proposal for strong, comprehensive federal regulation of the environment, calling, among other things, for national emissions standards and a partial shift in regulatory power from the states and localities to the federal government. In May a Nader-inspired report on the air pollution problem, *Vanishing Air*, was published. It was sharply critical of Muskie for creating unworkable institutions—accusing him, in effect, of selling out to the opponents of effective regulation.[44]

Muskie got religion in a hurry. Over a period of a few months, he and his subcommittee came up with a bill far bolder than Nixon's proposal. It now provided for national air quality standards and a much stronger role for the federal government. It explicitly stated that economic costs were not to be taken into account in setting standards. Perhaps most important of all, the designers had aggressively searched for mechanisms by which air pollution agencies could be forced to do a good job. This search led to the arsenal of structural weapons for which the Clean Air Act of 1970 is now famous: painfully explicit goals and criteria, lists of specific substances to be regulated, exact deadlines for agency action and goal attainment, detailed procedures to be followed in setting and enforcing standards, citizen suits as a check on agency inaction, and pervasive opportunities for judicial review.

For environmental interests, the agency-forcing strategy was eminently reasonable. They were politically dominant now, but there was no guarantee that they could stay on top. By imposing strict requirements and deadlines on the agency—even though, given the daunting technical complexity of the issues involved, they could not be sure that these requirements and deadlines were technically justified or feasible—they reduced the likelihood that resurgent business and state-local interests could someday turn agency discretion to their own advantage. Scientifically, this strategy was surely unwise. Politically, it made good sense.

This is only reinforced by the institutional heritage the environ-

44. John C. Esposito, *Vanishing Air: The Ralph Nader Study Group Report on Air Pollution* (Grossman, 1970).

mentalists were forced to accept in delegating authority—namely, NAPCA and its counterpart agencies in the states and localities. None of this would or could be destroyed. Like the agencies responsible for water pollution and a number of other environmental programs, they would simply be relocated under the organizational rubric of the Environmental Protection Agency. Thus environmentalists were constrained to work through the same basic set of institutions and personnel that had failed them in the past. With so many of the usual design options foreclosed, environmentalists were compelled to channel their reforms into the kinds of agency-forcing restrictions the Clean Air Act is known for.

The Senate, its agenda skillfully controlled by Muskie and his subcommittee, was a bastion of environmentalist power and the chief institutional proponent of agency-forcing legislation. The House, where the environmentalists also had pervasive influence, was a more receptive arena for the interests of business and state and local governments. The bill that passed the House, accordingly, was different from the Senate's in ways one would expect. It shifted standard-setting and enforcement power less drastically in favor of the federal government. It gave bureaucrats discretion rather than binding their decisions by procedural restrictions and deadlines. It forced the EPA to rely on Justice rather than authorizing autonomous legal action. It made no allowance for citizen suits against violators or the EPA in cases of nonenforcement. It cut the auto companies more slack in forcing a timely reduction in emissions.

The Senate and its environmentalist supporters, however, won out in conference, and their strikingly tough set of particulars became law with only minor amendment in late December 1970. The EPA, which had begun its bureaucratic life only a few weeks earlier, would have to hit the ground running. It had deadlines to meet. As its new administrators and everyone else were soon to find out, however, there was no way the new agency could run fast enough to meet the crushing burden of its legal obligations.

Meanwhile, Congress turned its attention to the Water Quality Act.[45] As it did, it braced for a new political firestorm. Due to the

---

45. See Marcus, *Promise and Performance,* pp. 141–62; Davies and Davies, *The Politics of Pollution;* "Clean Water: Congress Overrides Presidential Veto," *Congressional Quarterly Almanac,* vol. 28 (1972), pp. 708–22; Jamie Heard, "Water Pollution Proposals to Test Blatnik's Strength as Public Works Chairman," *National Journal,*

wildly popular construction grant program, the water bill stood to be "the most expensive environmental protection legislation ever contemplated by Congress."[46] It also threatened to impose extraordinary pollution control costs on business, making it "the most significant legislative test to date between the goals of environmental quality and economic development."[47]

Nixon again tried to get out front. In his February 1971 message to Congress, he outlined his own proposal for a much stronger, procedurally streamlined system of federal-state regulation of water pollution; it even included a limited provision for citizen suits. While this was a genuine proposal for major change, environmentalists found it weak in predictable ways: it gave bureaucrats too much discretion and granted too much power to the states. Its $6 billion authorization request, moreover, was skimpy.

The Muskie subcommittee did not disappoint. Before 1971 was out, it had come up with an extremely ambitious bill. Among other things, it set national policies of making all navigable waters safe for fish, wildlife, and recreation by 1981 and eliminating *all* discharges of pollutants into the water by 1985; required polluters to adopt the "best practicable" technology by 1976 and the "best available" technology by 1981; established a state-run permit program for regulating discharges and authorized the EPA to set guidelines and exercise permit-by-permit veto power over state decisions; and authorized any citizen to sue polluters or the EPA to demand enforcement of the act.

The administration charged "that the bill set technologically impossible goals, that it was too costly, and that it would destroy the states' role."[48] It had plenty of support. William Ruckelshaus, first administrator of the EPA, had tried to convince senators from the beginning that their strict goals and deadlines, while politically attractive, were impossible to achieve and would lead to administrative nightmares. Lobbyists representing the states were livid

---

vol. 3 (August 14, 1971), pp. 1717–23; Claude E. Barfield, "Administration Fights Goals, Costs of Senate Water-Quality Bill," *National Journal*, vol. 4 (January 15, 1972), pp. 84–96; Barfield, "Economic Arguments May Force Retreat from Senate Water-Quality Goals," *National Journal*, vol. 4 (January 22, 1972), pp. 136–47; and Richard Corrigan, "President's Slash of Clean-Water Funds May Shift Debate from Congress to the Courts," *National Journal*, vol. 4 (December 2, 1972), pp. 1846–55.

46. Barfield, "Economic Arguments May Force Retreat," p. 136.
47. Barfield, "Administration Fights Goals, Costs," p. 85.
48. Barfield, "Economic Arguments May Force Retreat," p. 137.

about the bill's unrealistic goals and its encroachment on state powers. Industry opposition focused primarily on the tremendous costs the bill would impose on the private sector, and they were particularly bitter about the environmental fantasy of zero discharge. As one Harvard economist put it, "There isn't a single respectable economist in the country who would back the no-discharge goal adopted by the Senate."[49] All of this fell on deaf ears. Environmental interests were dominant in the Senate, and it did not matter much what others had to say.

The administration took the lead in mobilizing a coalition to wring concessions out of the House Public Works Committee. To the environmentalists' credit, the committee still produced a strong bill. But they did lose ground on a number of structural issues, including each of those listed above, and the House bill proved to be so different from the Senate's that the conference committee had to meet forty times before the necessary compromises could be hammered out. In the final bill, the Senate's safe-water and no-discharge "policies" were transformed into purposely vaguer "goals." The deadline for installation of "best practicable" technology was pushed back to 1977 and that for "best available" technology to 1983, and a national commission was set up to study the costs and benefits of achieving those deadlines. The EPA's permit-by-permit authority was revoked, reserving greater control for the states. Citizens were allowed to sue for enforcement only if their interests were directly affected. Finally, there was a nice bonus for state-local interests, courtesy of the House's voracious appetite for pork barrel legislation: multiyear funding authorization was raised from an already astounding $20 billion to an unbelievable $24.6 billion. President Nixon, outraged by the bill's budgetary excesses and concerned about its consequences for economic growth, vetoed it—only to have it overriden by huge bipartisan majorities in both houses. The combination of environmentalist power and pork barrel politics was unbeatable.

Structure, Performance, and the Recurrent Battle

In the air and water pollution struggles, environmentalists had won smashing legislative victories. But these victories did not translate automatically into effective policy. Their victories were

49. Quoted in ibid., p. 141.

structural, and they translated into a forbidding maze of detailed instructions, procedures, requirements, criteria, and deadlines—all of them tacked onto entrenched institutions inherited from a powerless past. There were compelling political reasons for burdening the EPA with all this baggage, but, as the young agency struggled to pursue its mandate, the load would take a heavy toll on its capacity for effective performance.

The EPA was plagued by several different kinds of structural problems. In the first place, the agency was never designed as a coherent organization. Its presidential creators pulled together disparate programmatic units under one roof, viewing this as a first step toward a coherent organizational structure; but because the White House and the EPA were not willing to waste time and political capital on a reorganization fight, these units were left separate and largely unintegrated, wedded to their own norms, cultures, and characteristic ways of doing things. The situation has never been corrected. Throughout its life, the EPA has been hobbled by its programmatic inheritance.[50]

Second, the EPA neither inherited nor was able to amass the scientific knowledge necessary to formulate well-conceived standards in a timely fashion. Punctuality was mandated, scientific validity was not. All too often this would cause the EPA to rush to judgment on the basis of sketchy evidence that even its own people did not find adequate. This began to happen immediately after the Clean Air Amendments went into effect, as Ruckelshaus, required to issue national ambient air standards within thirty days, promulgated standards that neither he nor his chief scientific adviser thought were technically justified.[51] As the EPA's head economist was to put it years later, "The ultimate difficulty lay in the law. EPA was forced by legislative deadlines, often imposed on the administrator by court decisions in response to citizen suits, to act on the basis of weak technical knowledge."[52]

Third, EPA's rulemaking procedures—variously imposed to protect business, to ensure environmentalist participation, to satisfy the courts and, of course, to ensure that scientific evidence is somehow taken into account—are so tortuously complex it is a wonder

50. Marcus, *Promise and Performance.*

51. Ibid.

52. Robert L. Sansom, *The New American Dream Machine: Toward A Simpler Lifestyle in an Environmental Age* (Anchor Books, 1976), p. 35.

anything at all emerges from them. In great measure, they provide a framework of rules within which the political battle continues, whatever science might appear to require. As the EPA's own frustrated leaders have acknowledged, environmental problem solving is often not the essence of what is going on.[53]

Fourth, the institutional legacy of American environmental policy has forced the EPA to rely on a complicated, confusing diversity of state and local agencies. Effective coordination and control are extremely difficult under the best of circumstances and are worsened by legislative design: the EPA is not supposed to have sufficient authority to take charge. The opponents of effective regulation and the protectors of state and local interests have seen to it over the years that this is so. This pervades the EPA's regulatory organization.[54]

Finally, the EPA has been hemmed about by the judiciary. Virtually every decision the agency has made has been subject by legislative design to judicial review. Business has consistently attacked agency standards for being too restrictive, environmentalists have attacked them for being too lax, and both have pressed whatever arguments the courts might respect: that proper procedures were not followed, that decisions were not based on the record, that scientific evidence was lacking, that the agency exceeded or failed to exercise its authority. Decisionmaking, as a result, has dragged on in a continual state of uncertainty until judicial approval finally has been granted. Moreover, the EPA has been forced to build a host of complications into its decision procedures to ensure that their results would stand up under judicial scrutiny, adding heavy bureaucratic baggage to an already overloaded system.[55]

While the EPA was struggling under the weight of its own structure, the politics of structure raged on in Congress. It has never really ended. Some of these battles arose from environmentalist efforts to grant the EPA new authority over more specialized problem areas: toxic chemicals, hazardous wastes, noise, radiation, pesticides. With environmentalist successes came not only new authority, but also new procedures, new deadlines, new organiza-

53. Bryner, *Bureaucratic Discretion*, especially chap. 5; and National Academy of Sciences, *Decision Making in the Environmental Protection Agency* (National Academy of Sciences, 1977).

54. Bryner, *Bureaucratic Discretion*; and Marcus, *Promise and Performance*.

55. Bryner, *Bureaucratic Discretion*.

tional headaches—and new regulated interests sharpening their knives for the administrative fights ahead.

Legislatively, however, the greatest attention centered on the core of the EPA's environmental mandate, the Clean Air Amendments of 1970 and the Federal Water Pollution Control Act Amendments of 1972. From the moment these bills passed into law, business desperately wanted to eviscerate them, environmentalists wanted to protect and strengthen them, and states wanted greater autonomy from EPA oversight, control, and maddening red tape. Episodic fights aside, all looked ahead to 1976–77, when both acts came up for reauthorization. A major conflagration was unavoidable.[56]

The economic context had changed since the 1970 and 1972 battles. The nation was plagued by serious economic problems; considerations of cost, economic growth, and international competitiveness were now far more politically potent. And the energy crisis gave rise to strong pressures for relaxing environmental standards in the interests of fuel economy and lessened dependence on foreign oil. All of this played into the hands of industry and the opponents of strict regulation. But the major difference in legislative politics was not economic: the structural status quo had shifted. The acts of 1970 and 1972, the environmentalist triumphs, were the new status quo—and, as always in the American separation-of-powers system, any major change would be extremely difficult to achieve by either side. Since the two sides were now better balanced in political power, the inevitable war was not likely to produce much. And indeed, when the dust cleared, the 1977 amendments to both acts left the core legislation intact. Deadlines were extended, and exceptions and conditions were introduced to soften the rigid, infeasible requirements of the earlier legislation. Business won additional procedural protections. The EPA would have a bit more discretion.

After the 1977 adjustments, legislative politics surrounding the air and water acts remained just as intense and explosive, but for

56. On the politics of the 1977 amendments, see Marcus, *Promise and Performance*; Bryner, *Bureaucratic Discretion*; Melnick, *Regulation and the Courts*; "Water Pollution," *Congressional Quarterly Almanac*, vol. 32 (1976), pp. 166–70; "Clean Air Amendments Die at Session's Close," *Congressional Quarterly Almanac*, vol. 32 (1976), pp. 128–43; "Major Clean Air Amendments Enacted," *Congressional Quarterly Almanac*, vol. 33 (1977), pp. 627–46; and "Water Pollution Compromise Enacted," *Congressional Quarterly Almanac*, vol. 33 (1977), pp. 697–707.

the next decade the contending forces were in total deadlock. The election of Ronald Reagan and the resurgence of business political power did not shift the political balance sufficiently to shatter the status quo. Both acts were due for reauthorization in 1982. The legislative machinery cranked up, the inevitable fights broke out, but 1982 came and went with Congress incapable of passing new legislation.[57] So did 1983. Finally, in 1986, Congress coughed up amendments to the water act, which "merely fine-tuned and up-dated the basic law."[58] Action on the Clean Air Act remained stalled.

Presidential Bureaucracy

In the environmental politics of structural choice, the major force for change since the statutory breakthroughs of 1970 and 1972 has not been legislative. It has been presidential. The EPA is the largest federal regulatory agency; it regulates the whole economy; it controls a huge budget; and it imposes enormous costs on American industry, with real consequences for inflation, unemployment, trade, and the nation's general economic well-being. Because presidents are held directly responsible for all these things, they have had strong incentives to try to exercise control over the EPA. And that is precisely what they have done, Republican and Democrat alike.[59]

Presidential control began even before the EPA was created. The Nixon people knew that their environmental agency would generate costly rules, and they took steps to ensure its decisions could be moderated and controlled in the interests of competing presidential concerns. As a countervailing force, they created a new advisory committee of business executives within the Commerce De-

57. It did reauthorize the grant program, but, owing to strong opposition by the Reagan administration, reduced its scope and funding. See "Congress Begins Rewrite of Clean Air Act," *Congressional Quarterly Almanac*, vol. 37 (1981), pp. 505–13; "Congress Clears Sewer Grant Legislation," *Congressional Quarterly Almanac*, vol. 37 (1981), pp. 515–20; and "Congress Fails to Act on Clean Air Rewrite," *Congressional Quarterly Almanac*, vol. 38 (1982), pp. 425–34.

58. "Environment/Energy," *Congressional Quarterly Almanac*, vol. 43 (1987), p. 289.

59. My discussion of presidential control of the EPA relies on Marcus, *Promise and Performance*; Sansom, *New American Dream Machine*; Quarles, *Cleaning Up America*; Whitaker, *Striking a Balance*; Bryner, *Bureaucratic Discretion*; and V. Kerry Smith, ed., *Environmental Policy under Reagan's Executive Order: The Role of Cost-Benefit Analysis* (University of North Carolina Press, 1984).

partment to provide input on EPA initiatives. They also added an enhanced environmental research and analysis component to Commerce for challenging EPA rules on scientific and economic grounds. Once EPA was up and operating, they set up a formal review process through the OMB for assessing the broader economic effects of EPA rules and forcing it to justify its decisions.

The EPA was at a serious disadvantage. It lacked the capacity to carry out sophisticated economic analysis and could not justify its decisions. It responded by building its own team of economic analysts, allowing it to play the game on a more equal footing. But the combination of OMB review and economic analysis had the presidentially intended effect: the EPA now took economic costs into account in formulating rules. This was not contemplated by either the air or water acts and appeared to violate their intent. The presidential hierarchy had imposed a new structure, and it was working to redirect agency behavior.

This continued under Ford and Carter, both of whom were seriously concerned with inflation, unemployment, the energy crisis, and related economic problems of enormous national significance. As outlined in the discussion of OSHA above, both presidents took various steps to bring rulemaking by federal agencies under presidential control. The EPA was an integral part of this, but in practice it was regarded as being in a class by itself. Its rules were likely to be the most costly and far-reaching in their economic impact, and they were given especially critical scrutiny.

During the Reagan administration, the EPA found itself constrained ever more tightly by presidential control as the review process became increasingly strict and centralized in the OMB. At least for the first few years, however, much of this hierarchical direction was unnecessary—for Reagan had used his appointment power to install a team of policymakers at the EPA who were far more dedicated to the president's mission than the agency's. The tension that had always existed between White House and EPA officials essentially disappeared.

The president's agent was EPA administrator Anne Gorsuch, who immediately began to change the EPA's regulatory strategy to one of cooperation with business and delegation of enforcement responsibilities to the states. Under Gorsuch, the EPA shelved virtually all rules except those designed to reduce the costs of current regulations, abolished the Office of Enforcement to pave the way toward a system of voluntary compliance, and reduced the number of enforcement cases scheduled for court action.[60] This probably could have gone on for some time in the hands of a more politically skilled administrator, but Gorsuch allowed herself to get snared in a scandal involving manipulation of the agency's "superfund" for hazardous wastes, and she was forced to resign in 1983 along with about a dozen other top appointed officials. They were replaced by William Ruckelshaus and his own hand-picked team, who injected new life and vigor into EPA regulation. Yet the OMB and its routine review process remained, as did White House insistence on subordinating the agency to presidential priorities. Ruckelshaus and his successor, Lee Thomas, were not Reagan revolutionaries, but neither could they free themselves from the pressing constraints of presidential management. The EPA remained underfunded, undermanned, and well integrated into the structure of presidential bureaucracy.

None of this was ever intended when the core enabling acts were written in 1970 and 1972. The rise and power of presidential bureaucracy were phenomena that environmentalists could do little about, but that structured environmental policymaking by the EPA just as surely as their own legislative successes did. Presidents have had a decided historical advantage in shifting the structural balance over time: they have not needed to act through affirmative legislative choice. While environmentalists and industry have battled it out in Congress, with neither side able to clear the uncountable hurdles that stand in the way of legislative victory, presidents have been able to take unilateral action in imposing structures conducive to their own interests. Thus the EPA has grown into a confounding mixture of congressional and presidential bureaucracy.

Conclusion: The EPA and the Politics of Structure

From its creation in 1970 to the present, then, the EPA has had to struggle against overwhelming disadvantages in seeking to engineer a better environment. Its supporters, driven by political uncertainty and forced to build on failed institutions, have responded by burdening the EPA with goals and deadlines impossible to meet and procedures so complex little could be done. Its opponents—including, in effect, the defenders of its institutional inheritance—

60. Bryner, *Bureaucratic Discretion*; and "Environment," *Congressional Quarterly Almanac*, vol. 37 (1981), pp. 503–04.

have exacted structural concessions that promoted fragmentation, decentralization, procedural complexity, and delay. Presidents have targeted the EPA for strict hierarchical control, layering rules and procedures of their own on top of the already unwieldy hodge-podge of congressional bureaucracy.

The resulting set of arrangements conforms to no one's idea of what an effective bureaucracy ought to look like. However popular the EPA might be with the public, and despite the fact that air and water pollution have been reduced over the years, few would claim the EPA has done an effective job of pursuing its mandate. Deadlines go unmet. Standards are slow in coming and often inappropriate. Enforcement is spotty. Coordination and coherence are intractable problems. But, then, what else should one expect? The EPA is a creature of politics—and in politics, organizations are not designed to be effective.

CONCLUSION

The Consumer Product Safety Commission, the Occupational Safety and Health Administration, and the Environmental Protection Agency are all prime examples of the new social regulation. In each case, a coalition of groups representing broad social interests triumphed over the narrower, more concentrated interests of business in committing the nation to bold new policies and creating bureaucratic arrangements for carrying them out.

The policies, however, were never explicitly fought over. They were broadly popular among the electorate, and political elites of all stripes, including leaders within the business community, were quick to voice support for governmental action. All this was symbolic. The real battles over policy took place within an arcane realm of politics remote from the concerns of ordinary citizens: the politics of structural choice. The struggles of genuine consequence were about bureaucratic arrangements, about powers and procedures and criteria. These were the choices that would determine whether the bold new policies of social regulation would mean anything at all in practice. Interest groups speaking for the consumer, labor, and environmental movements were counted as victorious not because they committed government to laudable social goals, but because they won most of the battles over structure.

The bureaucracies of the new social regulation are the products of these battles over structure, and they have to be understood as such. Popular academic theories—whether about regulatory capture or about the technical requirements of organizational effectiveness—doubtless entered the thinking of various participants as they settled on the structures most conducive to their own interests. But by no stretch of the imagination was there any substantial coherence, theoretical or otherwise, to the bureaucracies they created. Nor is there reason to expect any. Bureaucracies do not emerge from analytical exercises in applied theory, nor do they emerge from public-spirited efforts to find the most effective structural means for achieving the goals of public policy. Politics has a way of overwhelming these sorts of "good government" concerns and driving them out—even when the major interest groups claim to be forces for good government themselves.

The three modern agencies explored here were endowed with very different designs. The CPSC is an independent regulatory commission, a structural form that consumerists pressured strongly for, despite their rhetoric over the years about the vulnerability of commissions to capture. Things somehow looked a little different to them once they got in the driver's seat. OSHA is safely (or so labor expected) located within the Labor Department. But enforcement responsibilities quite central to OSHA's regulatory functions were delegated to a separate independent agency, the Occupational Safety and Health Review Commission. This was done, quite deliberately, to undermine the effectiveness of OSHA regulation, not to enhance it. The EPA is not within a department at all and is headed by a single administrator rather than a commission, making it fundamentally different from both OSHA and the CPSC. Any notion that these agencies were all crafted according to some coherent body of modern ideas about bureaucratic organization needs a lot of explaining.

Much the same applies if these structural arrangements are assessed one at a time: each is a grotesque combination of organizational features that clearly are not conducive to effective performance. Each sports its own peculiar set of complicated, cumbersome, time-consuming procedures for rulemaking. Each is burdened by a distinctive and troublesome array of judicial checks on its decisions. The EPA suffers from a motley assortment of programmatic structures it inherited from its institutional past and can do little about. OSHA and the EPA are forced into a clumsy, fragmenting reliance on disparate state agencies. And, as components of the executive branch, they are also drawn tightly into the hierarchy of presidential bureaucracy and forced to comply with rules and procedures that fit awkwardly, if at all, with those imposed by Congress.

This is basically what one ought to expect from American government. At the risk of oversimplifying, there are three major reasons that help explain why this is so and thus why public bureaucracy cannot be organized for effective performance. First, even the group that successfully pressures for the creation of a public agency—consumers for the CPSC, labor for OSHA, environmentalists for the EPA—will not demand an effectively designed organization. While it certainly wants a bureaucracy that will do the best job possible, it must also reckon with political uncertainty: its political enemies may soon gain sufficient power to exercise legitimate authority over the winning group's agency. Something must therefore be done to protect the group's accomplishments from being captured or destroyed.

Consumers were responding to political uncertainty when they chose an independent commission, a form they had loudly damned in earlier days. Perhaps the most pervasive examples, though, are the host of agency-forcing mechanisms that all the winning groups employed in imposing detailed and onerous requirements on their agencies, the EPA being the extreme case. There is little doubt that these formal constraints were debilitating and a direct cause of ineffective performance. There is also little doubt, especially in the EPA's case, that many of these agency-forcing requirements were technically unjustified. The experts clearly could have done a much more competent job if they had been granted the discretion to put their expertise to proper use.[61] But the groups had no intention of granting them discretion. By directing bureaucratic behavior themselves via detailed formal requirements—even if these requirements were technically ill advised and took a toll on agency performance—the groups were removing crucial decisions from the realm of future influence by business. This was tremendously valuable, and they were willing to pay a price for it. As a result, they purposely created bizarre

61. For a discussion of this point in application to the EPA, see Ackerman and Hassler, *Clean Coal/Dirty Air.*

administrative arrangements that were not well suited to effective regulation.

Second, the winning group must usually compromise with the losing group when structural choices are being made. This is democracy in action. Unfortunately, the losing group is dedicated to crippling the agency in whatever ways it can and gaining a measure of control over agency decisions. Thus it will pressure for fragmented authority, labyrinthine procedures, mechanisms of presidential and congressional intervention, and other structures that impede vigorous agency performance. This is precisely why OSHA is hobbled by the OSHRC, why OSHA's and the EPA's regulatory arrangements are so heavily reliant upon the states, why the CPSC was slapped with a congressional veto, and why all these agencies must give business procedural protections that go well beyond those required by the Administrative Procedure Act and the courts. In the private sector, structures are generally designed by participants who want the organization to succeed. In the public sector, bureaucracies are designed in no small measure by participants who explicitly want them to fail.

Third, presidents have the power and incentive to impose their own layer of structure on top of the one that the legislative process has already produced. Although presidents have a direct stake in how well government performs, they are a constant threat to impose structures that undermine the policy goals of individual agencies and their group supporters. Most obviously, presidents have electoral coalitions that may dispose them to favor an agency's opponents. Clearly, business has successfully worked through Republican presidents in putting a structural rein on the regulatory agencies, particularly OSHA and the EPA.

In addition, though, all presidents have broader social concerns that thrust them into the enemy's role. For agencies are single-minded in pursuit of their mandates, and presidents do not want them to be. Presidents want them to give balanced consideration to economic growth, inflation, and other issues of national concern. This means they must prevent agencies from simply doing a good job at what their designers intended for them to do. This may or may not be in the best interests of society. But whatever the case may be, the structures imposed on agencies will be even more byzantine and convoluted because of the president's superimposed layer, and they will be even less well suited to the achievement of congressionally ordained goals.

This is a sorry picture. But if the basic institutions of American democracy are taken pretty much as given, along with the characteristic ways in which they structure the incentives and opportunities of the influential players in and out of government, then there appears to be little that can be done about it. Politicians will be responsive to group interests and demands in making choices about the structure of public bureaucracy. Because democratic politics, by its very nature, raises uncertainties about who will control public bureaucracy, winning groups will have strong incentives to demand protective structures they know are impediments to effective performance. Because American politics, by its very nature, makes compromise a virtual necessity in the legislative process, losing groups will have opportunities to impose structures fully intended to promote failure and conflict. And because presidents are constitutionally empowered and politically induced to control executive agencies, they cannot be stopped from acting to impose structures of their own that may be quite incompatible with those prescribed by Congress.

There is some reason to believe, in fact, that the current administrative tangle may actually get worse over time. Consider the following.

—The kinds of socioeconomic problems government is called upon to address seem to be growing increasingly interdependent and complex. Even reasonably adequate bureaucratic solutions require extensive technical knowledge and professionalism—and the discretion necessary for their productive employment. Yet, in a democratic system fraught with political uncertainty, enemy designers, and contending institutional authorities, severe constraints tend to be placed on bureaucratic discretion for political reasons, and these constraints directly undermine the technical capacity so necessary for effective performance. The greater the technical requirements of society's problems, the more poorly designed American bureaucracy is likely to prove as it struggles to address them.

—Politics has become much more competitive in the last decade or two, as an interest group system heavily weighted in favor of business has been transformed by groups representing consumers, women, blacks, environmentalists, and other broad social interests. For good reason, scholars have regarded this as a healthy development for American democracy. As it affects bureaucracy, in particular, group competition has worked against capture, iron triangles, and other monopolistic arrangements, freeing public administration from the grip of business. In all likelihood, however, it has also contributed to the structural disarray that plagues American government: for as the group system has become more competitive, political uncertainty and political compromise have dramatically increased, and, in the politics of structure, both generate a proliferation of structural forms ill suited to effective organization. It is well known that public agencies have become increasingly formalized and proceduralized during the 1970s and 1980s, in part because of restrictions imposed by the courts.[62] Group competition may well have been at least as consequential. And the more vital and competitive American democracy becomes in the future, the worse its "bureaucracy problem" will get.

—The intrusive structural designs of presidents are only going to become more intrusive over time. The development of an institutional capacity to control the bureaucracy is not something peculiar to Republican presidents, nor is the aggressive use of this capacity going to fade into the past with the Reagan presidency. All modern presidents have strong political incentives to bring the federal bureaucracy under their control, and future presidents of both parties can be expected to protect and elaborate upon the managerial institutions that their predecessors have built.[63] The layering of presidential bureaucracy upon congressional bureaucracy, then, will continue apace, and will likely become a still more consequential—and organizationally disruptive—feature of American government in the future.

It would be nice to say that there is an easy way out of all this, that the nation can have an effective public bureaucracy if only it wants one. But this is probably not so. A bureaucracy that is structurally unsuited for effective action is precisely the kind of bureaucracy that interest groups and politicians routinely and deliberately create. Most of them, taken singly, would not want it that way. Each actor, if able to design and control a bureaucracy without interference by opposing interests, would create the most effective

---

62. Melnick, *Regulation and the Courts*; and Bryner, *Bureaucratic Discretion*.
63. Moe, "The Politicized Presidency."

organization possible and take steps to keep it that way. No one, however, has the power to make these political choices alone. Various actors with various interests have to do it collectively, democratically. And because they are forced to design bureaucracy through a democratic process, their structural choices turn out to be very different indeed from those intended to promote effective organization.

This is no one's fault. The problem is inherent in our democratic system as a whole, and it is our basic framework of political institutions, not the bureaucracy, that must be reformed if solutions are ever to be found. This is a big job, and perhaps an impossible one. In the meantime, the blame should at least be directed where it belongs. The bureaucracy itself is not the problem.

Index

331